The Essential Civil War

The Essential Civil War

A Handbook to the Battles, Armies, Navies and Commanders

JAYNE E. BLAIR

McFarland & Company, Inc., Publishers

Jefferson, North Carolina, and London

LIBRARY OF CONGRESS CATALOGUING-IN-PUBLICATION DATA

Blair, Jayne E.
The essential Civil War : A handbook to the battles,
armies, navies and commanders / Jayne E. Blair.
p.   cm.
Includes bibliographical references and index.

ISBN-13: 978-0-7864-2472-6
ISBN-10: 0-7864-2472-9 (softcover : 50# alkaline paper) ∞

1. United States—History—Civil War, 1861–1865.
2. United States—History—Civil War, 1861–1865—Miscellanea.
3. United States—History—Civil War, 1861–1865—Chronology.   I. Title.
E468.B55 2006   973.7'3—dc22   2006014824

British Library cataloguing data are available

Cover photograph ©2006 Pictures Now

Manufactured in the United States of America

*McFarland & Company, Inc., Publishers
Box 611, Jefferson, North Carolina 28640
www.mcfarlandpub.com*

Acknowledgments

It takes many people, both directly and indirectly, to bring a book of this kind to publication. Had it not been for my many friends and co-workers, this project would have never advanced beyond my library shelf.

I want to thank my dear friend Susan Sadler. Susan spent many an hour listening to me while I described the war to her, going so far as to draw maps and battle plans on napkins as we ate dinner. She listened and did not laugh at my anger as I, very upset, described how a commander was killed when he accidentally rode into an enemy's camp.

My thanks and appreciation are extended to the following individuals in Texas, where I first started on this project: Sr. Cpl. Keith Caruso, Jerry Coker, Sgt. Robert J. Crider, Jennifer Gammill, Cathi Gumpert, Karen Hartman, Marvin Marks, Lt. Todd Thomasson, and my former co-workers at Dallas Love Field — the members of the Dallas Police Department and Airport Operations.

Upon retirement, I left the great state of Texas and moved to the Commonwealth of Virginia. This project reached maturity there because of the help and support of the following individuals, to whom I am very grateful: Carolyn Amundson, Marion Coss, Pat Dietch, Rick Moyer, Eugenia Gladwell Visaggio and the wonderful guide staff at Montpelier.

Most of all I want to thank my family, Ronald and Judy Harris and Donna Blair, for their continual support and encouragement. Had it not been for them, this project may never have been started at all.

Contents

List of Charts

This list does not include the various charts of the battles/fights/skirmishes, which are located within the year the battle/fight/skirmish was fought.

Preface

In 1992, as I drove across this country, I saw a sign outside of Memphis, Tennessee, directing visitors to the Shiloh Battlefield. Having never visited a battlefield, I had no idea what to expect. At Shiloh, I saw rows upon rows of small white stones, each bearing a number on its top. Nearby, a sign indicated that the stones were the graves of the unknown dead of that battle. The term "unknown" piqued my curiosity. These were men who before the battle were known to their comrades and, now in death, were unknown, their names lost forever in the annals of time. After I visited the Gettysburg Battlefield, the spark ignited at Shiloh turned into a full-blown quest for information. What caused these men to take up arms and die for their beliefs? I wanted to know more about the Civil War other than what was printed in a park brochure.

When I visited libraries and bookstores, I found many books covering every aspect of the Civil War, from the various battles to the various commanders and everything in between. Where does one start to search for information? I just wanted basic information, not to be bogged down in the strategy that played out on the field. In essence, I just wanted the essential facts, plain and simple.

There were several reference books on the market, including Patricia Faust's *Historical Times Illustrated: Encyclopedia of the Civil War.* This book contained information on the battles, commanders and ships and also included definitions, all arranged alphabetically. However, as a novice, the only way I could use the book was if I knew what I was looking for, which most of the time I did not. I discovered another book, *The Civil War Day by Day*, written by E.B. and Barbara Long, which followed the war on a daily basis. I thought I had found what I was seeking. This book, arranged chronologically, covered political events, planning and strategy sessions, as well as the battles, each discussion confined to several paragraphs. I now had the information, but not in a condensed form.

I was hooked, not only on the events of the war, but also the small incidents or strange quirks that occurred, both on and off the battlefield. I began to make notes from many and varied sources. Magazines, such as the *Civil War Times Illustrated, America's Civil War,*

1

and *North and South*, contained many stories on the various battles and individuals and supplied statistical information. The Ken Burns PBS series on the Civil War as well as A&E's *Civil War Journal* added fascinating stories and tidbits. The Internet opened many other sources, especially on regimental histories and the various ships of the navies.

After compiling all my notes, I put them into a bound booklet. As the years passed and my interest in the Civil War grew, my thirst for information increased, as did the size of my library. However, I found I was using this booklet more and more; it had become one of my most valued resources in my library. I had a place to find basic information quickly and it made the Civil War plain and simple to understand and follow. I did not have to wade through volumes to find the information I was seeking.

This book will be a great source of information for the Civil War novice whose appetite for just basic information on the war has been whetted. In addition, the Civil War enthusiast or historian will have a useful resource to locate that certain piece of information needed to complete a project or to remember a certain date, a certain battle, or other essential detail on the war. Sometimes a person just needs a place to start their search, a helping hand to guide them on their way.

How to Use This Book

1. How to locate a battle, a fight or a skirmish

Study of the Civil War can be a confusing endeavor and often information on a certain battle is difficult to find, as one battle was sometimes known by different names. The North tended to refer to a battle after the nearest landmark, usually a river or stream. The South would name or call the same battle after the nearest town or region where the fight took place. As if that is not enough to create utter confusion for the Civil War novice, not all fights or conflicts were considered battles, for there were certain requirements necessary to meet the definition of a battle. In addition to the battles, there were skirmishes, actions, engagements and raids. To obtain information on a particular fight, look up the name of the incident in "The Battles" section of the book. There the name of the battle/skirmish/action/engagement is listed alphabetically with the date of the event. The outcome or the agreed upon conclusion of many historians is also listed. If there was no clear-cut victor, the outcome is listed as "undetermined." If the event is known by another name, that name is listed. Refer to that name to obtain the date and the agreed upon victor.

EXAMPLE A:

1. If searching for information on the Battle of Trevilian Station, first locate Trevilian Station in "The Battles." The date listed for the battle is June 12, 1864.

Tom's Brook	October 9, 1864	Union
Totopotomoy	May 28–30, 1864	Undetermined
Tranter's Creek	June 5, 1862	Union
Trevilian Station	*June 12, 1864*	*Confederate*
Tupelo	July 14, 1864	Confederate

2. Now, go to the chapter titled "1864" and look up June 12. The information on the Battle of Trevilian Station is provided there.

12   *Battle of Trevilian Station, Virginia* (**Confederate Victory**)
In an effort to shield the army's movement toward Petersburg, General Grant ordered his cavalry commander to create a diversion. By moving westward, Sheridan hoped Lee's cavalry would follow, thus depriving Lee of his "eyes and ears." Sheridan was also to link up with Hunter and destroy the Confederate rail system from central Virginia. His first movement was toward Trevilian Station and there he was met by Confederate cavalry. The fight between the two cavalry units was described by some as "a wild melee of saber strokes and pistol shots." With his defeat at Trevilian Station, Sheridan's planned cavalry raids in the Shenandoah were stopped.

	U.S.A.			C.S.A.	
	Philip Sheridan, George Custer			Wade Hampton, Fitzhugh Lee	
	Troops	*Killed*	*Wounded*	*Missing/Captured*	*Total Casualties*
U.S.A.	8,000	150	738	624	1,512
C.S.A.	5,000				612

EXAMPLE B:

1. For information about what took place at Fort Davidson, look up the name Fort Davidson in "The Battles."

Fort Brooke	October 16–18, 1863	Union
Fort Davidson	*See Pilot Knob*	
Fort DeRussy	March 14, 1864	Union

2. Under Fort Davidson is a notation to see Pilot Knob. Look up Pilot Knob in the same section.

Piedmont	See Staunton	
Pilot Knob	*September 26–27, 1864*	*Union*
Pine Bluff	October 25, 1863	Union

3. Look for September 26 in the chapter titled "1864." The information listed below is given about the incident at Pilot Knob.

26–27   *Engagement at Pilot Knob (AKA Fort Davidson), Missouri* (**Union Victory**)
General Sterling Price approached Pilot Knob where General Thomas Ewing, Jr., was defending Fort Davidson, a six-sided earthwork fort protected by a 12 foot wide by 9 foot deep moat. Price could have bypassed the fort but upon hearing that Ewing was present, he decided to attack, for he disliked Ewing and the cruel manner in which he treated pro–Confederate supporters. On the third attempt to take the fort, Price's men were able to reach the moat but were slaughtered by rifle fire and hand thrown grenades. Price called off the attack and Ewing withdrew during the night. It was considered a Union victory; though Price continued the raid, he did not try to take the city of St. Louis.

		U.S.A.				C.S.A.	

	General Thomas Ewing					General Sterling Price	
	Troops	*Killed*	*Wounded*	*Missing/Captured*	*Total Casualties*		
U.S.A.	6,000	28	56	100	184		
C.S.A.	9,000				unknown		

2. *To find armies*

Prior to the start of the Civil War, the United States had a small standing army whose main responsibility was the defense of the frontier while the Confederacy had no standing army. By the end of the war, over forty armies had been created. The Union would have from fourteen to sixteen while the Confederacy ended up with twenty-one to twenty-three, depending upon what at the time constituted an army. For an army to function properly there must be a command structure. At the end of the chapter titled "The Armies" is a chart with the breakdown of the command structure, the uniform designations for the Union and Confederate armies and the structure and chain of command for infantry, artillery and cavalry regiments. For a list of the various armies formed by both the United States and the Confederate States during the Civil War, see Appendix II.

3. *Naval information*

At the start of the war, the United States had a small naval force whose primary responsibility was to protect the coast of the United States. The Confederate States had no navy at the beginning of the war, but quickly acquired one. Many times, ships were captured or seized and placed back into immediate service under the flag of the new owner. Sometimes, the only change, other than manpower, was in the designation from *USS* to *CSS* or vice versa. In Appendix III, ships of both navies are listed, arranged alphabetically by allegiance, with brief descriptions for many of the ships.

4. *Commander information*

To find out personal information about a commander, look up the commander's name in Appendix IV. The names are listed alphabetically without regard to allegiance. The reader will find basic information on the commanders as to allegiance (U.S.A. or C.S.A.), date and place of birth, date and place of death, and where he is buried, if known.

EXAMPLE C:

1. For Sterling Price, Appendix III lists the following:

Price, Sterling. C.S.A.— Major General. Born September 20, 1809, in Prince Edward County, Virginia. Died September 29, 1867, in St. Louis, Missouri. Buried in Bellefontaine Cemetery, St. Louis, Missouri.

5. *Definitions*

Many words used in descriptions of the war are unfamiliar to the modern reader. Appendix I is a glossary of the more unusual terms.

Introduction

"There will never be anything in America more interesting than the
Civil War — never."
                                        — *Gertrude Stein, 1937*

Why write another book on the Civil War? There are already so many books on the
market today covering every Civil War topic imaginable that a reader has an enormous task
just to sort through it all. As an amateur Civil War buff, I wanted to know just the facts.
When was a certain battle fought? What led up to the fight? Who were the commanders
and what was the outcome? How many men were killed or injured in a particular battle or,
for that matter, in all the war? In order to obtain this information it was necessary to locate
and go through various books, magazines and other sources. Why not a book with only
the basic facts?

In 1992, after trying to find certain facts and being unable to do so, I decided to gather
information for myself so I could better understand the Civil War. At the same time, I
would streamline all the information that was available. As I started gathering facts, I mentioned to a few friends and co-workers what I was doing. They liked the idea and started
to ask me questions as to what happened or why it was important. I did not realize how
many people were interested in the Civil War, nor did I realize how many were interested
in only a brief outline of the war. Therefore, I did not concentrate so much on the strategy that was played out on the field or the plans drawn up the night before a battle, but
instead just the facts.

While searching for and gathering information, I discovered a possible reason why
this war is of interest to so many people. It is not difficult to be caught up in the emotions
of the times. This war played out on American soil and involved American soldiers. It was
a family fight, in which men fought brothers, fathers, cousins and even in-laws. As I read
about various battles and followed a company, a regiment, a brigade, a division or a corps
through their campaigns, I was devastated when the leader of that unit was killed or when

one died needlessly in a duel. When I read of their deaths, I became angry and upset, although these men died well over a century ago.

There had been talk of possible secession since our country's beginning. When war did break out, men on both sides immediately joined the fight. By July 1861, three months after the start of the first hostilities, the Union's military strength stood at 219,400 men while the South had a mere 114,000. The men that joined the army really did not know the horrors that would last for the next four years. Neither did the country.

While studying the war and its battles, I thought of all the men who lined up shoulder-to-shoulder, muskets in place, and marched across an open field towards the enemy. What thoughts crossed their minds as they stepped out? Did they think they would be victorious and return to camp unscathed? Were their thoughts on the objective or were their thoughts on the loved ones waiting for them back at home? It must have been frightening to walk across an open field into the face of cannon fire. Knowing this, why then did they so readily line up and march directly into danger? Was it patriotism, or old fashioned gallantry? Or did they instead go about following orders, doing their duty to God, their country and their fellow man? We will never know the answers to these questions. All we can do is surmise the answers, for the men's deeds speak volumes.

This war is known by many names; most call it the Civil War and that is almost by default. Many Southerners called it the War for Southern Independence while in the North, particularly New England, it was called the War of the Rebellion. In some areas, it was known as the War of Northern Aggression or the War of Southern Aggression, depending on where you lived. Even today, those last two terms are met with intensely partisan feeling and, in some cases, the terms are considered "fighting words." The War Between the States, like the Civil War, is a nonpartisan term that never really achieved common usage at the time.

In July 1861, the first real battle of the war occurred. It was known as Bull Run or Manassas, both being the same place. The Union and Confederate forces often referred to the same battle by different names. The Union tended to name a battle after the nearest landmark, usually a river or stream such as Bull Run, the Confederacy after the nearest town, such as Manassas. In the North, Sharpsburg was better known as Antietam. Stone's River was known in the South as Murfreesboro; Opeqon Creek was called Winchester. The South named one battle, Shiloh, after a church that was near the location where they fought; the North called this same battle Pittsburg Landing because that was where the troops were encamped.

When actual combat broke out, people of this country were unfamiliar with the horrors of war. In early July 1861, when it was discovered that a battle was to be fought, people came from all areas to watch. Some packed a picnic basket, grabbed the kids, piled them in a wagon, and traveled down from Washington, D.C., and the surrounding counties. They were going to make a day of it. A festive atmosphere greeted the people as they arrived. They spread their blankets out and proceeded to have lunch while men on both sides prepared to "do battle." Bands played, flags waved in the breeze, and young children played games of hoops. This was going to be a show well worth the trip. In the background, drums could be heard calling the soldiers to assembly. However, once the firing of guns began, the horror of war became a reality. Men actually fell down and bled. Their cries of pain and agony were real. Both soldier and civilian alike were dazed. Confusion reigned on the field as many, including soldiers, fled in all different directions as if to put a distance between themselves and the fighting. This war, this terrible war, would exact a high price.

Many historians believe the Civil War marked the beginning of modern warfare and new inventions. Before this war, soldiers studied the Napoleonic Wars and at the start of the fighting employed the same technologies. In fact, one of the required courses at West Point Military Academy was French so that future military commanders would be able to read and understand the latest European military manuals. However, as the war progressed, changes occurred. It was this war that saw the first use of trenches and wire entanglements. The telegraph had its first practical use. This war also was the first to use railroads to move troops and equipment, the first with repeating infantry rifles, and the first to employ armored ships, the ironclad and the submarine. One of the technological innovations used by the Union was the observation balloon. Such hot air balloons helped in tracking troop movements and the accuracy of artillery fire. Both the Union and the Confederacy employed the military draft for the first time in America. Not only did this country lose its childhood, but warfare would never be the same. The way men fought would change. Their weaponry would change. Moreover, this country would change — it would be stronger than ever before because of it. This country grew up within a short span of four years.

The carnage was enormous. Over a million men were killed, wounded or died of other causes related to the war. Even though warfare improved, medical practices did not. Doctors quickly amputated arms, legs, hands and feet in record numbers, as they believed amputation was the only way to save a man's life when there was damage to the bone. Head and stomach wounds were treated with a dose of whiskey to ease the man's suffering until death relieved him of his life. Wounds were poorly treated and the idea of sterile dressings was still years off. Wounds became infected and caused more deaths than bullets.

Many soldiers returned to camp after a fight leaving a relative or friend dead or dying on the battlefield. If it were possible and time permitted, burial details were formed and the dead laid to rest. Perhaps a wooden marker was placed on the grave to mark the final resting place of the soldier. If time permitted and the inclination was there, a letter was sent to the soldier's family telling them of his death and perhaps his burial place, if known. Families anxiously awaited news from their loved ones, hoping all were safe. This was also the time when many soldiers could not read or write and many a family never heard from their loved ones. Sometimes a notice would be posted at the courthouse or news office listing the names of the dead and wounded. There were numerous occasions when the family never heard and, after months of not hearing, concluded their loved one was dead.

After a battle and especially after the loss of a friend, a comrade or a close relative, soldiers were not given the time to recoup or to grieve. There was no R and R for the soldier and furloughs were hard to come by or non-existent. If they were lucky enough to get a furlough, most could not afford the trip home. Mental anguish and mental fatigue were never considered. Men were expected to march all day and then, when called for, fight. When the war was over, the men were expected to return home and resume their lives as if nothing happened. "Get over it and get on with your life" was the way most handled the flashbacks and nightmares that plagued them. The idea of treating the mind and emotions after a traumatic event was not an accepted practice and would not be so for more than a hundred years. Many men who fought bravely returned home not the same person they were when they left. Some just could not pick up the pieces and resume their lives. This war affected future generations in ways too numerous to mention or consider.

Not only was the war costly in lives, but it was costly in terms of dollars to the governments. It cost the U.S. government approximately two million dollars a day to conduct the war, for an estimated total cost of more than six billion dollars. The total cost to the Confederacy has been estimated at four billion dollars. The price does not include the loss of land, buildings, livestock to the citizenry nor the amount paid to restore, replenish or revitalize the country when the war was over.

Given the scope of this war, the volumes that could be written about it are endless. After finishing my initial project, I found that the notes I put together were the most consulted of all my references on the Civil War. The notes contained just the facts, which were easy to find. I did not have to wade through volumes to find when an engagement occurred or what its outcome was. The more I consulted it, the more I thought others, perhaps, would find it just as useful.

The object of this work is just to give the barest facts. If readers find something interesting and want further information on it, head towards the nearest bookstore or library to find numerous books on battles, leaders and the war itself. Happy reading.

Chapter 1

The Armies

"We must train and classify the whole of our male citizens, and
make military instruction a regular part of collegiate education."
— *Thomas Jefferson to James Monroe, June 18, 1813*

Prior to the start of the Civil War, the United States had a small standing army made up of 16,367 officers and men distributed over 198 fighting units. Most units were in the west to deal with issues among the settlers and the Indians. The Army of the East had fewer than a thousand men by the time President-elect Lincoln arrived in Washington. With the looming threat of war, the army began transferring men and divisions from the western frontier to the East. By April 1861, the Second Infantry was transferred from Kansas, Nebraska and Minnesota while the Fourth Infantry was recalled to the East after spending the previous ten years in the Pacific Northwest. By the spring of 1862, most Regular army units would be part of the 5th Army Corps assigned to the Army of the Potomac in the East.

At the same time, recruiting increased. After the firing on Fort Sumter, President Lincoln called for 75,000 volunteers to join the army to help "put down the rebellion." Men flocked to their local recruiting areas and by the end of the war, the Union would have 3,559 fighting units. The Volunteer units were accepted into service or "mustered in" and given certain designations, a number plus the state where the unit originated. (Example: 83rd Pennsylvania — the 83rd unit formed in Pennsylvania.) The United States, though, kept the Regular army as a separate unit, designating it as such, but parceling it out to the various armies depending on the need of the unit. They would be known as the "U.S. Regulars" (1st U.S. Regulars, 2nd U.S. Regulars, 3rd U.S. Regulars, etc.). Many Regular officers were permitted to take a leave of absence to accept a position of higher rank within the volunteer army. At the conclusion of the war, these men were to return to their original unit with their former rank, while the volunteer army was disbanded or "mustered out."

The newly formed Confederacy had no standing army at all. Plans were on the drawing board for the creation of a "peacetime" army consisting of one corps, which would number approximately ten thousand men. Each state had its own local militia or Home Guard whose purpose was to defend and protect its residents. The number of men joining their local militia increased as raised voices called for secession. The new Confederacy began to make provisions for the creation of a fighting army with the Act of the Confederate Congress on March 6, 1861.

With the drums of war now beating louder, many influential Southern men began to raise armies and offer them to the state, which under the act allowed the state to offer them to the Confederate government. The state retained authority over the raising, the organizing and the appointment of officers. This changed in May 1861, when the Confederate Congress gave authority to President Jefferson Davis to accept local units without state approval. Davis was also granted the right to name and appoint officers. As the war progressed, the Confederate government exercised more and more control over the armies and, in essence, removed them from state control.

The states, though, did maintain control over the local militia and Home Guards. These units provided defense for the local regions and also provided a way for those who could not serve in the armed forces for being too young, too old or other reasons. These local militias or Home Guard would be given the responsibility, at first, of handling the Conscription Laws, which would be enacted later in the war. By the end of the war, the Confederate government had 1,526 fighting units.

Both the North and the South during the course of the war created over forty armies. At the start of the war, the United States had just one army composed of four artillery units, five cavalry regiments and ten infantry regiments. By the end of the war, the Union had fourteen different armies consisting of 2,144 infantry regiments, 9 light infantry battalions, 272 cavalry regiments, 61 heavy artillery units, 432 separate batteries and 13 engineer units. The Confederacy went from no armies in the beginning to twenty-one armies created by the various state and central governments. By the end of the war, the Confederate military would have 642 infantry regiments, 137 cavalry regiments and 16 artillery regiments consisting of 227 batteries. Many of the armies existed for a short time or were merged into others. The Confederacy had one army, the Army of West Tennessee/Mississippi, which ceased to exist when its commander, John C. Pemberton, surrendered it to Union forces upon the fall of Vicksburg in July 1863. Appendix II is a list of the various armies formed with a brief history for each and the names of men who commanded them.

On March 6, 1861, almost a month prior to the firing on Fort Sumter, the Act of the Confederate Congress launched the organization of an army. When forming its army, the Confederate government looked to individuals familiar with military matters. Men who had formerly served in the U.S. military but had resigned their position to go with the Confederacy decided on its organization. As a result, the Confederate army resembled the United States army in almost every way. The same rules and regulations applied, as did the same training and the military protocol. The Confederate Constitution, similar to the U.S. Constitution, provided for the president to be the commander-in-chief of all military forces. Confederate President Jefferson Davis was a graduate of West Point Military Academy and had served as secretary of war under President James Buchanan.

In the beginning, both the northern and southern armies were commanded by a major-general. However, in October 1862, the Confederate government decided, with the additional armies coming into formation, that each should be commanded by a new rank — lieutenant general. During the course of the war, the Confederacy would have seventeen lieutenant generals. On the other side, it would not be until March 12, 1864, that the Union established the rank of lieutenant general, and there would only be one. Ulysses S. Grant was promoted to that rank and at the same time he was placed in command of all the Union armies. Each army commander would report directly to General Grant, who issued all military orders. Grant established his headquarters with the Army of the Potomac, which was under the command of Major General George G. Meade. A year later, in March 1865, the Confederate government gave that same authority to one man, General Robert E. Lee.

Before establishing the position of lieutenant general, Union commanders in the field reported to the general-in-chief, who issued all directives and orders. He in turn reported to the secretary of war. At the start of the conflict, Winfield Scott held the position as brevet lieutenant general in charge of all military matters. However, because he was 75 years old (born June 13, 1786) and in poor health, he was soon replaced by Major General George B. McClellan (November 6, 1861, to March 11, 1862). It was reported that Scott could not sit a horse because of his weight and girth, and thus could not take to the field to oversee matters. He relied on the written report. Major General Henry W. Halleck assumed the position as general-in-chief from March 11, 1862, to March 12, 1864, after which Lieutenant General Ulysses Grant took command of all the various northern armies.

The Confederate military leaders in the field reported either to the secretary of war or to President Jefferson Davis directly. Davis had problems keeping a secretary of war, having six over the course of the war years. The men who served in that position were: LeRoy P. Walker, February 21, 1861, to September 17, 1861; Judah P. Benjamin, September 17, 1861, to March 17, 1862; George W. Randolph, March 17, 1862, to November 17, 1862; Gustavus W. Smith, November 17, 1862, to November 21, 1862; James A. Seddon, November 21, 1862, to February 6, 1865; and John C. Breckinridge, February 2, 1865, to the end of the war. With the threat of defeat, the Confederate government placed Robert E. Lee in command of all southern armies with the hope he could pull the Confederacy from the brink of disaster.

Both the northern and southern armies consisted of regiments, brigades, divisions and finally corps. Each regiment, on both sides, had ten companies at the start of the war. These companies were designated by letters—"A" company, "B" company, etc. The letter "J" was not used, for when spoken or hollered in the heat of battle, "J" often sounded like "A" and could result in misunderstanding and confusion. In the north, when the men enlisted, they were assigned to the company being formed at the time. Once that company reached its quota, which was usually one hundred men, the next men would be assigned to the next company forming. Most companies in the Confederate army were formed with men from the same area. These companies were then assigned to a regiment from the same locality in the belief this would foster good morale, loyalty and bravery. In both armies, a captain normally commanded the companies while a colonel usually commanded a regiment.

Usually four to five regiments formed a brigade. In the north, the brigades would be commanded by the senior ranking colonel, while in the Confederate army, a brigadier general was placed in command. Three to four brigades made up a division. A brigadier general commanded a northern division while a major general commanded a southern division. Two to three divisions made up a corps, which were commanded by a major general in the Union armies and a lieutenant general in the Confederate army. The northern army usually consisted of five to seven corps commanded by a major general, who was also known as the commanding general. He usually was the most senior ranking officer. Sometimes, though, political appointees would be named to head the corps. For the southern armies, the army was usually made up of two to three corps and commanded by a lieutenant general. Most of these positions were the senior ranking men, but there were also political appointees named to the position.

An army usually was made up of different elements or units—infantry, artillery, cavalry, engineers and topographers. The infantry was and is considered the main fighting force being trained, armed and equipped to fight on foot. During the Civil War, the infantry marched everywhere they went and soon earned the nickname "foot soldier." Some men were assigned to the artillery where they were trained, armed and equipped to use the large caliber guns: napoleons, parrots, howitzers or mortars. (See Appendix I for definitions of these guns.)

The cavalry was not only considered a fighting force, but also acted as scouts and guards for wagon trains and supply lines. As the war progressed, cavalrymen would serve as couriers and messengers and some acted as provost guards for prisoners captured after a battle. In some instances, they were sent out as an advance guard with instructions to ascertain the enemy's location or strength. In the Confederate cavalry, most men were expected to furnish their own horses. If he lost his horse in battle, he had to get another mount or risk being transferred to the infantry. Most Union cavalrymen had their mounts furnished by the government, though many did purchase their own.

To differentiate among the various services, both sides used color designations. It was discovered that on the battlefield, commanders had a hard time distinguishing infantry from cavalry or artillery. Color on a man's cap made the recognition possible. Blue represented infantry, while red indicated artillery and yellow signified cavalry. Later the Union further devised a system of corps badges to indicate which corps the soldier belonged to. The corps badge was affixed to the man's hat, and, though the use of the various colored corps badges, the man's division was identifiable.

When the war started, both armies were at full strength with regiments of approximately one thousand men each. As the war progressed, the size of the regiments varied greatly. By the end of the war, some regiments had fewer than three hundred. When a new regiment reached the field, it often had fewer than 800 men available for combat. Men who fell ill or who were serving as cooks, teamsters, orderlies, and clerks accounted for the reduced numbers. In many of the larger battles, the fighting strength of some regiments was less than 500. In 1862, the average full strength of a regiment was roughly 500 to 600 men, but that total was almost cut in half the following year. By 1863, the average full strength of most fighting infantry regiments fell to 300 or 400 men. In the final stages of the war, some regiments could not muster enough men to form ten companies. It was then that the regiments either were combined with other units or were delegated as battalions. Battalions were usually was made up of two to nine companies.

It was expensive to equip an army. The total Union expenditures for land operations were estimated at $2,713,568,000; for the naval war, it was estimated that $314,223,000 was spent. The total cost of the war was about $3,027,791,000. The cost to the Confederacy is hard to determine, for many records were destroyed. It has been estimated by some experts to be around $1,356,784,222 for land operations and $93,045 for naval operations, with a combined total cost of $1,449,830,176.

CHAIN OF COMMAND

The President (United States or Confederate States)
General-in-Chief

Command	Commanded By	Basic Information
Corps	Major General	Usually 3 Corps were under each Army Commander. Union army had a total of 40 corps (37 infantry, 3 cavalry), some combined with others, while the Confederate armies had a total of 11 (8 infantry and 3 cavalry).
Division	Major General or Brigadier General	Usually 3 Divisions were under each Corps Commander
Brigade	Brigadier General or a Colonel	Usually 4 Brigades were under each Division Commander
Regiment	Colonel	Usually 4 Regiments were under each Brigade Commander
Company	Captain	Usually 10 Companies were under each Regiment Commander

REGULAR INFANTRY REGIMENT

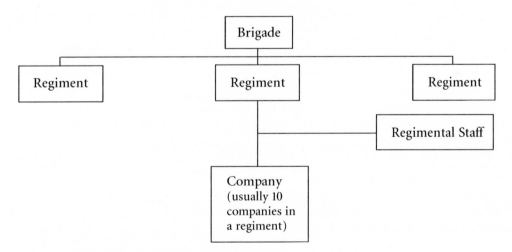

Regimental Staff comprised of	*Company comprised of*
Colonel (Commanding)	Captain (Commanding)
Lt. Colonel	First Lieutenant
Regimental Adjutant	Second Lieutenant
Regimental Quartermaster	4 Sergeants
Drum Major	8 Corporals
	82 Privates

BREAKDOWN OF A COMPANY

A company was commanded by a captain, one first lieutenant, one second lieutenant, one first sergeant, four sergeants and eight corporals. When the company was divided into platoons, a lieutenant commanded each platoon. Each section was commanded by a sergeant and each squad commanded by a corporal.

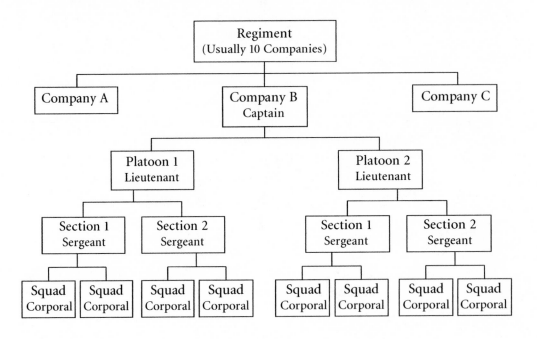

REGULAR CAVALRY REGIMENT

When fighting as dismounted cavalry, one man in four was assigned to hold and guard the horses.

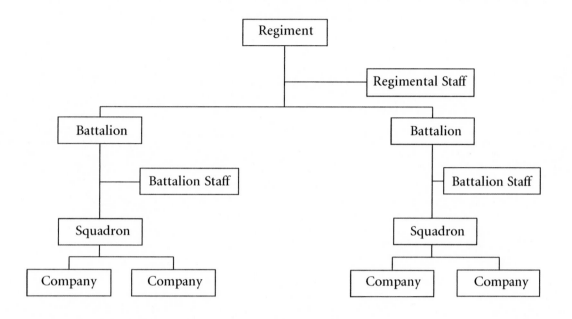

Regimental Staff consists of	Battalion Staff consists of	Company consists of
Colonel (Commanding)	Major (Commanding)	Captain (Commanding)
Lt. Colonel	Battalion Adjutant (usually a Lt.)	First Lieutenant
		2nd Lieutenant
Regimental Adjutant	Battalion Quartermaster (usually a Lt.)	First Sergeant
Regimental Quartermaster		Quartermaster Sgt.
2 Buglers	Sergeant Major	4 Sergeants
	Commissary Sergeant	8 Corporals
	Hospital Steward	2 Farriers
	Saddler Sergeant	1 Wagoner
	Veterinary Sergeant	1 Saddler
		72 Privates

REGULAR ARTILLERY REGIMENT

The smallest artillery unit in a regular regiment was the section. A section had two guns, each with a team and limber (a horse drawn carriage for artillery). A battery of three sections would have 6 caissons and limbers in reserve with a field forge and battery wagon. Artillery rarely fought as a regiment and were usually loaned out in batteries to infantry brigades, divisions and corps.

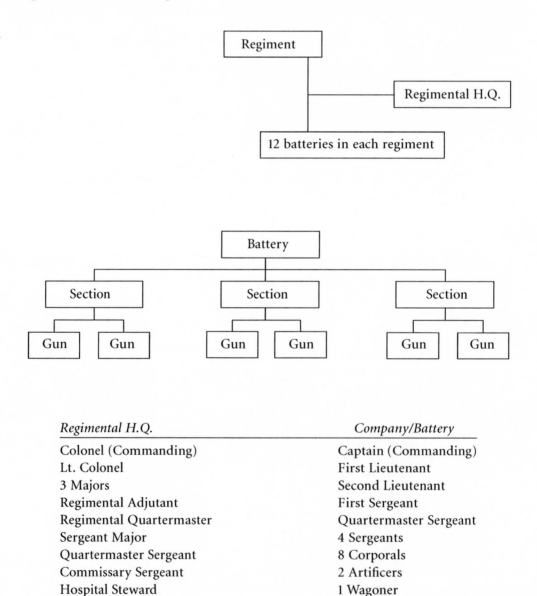

Regimental H.Q.	Company/Battery
Colonel (Commanding)	Captain (Commanding)
Lt. Colonel	First Lieutenant
3 Majors	Second Lieutenant
Regimental Adjutant	First Sergeant
Regimental Quartermaster	Quartermaster Sergeant
Sergeant Major	4 Sergeants
Quartermaster Sergeant	8 Corporals
Commissary Sergeant	2 Artificers
Hospital Steward	1 Wagoner
Drum Major	122 Privates

Chapter 2

The Battles

"There is no glory in battle worth the blood it costs."
— *Dwight Eisenhower*

It can be confusing and sometimes difficult to locate information on a certain battle. There are many reasons why this is so, but the major reason is battles often had more than one name. The North tended to name a battle after the nearest landmark, usually a river or stream. The South would name the same battle after the nearest town or region where the fight took place.

As if that's not enough to create utter confusion for the Civil War novice, not all fights or conflicts were battles; some did not meet all the requirements to be defined as such. In addition to battles, there were skirmishes, actions, engagements and raids. When I was searching for information on a fight at either Trevilian Station or Jack's Shop, I could find nothing, for they are not classified as battles but instead as skirmishes. In fact, there were 6,337 skirmishes. *Dyer's Compendium*, a noted Civil War reference book containing facts on armies and men, lists 10,455 types of events that ran twenty-five pages. In an effort to define the various military conflicts, the following definitions are included for easy reference. In descending order, depending on the incident, the fight is listed as an operation, campaign, action/battle, engagement, skirmish, assault, demonstration, and affair.

- **Action**—Widely used term for an engagement between enemy forces, often used interchangeably for battle.
- **Affair**—An engagement of minor size.
- **Assault**—A military attack such as one launched against a fortified area or place, or a concluding stage of an attack in which close combat took place with an enemy.
- **Battle**—A wide scale engagement between major forces of independent command and usually directed by a commanding general.
- **Campaign**—A series of military operations undertaken to accomplish a purpose or objective.

- **Engagement**—A fight involving combat between regiments, divisions or brigades or detachments of main armies. In size, an engagement would be classified as being just above a skirmish but below a battle. When the main body was involved, the incident was usually termed an engagement.

- **Operation**—A military campaign or mission to achieve an objective that may involve various campaigns.

- **Raid**—A swift and usually fast moving strike behind enemy lines to either burn, destroy, wreck or confiscate a strategic target or supplies. It was also performed sometimes to draw manpower away from one area. Cavalry units usually conducted raids.

- **Reconnaissance**—Exploring an area in an effort to determine the enemy's location or position or an attempt to gain information as to manpower or other military information.

- **Siege**—The surrounding or blockading of a position for a prolonged period in an attempt to gain possession or control of it. Usually this was accomplished by refusing supplies or manpower to resupply or reinforce an area.

- **Skirmish**—A clash or minor battle of the smallest scope involving limited manpower or units, and where the main army was not involved. Usually a skirmish involved opposing troops assigned to guard or to protect the front or flanks of a moving army. A skirmish could lead to a full-scale battle.

Below are the approximate numbers of the various military affairs between 1861 and 1865.

MILITARY AFFAIRS

Type		Type		Type	
Actions	1,026	Combats	46	Reconnaissance	252
Affairs	639	Engagements	310	Scouts	434
Assaults	29	Expeditions	727	Sieges	26
Battles	76	Occupations	82	Skirmishes	6,337
Campaigns	29	Operations	299		
Captures	79	Raids	64	**Totals**	10,455

The South had more military activity than the North. Several times during the conflict, efforts were made to take the war northward, but all the attempts met with disaster. Virginia saw more action than any other state, for she not only had the capital of the Confederacy but was also a border state and considered a leader in the fight.

MILITARY EVENTS WITHIN A STATE

1. Virginia	2,154	8. Georgia	549	15. Texas	90
2. Tennessee	1,462	9. Kentucky	453	16. Indian Territory	89
3. Missouri	1,162	10. Alabama	336	17. California	88
4. Mississippi	772	11. North Carolina	313	18. New Mexico	
5. Arkansas	771	12. South Carolina	239	Territory	75
6. West Virginia	632	13. Maryland	203	19. Other states	333
7. Louisiana	566	14. Florida	168	**Total**	10,455

Battles and Other Actions

Many battles were fought over a wide area. Some of those areas were given descriptive names by the men who fought there or by newspapermen or historians who wrote of the battle immediately afterwards. The asterisk (*) beside the name of the main battle indicates that this was one of those areas.

West Virginia didn't exist as a state until June 20, 1863, when it officially split from Virginia because of its pro–Union stance. Battles in the soon-to-be state are referred to as being in Western Virginia.

Event	Dates	Outcome
Adairsville (Georgia)	May 17, 1864	Confederate
Albemarle Sound (North Carolina)	May 5, 1864	Undetermined
Aldie (Virginia)	June 17, 1863	Undetermined
Allatoona (Georgia)	October 5, 1864	Union
Alsop's Farm (Virginia) *see* Spotsylvania		
Andrew's Raid (Georgia)	April 12, 1862	Confederate
Antietam (Maryland)	September 17, 1862	Union
Apache Canyon (New Mexico Territory)	March 26, 1862	Union
Appomattox (Virginia)	April 8–9, 1865	Union
Arkansas Post (Arkansas)	January 11, 1863	Union
Athens (Missouri)	August 5, 1861	Union
Athens (Alabama)	January 26, 1864	Union
Atlanta (Georgia)	July 22, 1864	Union
Auburn (Virginia)	October 13–14, 1863	Undetermined
Averasborough (North Carolina)	March 16, 1865	Union
Baker's Creek (Mississippi) *see* Champion's Hill		
Ball's Bluff (Virginia)	October 21, 1861	Confederate
Barbourville (Kentucky)	September 19, 1861	Confederate
Barhamsville (Virginia)	May 7, 1862	Confederate
Baton Rouge (1st) (Louisiana)	May 12, 1862	Union
Baton Rouge (2nd) (Louisiana)	August 5, 1862	Union
Battery Wagner (South Carolina)	July 10–18, 1863	Confederate
Battle of the Clouds—Lookout Mountain*		
Baxter Springs (Kansas)	October 6, 1863	Confederate
Bayou Bourbeau (Louisiana)	November 3, 1863	Undetermined
Bayou Forche (Arkansas)	September 10, 1863	Union
Bean's Station (Tennessee)	December 14, 1863	Confederate
Bear River (Idaho)	January 29, 1863	Union
Beaver Dam (Virginia) *see* Mechanicsville		
Belmont (Missouri)	November 7, 1861	Confederate
Belle Grove (Virginia) *see* Cedar Creek		

Event	Dates	Outcome
Bentonville (North Carolina)	March 19–21, 1865	Union
Berryville (Virginia)	September 3–4, 1864	Undetermined
Bethesda Church (Virginia) *see* 2nd Cold Harbor		
Beverly's Ford (Virginia) *see* Brandy Station		
Big Bethel (Virginia)	June 10, 1861	Confederate
Big Black River (Mississippi)	May 17, 1863	Union
Big Blue River (Missouri)	October 21, 1864	Confederate
Blackburn's Ford (Virginia)	July 18, 1861	Confederate
Blair's Landing (Louisiana)	April 12–13, 1864	Union
Bloody Angle — Gettysburg*		
Bloody Angle — Spotsylvania*		
Bloody Lane — Antietam*		
Bloody Pond — Shiloh*		
Bloody Salient — Spotsylvania*		
Blountsville (Tennessee)	September 22, 1863	Union
Blue Springs (Tennessee)	October 10, 1863	Union
Boonville (Missouri)	June 17, 1861	Union
Boteler's Ford (Maryland)	September 19–20, 1862	Confederate
Boydton Plank Road (Virginia) *see* Hatcher's Run (First)		
Brandy Station (Virginia)	June 9, 1863	Union
Brentwood (Tennessee)	March 25, 1863	Confederate
Brice's Crossroads (Mississippi)	June 10, 1864	Confederate
Bristoe Station (1st) (Virginia) *see* Manassas Junction		
Bristoe Station (Virginia)	October 14, 1863	Union
Brown's Ferry (Tennessee)	October 26–27, 1863	Union
Buck Head Creek (Georgia)	November 28, 1864	Union
Buckland Mills (Virginia)	October 19, 1863	Confederate
Buffalo Mountain (Virginia) *see* Camp Alleghany		
Bull's Gap (Tennessee)	November 11–13, 1864	Confederate
Bull Pasture (Virginia) *see* McDowell		
Bull Run (1st) (Virginia)	July 21, 1861	Confederate
Bull Run (2nd) (Virginia)	August 29–30, 1862	Confederate
Burgess Mill (Virginia) *see* Hatcher's Run (First)		
Byrum's Ford (Missouri)	October 22–23, 1864	Union
Cabin Creek (Oklahoma)	July 1–2, 1863	Union
Camp Alleghany (Virginia)	December 13, 1861	Undetermined
Campbell Station (Tennessee)	November 16, 1863	Union
Cape Girardeau (Missouri)	April 24, 1863	Union
Carnifix Ferry (Virginia)	September 10, 1861	Union
Carrick's Ford (Western Virginia) *see* Corrick's Ford		

Event	Dates	Outcome
Carthage (Missouri)	July 5, 1861	Confederate
Cedar Creek (Virginia)	October 19, 1864	Union
Cedar Mountain (Virginia)	August 9–10, 1862	Confederate
Cemetery Ridge — Gettysburg*		
Chaffin's Farm (Virginia) *see* Fort Harrison		
Chalk Bluff (Arkansas)	May 1, 1863	Confederate
Champion's Hill (Mississippi)	May 16, 1863	Union
Chancellorsville (Virginia)	May 1–4, 1863	Confederate
Chantilly (Virginia)	September 1, 1862	Confederate
Chaplin Hills (Kentucky) *see* Perryville		
Charleston (South Carolina)	April 7, 1863	Confederate
Charleston (South Carolina)	February 18, 1865	Union
Chattanooga (1st) (Tennessee)	June 7, 1862	Union
Chattanooga (2nd) (Tennessee)	November 23–25, 1863	Union
Cheat Mountain (Western Virginia)	September 11, 1861	Union
Chester Station (Virginia)	May 10, 1864	Undetermined
Chickahominy (Virginia) *see* Gaines Mill		
Chickamauga (Georgia)	September 19–20, 1863	Confederate
Chickasaw Bayou (Mississippi)	December 27–29, 1862	Confederate
Cloyd's Mountain (Virginia)	May 9, 1864	Union
Cold Harbor (1st) (Virginia) *see* Gaines Mill		
Cold Harbor (2nd) (Virginia)	June 1–3, 1864	Confederate
Collierville (Tennessee)	November 3, 1863	Union
Columbia (South Carolina)	February 17, 1865	Union
Columbia (Tennessee)	November 24–26, 1864	Confederate
Cool Spring (Virginia)	July 17–18, 1864	Confederate
Corbin's Bridge (Virginia) *see* Spotsylvania		
Corinth (Mississippi)	October 3–4, 1862	Union
Corn Field — Antietam*		
Corrick's Ford (Western Virginia)	July 13, 1861	Union
Corydon (Indiana)	July 8, 1863	Confederate
Cove Mountain (Virginia)	May 10, 1864	Undetermined
Crampton's Gap (Maryland)	September 14, 1862	Confederate
Crater (Virginia)	July 30, 1864	Confederate
Cross Keys (Virginia)	June 8, 1862	Confederate
Cross Lanes (Western Virginia)	August 26, 1861	Confederate
Cumberland Church (Virginia)	April 7, 1865	Confederate
Cumberland Gap (Tennessee)	September 9, 1863	Union
Cynthiana (Kentucky)	June 11–12, 1864	Union
Dabney's Mill (Virginia) *see* Hatcher's Run (2nd)		

Event	Dates	Outcome
Dallas (Georgia)	May 28, 1864	Union
Dalton (Georgia)	August 11–15, 1864	Union
Dandridge (Tennessee)	January 17, 1864	Confederate
Darbytown Road (1st) (Virginia)	October 7, 1864	Union
Darbytown Road (2nd) (Virginia)	October 13, 1864	Confederate
Darbytown Road (3rd) (Virginia)	October 27–28, 1864	Confederate
Davis Bridge (Tennessee)	October 5, 1862	Union
Day's Gap (Alabama)	April 30, 1863	Union
Decatur (Alabama)	October 26–29, 1864	Union
Dead Angle — Kennesaw Mountain*		
Deep Bottom (1st) (Virginia)	July 27–29, 1864	Confederate
Deep Bottom (2nd) (Virginia)	August 13–20, 1864	Confederate
Deep Gully (Kentucky) *see* Fort Anderson (Kentucky)		
Devil's Backbone (Arkansas)	September 1, 1863	Union
Dinwiddie Court House (Virginia)	March 30, 1865	Confederate
Donaldsonville (Louisiana)	June 28, 1863	Union
Dover (Tennessee) *see* Fort Donelson (2nd)		
Dranesville (Virginia)	December 20, 1861	Union
Drewry's Bluff (1st) (Virginia)	May 15, 1862	Undetermined
Drewry's Bluff (2nd) (Virginia)	May 16, 1864	Confederate
Droop Mountain (West Virginia)	November 6, 1863	Union
Dunker Church — Antietam*		
Ebenezer Church (Alabama)	April 1, 1865	Union
Elizabeth City (North Carolina)	February 10, 1862	Union
Elkhorn Tavern (Arkansas) *see* Pea Ridge		
Elkin's Ferry (Arkansas)	April 3–4, 1864	Union
Ellerson's Mill (Virginia) *see* Mechanicsville		
Erza Church (Georgia)	July 28, 1864	Union
Evelington Heights (Virginia)	July 3, 1862	Union
Fair Garden (Tennessee)	January 27, 1864	Union
Fair Oaks (Virginia)	May 31–June 1, 1862	Undetermined
Falling Waters (Western Virginia) *see* Hoke's Run		
Farmington (Tennessee)	October 7, 1863	Undetermined
Fisher's Hill (Virginia)	September 22, 1864	Union
Five Forks (Virginia)	April 1, 1865	Union
Fleetwood Hill (Virginia) *see* Brandy Station		
Folck's Mill (Maryland)	August 1, 1864	Undetermined
Fort Anderson (North Carolina)	March 15, 1863	Union
Fort Anderson (Kentucky) *see* Paducah		
Fort Bisland (Louisiana)	April 12–13, 1863	Union

Event	Dates	Outcome
Fort Blakely (Alabama)	April 9, 1865	Union
Fort Brooke (Florida)	October 16–18, 1863	Union
Fort Davidson (Missouri) *see* Pilot Knob		
Fort DeRussy (Louisiana)	March 14, 1864	Union
Fort Donelson (1st) (Tennessee)	February15, 1862	Union
Fort Donelson (2nd) (Tennessee)	February 3, 1863	Union
Fort Fisher (1st) (North Carolina)	December 23–27, 1864	Confederate
Fort Fisher (2nd) (North Carolina)	January 15, 1865	Union
Fort Gregg (Virginia)	April 2, 1865	Union
Fort Gilmer (Virginia) *see* Fort Harrison		
Fort Harrison (Virginia)	September 29, 1864	Union
Fort Hatteras (North Carolina)	August 27–29, 1861	Union
Fort Henry (Tennessee)	February 6, 1862	Union
Fort Hindman (Arkansas) *see* Arkansas Post		
Fort Jackson (Louisiana)	April 18–26, 1862	Union
Fort McAlister (Georgia)	March 3, 1863	Confederate
Fort McAlister (Georgia)	December 13, 1864	Union
Fort Macon (North Carolina)	March 23–24, 1862	Undetermined
Fort Philip (Louisiana)	April 18–26, 1862	Union
Fort Pillow (Tennessee)	April 12, 1864	Confederate
Fort Pulaski (Georgia)	April 11, 1862	Union
Fort Sanders (Tennessee)	November 29, 1863	Union
Fort Stedman (Virginia)	March 25, 1865	Union
Fort Sumter (1st) (South Carolina)	April 12, 1861	Confederate
Fort Sumter (2nd) (South Carolina)	September 8, 1863	Confederate
Fort Sumter (3rd) (South Carolina)	February 18, 1865	Union
Fort Wagner (South Carolina)	July 18, 1863	Confederate
Fort Walker (South Carolina) *see* Port Royal		
Franklin (1st) (Tennessee)	April 11, 1863	Union
Franklin (2nd) (Tennessee)	November 30, 1864	Union
Franklin's Crossing (Virginia)	June 5, 1863	Confederate
Frayser's (Frazier's) Farm (Virginia)	June 30, 1862	Confederate
Fredericksburg (1st) (Virginia)	December 13, 1862	Confederate
Fredericksburg (2nd) (Virginia) *see* Chancellorsville		
Fredericktown (Missouri)	October 21, 1861	Union
Freeman's Ford (Virginia)	August 22, 1862	Confederate
Front Royal (1st) (Virginia)	May 23, 1862	Confederate
Front Royal (2nd) (Virginia) *see* Guard Hill		
Fussell's Mill (Virginia) *see* Deep Bottom (2nd)		
Gaines Mill (Virginia)	June 27, 1862	Confederate

Event	Dates	Outcome
Galveston (Texas)	January 1, 1863	Confederate
Garnett's Farm (Virginia)	June 28, 1862	Confederate
Gettysburg (Pennsylvania)	July 1–3, 1863	Union
Glasgow (Missouri)	October 15, 1864	Confederate
Glendale (Virginia) *see* Frayser's Farm		
Globe Tavern (Virginia) *see* Weldon Railroad (2nd)		
Glorietta Pass (New Mexico Territory)	March 28, 1862	Union
Goodrick's Landing (Louisiana)	June 29–30, 1863	Undetermined
Grand Gulf (Mississippi)	April 29, 1863	Confederate
Greenbrier River (Western Virginia)	October 4, 1862	Confederate
Grimball's Landing (South Carolina)	July 16, 1863	Undetermined
Griswoldville (Georgia)	November 22, 1864	Union
Groveton (Virginia)	August 28, 1862	Confederate
Guard Hill (Virginia)	August 16, 1864	Confederate
Hancock (Maryland)	January 3, 1862	Undetermined
Hanover (Pennsylvania)	June 30, 1863	Undetermined
Hanover Court House (Virginia)	May 26, 1862	Union
Harpers Ferry (Western Virginia)	September 15, 1862	Confederate
Harris Farm (Virginia)	May 18–19, 1864	Undetermined
Harrison Landing (Virginia) *see* Evelington Heights		
Hartsville (Missouri)	January 9–11, 1863	Confederate
Hartsville (Tennessee)	December 7, 1862	Confederate
Hatcher's Run (1st) (Virginia)	October 27–28, 1864	Confederate
Hatcher's Run (2nd) (Virginia)	February 5–7, 1865	Confederate
Hatcher's Run (3rd) (Virginia) *see* White Oak Road		
Hatchie's Bridge (Tennessee) *see* Davis Bridge		
Haw's Shop (Virginia)	May 28, 1864	Undetermined
Helena (Arkansas)	July 4, 1863	Union
Hell's Half Acre — Stone River*		
Hell's Hallow — Shiloh*		
High Bridge (Virginia)	April 6–7, 1865	Undetermined
Hoke's Run (Western Virginia)	July 2, 1861	Union
Holly Springs (Mississippi)	December 19–20, 1862	Confederate
Honey Hill (South Carolina)	November 30, 1864	Confederate
Honey Springs (Oklahoma)	July 17, 1863	Union
Hoover's Gap (Tennessee)	June 24–26, 1863	Union
Hornet's Nest — Shiloh*		
Independence (Missouri)	October 22, 1864	Confederate
Irish Bend (Louisiana)	April 14, 1863	Union
Island No. 10 (Missouri)	April 8, 1862	Union

Event	Dates	Outcome
Iuka (Mississippi)	September 19, 1862	Union
Ivey's Farm (Mississippi) *see* Okolona		
Ivy Mountain (Kentucky)	November 8, 1862	Confederate
Jack's Shop (Virginia)	September 22, 1863	Undetermined
Jackson (Mississippi)	May 14, 1863	Union
Jenkins Ferry (Arkansas)	April 30, 1864	Union
Jerusalem Plank Road (Virginia) *see* 2nd Weldon Railroad		
Jetersville (Virginia)	April 4, 1865	Union
Johnson Farm (Virginia) *see* Darbytown Road		
Johnsonville (Tennessee)	November 4–5, 1864	Confederate
Jonesboro (Georgia)	August 31– September 1, 1864	Union
Kelly's Ford (Virginia)	March 17, 1863	Confederate
Kennesaw Mountain (Georgia)	June 27, 1864	Confederate
Kernstown (1st) (Virginia)	March 23, 1862	Union
Kernstown (2nd) (Virginia)	July 24, 1864	Confederate
Killdeer Mountain (North Dakota)	July 28, 1864	Union
Kingston (North Carolina)	March 8–10, 1865	Union
Kinston (North Carolina)	December 14, 1862	Union
Kock's Plantation (Louisiana)	July 12–13, 1863	Confederate
Kolb's Farm (Georgia)	April 22, 1864	Union
LaFourche Crossing (Louisiana)	June 20–21, 1863	Union
Laurel Hill (Virginia) *see* Spotsylvania		
Leesburg (Virginia) *see* Ball's Bluff		
Levyville (Florida)	February 13, 1865	Confederate
Lewis Farm (Virginia)	March 29, 1865	Union
Lexington (1st) (Missouri)	September 12–20, 1861	Confederate
Lexington (2nd) (Missouri)	October 19, 1864	Confederate
Limestone Station (Tennessee) *see* Telford		
Lookout Valley (Tennessee) *see* Wauhatchie		
Lookout Mountain (Tennessee) *see* 2nd Chattanooga		
Lovejoy's Station (Georgia)	August 20, 1864	Confederate
Lynchburg (Virginia)	June 17–18, 1864	Confederate
McDowell (Virginia)	May 8, 1862	Confederate
Malvern Hill (Virginia)	July 1, 1862	Confederate
Manassas (1st) (Virginia) *see* Bull Run (1st)		
Manassas (2nd) (Virginia) *see* Bull Run (2nd)		
Manassas Junction (Virginia)	August 27, 1862	Confederate
Mansfield (Louisiana) *see* Sabine Crossroads		
Mansura (Louisiana)	May 16, 1864	Union

Event	Dates	Outcome
Marais des Cygnes (Missouri)	October 25, 1864	Union
Marion (Virginia)	December 17–18, 1864	Union
Mark's Mill (Arkansas)	April 25, 1864	Confederate
Marmiton River (Missouri)	October 25, 1864	Union
Marye's Heights— 2nd Fredericksburg (Chancellorsville)*		
Maryland Heights (Maryland) see Crampton's Gap		
Mechanicsville (Virginia)	June 26, 1862	Confederate
Memphis (Tennessee)	June 6, 1862	Undetermined
Meridian Campaign (Mississippi)	February 3, 1864	Undetermined
Messilla (New Mexico Territory)	July 25, 1861	Confederate
Middle Creek (Kentucky)	January 10, 1862	Union
Middleburg (Virginia)	June 17–19, 1863	Undetermined
Mill Springs (Kentucky)	January 19–20, 1862	Union
Milliken's Bend (Louisiana)	June 7, 1863	Union
Mine Creek (Missouri)	October 25, 1864	Union
Mine Run (Virginia)	November 26– December 1, 1863	Confederate
Missionary Ridge (Tennessee) see 2nd Chattanooga		
Mobile Bay (Alabama)	August 5, 1864	Union
Monett's Ferry (Louisiana)	April 23, 1864	Union
Monitor vs. Merrimack	March 9, 1862	Undetermined
Monocacy (Maryland)	July 9, 1864	Confederate
Monroe's Crossroads (North Carolina)	March 10, 1865	Union
Moorefield (West Virginia)	August 7, 1864	Union
Morris Island (South Carolina) see Fort Wagner		
Morton Ford (Virginia)	February 6–7, 1864	Confederate
Mossy Creek (Tennessee)	December 29, 1863	Union
Munfordville (Kentucky)	September 13–17, 1862	Confederate
Murfreesboro (1st) (Tennessee)	June 13, 1862	Confederate
Murfreesboro (2nd) (Tennessee)	July 13, 1862	Confederate
Murfreesboro (3rd) (Tennessee) see Stone River		
Murfreesboro (4th) (Tennessee)	December 5–7, 1864	Union
Namozine Church (Virginia)	April 3, 1865	Undetermined
Nashville (Tennessee)	December 15–16, 1864	Union
Natural Bridge (Florida)	March 6, 1865	Confederate
New Bern (1st) (North Carolina)	March 14, 1862	Union
New Bern (2nd) (North Carolina)	February 1–2, 1864	Union
New Creek (West Virginia)	November 28, 1864	Confederate
New Hope Church (Georgia)	May 25–June 4, 1864	Undetermined
New Madrid (Missouri)	March 14, 1862	Union

Event	Dates	Outcome
New Market (Virginia)	May 15, 1864	Confederate
New Orleans (Louisiana)	April 25–May 1, 1862	Union
Newtonia (Missouri)	October 28, 1864	Union
North Anna (Virginia)	May 23–26, 1864	Undetermined
Oak Grove (Virginia)	June 25, 1862	Confederate
Okolona (Mississippi)	February 22, 1864	Confederate
Old Church (Virginia)	May 30, 1864	Union
Old River Lake (Arkansas)	June 6, 1864	Union
Olustee (Florida)	February 20, 1864	Confederate
Opequon Creek (Virginia) *see* Winchester (3rd)		
Orchard (Virginia) *see* Oak Grove		
Orchard Knob (Tennessee) *see* 2nd Chattanooga		
Osage (Missouri) *see* Mine Creek		
Overall Creek (Tennessee)	December 4, 1864	Union
Ox Hill (Virginia) *see* Chantilly		
Paducah (Kentucky)	March 25, 1864	Confederate
Palmito Ranch (Texas)	May 12–13, 1865	Confederate
Parker's Cross Roads (Tennessee)	December 13, 1862	Confederate
Pea Ridge (Arkansas)	March 6–8, 1862	Union
Peach Orchard — Shiloh*		
Peach Orchard — Gettysburg*		
Peachtree (Georgia)	July 20, 1864	Union
Peeble's Farm (Virginia)	September 29–30, 1864	Union
Perryville (Kentucky)	October 8, 1862	Undetermined
Petersburg (Virginia)	June 15–18, 1864	Confederate
Petersburg Mine (Virginia) *see* Crater		
Philippi (Western Virginia)	June 3, 1861	Union
Pickett's Charge — Gettysburg*		
Pickett's Mill (Georgia) *see* New Hope Church		
Piedmont (Virginia) *see* Staunton		
Pilot Knob (Missouri)	September 26–27, 1864	Union
Pine Bluff (Arkansas)	October 25, 1863	Union
Pittsburg Landing (Tennessee) *see* Shiloh		
Plain's Store (Louisiana)	May 21, 1863	Union
Pleasant Hill (Louisiana)	April 9, 1864	Union
Pleasant Hill Landing (Louisiana) *see* Blair's Landing		
Plum Run Bend (Tennessee)	May 10, 1862	Union
Plymouth (North Carolina)	April 17–20, 1864	Confederate
Poison Springs (Arkansas)	April 18, 1864	Confederate
Poplar Spring (Virginia) *see* Pebble's Farm		

Event	Dates	Outcome
Port Gibson (Mississippi)	May 1, 1863	Union
Port Hudson (1st) (Louisiana)	May 27, 1863	Confederate
Port Hudson (2nd) (Louisiana)	June 14, 1863	Confederate
Port Hudson (3rd) (Louisiana)	July 8, 1863	Union
Port Republic (Virginia)	June 9, 1862	Confederate
Port Royal (South Carolina)	November 7, 1861	Union
Port Walthall Junction (Virginia)	May 6–7, 1864	Union
Prairie D'Ane (Arkansas)	April 10–13, 1864	Union
Prairie Grove (Arkansas)	December 7, 1862	Union
Proctor's Creek (Virginia)	May 12–16, 1864	Confederate
Rappahannock Station (1st) (Virginia) *see* Freeman's Ford		
Rappahannock Station (2nd) (Virginia)	November 7, 1863	Undetermined
Raymond (Mississippi)	May 12, 1863	Union
Reams Station (1st) (Virginia)	June 29, 1864	Confederate
Reams Station (2nd) (Virginia)	August 25, 1864	Confederate
Resaca (Georgia)	May 14–15, 1864	Union
Rice Station (Virginia)	April 6, 1865	Union
Rich Mountain (Western Virginia)	July 11–13, 1861	Union
Richmond (Kentucky)	August 30, 1862	Confederate
Ringgold Gap (Georgia)	November 27, 1863	Confederate
Rio Mills (Virginia)	February 29, 1864	Confederate
Rivers' Bridge (South Carolina)	February 3, 1865	Union
Roanoke Island (North Carolina)	February 8, 1862	Union
Rochelle (Virginia) *see* Jack's Shop		
Rocky Gap (West Virginia)	August 26, 1863	Confederate
Rocky Face Ridge (Georgia)	May 7–13, 1864	Union
Rowlett Station (Kentucky)	December 17, 1861	Undetermined
Rutherford's Farm (Virginia)	July 20, 1864	Union
Sabine Crossroads (Louisiana)	April 8, 1864	Confederate
Sabine Pass (1st) (Texas)	September 24–25, 1862	Union
Sabine Pass (2nd) (Texas)	September 8, 1863	Confederate
Sacramento (Kentucky)	December 28, 1861	Confederate
Saint Mary's Church (Virginia)	April 22, 1864	Undetermined
Salem Church — Chancellorsville*		
Sappony Church (Virginia)	June 28, 1864	Confederate
Saltville (Virginia)	October 2–3, 1864	Confederate
Saltville (Virginia)	December 20–21, 1864	Union
Sand Creek (Colorado Territory)	November 29, 1864	Union
Savage's Station (Virginia)	June 29, 1862	Confederate
Sayler's Creek (Virginia)	April 6, 1865	Union

Event	Dates	Outcome
Secessionville (South Carolina)	June 16, 1862	Confederate
Second Fair Oaks (Virginia) *see* 3rd Darbytown Road		
Selma (Alabama)	April 2, 1865	Union
Seminary Ridge — Gettysburg*		
Seven Day Campaign (Virginia)	June 25–July 1, 1862	Confederate
Seven Pines (Virginia) *see* Fair Oaks		
Sharpsburg (Maryland) *see* Antietam		
Shiloh (Tennessee)	April 6–7, 1862	Union
Slaughter Mountain (Virginia) *see* Cedar Mountain		
Slaughter Pen — Gettysburg*		
Smithfield Crossing (West Virginia)	August 29, 1864	Undetermined
Snake Gap (Georgia)	May 9, 1864	Confederate
Snicker's Ferry (Virginia) *see* Cool Spring		
Snyder's Bluff (Mississippi)	April 29–May 1, 1863	Confederate
South Mills (North Carolina)	April 18, 1862	Undetermined
South Mountain (Maryland)	September 14, 1862	Union
Spanish Fort (Alabama)	March 27–April 8, 1865	Union
Spotsylvania (Virginia)	May 8–21, 1864	Undetermined
Spring Hill (Tennessee)	November 29, 1864	Union
Springfield (Missouri)	January 8, 1863	Union
St. Albans Raid (Vermont)	October 19, 1864	Confederate
St. Phillip (Louisiana)	April 18–25, 1862	Union
Staunton (Virginia)	June 5, 1864	Union
Staunton River Bridge (Virginia)	June 25, 1864	Confederate
Stirling (Sterling) (Louisiana)	September 29, 1863	Confederate
Stone River (Tennessee)	December 31, 1862	Undetermined
Stone Wall — Fredericksburg*		
Stone Wall — Chancellorsville*		
Strawberry Plains (Virginia) *see* Deep Bottom (2nd)		
Summit Point (West Virginia)	August 21, 1864	Undetermined
Sunken Road — Antietam*		
Sunken Road — Fredericksburg*		
Sutherland Station (Virginia)	April 2, 1865	Union
Swift Creek (Virginia)	May 9, 1864	Undetermined
Tampa (Florida)	June 30–July 1, 1865	Confederate
Telford (Tennessee)	September 8, 1863	Confederate
Thompson's Station (Tennessee)	March 4, 1863	Confederate
Todd's Tavern (Virginia)	May 7, 1864	Union
Tom's Brook (Virginia)	October 9, 1864	Union
Totopotomoy (Virginia)	May 28–30, 1864	Undetermined

Event	Dates	Outcome
Tranter's Creek (North Carolina)	June 5, 1862	Union
Trent's Reach (Virginia)	January 23–24, 1865	Union
Trevilian Station (Virginia)	June 12, 1864	Confederate
Tupelo (Mississippi)	July 14, 1864	Confederate
Union City (Tennessee)	March 24, 1864	Confederate
Upperville (Virginia)	June 21, 1863	Undetermined
Utoy Creek (Georgia)	August 5–7, 1864	Undetermined
Valley of Death — Gettysburg*		
Valverde (New Mexico Territory)	February 21, 1862	Union
Vaught's Hill (Tennessee)	March 4, 1863	Union
Vermillion Bayou (Louisiana)	April 17, 1863	Union
Vicksburg (Missouri)	July 15, 1862	Undetermined
Vicksburg (Missouri)	July 4, 1863	Union
Ware Bottom Church (Virginia)	May 20, 1864	Confederate
Washington, D.C.	July 11–12, 1864	Union
Washington (North Carolina)	March 30–April 20, 1863	Undetermined
Wauhatchie (Tennessee)	October 28–29, 1863	Union
Waynesboro (Virginia)	March 2, 1865	Union
Waynesborough (Georgia)	December 4, 1864	Union
Weldon Railroad (1st) (Virginia)	April 22, 1864	Confederate
Weldon Railroad (2nd) (Virginia)	June 22, 1864	Confederate
Weldon Railroad (3rd) (Virginia)	August 18–21, 1864	Union
Westport (Missouri)	October 23, 1864	Union
Wheatfield — Gettysburg*		
White Oak Road (Virginia)	March 31, 1865	Union
White Oak Swamp (Virginia) see Frayser's Farm		
Whitestone Hill (North Dakota)	September 3–5, 1863	Union
Wilderness (Virginia)	May 5–7, 1864	Undetermined
Williamsburg (Virginia)	May 5, 1862	Confederate
Wilmington (North Carolina)	February 12–22, 1865	Union
Wilson's Creek (Missouri)	August 10, 1861	Confederate
Wilson's Wharf (Virginia)	May 24, 1864	Union
Winchester (1st) (Virginia)	May 25, 1862	Confederate
Winchester (2nd) (Virginia)	June 14–15, 1863	Confederate
Winchester (3rd) (Virginia)	September 19, 1864	Union
Wise's/Wyse Forks (North Carolina) see Kingston		
Yellow Bayou (Louisiana)	May 18, 1864	Union
Yellow Tavern (Virginia)	May 11, 1864	Confederate
Yorktown (Virginia)	April 5, 1862	Union

Chapter 3

The Officers

"The art of war is simple enough. Find out where your enemy is.
Get at him as soon as you can. Strike at him as hard as you can and
as often as you can, and keep moving on."
— *General Ulysses S. Grant*

The Civil War was unique in every sense of the word. It was a war fought on American soil by Americans against Americans. It was a war where brother fought brother; father was against son and friend was against friend. It was a war that produced oddities, coincidences and strange twists of fate, many of which tested the remarkable abilities of the men involved in ways that still resound to this day.

When war clouds loomed on the horizon in 1860, military personnel prepared for the possibility of armed conflict. Armies were formed, men recruited, supplies gathered and experienced commanders were sought to direct it all. The United States had roughly one thousand officers, many of whom had previous war experience. The Confederate states in 1860 had local militias and very few experienced commanders. With the secession of South Carolina in December 1860, many general officers resigned their commissions with the U.S. military to offer their services to the fledgling government. Some of these men had positions of higher rank before tendering their resignations.

Some struggled with the idea of leaving the federal government. They owed their loyalty to their country, the one they had sworn to protect and defend. At the same time, they had strong ties and loyalty to their state. It had been less than seventy-five years since the formation of the country under the U.S. Constitution. Before that, the thirteen states had acted as countries unto themselves. The United States was smaller then and the vast majority of the people never traveled far from their homes and communities. The outside world was down the road and somewhere else.

Two hundred thirty-nine officers eventually left the Union to take up arms against their former comrades. The best known was Robert E. Lee. Lee had devoted his life to the

United States military and he was highly thought of in the upper echelon of command. After hostilities broke out in April 1861, he was offered command of all Union forces but is reported to have agonized over the decision. In the end, Lee declined the appointment, tendered his resignation and went with his state when Virginia seceded from the Union.

Many of the officers who resigned had graduated from West Point, a prestigious military academy established in 1802 by President Thomas Jefferson. As secretary of state, Jefferson, along with President Washington, wanted to eliminate the need for the military to depend on foreign engineers and artillerists. The academy, in addition to teaching the science of warfare, furnished America with some of the foremost civil engineers of the time. It would be West Point and other military academies, Virginia Military Institute (VMI) and the South Carolina Military Academy, that would furnish the bulwark of military officers that served in the Civil War.

When war was declared, many of the cadets attending West Point were from the seceding states. Numerous arguments and fights broke out at the academy between the cadets as tensions ran high. Fearing disloyalty, the school issued an order requiring all the West Point cadets to swear an oath of allegiance to the United States. Failure to do so would result in immediate termination. Two hundred seventy-eight cadets resigned or were discharged for refusing to take the oath.

Robert E. Lee served as commandant and superintendent of West Point for a three-year period from 1852 to 1856. Of Lee's last class, twenty-three cadets served the Union, fourteen served the Confederacy. In January 1861, a new superintendent was named to take the helm of West Point — P.G.T. Beauregard. When it was learned he had southern sympathies, Beauregard's resignation was requested. Not only did he offer his resignation as commandant, but he also resigned his U.S. commission effective March 1, 1861. Before submitting his resignation, he had secured an appointment as a brigadier general in the newly formed Confederate Provisional Army. His first assignment was the command of operations at Charleston Harbor, South Carolina. On April 12, 1861, Beauregard gave the order to fire on Fort Sumter, signaling the start of hostilities.

Ulysses S. Grant and Simon Bolivar Buckner were classmates at the academy, graduating in 1843. They had remained good friends over the years. In the 1850s, when Buckner learned his friend was in a financial crisis and down on his luck, he loaned Grant money to help him get on his feet. In 1862, Buckner was a Confederate general and one of the commanders of Fort Donelson, along with John B. Floyd. As the Union forces threatened the fort, Floyd fled, leaving Buckner to face the consequences. Buckner asked the Union commander what terms he would offer for the surrender of the fort. It was here that Grant replied he would accept nothing but "unconditional surrender." Buckner surrendered the fort and was taken prisoner. Later when Grant found out that Buckner was in financial hardship, he repaid the earlier favor by sending him the money he needed.

Another friend of Grant's was James Longstreet, who was in the class just before Grant at West Point. They had developed a strong and lasting friendship. After his graduation, Grant was assigned to the Jefferson Barracks where he resumed his friendship with Longstreet, who was also there. When off duty, Grant and Longstreet often visited the plantation of a former classmate of Grant's, the family of Frederick Dent. Longstreet's mother was a cousin of the Dents. There Grant met the love of his life, Julia Dent, whom he would later marry. After the war, Longstreet and Grant resumed their friendship when Longstreet approached Grant seeking to obtain his citizenship, for Grant by now was president.

Longstreet, along with many of the Confederate upper echelon, had lost the right of citizenship and could only get it back with the permission of the president of the United States. Longstreet had applied to President Andrew Johnson, but his request was declined. Johnson, according to James Longstreet, told him that he would not honor his request or that of Lee or Jefferson Davis. Grant not only returned Longstreet's citizenship to him, but also secured a government appointment for his friend and former adversary.

Confederate General Stephen D. Ramseur was mortally wounded during the Battle of Cedar Creek on October 19, 1864, and was left in Union hands when the Confederates were forced to withdraw. He was carried into the quarters of General Philip Sheridan. Many of his former classmates from West Point, now Union officers, gathered at his bedside to comfort the dying man as he breathed his last. This time they were friends comforting a comrade, whereas but hours earlier, they had been enemies trying to destroy one another.

The Mexican War was another bond that cemented relationships and friendships among many of the officers. During the Mexican War, Pierre Gustave Toutant Beauregard and George B. McClellan both served on the staff of General Winfield Scott. Captain Robert E. Lee once commended a young lieutenant on his capture of Mexico City. Lee would meet this young man once more at Appomattox when he would surrender the Army of Northern Virginia to Ulysses S. Grant. An officer who assisted Lt. Grant in the capture of Mexico City was Lieutenant John C. Pemberton, who later faced Grant in 1863 at Vicksburg. James Longstreet and Winfield Scott Hancock, who would oppose each other at Gettysburg, had worked together at Churubusco. Colonel Jefferson Davis, a future Union General (no relation to Jefferson Davis, the president of the Confederacy) commanded Mississippi volunteers at Buena Vista and future Union commander George H. Thomas and Braxton Bragg, later a Confederate leader, were fellow artillery officers in the attack. At Monterey, Joseph Hooker and Albert Sidney Johnston were comrades in arms while Joseph E. Johnston and George Meade were engineer officers during the siege of Vera Cruz.

The officer corps was small before the war, fewer than 1,500 men. Overall, the majority were outstanding leaders and conscientious men. They considered the welfare and safety of the troops under them and were able to analyze the enemy, the location and the situation. James Longstreet, though a subordinate of Robert E. Lee, disagreed with him over the plans for the third day's battle at Gettysburg in what became known as the "Pickett/Pettigrew Charge." Knowing and believing many would lose their lives in that charge, Longstreet hesitated to give the command for the advance, leaving it to a subordinate.

Some commanders could inspire their men on to feats of glory and victory, or comfort them in defeat. Joshua Chamberlain, his troops out of ammunition and under heavy attack by the Confederates at Gettysburg, was able to inspire his men by yelling, "Fix bayonets!" and leading them down Little Round Top. General Lee never placed the blame on anyone but himself when things went wrong on the battlefield.

As with any situation in dealing with people and positions of authority, there were ambitious men who, without any military experience whatsoever, politically acquired a command. They would use their command to feather their own nest, politically, financially, or both. Some of these "political generals" proved to be embarrassments. The heavy-handed conduct of Ben Butler in New Orleans was criticized throughout the war. Dan Sickles of New York had a poor battle record but was always able to secure a command. General Grant relieved John McClernand for undermining his authority. Many relied on their friendship with the powerful bureaucrats to either keep their commands, or once relieved of them, to get another. John B. Floyd, though relieved of his command for deserting Fort Donelson, pleaded to his friend Jefferson Davis to intercede on his behalf. Davis did and rewarded Floyd with another command.

Both President Lincoln and President Davis exercised command of the military and its operations, many times overruling their military advisors. President Lincoln took a personal interest and command of the Army during the first stages of the war. He wanted action; his generals did not. Many officers, believing that their men were not ready for battle or too tired from the previous day's battle, often hesitated or refused to instigate a fight. General George B. McClellan often disagreed with Lincoln over sending raw recruits into battle and General Ambrose Burnside was slow to send his men into the fray. Both men were relieved of their command by Lincoln. Jefferson Davis was often seen in the field meeting with Lee to discuss movement of troops or calling his commander to Richmond to discuss attacks, assaults or troops movements. As the war progressed, both Lincoln and Davis came to realize that their officers were better equipped to make the needed decisions and both presidents backed off from direct supervision.

Marriage often makes strange bedfellows and that can be seen in some of the marriages of the participants of the Civil War. General Henry A. Wise, an ex-governor of Virginia and a Confederate general, had married the sister of General Ulysses S. Grant. When J.E.B. Stuart made his ride around the entire Union army during the Seven Days Battle, he was pursued by a Virginian who had remained loyal to the Union, Major General Philip St. George Cooke, his father-in-law. Philip's father, John Rogers Cooke of Missouri, served the Confederacy.

Two West Point graduates courted Ellen Marcy: Ambrose Powell Hill and George B. McClellan. She selected McClellan. During the war, McClellan served the Union while Hill served the Confederacy. Confederate General Louis A. Armistead at one time courted the future wife of General Winfield Scott Hancock. Ironically, Hancock and Armistead were both wounded within yards of one another on the third day of the Battle of Gettysburg. General Armistead had managed to breach the Union line before he was shot down near a copse of trees. He reportedly had in his jacket a bible he wanted to give to General Hancock's wife. A few hundred yards away and approximately the same time, Hancock was also wounded as he watched the Confederate advance. A portion of a shell struck his saddle horn, sending nail fragments into his groin. Armistead would not survive his wounds. Hancock not only survived, but would later run for president of the United States twice.

Speaking of the presidency, George B. McClellan would oppose Lincoln in the election of 1864 and would lose by a wide majority. Two future presidents would fight side by side during the Battle of Lynchburg, Virginia, in June 1864: General Rutherford B. Hayes and Major William McKinley. Seven Union generals were eventually elected president of the United States: in addition to Hayes and McKinley, they were Andrew Johnson, Ulysses S. Grant, James A. Garfield, Chester A. Arthur, and Benjamin Harrison. A former U.S. vice president, General John C. Breckinridge, was declared a traitor when he took up arms for the Confederacy. Breckinridge had been vice president of the United States under James Buchanan. When he accepted a Confederate command, Breckinridge was indicted for treason but was never tried.

The war strained many family relations. General John Gibbons was born and raised in North Carolina and had secured an appointment to West Point. When the war broke out, Gibbons remained loyal to the Union while his three brothers served the Confederacy. Thomas L. Crittenden, the son of Senator John Crittenden, joined the Union Army and rose to the rank of major general while his younger brother George became a major general in the Confederate Army. Major Henry B. McClellan, a first cousin of George B. McClellan, served on the staff of Confederate General J.E.B. Stuart.

There were many generals in the war. The North had 583; of these 217 were graduates of West Point. The average age of a northern general was 381/2 years old. The oldest, other than Winfield Scott, age 75, was Daniel Tyler, who was 62 when promoted to the rank. The youngest was Galusha Pennypacker, who was but twenty years old when promoted to brigadier general in April 1865, one month before his twenty-first birthday. He enlisted at age sixteen, received a captain's commission at seventeen and, in 1867, was promoted to major general at the age of twenty-three.

The smallest of the Union generals has been listed as Philip Sheridan, who stood approximately five feet tall. He was always photographed sitting in a chair. On the Confederate side, the shortest is believed to have been John C.C. Sanders, who stood five feet, two inches tall. The heaviest Confederate General was William R. Peck who was six feet tall and weighed over 300 pounds. On the Union side, the heaviest man was Winfield Scott, who stood at six feet, five inches, and weighed 300 pounds. Along with his age and girth, the fact that Scott could not sit a horse contributed to his retirement from the military.

The South had 425 generals by the end of the war: 336 brigadier generals, 72 major generals and 17 lieutenant generals. John Henry Winder was the oldest, having been born February 21, 1800. The youngest was William Paul Roberts, born July 11, 1841. General John Bell Hood was only thirty-three when he was appointed lieutenant general and Fitzhugh Lee was twenty-seven when promoted to major general. The youngest lieutenant general was Stephen D. Lee, who received his appointment at age thirty, while Leonidas Polk became the oldest when appointed at fifty-four years of age.

MILITARY EXPERIENCE OF THE COMMANDERS

Military Experience	*U.S.A.*	*C.S.A.*
West Point graduates	217	146
Nongraduates— dismissed/expelled	11	10
Other military academies	9	23*
Regular/Navy	36	19†
State militia officers	40	n/a
European émigré officers	20	3
Mexican war background	62	51
Inexperienced civilians	188	192
Totals	583	425

*Seventeen from VMI, four from South Carolina Military Academy and two from other academies.

†Two generals had fought in the Texas War of Independence and three had been officers in the U.S. Navy.

Many generals had military experience, having graduated from West Point or serving during the Mexican War. What about those who did not graduate from a military academy? What were their professions before the war? Some had been teachers and physicians while others were merchants and bankers. Many had received a college education; a few called themselves farmers. Below is a recap of the professions listed for the men prior to entrance into the military ranks.

PROFESSIONS OF THE GENERALS

Professions	U.S.A.	C.S.A.
Lawyers/jurists	126	129
Professional soldiers	194	125
Businessmen	116	55
Farmers	23	42
Politicians	47	24
Educators	16	15
Civil engineers	26	13
Students	8	6
Doctors	11	4
Ministers	1	3
Frontiersmen, peace officers	2	3
Indian agents	0	2
Naval officers	3	2
Editors	6	1
Unclassified	4	1
Totals	583	425

Both armies lost some of their commanding generals during the war. While a few resigned or left the service, others were killed in battle or died from other causes. Below are some of the reasons for the loss of commanding generals.

EXPLANATION FOR THE LOSS OF COMMANDING OFFICERS

Reason	U.S.A.	C.S.A.
Killed in action/died of wounds	47	77
Died of disease/accident	18	15
Killed in personal encounters/duels	1	2
Committed suicide	1	1
Resigned	110	19
Appointments canceled	22	5
Declined appointment	1	3
Retired	6	1
Cashiered/dismissed	3*	1
Other	0	2
Totals	209	126

*Three U.S.A. generals were court martialed and dismissed: James H. Leddlie, Edward Ferreir and Justis McKinstray.

Former classmates often found themselves opposing one another in battle. General P.G.T. Beauregard and General Irwin McDowell, both of the class of 1838, faced one another during the Battle of Bull Run (Manassas) while General McClellan often opposed a former classmate, "Stonewall" Jackson. They were both members of the class of 1846.

After the war, many of those that fought one another became the closest of friends.

The strangest relationship was the one between Confederate General Joseph E. Johnston and Union commander William T. Sherman. In the ending months of the war, Sherman pursued Johnston and his army through the Carolinas as they kept up their attacks. When Lee fled Petersburg, he had hoped to combine his forces with those of Johnston. When Johnston and Sherman met after Lee's surrender, they came to an agreement between themselves for the surrender of Johnston's army. The terms were extremely generous, but Sherman was not authorized to grant them. A series of meetings took place in which Sherman and Johnston agreed to the same terms offered to Lee. After the war, Johnston and Sherman often communicated and upon Sherman's death, Johnston stood bareheaded in the rain as his former foe was laid to rest. Johnston came down with pneumonia and died a few weeks later.

When the organizers of the Army of the Confederacy designed and set forth the regulations of their army, they copied and duplicated what they were familiar with — the Union Army. They copied it in all most every way from its ranks to its insignias. The color of their uniforms would be different, as would be the method for displaying rank, but for the most part, the armies were very similar. The Union officers wore their insignia of rank on rectangular shoulder straps rimmed with gold bullion on each side of their dark blue uniform blouse. The Confederate officers wore the insignia of rank on the front sides of a stand-up collar of the officer's jacket. This was very similar to the European custom of designating rank by collar insignias. When the war started, though, many officers removed their old shoulder epaulets and placed them on their new uniforms of gray.

OFFICER RANK INSIGNIA

Rank	Union Army*	Confederate Army†
Second lieutenant	Nothing on the shoulder strap	Single horizontal gold stripe
First lieutenant	Gold bar on each side	Two gold stripes— one above the other
Captain	Two gold bars on each side	Three gold stripes— one above the other
Major	Gold leaf on each side	A single 5 pointed star
Lieutenant colonel	Silver leaf on each side	Two stars
Colonel	Eagle in the center on each side	Three stars
Brigadier general	One star on each side	Three stars, one larger, one flanked by two smaller ones in a gold wreath.
Major general	Two stars on each side	Same as above
Lieutenant general	Three stars on each side	Same as above
Full general	Four stars on each side — position created for General Grant	No position in the Confederate army until February 1865

*The background colors of the shoulder straps indicated the officer's assignment. It would also apply to the Confederacy. Blue background — Infantry. Yellow background — Cavalry. Red background — Artillery

†In addition to the regulation on the design of the collar insignia for the Confederate officers, Confederate law also specified distinction in the cap and sleeve markings.

CONFEDERATE OFFICER SLEEVE MARKINGS

Lieutenants (both first and second)	a gold braid or "flogging" one wale (ridge of cloth) in width.
Captains and Majors	a gold braid or "flogging" two wales in width.
Colonel (both lieutenant and full)	a gold braid or "flogging" three wales in width.
General of all ranks	a gold braid or "flogging" four wales in width.

The only way to distinguish a brigadier general from a major general in the Confederacy was to look at the button arrangement on their jackets. General Order Number 6 stipulated the following: a major general was to have two rows of buttons on his jacket, nine in each row, placed in three sets of three. A brigadier general would be similar to that of a major general, except he would have only eight buttons in each row but these would be placed in pairs. Colonels, lieutenant colonels and majors were to have only seven buttons in each row while company grade officers would have "one row of nine buttons ... placed at equal distances."

The designation of generalship in the Confederate army was by one large star in the center with a smaller star on each side surrounded by a gold wreath. All generals, be they lieutenant, major or brigadier, wore the same design. General Robert E. Lee, though a full general and in command of an army, was usually seen wearing only three stars of equal size on his collar, the designation of a colonel. He also did not wear a cuff braid, but he was one of the most widely recognized of any of the generals and there was no doubt that he was in command.

Most every officer carried a side arm and was also authorized by regulations to carry a sword or a saber. In the Union army, the officer's sword usually was a standard issued model 1840 cavalry or an 1840 light artillery saber. Many carried special swords made for them. Most officers found the sword to be more ceremonial than practical. The sword was considered a symbol of office or rank. When used, it was usually waved overhead to signal the advance of his troops. Sometimes though, some commanders would use it to whack an errant private rather than for stabbing or cutting a foe. Very few wounds were attributed to the sword. The sword, as a badge of rank, was cherished and an officer rarely ever surrendered it under any circumstances.

Sometimes, no matter what an officer did or did not do, he would find himself placed under arrest by his superior for some infraction of the rules. Usually an officer was not jailed, but confined to his quarters until a hearing could be scheduled. If the army were on a march or about to engage in combat, the arrested officer would surrender his sword to his commander and take a position to the rear of his brigade or regiment. Thomas "Stonewall" Jackson was well known for placing junior officers under arrest for minor infractions. He had placed A.P. Hill under arrest for nine separate offenses one time, ranging from marching his men more than fifty minutes out of an hour to conducting drills on Sunday. If the enemy captured an officer, the officer's sword was confiscated and presented to the commander as a trophy. When Confederate General James Jay Archer was taken prisoner during the Battle of Gettysburg, he is said to have broken his sword in view of his capturers.

To assist the general in his various duties and responsibilities was a staff of junior officers and orderlies. These men not only handled the general's correspondence, his mail, and his orders to subordinates, but they also, in some cases, served him as a confidential aide. The size of a general's staff varied, as did his responsibilities; a corps commander would have a much larger staff than a company commander.

A regimental commander usually had an adjutant and perhaps an orderly or clerk. The latter was used to convey orders to the company commanders. He would also have a quartermaster and perhaps a surgeon assigned as a staff aide. The surgeon might or might not have several assistants under him, depending on the number in the regiment. There might be a chaplain in each regiment and perhaps a musician or two.

A brigade commander, in addition to the above, would also have a quartermaster to oversee the acquisition of and the disbursement of supplies. He may also have one of two aides-de-camp who were usually young lieutenants he could trust and rely on. The division commander, in addition to the ones listed above, would also have an ordnance officer and an engineer to assist him in the placement of his men in battle.

The corps commander had a rather large staff to help him in managing his responsibilities. Included were a chief engineer, a chief quartermaster, a chief ordnance officer responsible for having adequate ammunition on hand for the men and the guns, a chief surgeon, a judge advocate general responsible for handling military policy and law, a chief provost marshal to enforce military law, a chief of artillery responsible for the overall command of the batteries attached to the corps, and a chief of commissary. The commanding general would have several adjutants to help him in addition to clerks and orderlies. The young men who served as orderlies were normally enlisted men who were good horsemen, for they relayed messages and orders from the corps commander to the officers in the field.

In the Confederate army, a lieutenant general in command of a corps usually had four aides-de-camp, whereas a major general would have two and a brigadier had one. The scenario would be the same for the Union, with the major general in charge of a corps having from three to five aides, a division commander having two to three aides and a brigade commander usually having only one.

The commanders also had an adjutant general and an inspector general. These were usually young men holding the rank of lieutenant or captain and were officially listed as being an A.A.G, Acting Adjutant General, as each side had only one person filling the bill as adjutant general. The A.A.G was constantly at his commander's side and often served as his chief of staff. The A.A.G. could and often did sign his commander's name to orders and circulars.

A general would often have one or two officers on his staff that he trusted completely and confided in. He felt comfortable in conveying his plans and ideas to these men. The general's chief of staff became so familiar with the general that he could and often did anticipate his actions or movements. There were times, when engaged in a battle, a general found he could not be everywhere he needed to be as the action on the field unfolded. It was then that he placed his trust in his chief of staff to oversee actions on the opposite flank or area of fighting. The chief of staff usually had the commander's authority to issue or direct orders in the general's name.

The position of confidential officer or chief of staff was a prized and valued one — one that could and often did open the door for a future command. The best known and respected staff officer was Moxley Sorrell of General Longstreet's staff. He often operated on the field separate from Longstreet but yet issued orders under his name. They made a good team. Sorrell later wrote:

The General left much to me, both in camp and on the field. As chief of Staff it was my part to respond to calls for instructions and to anticipate them. The General was kept fully advised after the event, if he was not near by at the time; but action had to be swift and sure, without waiting to hunt him on a different part of the field. The change of movement of a brigade or division in battle certainly carried a grave responsibility, but it has often to be faced by the chief staff officer if the general happened to be out of reach.[1]

Then again, there were some generals who never revealed their plans to anyone, much less their staff. The most notable of these was Stonewall Jackson. Prior to an engagement, Jackson would formulate his plan of attack and not inform anyone of it. As the battle played out about him, he would supervise and direct the actions on the field. There were times, though, when action was called for on another part of the field. Precious time was spent in locating General Jackson to get authorization to either advance or to bring up additional elements, much to the consternation of the men in the field.

Brief biographies of some of the important or well-known leaders, both the Union and Confederate, are in Appendix IV. Only their personal information is given; date of birth, place of birth, date of death, place of death and place of burial if known. The highest rank achieved during the war and if the officer was a graduate of West Point are listed. No matter what side these men fought on, they were Americans before the war and Americans after it. They, along with their men, helped to make this country a stronger and better nation.

Chapter 4

The Men

"War loses a great deal of its romance after a soldier has seen his first battle."

— John Singleton Mosby, 1887

In 1861 when hostilities broke out, newspapers across the country waved the flag of patriotism in the air. Politicians called for men to come forth either to put down the rebellion or to defend the right to form a new nation. The Union Army was extremely small at this time and the Confederate army almost non-existent. Manpower was needed on both sides to accomplish their goals.

The call to patriotism ignited the spark that caused men to leave their families and take up arms in their nation's cause. Women's groups formed to support their men by making uniforms, flags and other supplies necessary to wage war. There are no accurate records to indicate just how many men really did enlist. Records were destroyed either during or after the struggle. Also, some men enlisted, deserted and then re-enlisted again under a different name in a different company. Many did so to claim the bounty that was paid for enlistments, others to avoid punishment for some infraction of the rules.

It has been estimated that approximately 3,528,304 men served in the armies, both North and South. Union records indicate there were 2,672,341 men who served in the Union Army. This figure includes 2,489,836 Whites, 178,975 Negroes and 3,530 Indians, whereas the Union Navy consisted of 105,963 sailors and officers. This gave the United States a combined fighting force estimated to be 2,778,304. Totals for the Confederate forces are estimates only. Many historians place the number between 600,000 and 1,400,000, with the average being roughly 750,000. The Confederate Navy was considerably smaller than the Union's, consisting of 3,674 men in 1864.

The vast majority of the men enlisted in the army. Some enlistments were for a short duration. In the beginning, that period was from six months up to three years. Later, enlistments were recorded for "duration of the war." The war really was not expected to drag on.

However, drag on it did and, as it did, enlistments declined while at the same time terms of enlistments expired. Additional manpower was desperately needed and both North and South enacted draft or conscription laws to meet the need. On April 16, 1862, the Confederacy enacted the draft and, within a short period, had conscription officers enforcing the induction of men into the armed services. The draft law enacted in 1863 by the Union brought an additional 249,259 men into the army. Of this total, 86,724 paid a total of $26,366,316.78 to the federal government for the right to be excused from service, leaving a balance of 162,535 to actually serve. Of this figure, 116,118 paid a substitute to serve for them while 46,417 men were actually drafted into the Union Army. Figures for the total men conscripted into the Confederate Army have not yet been located at this time.

Whenever a country goes to war, it is always the young men who pay the price. It is they who do the actual fighting and die while their politicians debate the merits of the war and their officers decide on the strategy. When the guns opened on Fort Sumter on that day in April 1861, not only was the fort attacked, but the guns also heralded the call to arms across the country. Young men on both sides rushed to join the fight.

The pay for serving in the army did not make a man rich. The pay for a private was $11 to $13 a month, whereas a colonel earned $95 per month and a brigadier general in the Union army earned a grand total of $124 a month. The men were supplied with uniforms, blankets, weapons and food. They were taught to march, drill and follow orders. Some of the men were unable to read or write; however, during the course of the war, many would learn. A strong revival in religion touched many. Religious worship prior to the start of the war was considered feminine until men saw and experienced the horrors of war. Now church services were faithfully attended as men knelt in prayer before, during and after a battle. In addition to attending church services, many soldiers were given a basic education. Many men longed to return home for a visit, but furloughs were hard to come by. Some soldiers never made it home.

Who were the men who left their homes, took up a rifle and marched across the country to face the enemy? What was their life like in the camp and how did they survive? Many had never been more than five miles from their homes and here they were marching clear across the country, meeting up with other boys and men from the far reaches of the world. Some did not know how to fire a rifle, dig a latrine or live off the land. Many, for the first time in their lives, were exposed to tobacco, alcohol, gambling and sex.

The average age of a soldier was a little under twenty-six, ranging from eighteen to forty-six. Approximately 3,988 were under the age of sixteen when they enlisted. Many of them would fight on the front lines, some for the Union and others for the Confederacy. One of the youngest was John Lincoln Clem, who was but ten years old when he ran off to join the war in 1861. He became a member of the 22nd Massachusetts. Clem, born August 13, 1851, would become known as the "little drummer boy of Chickamauga." He served throughout the war and beyond, finally resigning from the army in 1915 at the rank of brigadier general. He died of old age on May 13, 1937.

On the other end of the spectrum, there were 2,366 men over the age of fifty who fought for the Union. John Burns was born in 1789, two years after the U.S. Constitution was drafted in Philadelphia. During the Battle of Gettysburg that this War of 1812 veteran picked up his old musket and fought side by side with the young soldiers. On the first day of the battle, Burns approached Colonel John Benton Callis of the 7th Wisconsin and proudly announced he was ready to fight the "rebels." Colonel Callis attempted to persuade the old man to go home, but as shells whistled overhead, Burns pulled out his old flintlock and powder horn, informing Callis he either would fight with the 7th Wisconsin or he would fight alone. Callis ordered one of his men to give Burns a more modern weapon and Burns got in line with the soldiers. With his new "modern" weapon, Burns took aim at the charging Confederates. He put his rifle to his shoulder, took a steady aim and fired, hitting a Confederate officer sitting atop a large white horse. With his steadiness and aim, he was immediately welcomed as part of the 7th Wisconsin.

What did these men look like? Their average height was five feet, eight inches with the average weight being one hundred forty-three pounds. The tallest man in the Union Army was Captain David Van Buskirk of the 27th Indiana, who stood six feet ten, while the shortest man was in the 192nd Ohio. He was reported to have been only three feet, four inches tall. Roughly sixty-eight percent had dark hair while thirty-one percent had hair that could be classified as being blond, sandy or red. Only about one percent had gray hair at the start of the war, but that figure changed drastically as the war progressed. Robert E. Lee sported a head of black hair when he resigned his Union commission and took a position with the Confederate army. By the end of the war four years later, his hair had turned completely gray. Over forty-five percent of the men had blue eyes while the others had gray (24 percent), hazel (13 percent) and dark (18 percent).

These men were not always soldiers. Most had a previous occupation, which they left behind to take up a rifle in defense of their country. In the North, three percent were classified as being professional men while forty-eight percent were listed as farmers. Twenty-four percent were mechanics, sixteen percent were laborers, and five percent were merchants. The remaining four percent represented miscellaneous professions.

Confederate enlistees were similar to those in Union army. They also were farmers, planters, merchants, teachers, bankers, clerks, lawyers, doctors and a few politicians thrown in for good measure. Percentages for the Confederacy cannot be determined at this time for many of the records no longer exist. Politicians in both the North and the South joined up, although many did so only after securing supervisory positions in the officer corps.

Seventy-five percent of the men who served in the military were native-born Americans, while twenty-five percent had immigrated to this country. Over 500,000 foreigners served in the Union forces: 175,000 Germans and 150,000 Irishmen. They had come to this country searching mainly for freedom and independence and now they took up the cause of their new country in an effort to hold it together. Many of the newly arrived were offered generous rewards for their enlistment, while others were guaranteed citizenship and a pension for their service.

Based on the known information, the average soldier in either army was in all likelihood a private roughly twenty-six years of age. He stood about 5'8" and weighed one hundred forty-three pounds. He had dark hair with blue eyes and was probably a farmer in civilian life. He was probably married with a wife and two to five children waiting for him back at home. He had a limited education and, for the most part, was a devoted husband and a loyal soldier who would do his duty.

Most of the men went into the infantry, for the infantry was the backbone of the army. It was a fighting force that traveled on its feet, slept on the ground and suffered the most from the effects of not only rifle and musket fire, but also cannon fire and in some cases the point of the saber.

Upon enlisting in the army, the soldier would first be assigned to a camp and then would report to his company to learn the art of soldiering. Once assigned to a company, he had to find a place for himself. He would learn to share his quarters. The new soldier would be expected to fend for himself and, at the same time, be part of a group that not only formed his company, but his regiment, his brigade, his division and ultimately his corps. He learned how to take orders, some of which might come from a former neighbor or businessman from his old hometown.

The soldier learned that his company had not only a command staff made up of a captain, three lieutenants, five sergeants, and eight corporals, but also that he was one of approximately 72 privates. His company was divided into two platoons, and each platoon was further divided into two sections. When he and the rest of the company fell into two ranks, he learned quickly how to mark off thirteen inches and that the second rank was positioned thirteen inches behind the front rank.

Newly recruited soldiers, upon arrival in camp, had to learn two things right off the bat — how to follow orders and how to march. Both were a prerequisite to be learned and to be followed without question. The men's lives and their company's life depended upon it. Orders had to be followed automatically; a soldier should not have to think about what to do or how to act when the command was given. This ability to act instinctively was imperative in the heat of battle, when positions might have to be suddenly switched or movements executed to either advance or retreat. Thus, discipline was often hard, rash and severe. To teach soldiers to march correctly and automatically, drills were held every day, sometimes two to four times a day depending on the commander, the men and the situation at hand.

First, there would be squad drill, followed by company drills. These would normally be followed by regimental drill and perhaps later brigade drill. The soldier learned how to perform the quick step, which was walking at a rate of approximately 110 steps per minute. This meant each step taken was about twenty-eight inches from heel to heel. After learning this, he next learned to "double quick," which was more like a run than a march. It was used mainly to hasten troops on the march or to charge the enemy across the field. The double quick was approximately a thirty-three inch step totaling about 165 to 180 steps per minute.

The soldier quickly learned army discipline. He was expected to obey all orders given and not to shirk his duty. Usually the provost marshal was responsible for the administration of discipline, but as the army increased and was constantly on the move, regimental commanders meted out punishments for minor infractions. These would include shirking duty, improper handling of equipment or the failure to maintain a clean camp. Punishments for these offenses ranged anywhere from digging latrines to extra guard duty, cutting wood or walking a post. Some officers went so far as to tie an offender up by his thumbs.

More serious infractions such as insubordination, straggling, thievery, drunkenness, or sleeping on duty subjected the transgressor to arrest and court-martial. Here the punishments ranged all the way from public humiliation to imprisonment and even death. Public humiliation took many strange forms, depending on who was administering it. Punishments would consist of either wearing a placard on one's back announcing his crime, or riding the wooden horse. To ride the wooden horse, a soldier was forced to sit for hours atop a narrow rail set high enough so his feet did not touch the ground. On other occasions, the transgressor might be assigned to wear a barrel shirt designed more for humiliation than anything else. The barrel shirt was a barrel in which holes were cut on the side for the arms and in the top for the head. Sometimes the soldier, especially in the Southern army, was subjected to being bucked and gagged. In this, the poor soldier was seated on the ground with his knees drawn up to his chest with his arms wrapped around his knees. His hands were tied at the wrist with a stick placed between his arms and his knees preventing the soldier from moving or straightening his arms or legs. He would stay this way for a few hours. If in the cavalry or the artillery, the errant the soldier could be tied spread-eagle to the gun carriage wheel for several hours.

An act of Congress outlawed flogging in the Union army on August 5, 1861, while it would not be until 1863 before the Confederacy would outlaw the use of the whip. Desertion, spying, murder, threats on an officer's life or crimes against civilians could and often did bring the death penalty. Death by firing squad was the usual form of execution for deserters while hanging was reserved mainly for spies and common criminals.

Soldiers learned how to march, carrying all of their equipment and personal belongings on their backs. At the start of the war, the soldier carried on his person a knapsack that contained all his belongings: a change of underwear, a pair of extra socks, a toothbrush, and perhaps a razor, eating utensils, some writing paper, a pencil and some stamps. He also had slung over his shoulder a haversack, which at first carried his food and perhaps some coffee and tobacco. On his belt would be his canteen, his cup, his cartridge box, his cap box, and a bayonet. Somewhere amid all of this would be his blanket, a poncho and perhaps a canvas tent, which was his home away from home. Later, as the war progressed, the men found less was more, especially among the Southern soldiers. All the baggage he carried weighed him down. It was extremely difficult to run carrying all on his back and, in the heat of battle, life was more important than possessions. When in a fight, many would throw their knapsacks and other belongs to the ground. In the end, the soldiers found it easier to wrap all their belongings in their blankets and tie it around their shoulders. Many men continued to carry their haversack across the shoulder in addition to the rolled blanket.

The soldiers spent more time in camp and on the march than they ever did in battle. Camp life was boring, dull, monotonous, and always regulated. The soldier awoke to reveille and went to bed with taps. Once awake, the first order of the day was the policing of the camp. The appearance of the camp was often thought to have been indicative of the unit's readiness for battle. A clean camp was a disciplined camp and a disciplined camp was ready for anything. A sloppy camp was indicative of sloppy, untrained troops.

Whenever the soldiers had time to themselves, it was usually spent writing letters home. In addition, soldiers spent time fishing if possible, reading newspapers and trying to find out the news from home. Many times, a dime novel would find its way through the camp as the book was passed from one to another. Though gambling was prohibited, many did find ways to do so, as card games and the rolling of the dice took place. Some soldiers, it has been reported, went so far as to place bets on the occasional cockroach or lice races. Literary societies were formed in some of the camps and an occasional play was staged for the troops. In the wintertime with the snow on the ground, mock battles were staged in snowball wars between huts, camps, companies or regiments.

Church services and music also occupied the soldiers' lives, not only in camp, but also on the march and in battle. Church services were normally full on Sundays and many companies and regiments had chaplains assigned to them. Before a major battle, men would gather on the field to pray to their God for success and their safety. Many times, a chaplain would lead the soldiers in prayer as the drums sounded assembly. Music provided a soothing sound for many while in camp at night and stimulated them as they marched.

As the war progressed, the Union army started to place the soldier's regiment number on his hat. Later, each division within a corps would be designated by a color and each corps would have its own symbol. This came about because on the field, commanders had no idea whose troops they saw, especially in a fight as several different divisions became mixed. Sometimes a commander, seeing soldiers on the field which he believed belonged to him, would issue directives to them, only to find out they belonged to another commander. This created confusion on the field not only for the soldier, but also for the commander. Many times the orders given countermanded those already in effect. While no battle can be said to have been lost because of this, years later, the men and officers still complained about the inefficiency of orders given in the field by the various commanders.

To solve this problem, especially in the Union army, each man had his regiment number attached to his cap. On March 23, 1863, orders were issued for the use of corps badges. Each Union corps would have a different emblem to represent them and each division with the corps would also have a different color. Red on a cap badge meant the soldier was a member of the First Division. White signified the Second Division and blue represented the Third Division. The Fourth Division had the color green while the Fifth Division used orange.

The food that the soldiers ate was not the best but it was sufficient to sustain a fighting force. The soldiers did not have the opportunity like their officers to sit around a table and quietly and calmly eat a meal. Their meals were fixed in the field and would consist of whatever was available to eat. The soldiers were supposed to get rations, but by the latter stages of the war, most soldiers would have to settle for hardtack and water. Hardtack was a large cracker made from flour, water and sometimes fatback. Usually this would be eaten while on the march and, at times, soaked in water or crumbled in soup. Sometimes it was fried and mixed with pork and beans. Soldiers at first did have a variety of foods, including peas, rice, beans, dried fruit and potatoes. As the Confederate soldiers approached Gettysburg in June 1863, many made themselves sick by consuming large amounts of fresh fruits. Many of them had dropped out of the ranks to pick apples, cherries and berries from the northern fields before rejoining the march, then became sick with cramps and diarrhea. Men on both sides enjoyed a good cup of coffee and the northern soldiers had a good supply of it. The southern soldiers learned how to make coffee with parched corn, beans or whatever grounds they could find. Many reports exist about the midnight swap of supplies between the soldiers on picket duty. Sometimes when the pickets would be manning their posts, they would make contact with the opposing pickets and make arrangements for the exchange of coffee for tobacco or newspapers.

The life of the soldier was indeed a difficult one. He endured hardships, loneliness, pain from terrible wounds or diseases, and perhaps time as a prisoner of war. With the end of the war, he returned to his home hoping to pick up where he left off. The Union soldier might have a farm to return to or a business where he could find employment, but the southern lands had been ravaged. Crops, buildings and land in the South had been burnt or destroyed, livestock taken and the means of earning a livelihood was, in many cases, gone. This country, North and South, would have to be rebuilt, both physically and emotionally, and it would be rebuilt by those who had experienced the horrors of war.

Chapter 5

The War

"Both parties deprecated war; but one of them would make war
rather than let the nation survive; and the other would accept war
rather than let it perish. And the war came."
— *Abraham Lincoln's Second Inaugural
Address, March 4, 1865*

Before the election of Abraham Lincoln to the presidency in November 1860, the United States was a troubled and a divided nation. There were many issues, and given cooler times and cooler heads, perhaps the issues could have been resolved, discussed, and worked out or more compromises reached. However, this was not the time. With the election of Lincoln, a Republican, firebrands continued to preach and war clouds continued to gather over many town meetings. The differences between the states reached a boiling point. What were the differences? Well, it depended on who was doing the talking — the industrialized North or the agrarian South. The country was split between the viewpoints of those who believed it was the right of the federal government to control issues that affected the constitutional rights of the citizens, the states, the economy and the westward movement and those who wanted to maintain the status quo. The question really came down to just one issue: who had the right to govern the states— the states themselves or the central government? Who had the right to control the expansion of slavery into western territories— the state or the federal government? Could a state secede from the Union if the state disagreed with the federal government or could the federal government use force to prevent it? South Carolina had threatened to secede from the Union if a Republican was elected, and one had been.

Of the thirty-three states that made up the United States in 1860, fifteen[1] were considered slave-holding states. The votes in Congress were nearly equal, but with the addition of new states into the Union, that equality was in peril. This country was growing and there were several territories about to petition for statehood. Numerous arguments and

49

compromises had been made and voided in the process. It had been decided that the people residing in those territories were the ones to make the decision whether, upon admission, they would be free or not. Many fights, arguments and massacres occurred as the territory of Kansas knocked on the door of statehood asking to be admitted to the Union of States. Bands of thugs, outlaws and mercenaries had moved into Kansas in an effort to persuade the residents on how to cast their vote. On May 21, 1856, pro-slavery advocates raided Lawrence, Kansas, destroying and burning property of those who opposed the idea of slavery in the territory. A few days later, John Brown, a noted abolitionist, with a few of his sons, dragged five men from their cabins and hacked them to death. By the time "Bleeding" Kansas was admitted into the Union as a free state, over two hundred people had been killed in the struggle to control the vote. Now with Lincoln, an anti-slavery advocate, coming into the White House, things would change. The Southern states, fearing this change, talked of secession, arguing that the U.S. Constitution preserved states' rights. Talk of a new southern confederacy grew daily.

South Carolina seceded from the Union in December 1860. The federal government opposed it. Would sending forces prevent their leaving or would it trigger additional states to secede? Outgoing President James Buchanan did nothing, claiming he could find nothing in the federal Constitution to prevent secession. It was hoped that the new Congress could agree upon a solution, or at least come up with some type of compromise, to solve the issue of secession. Congress did little but talk while the president-elect opposed any form or type of compromise. To Lincoln, compromise was not the answer. Neither side appeared willing to accept any real settlement. It was more than probable that other Southern states would follow South Carolina, but the federal government would take a wait and see attitude as 1861 approached.

As 1861 dawned, citizens on both sides of the issue of secession looked for answers to the many questions that arose. Many people wondered whether Buchanan would do anything to prevent additional states from seceding before he left office. If he did not act, what would Lincoln do? Many wondered if after his inaugural, Lincoln would take immediate action to force the seceding states back to the Union. No one had the answer, but many offered their opinions.

"Let the South go," cried some on both sides, believing secession was the natural right of sovereign states. Others cried that the Union was indivisible and that the founding fathers had worked long and hard to preserve this Union. The man many considered the "Father of the Constitution," James Madison, Jr., wrote in 1834, "The advice nearest to my heart and deepest in my conviction is that the Union of the States be cherished and perpetuated. Let the open enemy to it be regarded as a Pandora with her box opened; and the disguised one, as the Serpent creeping with his deadly wiles into Paradise."[2] With the secession of South Carolina, that Pandora's Box was now opened. It was a time of fearful tension and hopeful waiting.

When Lincoln took the oath of office on March 4, 1861, he said that there would be no interference with the institution of slavery where it existed. In his inaugural address, he stated that the disruption of the Union "is now formally attempted, but the Union of the States is perpetual." Lincoln argued that the Union could not be dissolved, and any acts of violence against the United States were "insurrectionary or revolutionary." Lincoln further stated that there need not be bloodshed or violence, and that there would be none, unless "it is forced upon the national authority ... in your hands, my dissatisfied fellow countrymen, and not in mine, is the momentous issue of civil war. The government will not assail you. You can have no conflict, without being yourselves the aggressors."[3] He would not fire the first shot.

Several minor issues had been resolved as 1861 began, but their solutions made things only darker. South Carolina began to set up its own government as other states contemplated secession. The United States Congress still debated possible compromises but with little success and with little enthusiasm. Lincoln, though violently opposed to secession, was publicly silent, but privately concerned that there should be no compromise over the expansion of slavery.

As more and more states seceded, confusion and uncertainty reigned. A new nation was being established amid powerful opposition. The Southern states, now referred to as the Confederate States of America, were acting very much like a separate nation complete with its own government, a president and a constitution. Many questions remained unanswered. Could military conflict be avoided? Would the Southern states be able to gain foreign recognition? The young Confederacy sought recognition on the world stage but was disappointed when observers were sent rather than ambassadors.

As a prelude to a possible upcoming insurrection, Major Robert Anderson, in command of the small military garrison in Charleston Harbor, decided to abandon Fort Moultrie and move his men to the more secure fort on the other side of the harbor. Anderson, in addition to believing that Fort Moultrie was insecure and would soon fall to Confederate forces, also believed he would be in a better position to defend the much stronger Fort Sumter. During the middle of the night on December 26, 1860, with strict orders to remain quiet, Anderson took his entire command and slipped unobserved across the harbor into Fort Sumter. Confederate officials were quite upset upon discovering this and vowed that the Fort Sumter would not be resupplied. All comings and goings to the fort were strictly monitored.

The new government took steps to expel the Union from its territory. The southern government insisted all federal property was to be turned over to the Confederacy. The federal government refused to give up several of their forts, specifically Fort Sumter in Charleston Harbor and Fort Pickens in Florida. As the negotiations continued over these areas, Confederates worked hard and with great energy to build fortifications in Charleston Harbor. Finally, South Carolina officials, under General P.G.T. Beauregard, decided to take possession of "their" property and opened fire on Fort Sumter on April 12, 1861. The talk was over as the war began.

The North had its advantages. They had more than twenty-two million people. The population in the South was estimated at nine million, more than a third of them slaves. The North controlled ninety percent of the country's manufacturing capacity and two-thirds of its railroad mileage. The South had approximately nine thousand railroad miles compared to the North's twenty-two thousand miles. Control of the Atlantic Ocean gave the North access to the factories of Europe and the huge surpluses of food in the northern states could be sold to pay for ammunition. The South had no navy and very few ships.

The South, however, was not without advantages. The North would have to invade, and an invader needed substantial superiority in numbers to conquer. The Confederacy was large. Northern supply lines would be long and many troops would be needed to guard and protect them. The long Confederate coastline was beyond the blockade capacity of the Union navy. The most important factor, however, was that the South would be fighting to protect its homeland. The North would fight for the abstract idea of the Union. The South could win if the North lost its desire to pursue the war, but the North could win only if it destroyed the South's ability to fight.

The South was an agrarian society. Many of its people lived on small farms. As the men left to join the young Confederacy, the women were left to tend to the farms and do the work of the men. Many of the small farmers were not slave owners and thus the women were left to plow, to plant and to harvest. At first, when winter came, the men were able to leave the armies and return home to tend their crops and farms, but as the war progressed, the men could not be spared. Worse, as the Northern armies trampled Southern soil, they laid waste to the fields. Crops and livestock disappeared and, by the end of the war, buildings and any supplies of value were either confiscated, burned or destroyed. Many of the women, now widows and some with children, were forced to abandon their lands. Some sought the safety of neighbors or moved to the cities while others tried to support themselves however they could.

In the various states, both North and South, armies were organized and men gathered. Men and boys quickly signed up as state governments organized regiments and then offered these regiments, in a somewhat haphazard manner, to the government. For the South, not only an army had to be organized, but a navy had to be created. In the North, there were those who still opposed war and hoped for a settlement. There were also problems with how to equip the men with the necessary implements of war. Uniforms had to be made and guns manufactured as factories were converted to the war effort for the production of ammunition, wagons, caissons and limbers, in addition to harnesses and saddles.

Patriotism was on the upswing as each country flew its flag with pride and determination. Ladies societies were formed and many small communities presented special flags for their boys to carry on the field of battle. Meanwhile, those closer to the fighting fields rolled bandages and made coffins. Promises of undying devotion to the community, state and nation were uttered as many of the enlisted "promised to do" their duty.

In the North, the United States Congress had its hands full. Men and money were needed to continue the war effort. The delegates discovered they were able to pass new laws and regulations that had been stymied by their Southern brothers. Many of the laws enacted in the 37th Congress opened lands in the west and those lands would be free of slavery. Congress also passed a railroad act, which would establish rail lines into the western part of the country. The beginning of emancipation was taking hold. Washington enacted the "District Emancipation Act" which freed the slaves living in Washington, D.C.

As the nation went to war, slavery became a major issue. Many found it strange that Julia Dent, the wife of General Ulysses S. Grant, often brought her slaves with her when she visited her husband in the field. She had come from a slave-holding family and her husband never asked her to give them up. Others, in the South, thought it strange that the widow of President James K. Polk, though she supported the Confederacy, sold her slaves and declared her Tennessee property to be neutral territory.

The war affected families of previous presidents. President Martin Van Buren's widow sent blankets to Confederate prisoners confined in the Union prison of Elmira, New York, while the wife of President Franklin Pierce called for the destruction of the South, she being an avid abolitionist. President Benjamin Harrison was urged to pick up a rifle for the Union's cause. One former president's widow attempted to make a financial gain for herself and the Confederacy. The widow of President John Tyler was able to slip her cotton crop past a Union's blockade, selling it for good money in the Bahamas. President Tyler's son enlisted in the Confederate forces.

Both Jefferson Davis and Abraham Lincoln started their administrations about the same time. As both leaders struggled to organize their presidency and cabinets, they both also attempted to direct the war effort — one in order to establish the right to form a separate, independent country and the other to keep the Union together.

In the South, a strong central government had to be established. The same problems that faced George Washington sixty years earlier now faced Jefferson Davis. Washington had nothing to draw on except the guidance and wisdom of his advisers. Davis had the history of the United States government to draw upon, his own political experiences, and the experience of many politicians who had also been representatives of that now foreign government. The country the South was trying to establish looked and sounded very much like the government that they had left and rejected.

Events started to pile up on events, as battles and engagements were fought. Previously unknown places with unknown names became part of history. Arguments continued on both the social and the political fronts, but for the most part, the people remained hopeful on both sides. Military commanders became either heroes or villains as the newspapers of the day carried news of the war. Still, the ideals for which both sides fought were glamorous and fascinated the masses.

CABINETS OF THE TWO GOVERNMENTS

Position	*United States*	*Confederate States*
President	Abraham Lincoln	Jefferson Davis
Vice President	Hannibal Hamlin	Alexander Stephens
	Andrew Johnson	
Secretary of State	William H. Seward	Robert Toombs
Secretary of War	Simon Cameron	Leroy P. Walker
	Edwin M. Stanton	J.P. Benjamin
		G.W. Randolph
		G.W. Smith
		James Seddon
		J.C. Breckinridge
Secretary of the Navy	Gideon Welles	Stephen M. Mallory
Secretary of the Treasury	Samuel P. Chase	C.G. Memminger
Attorney General	Edward Bates	Judah P. Benjamin
Postmaster	Montgomery Blair	John H. Reagan

After the first year ended, both sides of the conflict went into winter quarters. In some parts of the armies, men were permitted to go home to get their lands ready for next year's crop. Surely cooler heads would prevail and the war would end before spring. Many men still held that belief. Unfortunately, the quick end forecasted by many seasoned politicians would not happen. Both armies called for additional men and many responded to the call. The song of patriotism was still loud and strong.

With the arrival of 1862 came new problems. Two nations were in a struggle to see if one could keep its newly proclaimed independence and the other to see if the nation would be indivisible. In the South, a full time regular government had been elected. Before this, there had been only a provisional government. Now that a permanent government was in place, the work of running the new country got off in earnest. The first Congress would meet in February 1862 and before it lay the awesome task of not only funding the country and the government, but also finding the monies necessary to continue the fight for independence. Foreign recognition also had to be obtained to make the government legitimate.

On the military front, it was thought that the Confederacy could not resist or oppose the federal government for long. It hastened to work on its western defense line while, in the North, excitement mixed with anxiety as doubt continued. The people of the two nations were mainly optimistic, but questions of all kinds were being asked, more and more frequently, as the Union began to invade the South.

In the east, President Jefferson Davis had named Joseph E. Johnston to be the commander of the army, which later became the Army of Northern Virginia. However, Johnston would fall in battle, being wounded at Fair Oaks in May 1862. At that time, Davis selected Robert E. Lee to replace him, but Lee would not have much success at first, for he was slow to take the offensive. Early in the war, Lee had earned the name of "Granny Lee" because of his slowness to act. Nevertheless, as 1862 progressed, Davis realized that in Lee he had found the one military commander he had confidence in, but more important, that he could trust.

Davis was having problems with some of his other war commanders. Albert Sidney Johnston had been placed in command of the forces in the west and was considered by many military experts to be the most able and qualified commander of all the southern generals. However, early in 1862, Davis lost Johnston when he was killed during the Battle of Shiloh.

Davis had a different type problem with another commander, a close friend, John B. Floyd. The secretary of war under former President James Buchanan, Floyd had been accused by Union officials of transferring arms to the southern arsenals prior to the outbreak of hostilities. As Union forces were about to seize Fort Donelson, Floyd, its commander, fled saying he was fearful of being arrested and tried by Union officials for treason. As he made his way to safety Floyd abandoned not only the fort, but left his men behind to handle the surrender.

Lincoln, like Jefferson Davis, was having difficulties with the war effort and choosing the right commanders. Some were proving difficult to handle. In the fall of 1861, Lincoln had named Major General Henry W. Halleck to command the area west of the Cumberland River while naming Brigadier General Don Carlos Buell to command the forces east of the river. It would have been helpful if these two men had been able to get along and cooperate with one another, but as 1862 came and passed, they could or would not, as Lincoln soon discovered. Neither Halleck nor Buell could agreed on what defenses should be erected or, for that matter, what or if an offensive should be planned.

Lincoln also discovered that he could not get Major General George B. McClellan to move with any regularity. McClellan made advancements into Southern territory but then would pull back, waiting for more and more reinforcements. It was later believed McClellan was always overestimating the strength of his opponent. Repeatedly, McClellan failed to take advantage of the hard-earned victories his men gave him. Initially, Lincoln had confidence in McClellan, naming him general in chief of the army in late 1861. However, as 1862 progressed, Lincoln relieved McClellan of that command, although he left him in command of the Army of the Potomac.

When the state of Virginia voted to secede from the Union, the western part of the state voted against it and vowed to remain in the Union. The residents of this region formed their own government, the "Restored Government of Virginia," declaring the Confederate government illegal. There would be many battles fought in this part of Virginia, not only for the right to secede from the Confederacy but also to join the Union. The Battle of Philippi in June 1861 played an instrumental role, as did the fights at Boteler's Ford, Carrick's Ford, Droop Mountain and the numerous attempts to control Harper's Ferry. As discussions between politicians centered on getting this western part of Virginia into the Union, the name proposed for the new state was "Kanawha." The elected delegates of this region went to Washington, where they proposed to secede from the state of Virginia. A crises was created, for the Constitution specially forbids a state from being formed from another state.[4] Nevertheless, this territory, admitted to the Union as a free and independent state on June 20, 1863, would be known as West Virginia. Its admission into the Union was accompanied by a provision stating that all slaves in the state were to be emancipated.

How to finance the war effort was the worry of both Congresses. The United States government had three ways to obtain financing: by taxation, by printing new currency and by borrowing. When it looked like war was imminent, Congress began deciding what to tax and how much. The idea of selling war bonds came to light. The credit for the idea has been given to Jay Cooke, a Philadelphia banker who often placed ads in newspapers and handbills urging people to purchase the bonds.

Manpower was proving to be an issue on both sides. In the beginning of the war, prisoners were exchanged and paroled. Later in the war, General Ulysses S. Grant decided to end the exchange of prisoners, stating this would deprive the Confederacy of the manpower it needed to continue the war. Each nation, both North and South, developed the resources it needed by adopting draft or conscription laws to encourage able-bodied men to serve in the military.

Many regiments and some brigades were composed entirely of men of one nationality, while others saw a mixture of many. Since many of the immigrants arrived in the northern ports, it was only natural that they would fight for the north. Some immigrants became "soldiers of fortune" as they made their way southward and took up arms for the Confederacy. Many of the immigrants coming to this country had seen revolutions and wars in their native countries. Germany, Italy, and Hungry had revolutions during the 1840s and 1850s, and, by the time the 1860s arrived, many of the refugees of those countries came to America to get away from the fighting, only to find themselves taking up arms in defense of their new nation. The potato famine in Ireland brought many new Irishmen to the eastern shore, and by the end of the war, both sides would boast of their Irish brigades, as the flag of Erin waved over the blood-soaked field of the United States.

The fear of war caused panic in the streets of the nation's capital, especially after the Battle of Bull Run, which took place a mere thirty miles from the city. By the end of the first year, the city was encircled with sixty enclosed forts, thirty-seven miles of trenches, twenty miles of rifle pits and ninety-three gun batteries.

Texas also saw the ugliness of war, especially with the introduction of the Confederate draft, which allowed for the imprisonment of those suspected of disloyalty. In 1862, thirty-four Union loyalists, in an attempt to avoid imprisonment, made a dash for the

Mexican border. They were captured on August 9. Nineteen of the men were shot; six were trampled to death in the confusion of the fight and nine men were wounded. Those nine men wounded in the fight were immediately executed. People's courts sprang up to try anyone suspected of being disloyal or who spoke out against the Confederacy. Hearsay evidence was accepted, and in Cooke County, Texas, forty-seven men were dragged to the edge of town to be hanged. In Wise County, an additional five men were executed based on the whispers and gossip of neighbors. In Grayson County, Texas, another forty were sentenced to death, but were found not guilty.

Newspapers brought the war home to the people. Many papers sent reporters to the field to write articles about what they witnessed. Many families learned of the death of a loved one by reading his name in the local papers. Sometimes, a list would be posted in front of the news office and groups would gather daily to see if their husband, brother or son was listed. Some reporters were able to get themselves "imbedded" with certain military commanders and were able to accompany the officers and men when they entered the field of battle. Some of those commanders used the reporter for his own personal interest, especially those commanders who had been political appointees. Others, like General Grant, opposed the idea of having a newspaper reporter in camp and often ran them out, sometimes accompanied by an armed patrol to make sure the reporter left. Many news stories were sent via telegraph wires, but this sometimes proved to be haphazard, for many operators failed to send the entire message. Thus an idea was instigated which is still in effect to this very day. The lead paragraph of a news story would cover the entire gist of the story as to who, what, where, why and perhaps how.

Some of the newspapers employed artists who were adept at drawing or sketching. Their pictures appeared in the papers and, for the first time, the people on the home front were able to see the war through another's eyes. Battle sketches and soldiers' lives were popular topics. The pictures took on an added meaning especially to those who could not read or write. Many of the drawings and sketches appeared in *Harper's Weekly* magazine. Near the end of 1862, the idea of sending photographers to the field took hold and soon actual photographs of battle scenes accompanied the stories of the fighting.

The idea of slavery was now beginning to take some precedence over the idea of states' rights. Many called for the emancipation of all the slaves but President Lincoln was not yet ready to do so, for in the fading months of 1862, the war was going badly for the Union cause. However, in September 1862, things began to turn around for the Union with its victory at Antietam.

When 1863 arrived, President Lincoln was finally able to pacify the staunch opponents of slavery. He had been urged since the war began to make a stand on the issue of slavery by issuing a proclamation declaring an end to "that evil institution." In January 1863, Lincoln issued the Emancipation Proclamation, which freed the slaves held where "the people whereof shall then be in rebellion against the United States."

As the war reached the halfway point, the ravages had affected life everywhere. With more and more men needed for military service, businesses were unattended and fields were left unplowed. More and more men were in need of medical attention so homes, hotels and, in some cases, churches, were converted into hospitals.

Both presidents experienced problems with their military commanders, but by the spring of 1864, President Lincoln had found the one man who would not shrink from adversity, criticism or political aspirations. That man was Ulysses S. Grant. Once named as supreme commander of all Union forces, the fate of the South, in essence, was sealed. Grant had the bulldog ferociousness necessary to end the war. He would not pull back. He would leave his dead and wounded on the field as his armies drove the Confederacy in a narrowing circle. In the spring of 1864, Grant initiated a three prong assault on the South, which within a year would encircle it like a vise and then tighten it ever tighter until the Confederate army had been diminished in strength and had nowhere to maneuver.

With the reelection of Lincoln in November 1864 and increasing Union victories, the federal government began to think of how to re-unite the country. Decisions had to be made on what steps or what requirements would be necessary for the errant states to be readmitted to the Union. A question was asked whether the states should be punished. What about those who had taken up arms against the Union — should they ever be allowed to resume the privileges of citizenship? That question had to be answered, as would the question of the soon-to-be freed slaves.

It was a long war — four long years that changed the course of the country's future. The war divided a nation as it divided families. Brothers had fought against brothers, sons had fought against fathers and people everywhere wondered where all this foolishness would end. There were many questions and the answers would affect the country for years to come. This nation would never be the same again.

What follows is a recap of those four tumultuous years and the major events on the field of battle. Not every event is covered, nor every battle or skirmish. Not every convention, proclamation, campaign or every meeting is covered. This is a guide consisting of just the facts. For each battle, engagement, or skirmish, a brief explanation is given along with the apparent victor. A chart shows the approximate strength for each opponent, if known, the names of the commanders, and the loss if known.

Chapter 6

1861

"In your hands, my dissatisfied fellow-countrymen, and not in mine, is the momentous issue of civil war. The Government will not assail you. You can have no conflict without yourselves the aggressors. You have no oath registered in heaven to destroy the Government while I shall have the most solemn one to 'preserve, protect, and defend it.' ... We are not enemies, but friends. We must not be enemies. Though passion may have strained it must not break our bonds of affection. The mystic chords of memory, stretching from every battlefield and patriot grave to every living heart and hearthstone all over this broad land, will yet swell the chorus of the Union, when again touched, as surely they will be, by the better angels of our nature."
— *Abraham Lincoln, First Inaugural Speech,*
Monday, March 4, 1861

January 1861

2   South Carolina troops seized Fort Johnson, located in Charleston Harbor. It had been discovered that Robert Anderson, who was in command of Fort Moultrie, managed to move his entire command to the more secure Fort Sumter in the dead of night on December 26, 1860.

5   With the Confederacy in charge of Charleston Harbor, Fort Sumter was denied the ability to be resupplied with food, ammunition or men. Mail, newspapers and military dispatches, however, were permitted to reach the fort. The *Star of the West* set sail for Fort Sumter from New York after United States military officials decided to resupply the fort.

9   Mississippi seceded from the Union, becoming the second state to do so. South Carolina had been the first when it seceded on December 20, 1860.

10   Florida seceded from the Union.

11   Alabama seceded from the Union.

11   The Confederates established a blockade in an effort to control shipping on the Mississippi River near Vicksburg.

12   The *Star of the West* returned to New York after being denied access to Charleston Harbor.

19   Georgia seceded from the Union.

21   Jefferson Davis, along with David L. Yulee, Stephen R. Mallory, Clement C. Clay, and Benjamin Fitzpatrick, resigned from the U.S. Senate.

26   Louisiana seceded from the Union.

29   Kansas was admitted into the Union as the 34th state.

February 1861

1   Texas seceded from the Union.

4   Thirty-seven delegates representing six southern states met in Montgomery, Alabama, to form a provisional government for the seceding states.

8   The Montgomery Convention unanimously adopted a new constitution for the provisional Confederate government. The constitution adopted was very similar to the U.S. Constitution except slavery would be recognized and protected.

9   Jefferson Davis was named the provisional president of the Confederacy and Alexander H. Stephens of Georgia was named as the provisional vice president.

9   The USS *Brooklyn* arrived off the coast of Pensacola Bay, Florida, with supplies for Fort Pickens but was ordered to remain offshore unless the fort was actually attacked. First Lieutenant Adam Slemmer commanded Fort Pickens.

11   Each of the two newly elected presidents left for their respective capitals; Abraham Lincoln departed Springfield, Illinois, for Washington, D.C., while Jefferson Davis left his plantation in Mississippi for Montgomery, Alabama.

15   The Montgomery Convention resolved to do what was necessary to take possession of all federal property held in the southern states, such as Fort Sumter in South Carolina and Fort Pickens in Florida. Three commissioners were appointed and sent to Washington to negotiate the surrender of federal property in southern territories.

18   Jefferson Davis and Alexander Stephens were inaugurated as president and vice president of the Confederacy.

18   General David E. Twiggs surrendered all federal property in Texas to Confederate forces. He was later called a traitor for his actions.

20   The Confederate government officially established a navy with Stephen Mallory as the new secretary of the navy.

23   Lincoln finally arrived in Washington, D.C., early in the morning, after Alan Pinkerton informed him that Pinkerton had discovered a plot to assassinate the newly elected president.

March 1861

4   Abraham Lincoln was sworn in as the 16th president of the United States. In his inaugural address, Lincoln stated that secession would not be tolerated. He further said that the nation cannot nor should not be separated. He assured the states that there would be no violence unless others forced it upon the Union.

6   The Confederate government called for 100,000 volunteers to staff the provisional army.

11   A permanent Confederate Constitution was adopted, resembling the U.S. Constitution but with its differences spelled out. Slavery was recognized as being legal. The fugitive slave act was not only fortified but strengthened. Though the right of secession was not mentioned, it was implied. Cabinet members were to hold seats in both houses of Congress and the president was to be given the right to use line-item veto while approving the rest of a bill. Presidential terms were to be one term of six years. Free states could only be admitted to the Confederacy with a majority vote.

29   Lincoln ordered a secret relief expedition sent to resupply Fort Sumter.

April 1861

8   Lincoln notified Governor Pickens of South Carolina that he would send supplies to Fort Sumter.

11   South Carolina asked for the surrender of Fort Sumter and that request was denied.

12   The USS *Brooklyn* finally was able to send supplies to Fort Pickens.

12   The first shots of the Civil War were fired at 4:30 a.m. as South Carolina militia opened fire on the federal stronghold at Fort Sumter in Charleston Harbor.

13 Cut off from any means of reinforcement, Major Robert Anderson surrendered Fort Sumter to South Carolina officials. Only one death was recorded when a gun accidentally exploded inside the fort, killing Private Daniel Hough. Hough unofficially became the first casualty of the war.

15 Lincoln declared a state of insurrection and issued a call for 75,000 volunteers to join the military in order to put down the rebellion.

17 The Virginia State Convention passed an Ordinance of Secession.

18 Union soldiers stationed at Harper's Ferry learned that a Confederate contingent under Captain Turner Ashby was en route to take possession of the fort. After destroying what weapons and supplies they could, the Union abandoned Harper's Ferry, giving the Confederacy control of the long section of the Baltimore and Ohio Railroad, a major lifeline supplying the city of Washington, D.C.

19 The Sixth Massachusetts commanded by Colonel Edward F. Jones, while on its way to Washington, clashed with a mob of Confederate sympathizers in Baltimore. Four soldiers were killed.

19 Lincoln called for the blockade of all southern ports. Union gunboats patrolled the Chesapeake Bay and the coast of Virginia.

20 Robert E. Lee was offered command of all Union forces, but resigned to serve Virginia and the South, saying, "How can I draw my sword upon Virginia, my native state?"

21 Confederate forces took control of the Gosport Naval Yard near Norfolk, Virginia, after its U.S. military commander, General Charles S. McCauley, ordered all ships to be burned or scuttled. Three ships survived. One, the USS *Merrimack*, was salvaged and after repair became the CSS *Virginia*.

May 1861

3 Lincoln called for an additional 42,000 three-year volunteers.

6 The Confederate Congress declared that a state of war existed with the United States.

6 Arkansas seceded from the Union.

6 Tennessee voted for secession from the Union.

9 Shots were exchanged between the USS *Yankee* and a Confederate battery at Gloucester Point, Virginia.

10   Robert E. Lee assumed command of Confederate forces in Virginia.

10   Captain Nathaniel Lyon took control of St. Louis, Missouri, and the St. Louis Armory, after putting down a riot between pro–Union and pro-slavery elements.

13   Queen Victoria declared England would remain neutral. With the declaration of neutrality, belligerent status was not only granted to the Confederate government but also to the United States. This allowed the South to purchase materials from England and to buy ships as long as they were not fitted with guns in British ports. This was, in a way, the first step towards formal recognition of the Confederacy as an independent nation.

16   Confederate Congress authorized the recruitment of 400,000 volunteers.

18   The USS *Monticello* and a Union steamer out of Old Point engaged in a duel with Confederate batteries on Sewell's Point near Norfolk, Virginia. The Union ships were attempting to enforce the blockage of Hampton Roads.

20   North Carolina seceded from the Union.

20   Kentucky proclaimed its neutrality.

20   Confederate Congress voted to move the capital of the Confederacy to Richmond, Virginia.

23   Virginia voted to join the Confederacy.

23   Colonel Thomas J. Jackson established a barricade on the train tracks near Harper's Ferry, trapping forty-two locomotives with 386 railroad cars, which he converted for use by the Confederacy. He later ordered the destruction of thirty-six miles of that track.

24   Ten thousand federal troops occupied Alexandria, Virginia. As Major Ephriam Ellsworth attempted to remove a Confederate flag flying above the Marshall House Hotel, he was shot and killed by innkeeper James W. Jackson. Jackson was shot dead on the spot by Ellsworth's comrades. Ellsworth became the first officer killed in the war.

26   General George B. McClellan, commander of the Army of the Ohio, ordered his men to enter the western area of Virginia to protect the railroad lines and bridges between the western portion of Virginia and the Ohio River.

28   Brigadier General Irvin McDowell was appointed commander of the Federal Department of Northeastern Virginia.

29   Union forces occupied Newport News, Virginia.

29   Three Union gunboats including the steamer *Mount Vernon* and the *Pocahontas* fired on Confederate batteries near Aquia Creek. The batteries had been placed there to protect the northern railroad terminal leading into Richmond. Fearing that a landing of federal troops was pending, Lee directed the removal of the Confederate batteries.

June 1861

3 Stephen A. Douglas, Lincoln's opponent in the 1860 election, died in Chicago, Illinois.

3 *Action at Philippi, Western Virginia* (**Union Victory**)
The first land battle of the war was fought as Confederate forces clashed with Union troops protecting the Baltimore and Ohio Railroad, whose main line between Washington and the West ran near the town. The Confederate force retreated toward Huttonsville. This skirmish influenced the separation of western Virginia from the state.

		U.S.A.		*C.S.A.*	
		T.A. Morris, B.F. Kelley, Ebenezer Dumont		G.A. Porterfield	
	Troops	*Killed*	*Wounded*	*Missing/Captured*	*Total Casualties*
U.S.A.	3,000		4		4
C.S.A.	800	6	9	11	26

10 Napoleon III of France declared that France would remain neutral.

10 *Engagement at Big Bethel, Virginia* (**Confederate Victory**)
A strong Union force marched and blundered through the night to attack Confederate positions in an attempt to dislodge them from Yorktown and their proximity to Fort Monroe. The attack, supposed to be a surprise, was discovered. After two hours of hesitant and uncoordinated fighting, the Union troops retreated, giving Major General Benjamin Butler a degrading defeat. This was the first land battle on Virginia soil.

		U.S.A.		*C.S.A.*	
		Benjamin F. Butler, E.W. Pierce, Major Theodore Winthrop (Killed)		John B. Magruder, Daniel H. Hill, George W. Randolph	
	Troops	*Killed*	*Wounded*	*Missing/Captured*	*Total Casualties*
U.S.A.	3,500	18	53	5	76
C.S.A.	1,200	1	7		8

11 Western Virginia organized a pro–Union government and moved to secede from Virginia to form a new Union state.

17 *Engagement at Boonville, Missouri* (**Union Victory**)
Claiborne Jackson wanted Missouri to secede from the Union and join the Confederacy and General Nathaniel Lyon was sent to take control of the Missouri government. General Lyon, after taking control of the state capital, pursued Jackson and the secessionist government, becoming embroiled in a minor skirmish with a small force under the command of Colonel John Marmaduke. This minor engagement was considered of no military

significance except it indicated the Union was in firm control of the Missouri River and would fight to keep Missouri in the Union.

	U.S.A.				C.S.A.
	Nathaniel Lyon				John S. Marmaduke

	Troops	Killed	Wounded	Missing/Captured	Total Casualties
U.S.A.	1,700				31
C.S.A.	unknown				50

21 McClellan, with 20,000 men, marched into western Virginia.

July 1861

2 *Skirmish at Hoke's Run, in Western Virginia* (**Union Victory**)
    Jackson, under orders to delay the Union advancement, encountered brigades under Abercrombie and Thomas on their way from Williamsport to Martinsburg near Hoke's Run to "rout troops near the point of crossing." Jackson withdrew upon seeing Patterson's larger force coming up to assist the other Union brigades. Jackson was under orders not to bring on an engagement. Patterson moved on to occupy Martinsburg and later withdrew to Harper's Ferry.

	U.S.A.				C.S.A.
	Robert Patterson, George Thomas, John J. Abercrombie				Thomas J. Jackson

	Troops	Killed	Wounded	Missing/Captured	Total Casualties
U.S.A.	10,000	8	15		23
C.S.A.	7,000	11	37	43	91

4 Congress approved Lincoln's war measures.

5 *Engagement at Carthage, Missouri* (**Confederate Victory**)
    Governor Jackson, in southwest Missouri with its Confederate government on the move, was concerned not only about the Union troops under the command of Lyon on his rear but also was concerned about the German troops under Sigel moving up on his front. With civilian soldiers, Jackson awaited the attack. With Confederate cavalry flanking both sides of the Union line, Sigel's troops fled.

	U.S.A.				C.S.A.
	Franz Sigel				Governor Claibourne Jackson, James S. Rains

	Troops	Killed	Wounded	Missing/Captured	Total Casualties
U.S.A.	1,100	13	31	5	49
C.S.A.	4,000	50	120		170

8 Brigadier General Henry Sibley ordered Confederate forces in Texas to expel the Union troops from the New Mexico territory. Union forces began to move toward Fort Fillmore.

11 *Engagement of Rich Mountain, Western Virginia* (**Union Victory**)
In an effort to clear Western Virginia of Confederate forces, McClellan directed General Rosecrans to secure Rich Mountain before moving on to capture Laurel Mountain. Rosecrans discovered a secret route to Rich Mountain but held off for several hours. Believing the Union charge had been repulsed, the Confederate force left their secured entrenchment and made a countercharge only to find a large Union force waiting for them. This victory cleared Western Virginia of a southern threat for a temporary period and established McClellan's pattern of "maneuvering" rather than fighting.

	U.S.A.			*C.S.A.*	
	William S. Rosecrans, T.A. Morris			John Pegram, Robert S. Garnett	
	Troops	*Killed*	*Wounded*	*Missing/Captured*	*Total Casualties*
U.S.A.	1,900	12	59		71
C.S.A.	1,310				555

13 *Action/Battle at Corrick's Ford, Western Virginia* (**Union Victory**)
Garnett attempted to retreat from Rich Mountain (Laurel Hill) with Morris in pursuit. This campaign, in addition to a few others, secured the control of Western Virginia for the Union. The citizens of this section of Virginia had opposed secession.

	U.S.A.			*C.S.A.*	
	George B. McClellan, T.A. Morris, William S. Rosecrans			Robert S. Garnett (Killed)	
	Troops	*Killed*	*Wounded*	*Missing/Captured*	*Total Casualties*
U.S.A.	12,000	13	40		53
C.S.A.	5,300	20	75	50	145

16 McDowell's army advanced upon Manassas.

18 *Skirmish at Blackburn's Ford, Virginia* (**Confederate Victory**)
The Union troops, moving down from Washington toward the railroad junction at Manassas, were prevented from crossing the creek.

	U.S.A.			*C.S.A.*	
	Irvin McDowell, R. Patterson, Israel B. Richardson, Daniel Tyler			P.G.T. Beauregard, James Longstreet, Joseph E. Johnston	
	Troops	*Killed*	*Wounded*	*Missing/Captured*	*Total Casualties*
U.S.A.	30,000	19	38	26	83
C.S.A.	22,000	15	53		68

20   Major General Joseph E. Johnston joined Brigadier P.G.T. Beauregard at Manassas.

21   *First Battle of Bull Run (Manassas), Virginia* (**Confederate Victory**)
The Battle of Bull Run, also known as the First Battle of Manassas, was the first major clash of armies in the Civil War. Bowing to demands for action from Washington authorities, Major General McDowell moved south across the Potomac River toward Richmond. To protect his flank and rear during the advance, he first had to seize the vital railroad junction at Manassas, some 30 miles from Washington. Confederate General Joseph E. Johnston massed an army of equal size. Although close to success at one point, the Union force was routed by a rebel counterattack after a determined stand by General Jackson had brought time for Confederate reinforcements under E. Kirby Smith to arrive. The battle resulted in the utter defeat of Union forces and dashed hopes that the war would be brought to a swift conclusion. The South was convinced that victory would be theirs.

U.S.A.				C.S.A.
Irvin McDowell, R. Patterson, Ambrose Burnside, Daniel Tyler				Thomas J. Jackson, P.G.T. Beauregard, C. Evans, Barnard Bee (Killed), Joseph E. Johnston, Seth Barton, James Longstreet

	Troops	Killed	Wounded	Missing/Captured	Total Casualties
U.S.A.	28,450	460	1,124	1,312	2,896
C.S.A.	32,230	387	1,582	13	1,982

23   Colonel Baylor with his 300 Texas troops entered the New Mexico Territory.

25   The U.S. Congress passed the Crittenden Resolution, which stated the object of the war would be the preservation of the Union rather than the end to slavery.

25   *Skirmish at Messilla, New Mexico Territory* (**Confederate Victory**)
Union forces under Major Isaac Lynde confronted Colonel John Baylor at Messilla in a half-hearted attempt to drive the Confederate forces from the New Mexico Territory.

U.S.A.				C.S.A.
Major Isaac Lynde				Colonel John R. Baylor

	Troops	Killed	Wounded	Missing/Captured	Total Casualties
U.S.A.	300	3	6		9
C.S.A.	400	0	0		0

26   Major I. Lynde, in command of Union forces at Fort Fillmore in the New Mexico Territory, surrendered all 410 soldiers and all Union property to Colonel John R. Baylor. The Union soldiers were paroled and left the territory.

27 Lynde was censured and dismissed from the Army for his poor performance and the surrender of his army to the Confederate force without firing a shot.

27 Major General George B. McClellan replaced McDowell in command of Union troops around Washington.

August 1861

5 *Skirmish at Athens, Missouri* (**Union Victory**)
Confederates attacked the Home Guard and Union loyalists at Athens, but the inexperienced Confederate soldiers were unable to drive the Home Guard from the city and fled when Colonel Moore launched a counterattack.

	U.S.A.			C.S.A.	
	Colonel David Moore			Martin Green, Stand Watie	
	Troops	*Killed*	*Wounded*	*Missing/Captured*	*Total Casualties*
U.S.A.	400				Unknown
C.S.A.	1,200				Unknown

6 The U.S. Congress passed the Confiscation Act, which called for the seizure of property (including slaves) used against the Union for insurrection.

10 *Action/Battle of Wilson's Creek, Missouri* (**Confederate Victory**)
Both the North and the South wanted the border state of Missouri because it was strategically located on the Mississippi and Missouri rivers. Most Missourians wanted the state to stay neutral, but there was a strong pro–Confederate element led by Governor Claiborne F. Jackson. This battle kept Missouri in the Union. It was often referred to as the "Bull Run of the West." Union troops commanded by General Nathaniel Lyon, a former state official, were defeated by Confederates commanded by General Benjamin McCulloch. Among the casualties suffered by both sides was Lyon himself, who was killed when a bullet pierced his heart.

	U.S.A.			C.S.A.	
	Nathaniel Lyon (Killed), Franz Sigel			Ben McCulloch, Sterling Price	
	Troops	*Killed*	*Wounded*	*Missing/Captured*	*Total Casualties*
U.S.A.	5,400	258	873	186	1,317
C.S.A.	11,000	279	951		1,230

14 Fremont placed the city of St. Louis under martial law.

26 *Action at Cross Lanes, Western Virginia* (**Confederate Victory**)
While Union troops commanded by Colonel Erastus Tyler were eating their breakfast, they were surprised when Confederate forces, under John B. Floyd operating in the Kanawha Valley, launched their attack.

| U.S.A. | | | | C.S.A. |
| Erastus Tyler | | | | John B. Floyd |
	Troops	Killed	Wounded	Missing/Captured	Total Casualties
U.S.A.	7,000	5	40	200	245
C.S.A.	10,000	3	26	11	40

27–29 *Engagement at Fort Hatteras, North Carolina* (**Union Victory**)
Confederate raiders had been a havoc on Union shipping. Secretary of the Navy Gideon Wells ordered the forts along the Atlantic coast from North Carolina to the Mississippi River to be secured. The largest inlet, known as the Hatteras Inlet, was guarded by two Confederate ports, Fort Hatteras (fifteen guns) and Fort Clark (five guns). The plan called for Union troops to land north of the forts and move on them as the Navy shelled the forts from the sea. The Navy opened up first on Fort Clark, causing the Confederates to flee to Fort Hatteras. On the 29th, Commodore Stringham turned his ten-inch guns on Fort Hatteras, forcing it to surrender.

| U.S.A. | | | | C.S.A. |
| S.H. Stringham (USN), Benjamin Butler | | | | Colonel William F. Martin |
	Troops	Killed	Wounded	Missing/Captured	Total Casualties
U.S.A.	2,000	1	2		3
C.S.A.	770				770

30 Fremont proclaimed martial law in Missouri and, in an effort to eliminate assistance to guerrillas, issued a proclamation declaring Missouri's slave laws to be illegal and freeing all slaves held in Missouri. His Confiscation Act of 1861 ordered the confiscation of property and slaves of anyone aiding the Confederacy.

September 1861

2 Kentucky, a border state, had divided loyalties and, as such, the governor declared the state to be neutral. He made the announcement that neither the Union nor Confederacy could enter. Both sides agreed to the neutrality status, though both sides encouraged men to join the respective armies. But on this date, Confederate forces under General Leonidas Polk with 20,000 men crossed into the state from Union City, Tennessee, while General Grant moved southward from Cairo, Illinois. Both sides were moving to take the city of Columbus, which was strategically an important position on the Mississippi River.

4 Confederate Major General Leonidas Polk seized Columbia, Kentucky, ending the state's attempt at neutrality.

6 Grant occupied Paducah, Kentucky, at the mouth of the Tennessee River.

8   Sherman assumed command of the Union army in central and eastern Kentucky.

10   General Albert S. Johnston took command of all Confederate armies in the West.

10   *Engagement at Carnifix Ferry, Virginia* (**Union Victory**)
Upon learning of Colonel Tyler's defeat at Cross Lanes, Rosecrans quickly moved men south to assist Tyler confronting Confederate General Floyd. Floyd ordered General Henry Wise, at Hawk's Nest, to rush to his support. Wise instead sent only a small contingent and Floyd was forced to retreat. Floyd assumed no responsibility, instead placing all the blame on General Henry Wise. Wise and Floyd had been bitter political enemies before the war and could not overcome their dislike of one another to work together for a common goal, to the benefit of federal forces.

U.S.A.			*C.S.A.*	
William S. Rosecrans			John B. Floyd, Henry A. Wise	
	Troops	*Killed*	*Wounded*	*Missing/Captured*	*Total Casualties*
U.S.A.		17	141		158
C.S.A.					92

11   Lincoln ordered General Fremont to ease his Missouri slave proclamation to conform to the National Confiscation Act.

11   *Skirmish at Cheat Mountain, Western Virginia* (**Union Victory**)
After Union victories at Philippi and Rich Mountain, much of pro–Union Western Virginia was securely in the control of the Union.
Confederate forces under Robert E. Lee attempted to take Cheat Mountain, a key position in Western Virginia that controlled traffic on the major turnpike and several mountain passes. Lee's plan for the attack was too complicated for his inexperienced commanders to follow and it fell apart. Lee was severely criticized for his actions and earned the nickname "Granny Lee" after this loss.

U.S.A.			*C.S.A.*	
John J. Reynolds			Robert E. Lee, William W. Loring, Albert Rust	
	Troops	*Killed*	*Wounded*	*Missing/Captured*	*Total Casualties*
U.S.A.	2,000		9	12	21
C.S.A.	15,000				100

19   *Skirmish at Barbourville, Kentucky* (**Confederate Victory**)
Union sympathizers in Kentucky underwent training at Camp Andrew Johnson located near Barbourville, Kentucky. Confederate troops, under the command of General Albert S. Johnston, who had been making raiding forays into Kentucky, and Colonel Battle decided to attack the training camp. The recruits had been dismissed by the time Colonel Battle arrived, leaving only the Home Guard to defend the camp.

U.S.A.				C.S.A.
Captain Isaac J. Black				Colonel Joel A. Battle

	Troops	Killed	Wounded	Missing/Captured	Total Casualties
U.S.A.	300	1	2	12	15
C.S.A.	800	1	4		5

12–20 *Siege of Lexington, Missouri* (**Confederate Victory**)

Mulligan had been ordered to hold Lexington, Missouri, at all costs. Price, a former governor of Missouri, moved to take the city by surrounding it as he waited for additional reinforcements. At one point, he had the water supply to the city cut off. On the 20th, he mounted his attack, forcing Mulligan to surrender his men and the city. Now, for the time being, the Confederates would be in command of the Missouri Valley.

U.S.A.				C.S.A.
J.A. Mulligan				Sterling Price

	Troops	Killed	Wounded	Missing/Captured	Total Casualties
U.S.A.	3,600	42	120	1,624	1,786
C.S.A.	18,000	25	72		97

29 The Union naval fleet arrived at the Head of the Passes, a wide bay on the Mississippi River downstream from New Orleans, and closed all river traffic to the Gulf of Mexico.

October 1861

3 *Skirmish at Greenbrier River, Western Virginia* (**Confederate Victory**)

In command of Cheat Mountain, Reynolds decided to remove the Confederate forces from the mouth of the river. The Confederates had anticipated Reynolds' move and were ready. They overwhelmed and drove Reynolds back to Cheat Mountain.

U.S.A.				C.S.A.
John J. Reynolds				Henry R. Jackson

	Troops	Killed	Wounded	Missing/Captured	Total Casualties
U.S.A.	5,000	8	36		44
C.S.A.	1,800	6	33	13	52

11 The Confederate Navy fleet, under the command of George N. Hollins, sailed down the Mississippi from New Orleans toward the Union flotilla. Near the Head of the Pass, Hollins ordered the ramming of the USS *Richmond*. Taken by surprise, the Union ships quickly moved southward toward the mouth of the river with two Union ships becoming stuck on a sandbar. The Confederate fleet pursued and a sea battle ensued involving the CSS *Ivy* and CSS *McRae* against the USS *Santee* and the USS *Richmond*. The Confederate fleet was unable to tolerate the firing and was forced to return to its home base. Hollins claimed a victory as the river was clear of the Union blockade.

21 *Engagement at Ball's Bluff, Virginia (aka Leesburg)* (**Confederate Victory**)

A Union reconnaissance force of 1,000 men crossed the Potomac to attack the Confederates camped near Leesburg, Virginia, and were met with disaster. The Union soldiers had to ascend a steep hill accessible only by a cow path, and, waiting at the top of the bluff was the large Confederate force. Confederates drove the Union soldiers back over the bluff to the river where rifle fire from above killed the commander, former Oregon senator Edward D. Baker, and half his force, while others were drowned. Oliver Wendell Holmes, Jr., later a justice of the U.S. Supreme Court, was among the wounded. The Ball's Bluff disaster had strong political ramifications and sparked the creation of the Congressional Joint Committee on the Conduct of the War, a watchdog agency that scrutinized closely all Union military movements thereafter.

U.S.A.			C.S.A.	
Edward D. Baker (Killed), Charles P. Stone			Nathan G. Evans	

	Troops	*Killed*	*Wounded*	*Missing/Captured*	*Total Casualties*
U.S.A.	1,700	49	117	714	880
C.S.A.	1,700	36	158	2	196

21 *Action at Fredericktown, Missouri* (**Union Victory**)

In an effort to increase Confederate activity and obtain much needed supplies, Confederate forces under Colonel Jeff Thompson moved toward Fredericktown but were confronted by Union forces that were able to force Thompson to retire. With the capture of Fredericktown, the Union forces were now in control of southeastern Missouri.

U.S.A.			C.S.A.	
J.B. Plummer, Leonard F. Ross			J. Thompson, A. Lowe	

	Troops	*Killed*	*Wounded*	*Missing/Captured*	*Total Casualties*
U.S.A.	4,500	1	27		28
C.S.A.	3,500	5	33	24	62

31 The "Rebel Legislature" voted Missouri out of the Union, but the state was still under control of the Union loyalists.

November 1861

1 McClellan was named general in chief of Union armies, succeeding the ailing Winfield Scott, who had tendered his resignation the day before.

2 Fremont was relieved of his command and replaced by David Hunter. A week after issuing his proclamation declaring slavery illegal in Missouri, Fremont notified President

Lincoln of his actions. Lincoln then requested Fremont to modify his proclamation to conform to the Confiscation Act of 1861, which freed only those slaves belonging to the Confederates who had taken up arms against the Union. Lincoln had not intended to grant a general abolition at the time. Fremont refused and was replaced.

6 Jefferson Davis was elected to a six-year term as president of the Confederacy. Davis had been serving as president of the Provisional Government and now was voted in as president of the permanent Confederate government.

7 *Engagement at Port Royal Sound (Fort Walker/Beauregard) South Carolina* (**Union Victory**)

To sustain and strengthen its blockade of Southern ports, the U.S. Navy needed a coaling, refitting and supply depot station located somewhere on the southern coast. Port Royal, being strategically between Charleston and Savannah, was that choice. As an added benefit, Port Royal held few Confederate defenders.

	U.S.A.			C.S.A.	
	Samuel F. DuPont, Thomas W. Sherman			Colonel R.G.M. Dunovant, S. Elliott, Commodore Josiah Tatnall	
	Troops	*Killed*	*Wounded*	*Missing/Captured*	*Total Casualties*
U.S.A.	12,000	8	23		31
C.S.A.	619	11	48	7	66

7 *Engagement at Belmont, Missouri* (**Confederate Victory**)

Forces under Grant were celebrating the looting of a nearby Confederate camp when they came under heavy fire from Polk's troops. Grant and his troops fought their way upriver to their transport ships and escaped. The whole affair was in fact a worthless waste of men and supplies. Belmont was of no strategic importance to either side.

	U.S.A.			C.S.A.	
	Ulysses S. Grant			Leonidas Polk, Gideon J. Pillow	
	Troops	*Killed*	*Wounded*	*Missing/Captured*	*Total Casualties*
U.S.A.	3,000	120	383	104	607
C.S.A.	5,000	105	419	117	641

8 Confederate Commissioners James M. Mason and John Sidell, ambassadors to England, had set sail from Cuba for Great Britain aboard the British ship *The Trent* when the USS *San Jacinto*, commanded by Captain Charles Wilkes, detained them. The commissioners were held prisoner aboard the United States ship. It was suspected the ambassadors were on their way to seek British support for the Confederacy in their struggle for independence.

8 *Engagement at Ivy Mountain, Kentucky* (**Confederate Victory**)

While Union troops solidified control of Kentucky, Confederate volunteers were gathering in the southeastern part of the state in an effort to form a detachment to send to Virginia to aid the Confederacy. Union commanders, upon learning of it, decided to stop them. The raw recruits held their own against an experienced army and were able to reach the safety of Confederate forces in Virginia, where they offered their service to the state and the Confederacy.

	U.S.A.				*C.S.A.*
	William Nelson, Joshua W. Sill				J.S. Williams
	Troops	*Killed*	*Wounded*	*Missing/Captured*	*Total Casualties*
U.S.A.	3,500	6	24		30
C.S.A.	1,000				263

9   Buell replaced Sherman in the Tennessee-Kentucky area.

18   Pro-southern leaders in Kentucky adopt secession.

19   General Henry Halleck assumed command of Missouri, replacing David Hunter, who had been sent to relieve John C. Fremont earlier in the month.

December 1861

13   *Engagement at Camp Alleghany (Buffalo Mountain), Virginia* (**Undetermined**)
In an effort to move from Cheat Mountain, Union forces ran into and tangled with Confederate troops moving toward Staunton, Virginia. After a brief engagement, both troops reversed their paths and retreated in the direction from which they came.

	U.S.A.				*C.S.A.*
	Robert Milroy				Edward Johnson
	Troops	*Killed*	*Wounded*	*Missing/Captured*	*Total Casualties*
U.S.A.	700	20	107	10	137
C.S.A.	2,000	20	98	28	146

17   *Action at Rowlett's Station, Kentucky* (**Undetermined**)
In an attempt to consolidate control of Union troops in Kentucky, General Don Carlos Buell sent troops under General Alexander McCook to Kentucky. As McCook moved toward the Green River near Munfordville, he found the Confederates had burned the Louisville and Nashville Railroad Bridge over the Green River. The Union forces built a pontoon bridge. A Confederate force was soon discovered in the woods and a small engagement occurred. Fearing for their flank, the Union troops retreated, as did the Confederate forces, thinking the Union reinforcements were en route.

	U.S.A.			*C.S.A.*	
	Alexander McCook			Thomas C. Hindman, B. Terry (Killed)	
	Troops	*Killed*	*Wounded*	*Missing/Captured*	*Total Casualties*
U.S.A.	375	11	22	7	40
C.S.A.	1,100	33	50	8	91

20   *Engagement at Dranesville, Virginia* (**Union Victory**)

Leading a forage expedition, J.E.B. Stuart encountered Union forces under Ord moving down the Georgetown Pike, also on a forging expedition. Stuart withdrew after first making sure his wagons were safe.

	U.S.A.				C.S.A.
	Edward O.C. Ord				J.E.B. Stuart
	Troops	*Killed*	*Wounded*	*Missing/Captured*	*Total Casualties*
U.S.A.	1,600	7	61	3	71
C.S.A.	1,200	43	143	8	194

28   *Action at Sacramento, Kentucky* (**Confederate Victory**)

As a Union cavalry unit stopped for water at a creek near Sacramento, they were spotted by a Confederate cavalry unit who charged, driving the Union horsemen off. This was the first fight for an up and coming Confederate cavalryman — Nathan Bedford Forrest.

	U.S.A.				C.S.A.
	E.H. Murray				Nathan B. Forrest
	Troops	*Killed*	*Wounded*	*Missing/Captured*	*Total Casualties*
U.S.A.	168	8	12		20
C.S.A.	300	2	3		5

26   Fearing war with Britain, after learning that the British were preparing to send 8,000 British soldiers to Canada, the United States released both Mason and Sidell.

Chapter 7

1862

"It is well that war is so terrible, else men would learn to love it too much."

— *Robert E. Lee, Fredericksburg, 1862*

January 1862

3 *Bombardment of Hancock, Maryland* (**Undetermined**)

This was a brief skirmish near Bath, Virginia, as Stonewall Jackson tried to break up the Baltimore and Ohio Railroad and destroy the dams on the Chesapeake and Ohio Canal. Upon reaching Hancock, Jackson opened fire with artillery when he discovered the town was occupied by Union troops under Frederick W. Lander. Unable to take the town, Jackson withdrew.

10 *Engagement at Middle Creek, Kentucky* (**Union Victory**)

The Confederates, on a recruiting expedition in Kentucky, were confronted by Union troops sent to force them out of the state.

U.S.A.				C.S.A.
James Garfield				Humphrey Marshall

	Troops	*Killed*	*Wounded*	*Missing/Captured*	*Total Casualties*
U.S.A.	2,350	1	20	6	27
C.S.A.	1,967	10	15	25	50

13 Lincoln replaced Secretary of War Simon Cameron with Edwin M. Stanton.

19–20 Engagement *at Mill Springs, Kentucky* (**Union Victory**)

The Confederates had moved back into Kentucky. Zollicoffer decided to place his winter quarters near Mill Springs and had fortified both sides of the Cumberland River. Union Commander General Thomas was sent to drive them out. Zollicoffer was killed as he rode into a Union camp thinking it was his. The Union commander of the unit shot Zollicoffer directly in the chest when he saw the Confederate leader in his camp giving orders to Union troopers. The battle was a small but strategically important one, for it broke whatever strength the Confederates had in eastern Kentucky. At the same time, it gave a boost for the Union cause among the people of Kentucky and eastern Tennessee.

U.S.A.			C.S.A.		
George Thomas			G.B. Crittenden, Felix K. Zollicoffer (Killed)		

	Troops	Killed	Wounded	Missing/Captured	Total Casualties
U.S.A.	4,000	39	207	15	261
C.S.A.	4,000	125	309	99	533

27   Lincoln ordered General McClellan to make a move and get into the action. McClellan ignored the order.

February 1862

6   *Capture of Fort Henry, Tennessee* (**Union Victory**)
    Fort Henry, a Confederate earthwork fort on the Tennessee River, was just south of Kentucky. It was one of a string of outposts built to protect Confederate territory. The fort, located on low ground, was subject to flooding and was also dominated by high ground on both sides of the river. Union forces were granted permission by General Halleck to attempt to capture the fort. Ships sailed up the Cumberland River to bombard it, as land troops would make the assault. Seeing the ships and aware of the situation, most of the Confederate troops were sent to Fort Donelson, leaving a small contingent to delay the Union assault. Unable to hold, the men surrendered the fort. The capture of Fort Henry opened the Tennessee River to not only Union shipping but also allowed Union gunboats to sail up and down the river unhindered.

U.S.A.				C.S.A.	
A.H. Foote				Lloyd Tilghman	

	Troops	Killed	Wounded	Missing/Captured	Total Casualties
U.S.A.	7 gunboats	11	31	5	47
C.S.A.	100	5	11	5	21

7   Albert S. Johnston retreated, pulling out of Kentucky.

8   *Battle of Roanoke Island, North Carolina* (**Union Victory**)
    To tighten the Union blockade of southern ports, Union troops moved to eliminate Confederate resistance by establishing a beachhead on the southern coast. After severe fighting on both land and sea, Colonel Shaw, commanding the Confederate forces, surrendered

the 2,500 men and 6 forts with 43 pieces of artillery to Union officials. Roanoke Island would remain under Union control for the duration of the war.

		U.S.A.		C.S.A.	
		Ambrose E. Burnside		Henry Wise, H. Shaw	
	Troops	*Killed*	*Wounded*	*Missing/Captured*	*Total Casualties*
U.S.A.	7,500	23	62		85
C.S.A.	2,500	37	214	2,249	2,500

10 *Action or Naval Engagement at Elizabeth City, North Carolina* (**Union Victory**)

After the fall of Roanoke Island, Confederate naval Captain Lynch moved his forces up the Pasquotank River to be resupplied. Union gunboats also moved up the river. A naval engagement ensued involving the CSS *Black Warrior, Seabird, Ellis* and *Fanny* against the USS *Commodore, Perry* and *Ceres*. Union ships were able to overpower the Confederate fleet and capture the city.

15 *Capture of Fort Donelson, Tennessee* (**Union Victory**)

The Battle of Fort Donelson would be a Union victory engineered by Brigadier General Ulysses S. Grant. The Confederate stronghold on the Cumberland River was a key element in Southern strategy for Kentucky and Tennessee. The fall of Fort Henry on the Tennessee River to the Union represented a significant setback for the Confederates in this region. Per General Albert Sidney Johnston, "Should Fort Donelson be taken, it will open the route to the enemy to Nashville, giving them the means of breaking the bridges and destroying the ferry-boats on the river as far as navigable."[1] The Confederates would have to hold Fort Donelson but the Union strength was too overwhelming. When it was discovered that the fort could not withstand the Union onslaught, General Buckner asked what conditions would be required for the surrender of the fort. Grant replied "nothing but the unconditional surrender."

		U.S.A.		C.S.A.	
		A.H. Foote (Wounded), U.S. Grant, John McClernand, Charles F. Smith		Simon B. Buckner, Gideon Pillow, Nathan B. Forrest, John B. Floyd	
	Troops	*Killed*	*Wounded*	*Missing/Captured*	*Total Casualties*
U.S.A.	27,000		2,108	224	2,832
C.S.A.	7,465				5,000

18–19 Burning *of Winton, North Carolina* (**Union Victory**)

Confederate forces under Colonel W.T. Williams opened fire on the Union ship USS *Delaware* as it moved up the Chowan River toward Winton. The ship withdrew but returned the following morning and shelled the city. The 9th New York Infantry landed, plundered the town and then set it ablaze.

20 William "Willie" Lincoln, the twelve-year-old son of President Lincoln, died of bilious fever.

21   *Engagement at Valverde, N.M. Territory* (**Confederate Victory**)
Confederate forces hoped to drive out Union forces in the New Mexico territory and then move on to capture Colorado before moving on to western California. The first obstacle in their path was Fort Craig but they were met at the ford near Valverde by Union troops.

	U.S.A.			*C.S.A.*	
	Edward R.S. Canby, Christopher "Kit" Carson			Henry H. Sibley, Thomas Green	

	Troops	*Killed*	*Wounded*	*Missing/Captured*	*Total Casualties*
U.S.A.	3,810	112	189	204	505
C.S.A.	2,600	31	180	12	223

22   Jefferson Davis took the oath of office as president of the Confederacy. His term was for six years.

25   Union troops occupied Nashville, Tennessee.

25   The U.S. Congress passed the first Legal Tender Act, which authorized the printing of $150 million in treasury notes. "Greenbacks" were printed on only one side with green ink. They could not be redeemable in gold or silver but would be honored for all debts. Since Congress could only "coin money" per the U.S. Constitution [2], there were many arguments whether this law was constitutional or whether paper money was legal.

March 1862

6–8   *Battle of Pea Ridge (Elkhorn Tavern), Arkansas* (**Union Victory**)
After the fall of Forts Henry and Donelson, Confederate General Earl Van Dorn attempted to outflank the Union forces by driving on to St. Louis. As he neared Pea Ridge, a small force under General Samuel Curtis confronted him. Van Dorn, being low on ammunition, withdrew.

	U.S.A.			*C.S.A.*	
	Samuel R. Curtis			Benjamin McCulloch (Killed), Earl Van Dorn, James M. McIntosh (Killed)	

	Troops	*Killed*	*Wounded*	*Missing/Captured*	*Total Casualties*
U.S.A.	17,000	64	1,019	201	1,284
C.S.A.	14,000				1,300

7   The CSS Virginia entered Hampton Roads and damaged three wooden U.S. warships.

9   *Battle of USS* Monitor *and the CSS* Virginia (**Undetermined**)
The first clash between ironclad ships took place off Hampton Roads near Norfolk, Virginia. The two vessels, the CSS *Virginia* (formally the USS *Merrimack*), commanded by

Franklin Buchanan, and the USS *Monitor*, commanded by Lt. John Worden, began their fight about 9 a.m. The ships continued to pound at one another within close range. The battle ended in a draw, as neither vessel could inflict any significant damage on its opponent. Both vessels withdrew after two hours of combat.

11 Major General Henry Halleck was named commander of all federal troops in the West.

11 General McClellan was removed as general-in-chief but remained as commander of the Army of the Potomac. At the same time, President Lincoln approved McClellan's Peninsula strategy.

12 A Union force moved in and captured Jacksonville, Florida.

13 President Davis gave Robert E. Lee command of Confederate military operations.

14 *Action at New Madrid, Missouri* (**Union Victory**)
With the fall of Forts Henry and Donelson, Confederates established a stronghold at Island No. 10 in which to defend the lower portions of the Mississippi River. Union forces under John Pope moved southward to attack the weakest point on the river, New Madrid, commanded by J.P. McCown. General Pope laid siege to the city on March 3. By the 14th, the Confederates determined it would be impossible to defend the city and abandoned it, moving to Island No. 10. When Union troops marched into New Madrid, they found it deserted.

14 *Battle of New Bern, N.C.* (**Union Victory**)
A serviceable base was established for inland expeditions after Union forces rendezvoused with the Union gunboats at Hatteras Inlet. The Confederates were driven out of their fortifications as the Union captured 9 forts and 41 heavy guns. They would hold this fort until the end of the war and used it as a vantage point for the pro–Union elements operating in North Carolina.

	U.S.A.			*C.S.A.*	
	Ambrose E. Burnside			Lawrence O'B. Branch	
	Troops	*Killed*	*Wounded*	*Missing/Captured*	*Total Casualties*
U.S.A.	3 brigades	90	361	20	471
C.S.A.	5 regiments	64	536		600

17 McClellan began his Peninsula Campaign.

23–April 26 *Siege of Fort Macon, N.C.* (**Union Victory**)
Part of Burnside's North Carolina expedition established a foothold below the Virginia border as the Union began a siege of Fort Macon. This fort commanded the channel.

U.S.A.	*C.S.A.*
John G. Parke	M.J. White

	Troops	Killed	Wounded	Missing/Captured	Total Casualties
U.S.A.	2 divisions				10
C.S.A.	500	20			500

23 *Battle of Kernstown, Virginia* (**Union Victory**)

Confederate cavalry leader Colonel Turner Ashby advised General Jackson that there was only a rear guard left in Winchester. Kernstown would be the first battle of Jackson's Shenandoah Valley campaign. He struck hard, but found Union forces strongly in place and blamed General Garnett for pulling back despite overwhelming odds. Jackson had Garnett placed under arrest for neglect of duty.

U.S.A.	C.S.A.
James Shields (Wounded), Nathan Kimball	Thomas J. Jackson, Richard B. Garnett

	Troops	Killed	Wounded	Missing/Captured	Total casualties
U.S.A.	9,000	118	450	22	590
C.S.A.	3,500	80	375	268	723

26 *Skirmish at Apache Canyon, N.M. Territory* (**Union Victory**)

Union forces attempted to move through a pass known as Apache Canyon, held by a strong Confederate force that had placed two small cannons on each side of the pass. The Union force eventually was able to drive the Confederates from the pass after engaging in hand-to-hand combat.

U.S.A.	C.S.A.
J. Chivington	Henry Sibley, William R. Scurry

	Troops	Killed	Wounded	Missing/Captured	Total Casualties
U.S.A.	418	5	14	0	19
C.S.A.	250	32	43	70	145

28 *Engagement at Glorietta Pass, New Mexico* (**Union Victory**)

Union and Confederate forces were on both sides of Glorietta Pass in the New Mexico territory. After a six-hour battle, the Union force withdrew with their weapons, making the Confederates believe they had won the battle. They soon learned that the Union force had moved in behind them and had burned 73 of the Confederates' supply wagons, and bayoneted 600 of their mules and horses before retreating. Thus, the Confederate invasion of New Mexico territory was halted.

U.S.A.	C.S.A.
J.M. Chivington, J.P. Sloan	William R. Scurry, C.L. Pyron

	Troops	Killed	Wounded	Missing/Captured	Total Casualties
U.S.A.	1,300	31	50	30	111
C.S.A.	1,100	36	60	25	121

April 1862

3 Lincoln held back McDowell's troops from the Peninsula Campaign in order to defend Washington from Jackson.

5–May 4 *Siege of Yorktown, Virginia* (**Union Victory**)
McClellan suspended his march down the peninsula after being convinced the Confederate force under J.B. Magruder was much larger than it actually was. McClellan instead ordered siege fortifications built.

6–7 *Battle of Shiloh, Tennessee (aka Pittsburg Landing)* (**Union Victory**)
The first major battle in the West occurred during the winter of 1861–1862, when the Army of Tennessee pushed south from St. Louis to capture Forts Henry and Donelson on the Tennessee and Cumberland rivers. Confederate General Albert S. Johnston was forced to abandon southern Kentucky and much of Tennessee, including Nashville. He instead established a new line of defense near the Memphis and Charleston Railroad, the only direct link to Richmond. He concentrated his men at Corinth, Mississippi. Union commander General Grant had not anticipated Johnston's withdraw and thus delayed moving his troops to Pittsburg Landing. While waiting to be joined by General Don Carlos Buell, Grant drilled his men instead of fortifying his position. Johnston, hoping to destroy the Union army, planned an all-out attack for the morning of April 4 but was forced to postpone it. His second-in-command, General P.G.T. Beauregard, thought that the element of surprise would be lost. When Johnston's men made the attack on the 6th, they discovered almost no Union patrols. The senior field commander, General William T. Sherman, had ignored reports of Confederate troops in the area. Once under attack, Union troops drove back the furious Confederate assault at Pittsburg Landing, where most of the April 6 fighting occurred. Killed in this battle was General Albert S. Johnston. General William T. Sherman was wounded. Because of the Union victory, Confederate forces were forced to evacuate much of Tennessee. The Confederate failure here to destroy Grant's army opened the way to Vicksburg.

	U.S.A.		*C.S.A.*	
	Ulysses S. Grant, Don C. Buell, William Nelson, William Harvey L. Wallace (Killed)		Albert J. Johnston (Killed), Benjamin M. Prentiss, P.G.T. Beauregard	

	Troops	*Killed*	*Wounded*	*Missing/Captured*	*Total Casualties*
U.S.A.	62,000	1,754	8,408	2,885	13,047
C.S.A.	40,000	1,723	8,012	959	10,694

7 *Action of Island No. 10, Missouri* (**Union Victory**)
Island No.10, forty miles below Columbus, Kentucky, on the Mississippi, led directly into the heart of the Confederacy. Here the Confederates were trapped between the Union flotilla sailing up the river and General Pope's forces moving down the river. Admiral Andrew H. Foote, in charge of the Union flotilla, began an aerial bombardment from two miles away instead of sailing directly up the river into the range of the guns at the fort. On April 6, Foote sent two Union ships which ran the gauntlet, making it through to join with

Pope's assault on the fort. Union troops were able to capture the vast majority of the Confederate soldiers as they fled from the fort and the area.

	U.S.A.				C.S.A.
	John Pope, Andrew H. Foote				William M. Mackall

	Troops	Killed	Wounded	Missing/Captured	Total Casualties
U.S.A.	23,000				
C.S.A.	7,000				5,000

11   *Capture of Fort Pulaski, Georgia* (**Union Victory**)

Fort Pulaski, under Confederate control, was located at the mouth of the Savannah River, which controlled access to the southern city of Savannah. Union troops were ordered to capture the fort and began to bombard it starting on the 10th. Confederate forces refused to surrender until the Union artillery hit the magazine within the fort. Realizing the danger, Confederate forces finally yielded. The fall of the fort closed the Savannah River to blockade runners.

	U.S.A.				C.S.A.
	David H. Hunter, Quincy A. Gilmore				C.H. Olmstead

	Troops	Killed	Wounded	Missing/Captured	Total Casualties
U.S.A.		1			1
C.S.A.	400	1		363	364

12   The *Andrews' Raid in Northern Georgia*

Twenty-two volunteers, under the command of Brigadier General Ormsby Mitchell, were ordered to assist Union spy James A. Andrews, who had planned to make a raid deep into Confederate territory. The original plan was to steal a train, rip up the railroad tracks, tear down telegraph wires and burn the bridges between Atlanta and Chattanooga, severing the vital Confederate communications line. After buying civilian clothes, the soldiers made their way to Marietta, Georgia, where they met with Andrews. They boarded the Confederate train known as the *General* and preceded to a point above Marietta called Big Shanty. There, the raiders uncoupled all but three boxcars, a tender and an engine. As they pulled out of the station, Confederate soldiers, camped across the tracks at Camp McDonald, watched unaware of what was happening. Andrews calmly stopped the train a mile up the track to rip out telegraph wires and tear up some more track, then he refueled before moving on. The raiders did not know that the train conductor, William Fuller, station superintendent Anthony Murphy, and the engineer of the *General* were pursuing on foot. When the pursuers came across a railroad handcar, they continued their pursuit by rail until they came to the ripped up track. Andrews and his men continued on to Cartersville, Georgia, where they were forced to wait almost an hour as a southbound train passed on the track. This delay enabled Fuller to catch up with the Union raiders. Now, Andrews realized he was being pursued. The train carrying Andrews and his raiders ran out of fuel ninety miles up the track from Big Shanty. Finding that they could not shake their pursuers, the raiders abandoned the *General*, having done little damage to the line. Attempting to escape on foot, they were captured with the help of dogs in a weeklong manhunt. Andrews and seven of the raiders were hung as spies on June 2, 1862. Ironically, at all times during the chase, the raiders outnumbered the pursuers, and could have possibly overpowered them and continued their work of ripping up the track.

16   First Confederate Conscription Act went into effect calling for men ages 18 to 35 to join the military. Enlistees were permitted to use substitutes. This was the first military draft in the history of the United States.

18–25   *Operations at Forts Jackson and St. Philip below New Orleans* (**Union Victory**)

In an effort to take New Orleans, Union forces first had to remove the two Confederate forts located above the Head of the Pass. The forts provided an impediment to Union naval forces trying to reach New Orleans. On the 18th, Union naval forces began bombarding the two forts while other ships attempted to run the pass. Once clear of the obstruction, David Farragut was able to head for New Orleans seventy miles away.

	U.S.A.			*C.S.A.*	
	D.G. Farragut, D.D. Porter			Johnson K. Duncan, J.K. Mitchell	
	Troops	*Killed*	*Wounded*	*Missing/Captured*	*Total Casualties*
U.S.A.		37	149		186
C.S.A.	1,400	61	43		104

18   *Engagement at South Mills, North Carolina* (**Undetermined**)

General Burnside learned of a Confederate plan to send naval ships from Norfolk to Dismal Swamp Canal to resist the Union control of the Hatteras Inlet and surrounding territory. Burnside sent soldiers to destroy the locks at South Mills where the canal joined the Pasquotank River. Hawkins, the commander of one wing of the expedition, got lost trying to find the road to South Mills and was forced to turn back. Reno, trying to take South Mills, ran low on ammunition and had to pull back.

	U.S.A.			*C.S.A.*	
	R. Hawkins, Jesse Reno			Ambrose R. Wright	
	Troops	*Killed*	*Wounded*	*Missing/Captured*	*Total Casualties*
U.S.A.	3,000	13	101	13	127
C.S.A.	1,200				28

25–May 1   *Capture of New Orleans, Louisiana* (**Union Victory**)

After passing Forts Jackson and St. Philip, Farragut moved on to New Orleans, demanding the city's surrender. The following day, the city of New Orleans surrendered.

May 1862

1   Benjamin Butler and Union troops moved into New Orleans. Butler set up what has been described as "one of the most corrupt administrations in the city's history."

3 *Siege of Yorktown, Virginia ends.*

The start of McClellan's Peninsular Campaign (an area covered by the James and York Rivers) began but McClellan was not enthusiastic about the campaign. He moved his men and equipment in a cautious manner up the peninsula, giving the Confederates adequate time to prepare and plan their defenses. While the Union forces built their fortifications and moved men and equipment into it, the Confederates were able to slip away quietly. Throughout the campaign, Lee was able to dictate when and where the battles would be fought.

3 *Start of Jackson's Shenandoah Valley Campaign.*

While McClellan was planning his Peninsula Campaign, Robert E. Lee made a suggestion to Jackson that it would be advantageous for him to operate in the Shenandoah Valley to relieve the pressure on Richmond. Jackson sent one-half of his army to the valley on the 3rd, while he took one-half of his army and marched eastward from the Shenandoah. This led Union officials to believe that Jackson was going to assist Confederate forces operating in Richmond. But when Jackson neared Charlottesville, he and his men boarded trains and rode back to Staunton and the valley. Jackson's rapid marches and his constant exploits gained him fame in both the North and the South. Jackson's men walked 45 miles in 36 hours and, during the campaign, covered 676 miles.

5 *Battle of Williamsburg, Virginia* (**Confederate Victory**)

The first battle of the Peninsula Campaign. The Confederates had pulled quietly out of Yorktown and moved toward Richmond. With Union forces in pursuit, a delaying action was needed, and forces under James Longstreet were ordered to delay the pursuit. There was a skirmish in the streets and on the campus of the College of William and Mary, as the Confederates were able to delay for several hours the advance of McClellan's Army up the James River. After the battle, Williamsburg became a key point in the Confederate defense of the Peninsula.

	U.S.A.			*C.S.A.*	
	George B. McClellan, Joseph Hooker, W.S. Hancock			James Longstreet, Daniel H. Hill	

	Troops	*Killed*	*Wounded*	*Missing/Captured*	*Total Casualties*
U.S.A.	40,000	456	1,410	373	2,239
C.S.A.	31,000	354	1,216	133	1,703

7 *Engagement at Barhamsville, Virginia* (**Confederate Victory**)

Union pursuit of Confederates continued following Williamsburg and the pursuit proceeded down the Pamunkey River. As the Union soldiers were about to disembark at Eltham's Landing, opposite West Point, Virginia, they were met by a Confederate force sent to prevent the landing.

	U.S.A.	*C.S.A.*
	William B. Franklin, John Newton	Gustavus W. Smith, William H.C. Whiting

	Troops	Killed	Wounded	Missing/Captured	Total Casualties
U.S.A.	20,000	48	110	28	186
C.S.A.	20,000	8	42		50

8 *Engagement at McDowell (Bull Pasture), Virginia* (**Confederate Victory**)

Jackson, moving northward, confronted Union forces sent to defend the valley. This was the first battle victory of Jackson's campaign. His forces were feared in the Shenandoah Valley and surrounding mountain country. Their rapid movement on foot was Jackson's trademark. In some circles, his men were often referred to as the "Foot Cavalry." After their defeat at McDowell, Union forces withdrew to western Virginia, leaving Jackson in command of the valley.

U.S.A.					*C.S.A.*
R. Schenck, R. Milroy					T.J. Jackson

	Troops	Killed	Wounded	Missing/Captured	Total Casualties
U.S.A.	6,500	26	227	3	256
C.S.A.	9,000	75	423		498

9 McClellan advanced on Richmond and forced the Confederates to abandon Norfolk, Virginia.

10 *Engagement at Plum Run Bend, Tennessee* (**Confederate Victory**)

The Union fleet was moored at Plum Run Bend in Tennessee in preparation for an attack on Fort Pillow, the last sizable Confederate river fort between Island No. 10 and Memphis. The Confederate naval fleet was anchored at Memphis and it was decided that this small fleet would sail up river to attack the larger Union fleet. Confederate ships were able to ram Union ships, sinking one and tearing a hole in another. Union ships managed to pull into shallow water where the Confederate ships could not follow. Since their guns were inferior to the Union's, they pulled back to Memphis after crippling the Union fleet. This battle was one of the few "fleet actions" of the war on a river.

U.S.A.					*C.S.A.*
C.H. Davis					J.E. Montgomery

	Troops	Killed	Wounded	Missing/Captured	Total Casualties
U.S.A.	7 ironclads	2	1		3 men
	16 mortar boats				2 ironclads
	1 gunboat				
C.S.A.	8 Converted river steamers				

10 Union forces occupied Pensacola, Florida.

11 *The Confederates sank the CSS* Virginia *(formerly the USS* Merrimack*).*

With the fall of Yorktown, the naval base at Norfolk was vulnerable and had to be evacuated. Since the CSS *Virginia* had a draft too deep to enter the river, it was deliberately sunk to keep it out of Union hands.

12   Union troops moved in and took possession of Baton Rouge, Louisiana.

13   *Battle between gunboats at Drewry's Bluff, Virginia* (**Confederate Victory**)

With the sinking of the CSS *Virginia*, the river route was now open to Richmond. It was decided that the Union fleet would advance up the James River toward Richmond. The only defense was Fort Darling located on Drewry's Bluff. The river below the fort was narrow and, as the Union ships came into view, they came under fire from heavy Confederate artillery. The Union force retreated.

U.S.A.				C.S.A.	
J. Rodgers				E. Ferrand, W. Mahone	
	Troops	*Killed*	*Wounded*	*Missing/Captured*	*Total Casualties*
U.S.A.	5 gunboats				24
C.S.A.	garrison	7	8		15

23   *Action at Front Royal, Virginia* (**Confederate Victory**)

Once known as "Hell Town" for the wild and colorful characters who gathered here, Front Royal became famous in the war for the activities of Belle Boyd, a southern spy. Boyd had extended an invitation to General Nathaniel Banks and his men when they occupied the city. Boyd later slipped away on horseback to tell Stonewall Jackson what she had learned. After receiving this important information, Jackson surprised and overran Union forces at Front Royal, capturing the city.

U.S.A.				C.S.A.	
J.R. Kenly				T.J. Jackson	
	Troops	*Killed*	*Wounded*	*Missing/Captured*	*Total Casualties*
U.S.A.	8,000	32	122	757	911
C.S.A.	17,000				35

25   *First Engagement at Winchester, Virginia* (**Confederate Victory**)

Winchester, known as the "gateway to the Shenandoah Valley," saw more action than any town west of Richmond, changing hands 72 times during the war. As Union forces fled from Front Royal and moved toward Winchester, Jackson pursued them. Thinking they had reached safety, Union forces occupied the city only to find the next morning there were Confederate forces on both ends of the Union line. The Confederates had now cleared all but a small portion of the Shenandoah Valley.

U.S.A.				C.S.A.	
N.P. Banks				T.J. Jackson, R.S. Ewell	
	Troops	*Killed*	*Wounded*	*Missing/Captured*	*Total Casualties*
U.S.A.	6,500	62	243	1,714	2,019
C.S.A.	16,000	68	329	3	400

26 *Engagement at Hanover Court House, Virginia* (**Union Victory**)

Union officials believed that a Confederate force at Hanover Court House presented a threat to the right flank of McClellan's army and also posed a hindrance to McDowell's army joining with McClellan.

	U.S.A.				*C.S.A.*
	F.J. Porter				L. O'B. Branch

		Troops	*Killed*	*Wounded*	*Missing/Captured*	*Total Casualties*
U.S.A.	Division	62	223		70	355
C.S.A.	Division					930

29 *Union forces occupy Corinth, Mississippi.*

After the Union victory at Shiloh, Union forces had moved toward Corinth, Mississippi, and Henry Halleck had assumed command of the Union forces, relieving Grant. Corinth, a centrally located railroad hub, was under Confederate control. Many of the Confederate soldiers were in poor shape after Shiloh, many dying of disease. When Union forces were well within range of the city, Beauregard decided to evacuate it and quietly moved his army to Tupelo. Their escape was not noticed until the following day.

31–June 1 *Battle of Fair Oaks (Seven Pines), Virginia* (**Undetermined**)

General McClellan divided his large force, placing three corps on the north side of the Chickahominy where he hoped to join up with McDowell's forces, who were expected to come from the north. Two corps were placed on the south side of the river, which was swollen with recent rains. After suffering criticism and lack of confidence from his superiors, Confederate General Joseph E. Johnston decided to launch an attack on the two corps south of the river. Longstreet was delayed in his attack, as he and his men took a wrong road, leaving the initial attack to D.H. Hill. McClellan had ordered Sumner to take his men across the river, but Sumner also was delayed because of collapsed bridges. However, his arrival did blunt the Confederate attack. Johnston was severely wounded and Robert E. Lee was named to take command of the Confederate army. Because of the recent rains, men fought in knee-deep water. Many of the wounded were propped up against trees to prevent them from drowning.

U.S.A.			*C.S.A.*		
E.V. Sumner, D. Couch			J.E. Johnston (Wounded), G.W. Smith, J. Longstreet, R.H. Hatton (Killed)		

	Troops	*Killed*	*Wounded*	*Missing/Captured*	*Total Casualties*
U.S.A.	42,000	790	3,594	647	5,031
C.S.A.	42,000	980	4,749	405	6,134

31 Robert E. Lee was appointed to take command of the Confederate Army, renaming it the Army of Northern Virginia.

June 1862

4   Confederate forces evacuated Fort Pillow.

5   *Skirmish at Tranter's Creek, North Carolina* (**Union Victory**)
   Union troops, on a reconnaissance, discovered a small Confederate force at a mill near Tranter's Creek. Confederates attempted to stop the Union forces from crossing the bridge over the creek, but when Union artillery opened, the Confederates retreated.

U.S.A.			C.S.A.	
F.A. Osborne			G. Singletary (Killed)	

	Troops	Killed	Wounded	Missing/Captured	Total Casualties
U.S.A. Regiments	7	11			18
C.S.A. Regiments					22

6   *Battle of Memphis, Tennessee* (Mostly fleet action) (**Union Victory**)
   After the Union defeat at Plum Run Bend, the Confederate fleet returned to Memphis. Upon learning that a large Union force was en route, Beauregard ordered not only the evacuation of Fort Pillow but also of Memphis, leaving only the Confederate navy to defend the city against the Union advance. The Union navy began the assault and quickly sank or captured all but one of the Confederate ships. The city soon surrendered and the Union flag was hoisted over the city. The fall of Memphis opened another part of the Mississippi to Union shipping.

U.S.A.			C.S.A.	
C.H. Davis, Charles Ellet (USN)			J.E. Montgomery, M.J. Thompson	

	Troops	Killed	Wounded	Missing/Captured	Total Casualties
U.S.A.	5 ironclads, 2 rams				1
C.S.A.	8 rams				180

7   *Skirmish at Chattanooga, Tennessee* (**Union Victory**)
   Brigadier General James Negley was ordered by Major General Ormsby Mitchell to capture Chattanooga. Local townsmen gave a spirited defense of the city as they faced the Union troops. When Confederate troops under General Kirby Smith arrived, they found that Union troops had left. This was classified as a Union victory because it demonstrated Union troops could launch attacks when and where they wanted.

7   General Benjamin Butler executed William Bruce Mumford for treason. Mumford had torn down a Union flag flying over the New Orleans Mint on April 26, before the city had officially surrendered and had ripped the flag apart. Butler wrote of Mumford: "He was tried, condemned and executed on the spot where he committed his heinous crime."[3]

8   *Battle of Cross Keys, Virginia* (**Confederate Victory**)
   Jackson faced two Federal columns coming up the Shenandoah, one to the West

commanded by Fremont, and the other to the north commanded by Shields. Jackson was attacked on the west side of the South Folk. While fighting Shields, Jackson sent Ewell to confront Fremont. After a tremendous artillery duel, Fremont was forced to withdraw.

		U.S.A.		C.S.A.	
		John C. Fremont, James Shields		Thomas J. Jackson, Richard S. Ewell	
	Troops	*Killed*	*Wounded*	*Missing/Captured*	*Total Casualties*
U.S.A.	11,500	114	443	127	684
C.S.A.	5,800	41	232	15	288

9 *Engagement at Port Republic, Virginia* (**Confederate Victory**)

The last battle of Jackson's Shenandoah Valley campaign. Jackson's army was now positioned between two Union armies, but Jackson thought he was in a good position to defeat each force. Port Republic was the place where the North River met the South River and Jackson controlled both crossings. With Ewell's defeat of Fremont at Cross Keys, Jackson tackled Shields. Jackson was able to drive Shield's men from the field with additional assistance of Confederate gunners and General Richard Taylor's troops, which had been summoned for assistance.

		U.S.A.		C.S.A.	
		James Shields, Erastus Tyler, John C. Fremont		Thomas J. Jackson, Richard S. Ewell, Richard Taylor	
	Troops	*Killed*	*Wounded*	*Missing/Captured*	*Total Casualties*
U.S.A.	3,500	67	393	558	1,018
C.S.A.	5,900				804

12–15 *Confederate Brigadier General J.E.B. Stuart rides around the Union Army*

After assuming command of the southern army, Lee wanted to launch an attack on Union forces near Richmond but needed to know their positions and their strengths. Stuart, accompanied by 1,200 horsemen, rode northward. The first Union force he came upon belonged to General Philip St. George Cooke, his father-in-law. In that encounter, Stuart lost only one man, Captain William Latane. He left Latane's body with the ladies on a nearby plantation who buried him in their family cemetery. Having ridden around the right flank of the Union army and into its rear, Stuart decided to encircle it completely instead of retracing his steps, believing the Union was waiting for him.

13 *Raid on Murfreesboro, Tennessee* (**Confederate Victory**)

Confederate forces under General Nathan B. Forrest attacked the Union garrison at Murfreesboro, taking the town and demanding the surrender of two Union garrisons located at the east and the west section of the town. Before leaving, Forrest captured 4 artillery guns, 40 wagons, 300 mules and 150 horses plus $300,000 worth of supplies. He destroyed not only the railroad tracks but also burned $200,000 worth of supplies he could not carry with him.

	U.S.A.			*C.S.A.*	
J.G. Parkhurst, H.C. Lester				Nathan B. Forrest	
	Troops	*Killed*	*Wounded*	*Missing/Captured*	*Total Casualties*
U.S.A.	1,200	29	120	1,051	1,200
C.S.A.	1,400	25	50		75

16   *Engagement at Secessionville, South Carolina* (**Confederate Victory**)

The Union began landing divisions on James Island, south of Charleston, South Carolina. They wanted to capture Charleston by land rather than risk a naval battle. The Confederates strengthened their line and were able to stop the Union attack. The outcome seriously hindered Union operations aimed at controlling Charleston Harbor.

	U.S.A.			*C.S.A.*	
Henry W. Benham, Horatio G. Wright, Isaac I. Stevens				Nathan G. Evans, T.G. Lamar	
	Troops	*Killed*	*Wounded*	*Missing/Captured*	*Total Casualties*
U.S.A.	6,600	107	487	89	683
C.S.A.	2,500	52	144	8	204

17   John C. Fremont resigned when informed that General John Pope was to take command of the newly created Army of Virginia. Fremont, being junior, would have to report to Pope, and this was something he did not want. At the same time, Braxton Bragg replaced P.G.T. Beauregard in the west. Beauregard was incapacitated at the time due to illness.

25–July 1   *Seven Day Campaign (AKA Great Skedaddle)*

This was part of the Peninsula Campaign, which ran from May 4 through August 26, 1862. During the seven days of battles and skirmishes, Confederate regiments attacked Union positions in an effort to remove the Union threat on Richmond. Faulty information had convinced Union commander McClellan that his army greatly outnumbered the Confederate forces defending Richmond. He also learned that Robert E. Lee had been named commander of Confederate forces. Lee's record at the time was termed as being "lackluster" and Lee had not yet earned the confidence of the Confederate army. In the meantime, Lee received vital information of Union movements from Stuart's ride around the Union army. Strongly entrenched and backed by artillery and cavalry, the Union force was able to inflict damage on the Confederates, but each of the battles was termed a Confederate victory since McClellan withdrew his forces. Eventually, he would be relieved of command.

25   *Engagement at Oak Grove (The Orchard), Virginia,* part of the Seven Days Campaign (**Confederate Victory**)

While Lee was moving his forces to the banks of the Chickahominy in anticipation of taking the offensive against McClellan, McClellan ordered his troops to take the area around Oak Grove Swamp. He wanted this area for the placement of his large siege guns.

	Troops	Killed	Wounded	Missing/Captured	Total Casualties
U.S.A.		51	401	64	516
C.S.A.		40	263	13	316

U.S.A. — Joseph Hooker, Cuvier Grover
C.S.A. — George Dole, Benjamin Huger

26 *Battle of Mechanicsville (Beaver Dam Creek, Ellerson's Mill), Virginia,* part of the Seven Days Campaign (**Confederate Victory**)

Lee took the offensive and ordered an attack on the right wing of the Union army, anticipating the arrival of Stonewall Jackson's forces. Jackson did not appear until late and did not participate in the battle. The Confederates were able to turn McClellan's flank and strike Porter with a superior force.

U.S.A. — Fritz J. Porter
C.S.A. — James Longstreet, A.P. Hill

	Troops	Killed	Wounded	Missing/Captured	Total Casualties
U.S.A.	15,631	49	207	105	361
C.S.A.	16,356				1,484

26 John Pope took command of the newly created Army of Virginia.

26 Farragut's fleet prepared to run past Vicksburg in an effort to help Grant capture that strategic fortification.

27 General Braxton Bragg took command of the Confederate Army of Tennessee.

27 *Battle of Gaines Mill (First Cold Harbor or Chickahominy), Virginia,* part of the Seven Days Campaign (**Confederate Victory**)

After Mechanicsville, Porter's force entrenched along the bank of the Chickahominy River near Cold Harbor. After a preliminary skirmish with A.P. Hill, who had come from Mechanicsville, Porter was hit hard by Lee's main force.

U.S.A. — Fritz J. Porter
C.S.A. — James Longstreet, John B. Hood

	Troops	Killed	Wounded	Missing/Captured	Total Casualties
U.S.A.	36,000	894	3,107	2,836	6,837
C.S.A.	57,000				8,750

28 *Action at Garnett's Farm,* part of the Seven Days Campaign (**Confederate Victory**)

As the fight continued at Gaines Mill, Magruder demonstrated against the Union forces south of the Chickahominy. Thought not technically a Confederate victory, it created a believable threat of a possible all-out Confederate attack.

	U.S.A.			C.S.A.	
Samuel P. Heintzelman				John B. Magruder	

	Troops	Killed	Wounded	Missing/Captured	Total Casualties
U.S.A.	70,000	37	227	104	368
C.S.A.	25,000				271

29 *Battle of Savage's Station, Virginia*, part of the Seven Days Campaign (**Confederate Victory**)

Confederate forces struck the retreating Union army under McClellan as they were pulling back from the siege of Richmond. The Confederates had to break off the action when expected support from Jackson failed to materialize.

	U.S.A.			C.S.A.	
Earl Sumner				John B. Magruder	

	Troops	Killed	Wounded	Missing/Captured	Total Casualties
U.S.A.	26,600				1,038
C.S.A.	14,000				473

30 *Battle of Frayser's/Frazier's Farm (or White Oak Swamp, or Glendale), Virginia*, part of the Seven Days Campaign (**Confederate Victory**)

McClellan began moving his army toward the James and, as he moved, his army was stretched out for miles. He placed a rear guard at the bridge near White Oak Swamp to buy time.

	U.S.A.			C.S.A.	
William Franklin				Thomas J. Jackson	

	Troops	Killed	Wounded	Missing/Captured	Total Casualties
U.S.A.		210	1,513	1,130	2,853
C.S.A.					3,647

30–July 1 *Firing at Tampa, Florida* (**Confederate Victory**)

A Union gunboat under Captain A.J. Drake sailed into Tampa Bay and opened fire upon the city and its crew demanded that the city surrender. Confederate forces under Captain J.W. Pearson refused and, at the same time, returned fire. Next day, the Union gunboat departed. No casualties occurred.

July 1862

1 *Battle of Malvern Hill, Virginia* (**Undetermined**)

The last of the Seven Days Battles. The steep slopes of Malvern Hill on the Union's left and the swampy bottoms on the right forced the Confederates to advance across open ground. The Union troops, who had not dug any defensive trenches, stood at their guns in battle formation as their artillery, consisting of 250 guns, shattered the ranks of the attacking Confederates. Unable to gain any ground and suffering huge losses, Lee had to pull back. Lee's inability to destroy McClellan's Army was countered by McClellan's inability to take Richmond. McClellan withdrew to his base at Harrison's Landing along the James River. (Harrison's Landing was part of the Berkeley Plantation, the home of William Henry Harrison, the 9th president of the United States.)

		U.S.A.			C.S.A.	
		George B. McClellan			Robert E. Lee, Daniel H. Lee	
	Troops	*Killed*	*Wounded*	*Missing/Captured*	*Total Casualties*	
U.S.A.	83,000	397	2,092	725	3,214	
C.S.A.	86,500				9,477	

Entire Seven Day Campaign

	Troops	*Killed*	*Wounded*	*Missing/Captured*	*Total Casualties*
U.S.A.	115,000	1,734	6,062	6,053	13,849
C.S.A.	88,000	3,286	15,909	946	20,141

1 Lincoln called for 300,000 three-year volunteers.

1 The Federal Income Tax Act was approved.

3 *Skirmish at Evelington Heights (Harrison Landing), Virginia* (**Union Victory**)
George B. McClellan had made camp at Harrison's Landing and considered his position invincible. His men controlled access to three sides, leaving only a hill, which they failed to secure. Stuart spotted it and hauled one howitzer to the top. Without waiting for additional troops, J.E.B. Stuart opened fire. McClellan sent men to remove the threat but Stuart, finding no additional troops coming to his assistance, withdrew.

4–28 John Hunt Morgan, with a 1,100 man cavalry, made lightning raids in Kentucky. As his troops rode into the various towns, they demanded the surrender of the Union garrisons stationed in the cities or the surrender of the Home Guards. Morgan was taking all supplies or equipment he could carry. By the time he returned to Tennessee on the 28th, he had covered 1,000 miles in less than 24 days. Morgan, in his report of July 30, 1862, said he had "captured seventeen towns, destroyed all the government supplies and arms in them, dispersed about fifteen hundred Home Guards, [and] paroled nearly twelve hundred regular troops."[4]

9 Lincoln visited McClellan at Harrison's Landing, where he expressed his disappointment with McClellan.

11 Henry W. Halleck was named general in chief of all Federal armies.

13 *Raid on Murfreesboro, Tennessee* (**Confederate Victory**)
Before the war, Murfreesboro served as a social center, and would later serve as the

command headquarters of Union Colonel W.W. Duffueld. Nathan Bedford Forrest had been ordered to disrupt the Union supply lines of Union Commander Don Carlos Buell. Buell was forced to surrender the city to Forrest. Forrest left the city with 1,200 prisoners, including Duffueld, and over a million dollars worth of captured arms, wagons and other supplies.

	U.S.A.				*C.S.A.*
	Thomas L. Crittenden, W.W. Duffueld				Nathan B. Forrest
	Troops	*Killed*	*Wounded*	*Missing/Captured*	*Total Casualties*
U.S.A.	1,200	19	120	846	985
C.S.A.	1,400				150

15   *Engagement near Vicksburg, naval engagement* (**Undetermined**)
The Union fleet, which was north of Vicksburg, met and fired on the CSS *Arkansas*, a new Confederate ironclad that had been recently commissioned. The Union fleet passed below the city dueling with both the land batteries and the CSS *Arkansas*. They were unable to damage the Confederate ship, but three Union ships were damaged in the encounter.

	U.S.A.				*C.S.A.*
	David G. Farragut				I. Brown
	Troops	*Killed*	*Wounded*	*Missing/Captured*	*Total Casualties*
U.S.A.		18	50	10	78
C.S.A.		10	15		25

16   Major General Ulysses S. Grant was named commander of Army of West Tennessee.

29   The CSS *Alabama* left Liverpool, England, to begin attacks on the northern shipping lanes.

August 1862

4   Lincoln called for an additional 300,000 men for a nine-month militia.

5   *Engagement at Baton Rouge, Louisiana* (**Union Victory**)
In an effort to regain Louisiana, Confederate forces would have to re-take Baton Rouge, the capital, which was under Union control. A land and sea assault was planned using the Confederate ram CSS *Arkansas*. The attack began and, at first, appeared to be successful in pushing back the Union defenders. As the Confederates approached the city, Union gunboats opened fire. The CSS *Arkansas* ran into mechanical difficulties and was unable to assist in the assault. After numerous attempts to drive the Union defenders from the city, the plan failed, forcing the Confederates to withdraw. They scuttled the ship and left the city in Union hands.

	U.S.A.			C.S.A.	
	Thomas Williams (Killed), Thomas W. Cahill			John C. Breckinridge	

	Troops	Killed	Wounded	Missing/Captured	Total Casualties
U.S.A.	2,500	84	266	33	383
C.S.A.	2,600	84	315	57	456

9–10   *Battle of Cedar Mountain (Slaughter Mountain), Virginia* (**Confederate Victory**)
The Union Army of Virginia, under General John Pope, advanced from Culpeper, Virginia, south toward Orange Court House with the intention of taking the rail station at Gordonsville. Jackson's corps was posted south of Culpeper, north of the Rapidan, and intended to attack each of the Union corps separately. General Banks managed to get the advantage until Jackson was reinforced by Hill's troops. After this battle, the Union abandoned the Peninsula Campaign and turned its attention to Northern Virginia.

	U.S.A.			C.S.A.	
	John Pope, Nathaniel Banks			Thomas J. Jackson, A.P. Hill, Charles S. Winder (Killed)	

	Troops	Killed	Wounded	Missing/Captured	Total Casualties
U.S.A.	8,030	314	1,445	622	2,381
C.S.A.	16,868				1,341

11   Confederates under William Quantrill rode in and captured Independence, Missouri, as they were on their way to take up the fight in Kansas.

13   The Army of the Potomac evacuated the peninsula as Lee moved north.

14   General E.K. Smith began the Confederate invasion of Kentucky at Knoxville.

17   Union cavalry almost captured J.E.B. Stuart as he awaited the arrival of his cavalry at Verdiersville, Virginia. He managed to flee, but as he did, he left behind his famous plume hat. Five days later, on August 22, Stuart captured General Pope's wagon train, and inside the wagon was Pope's dress uniform coat. Stuart was reported to have sent Pope the following message: "You have my hat and plume. I have your best coat. I have the honor to propose a cartel for fair exchange of the prisoners."[5] The coat was sent to Virginia Governor John Letcher, who had it hung in the State Library for all to see.

22   *Action at Freeman's Ford (AKA Rappahannock Station), Virginia* (**Confederate Victory**)
Stuart, coming across a portion of John Pope's army near Freeman's Ford, threw shells in their direction as Thomas J. Jackson moved upriver to cross. Jackson's column stretched over nine miles long. Union troops under Henry Bohlen set out to capture some of the trains but were assaulted by troops under Isaac Trimble who were concealed in the woods to protect the trains. Bohlen was killed.

27 *Skirmish at Manassas Junction (aka Bristoe Station)* (**Confederate Victory**)
After passing around Pope's right flank, Thomas J. Jackson attacked Bristoe Station, where he tore up the tracks of the Orange and Alexandria Railroad. After learning that the Union Supply Depot at Manassas Junction was thinly guarded, Jackson conducted a rare night maneuver. After a five-minute attack on the railroad, Jackson took his main force and moved on Manassas Junction. Whatever supplies he could not carry were burned. The attack forced Pope to pull back from his Rappahannock encampment. George W. Taylor, Union commander, was mortally wounded. Confederate troops under Isaac Trimble and J.E.B. Stuart also participated.

28 *Battle of Groveton, Virginia* (**Confederate Victory**)
After burning the supplies at Manassas Junction, Jackson went into hiding near Groveton, Virginia. Pope ordered his forces to move toward Centreville and as they did, they passed near Jackson's camps. Jackson decided to attack while awaiting the arrival of the rest of Lee's army. It was in this battle that Ewell lost his right leg.

	U.S.A.			C.S.A.	
	John Gibbon, Abner Doubleday			Richard S. Ewell, William B. Taliaferro	
	Troops	Killed	Wounded	Missing/Captured	Total Casualties
U.S.A.	2,800				900
C.S.A.	6,000				400

28 The Confederate Army of Tennessee commanded by Braxton Bragg began a campaign into Tennessee and Kentucky. In Frankfort, Bragg installed Richard Hawes as the Confederate governor of the state.

29–30 *Second Battle of Bull Run (Manassas), Virginia* (**Confederate Victory**)
Stonewall Jackson had previously captured Union supplies at Manassas Junction and had taken up a position in the woods at Groveton, near the old Manassas battlefield. Angered by the attack on his supplies, Pope abandoned the line at the Rappahannock and headed towards Manassas. Meanwhile, Lee and Longstreet moved up to join Jackson. To bring Pope to battle, Jackson struck at a Union column as it marched past Groveton and the Warrenton Turnpike. Believing that the Confederates were in retreat at this point, Pope ordered his men to pursue and, as they did, they ran into the combined forces of Lee, Longstreet and Jackson.

	U.S.A.			C.S.A.	
	John Pope, Fritz J. Porter, Gouverneur K. Warren			Robert E. Lee, Fitzhugh Lee, Thomas J. Jackson, James Longstreet	
	Troops	Killed	Wounded	Missing/Captured	Total Casualties
U.S.A.	75,000	1,724	8,372	5,958	16,054
C.S.A.	48,500	1,481	7,627	89	9,197

30 *Battle of Richmond, Kentucky* (**Confederate Victory**)
As Confederate forces moved into Kentucky, they came across Union troops stationed

near Richmond, Kentucky. A skirmish ensued which grew into a full-scale battle as artillery was brought up. After a concentrated Confederate attack on their right, Nelson's troops gave way.

U.S.A.				C.S.A.
William Nelson				Edmund K. Smith

	Troops	Killed	Wounded	Missing/Captured	Total Casualties
U.S.A.	6,500	206	844	4,144	5,194
C.S.A.	6,800	78	372	1	451

September 1862

1 *Engagement at Chantilly (Ox Hill), Virginia* (**Confederate Victory**)
    In an attempt to cut off Pope's retreat from the Second Battle of Bull Run (Manassas), Lee placed his men between the Union line and Washington. Alarmed and concerned for the safety of Washington, Union leaders decided the Confederates must be cleared from the Ox Hill region. After fighting to a standstill, Pope ordered his men to fall back to Washington. With the Union threat removed, Lee ordered his men to march across the Potomac into Maryland. General Philip Kearney was killed as he rode into the Confederate lines by mistake.

U.S.A.				C.S.A.
Isaac I. Stevens (Killed), Philip Kearney (Killed)				Thomas J. Jackson, Ambrose P. Hill

	Troops	Killed	Wounded	Missing/Captured	Total Casualties
U.S.A.	Division				1,300
C.S.A.	Division				800

1 Lincoln ordered McClellan to defend Washington.

3 Lee, with 50,000 men, crossed the Potomac River into Maryland to start the
    Maryland Campaign. He crossed east of the Blue Ridge Mountains to threaten both Washington and Baltimore, hoping Union officials would pull the remaining troops from the Shenandoah Valley. If they did, this would allow Lee to call additional men for his planned northern invasion. Confederate government officials felt that if Lee was able to secure a victory in the northern invasion, both England and France might grant recognition to the Confederate government.

4 Washington residents awoke to the fact that a large Confederate force had crossed the Potomac. At one point, it was reported that a farmer had raced down Pennsylvania Avenue on horseback shouting the news. The city was in a panic.

5 McClellan resumed command of the Army of the Potomac and marched northward with 15 divisions comprising 84,000 men.

7   The last of Lee's forces crossed the Potomac and gathered at Frederick, Maryland.

9   Lee issued Special Order No. 191, which outlined his plan for the invasion of Maryland. He ordered his army to divide into four separate sectors. He also sent Jackson to Harper's Ferry to prepare for an invasion of Pennsylvania should the Maryland invasion be a success.

11   McClellan learned Lee had left Frederick and was in possession of Hagerstown.

13   As McClellan's men arrive in Frederick, Maryland, Private Barton W. Mitchell, 27th Indiana Infantry Regiment, Company F, found a package containing three cigars wrapped in paper. The paper wrapped around one of the cigars was discovered to be a copy of Lee's Special Order 191, which was given to McClellan. It is suspected that the orders found belonged to General Daniel H. Hill. After the war, Hill denied the allegation. McClellan failed to act immediately upon learning that Lee had divided his forces.

13–17   *Siege of Munfordville, Kentucky* (**Confederate Victory**)
   Braxton Bragg sent General Chalmers toward Munfordville to destroy an important railroad bridge. At the same time, a Union force had been dispatched to protect the same bridge. Confederate forces demanded the surrender of the Union force but, upon their refusal, a skirmish broke out. Reinforcements were sent to assist the Union defenders and again their surrender was demanded. Once more, it was refused. Upon seeing a large Confederate force about to lay siege to not only the bridge but also the city, Union forces decided to surrender. With the surrender, the Confederates now had control of the transportation center and ultimately this would affect the movement of Union supplies and men.

	U.S.A.			*C.S.A.*	
	J.T. Wilder, C.L. Dunham			James R. Chalmers	

	Troops	*Killed*	*Wounded*	*Missing/Captured*	*Total Casualties*
U.S.A.	4,000				4,000
C.S.A.	10,000				714

14   *Battle of Crampton's Gap Maryland Heights, Maryland* (**Confederate Victory**)
   In preparation for the attack on Harper's Ferry, Lafayette McLaws was ordered to secure Maryland Heights, which dominated Harper's Ferry. The left wing of McClellan's army, under General William Franklin, had moved toward Crampton's Gap to relieve the Harper's Ferry garrison. They were also to cut off the Confederates from advancing on that stronghold. Franklin carried the pass against McLaws but, believing he was outnumbered, did not push on.

U.S.A.	*C.S.A.*
William B. Franklin, D.S. Miles, E. Sherrill	Lafayette McLaws, Joseph Kershaw, William Barksdale

14   *Battle of South Mountain, Maryland* (**Union Victory**)
   After his victory at the Second Bull Run, Lee had moved northward into Maryland. General D.H. Hill was in the vicinity of South Mountain when he was attacked by Pleasan-

ton's cavalry at Fox and Turner's gaps. With the arrival of General Reno and Hooker, the Confederates were forced to pull back. Reno was mortally wounded in the fray.

	U.S.A.			*C.S.A.*	
	Alfred Pleasanton, Joseph Hooker, Jesse Reno (Mortally wounded)			Daniel H. Hill, Samuel Garland (Killed)	
	Troops	*Killed*	*Wounded*	*Missing/Captured*	*Total Casualties*
U.S.A.	28,000	443	1,807	75	2,325
C.S.A.	18,000	325	1,560	800	2,685

15 *Capture of Harper's Ferry, Western Virginia* (**Confederate Victory**)

After securing the heights, Confederate artillery was moved into position and the attack was made on Harper's Ferry, as a part of Lee's invasion of the North. General Miles surrendered the entire garrison, but shortly afterwards he was mortally wounded when a shell from the artillery guns on Loudoun Heights struck him.

	U.S.A.			*C.S.A.*	
	D.S. Miles (Mortally wounded)			Thomas J. Jackson	
	Troops	*Killed*	*Wounded*	*Missing/Captured*	*Total Casualties*
U.S.A.	12,922	44	173	12,419	12,636
C.S.A.		39	247		286

16 McClellan moved into position near Sharpsburg to stem the Confederate movement northward.

17 *Battle of Antietam (Sharpsburg), Maryland* (**Union Victory**)

This encounter between McClellan's Army of the Potomac and Lee's Army of Northern Virginia marked the bloodiest single day of the Civil War with 26,000 casualties sustained by both sides. The fighting ranged from Dunker Church, Bloody Lane, and the Corn Field to the Sunken Road and Burnside Bridge, names that will live long in the memory of the war, as will Burnside Bridge. It was on this bridge that many men of Burnside's men were killed as the Confederates positioned themselves on the bluffs overlooking Rohrback Bridge that spanned the shallow Antietam Creek. Burnside would not allow his men to cross the creek, insisting they cross the bridge, making them easy targets. The Union's victory not only stopped Lee's Northern invasion, but also gave political leaders the victory that was desperately needed for President Lincoln to issue his Preliminary Emancipation Proclamation. Rohrback's bridge was soon called Burnside's Bridge.

	U.S.A.			*C.S.A.*	
	George B. McClellan, Ambrose Burnside			R.E. Lee, Ambrose P. Hill, Thomas J. Jackson	
	Troops	*Killed*	*Wounded*	*Missing/Captured*	*Total Casualties*
U.S.A.	75,000	2,010	9,416	1,043	12,469
C.S.A.	40,000	2,700	9,024	2,000	13,724

19   Lee withdrew to Virginia.

19   *Engagement at Iuka, Mississippi* (**Union Victory**)
Confederate forces under Sterling Price were ordered northward to Iuka to prevent the Union from reinforcing troops that had been sent to confront Bragg. Grant, believing Price was en route to support Bragg, decided to attack. Grant, leading the assault, attacked while Price was delayed waiting for the arrival of Van Dorn's army. Before the Union forces could launch a coordinated attack, Price moved toward the southwest.

	U.S.A.				C.S.A.
	Ulysses S. Grant, William S. Rosecrans			*Sterling Price, Earl Van Dorn*	
	Troops	*Killed*	*Wounded*	*Missing/Captured*	*Total Casualties*
U.S.A.	17,000	141	613	36	790
C.S.A.	14,000	263	692	561	1,516

19–20   *Skirmish at Boteler's Ford, Western Virginia* (**Confederate Victory**)
Shortly after dawn on the 19th, Lee's army crossed the Potomac heading back to Virginia. Union cavalry was in pursuit when they spotted the rear of Lee's army as it approached Boteler's Ford on the Potomac, near Shepherdstown. To guard the ford, Lee posted his chief of artillery, William Pendleton, with two brigades. Seeing the Union cavalry, Pendleton opened with his artillery only to have the Union quickly bring up their guns. Soon additional Union troops arrived. As darkness fell, the Confederates began to remove their guns when Union forces under Fritz J. Porter stormed across the field at them. After being advised that the Union had seized several of his guns, Lee ordered Jackson to get them back. Jackson sent A.P. Hill to get the guns and he not only recovered the guns, but also drove Union cavalry backwards.

22   Lincoln issued his Preliminary Emancipation Proclamation.

24–25   *Engagement at Sabine Pass, Texas* (**Union Victory**)
Union Naval ships bombarded Sabine Pass in an attempt to drive Confederate forces from the town. After a day of steady assault, the Confederates unable to inflict any damage on the Union ships and packed up their gear, spiked their guns and left the area. The town surrendered the next morning, giving the Union a foothold on the Texas coast.

27   *Capture of Augusta, Kentucky*
Confederate forces under Colonel Basil Duke attempted to capture Augusta, Kentucky. They had planned to use the city as a springboard to make future attacks on Cincinnati. However, with the river being patrolled by Union gunboats, the Confederates gave up on the city, as the fight was too intense and their ammunition was running low.

October 1862

3–4   *Battle of Corinth, Mississippi* (**Union Victory**)
The Confederates hoped to seize Corinth, a valuable transportation center, and then

sweep into middle Tennessee. Union forces had been building fortifications since they first entered the city after the Battle of Shiloh. It was hoped that Confederate presence in the area would take the pressure off Bragg, who was operating in Kentucky by keeping the Union forces from reinforcing Buell.

U.S.A.			*C.S.A.*	
William Rosecrans			Sterling Price, Earl Van Dorn	
	Troops	*Killed*	*Wounded*	*Missing/Captured*	*Total Casualties*
U.S.A.	23,000	355	1,841	324	2,520
C.S.A.	22,000	473	1,997	1,763	4,233

4 *Blockade of Galveston, Texas* (**Union Victory**)

Although Union forces had blockaded the Galveston Harbor, the town itself remained in Confederate hands. On the morning of October 4, Union forces sent a request under a flag of truce demanding the city's surrender. When no answer was received, a few guns sent shells into the city. A four-day truce was later requested and granted to allow innocent men, women and children to have a safe retreat from the city.

5 Engagement at Davis Bridge, Tennessee (AKA Hatchie's Bridge) (**Union Victory**)

Confederate forces fleeing from Corinth came across a Union detachment under General Edward Ord. Ord had been sent to help General Rosecrans at Corinth. An engagement followed and, while a portion of the Confederate force held back the Union pursuit, the majority of Price's and Van Dorn's forces were able to withdraw to Holly Springs.

U.S.A.			*C.S.A.*	
Edward O.C. Ord (Wounded)			Sterling Price, Earl Van Dorn	
	Troops	*Killed*	*Wounded*	*Missing/Captured*	*Total Casualties*
U.S.A.	5,000	46	493	31	570
C.S.A.	22,000				400

7 In England, Chancellor of the Exchequer William E. Gladstone indicated that even though the Confederate States of America was a new and independent nation, England would hold off formal recognition of it until it appeared they would be victorious in their quest for independence. The Union victory at Sharpsburg was believed to have delayed the recognition sought by the Confederacy.

8 *Battle of Perryville (Chaplin Hills), Kentucky* (**Union Victory**)

Union forces were sent to deter Confederate forces from the area and to drive them from Kentucky. The Confederates had previously threatened both Louisville and Cincinnati. After the battle, Bragg retreated to the southeast and no further major battles were fought on Kentucky's soil.

U.S.A.	*C.S.A.*
Don C. Buell, Philip H. Sheridan, William R. Terrill (Killed)	B. Bragg, J. Wheeler

	Troops	Killed	Wounded	Missing/Captured	Total Casualties
U.S.A.	55,000	845	2,851	515	4,211
C.S.A.	16,000	519	2,635	251	3,405

9–12   Stuart, with 1,600 cavalrymen, made another raid into the north, reaching as far as Chambersburg, Pennsylvania, which he captured. Lee had previously ordered Stuart to make the raid into Pennsylvania to destroy the vital railroad bridges at Chambersburg and to capture whatever supplies he could carry. In addition, Stuart was to gather as much information as he could on Union movements. Stuart's second ride around McClellan's army netted over $250,000 in supplies that were burned or destroyed. Stuart also took 1,200 horses in his three day, 130-mile ride raid.

25   Grant assumed command of the Department of Tennessee and began to make plans for a siege of Vicksburg.

November 1862

1   Union officials began a campaign to capture Vicksburg, Mississippi.

7   Lincoln relieved McClellan of his command for failing to follow up on Lee's retreat after the battle of Antietam. Ambrose E. Burnside was appointed to command the Army of the Potomac.

13   Moving toward Vicksburg, Union troops occupied Holly Springs, Mississippi.

17   Burnside moved toward Fredericksburg, Virginia, reaching the banks of the Rappahannock River opposite the city.

28   Major General John B. Magruder was named Confederate commander of military forces in Texas.

December 1862

7   *Battle of Prairie Grove, Arkansas* (**Union Victory**)
    En route to join in the defense of Vicksburg, Confederate General Hindman decided to remove Blunt's Union presence from northwest Arkansas. Aware that Blunt was to receive additional support, Hindman split his troops, ordering the larger contingent to attack the arriving support troops, which were commanded by General Herron. Blunt, when he heard the sound of battle and received a dispatch, went in support of Herron. Though both sides claimed victory, it is considered a Union victory, for Confederate presence in Arkansas was almost nil after the battle.

U.S.A.	*C.S.A.*
Francis J. Herron, James G. Blunt	Thomas C. Hindman

	Troops	Killed	Wounded	Missing/Captured	Total Casualties
U.S.A.	13,000	175	813	236	1,224
C.S.A.	10,000	164	817	336	1,317

7 *Action at Hartsville, Tennessee* (**Confederate Victory**)

John Hunt Morgan surprised Union troops guarding the crossing over the Cumberland River near Hartsville, Tennessee, when he penetrated their lines. Morgan's men were able to surround the Union soldiers, forcing the Union commander to surrender. This was a preliminary to the Confederate cavalry raids led by both Morgan and Nathan Bedford Forrest.

U.S.A.	*C.S.A.*
A.B. Moore	J.H. Morgan

	Troops	Killed	Wounded	Missing/Captured	Total Casualties
U.S.A.	1,855				1,855
C.S.A.					149

11 Pontoon bridges were laid across the Rappahannock River to enable Burnside and his men to cross. As they did, they were forced to dodge gunfire from Confederates posted in Fredericksburg and, at the same time, sharpshooters also opened fired on the crossing men, causing a great loss of manpower.

13 *Battle of Fredericksburg, Virginia* (**Confederate Victory**)

Union troops on the west side of the Rappahannock began their assault on Prospect Hill and Marye's Heights. Confederate troops posted on the bluffs could fire down on the advancing soldiers. "Wave after wave of courageous men dutifully attacked though out the afternoon," reported a noted historian, "and met their awful fate." Burnside called off his attack and withdrew back across the river.

U.S.A.	*C.S.A.*
Ambrose Burnside, Edwin V. Sumner, William B. Franklin, Joseph Hooker, Conrad F. Jackson (Killed), George Bayard (Killed)	R.E. Lee, James Longstreet, Thomas J. Jackson, Maxcy Gregg (Killed), Thomas R.R. Cobb (Killed)

	Troops	Killed	Wounded	Missing/Captured	Total Casualties
U.S.A.	114,000	1,284	9,600	1,769	12,653
C.S.A.	72,500	595	4,061	653	5,309

14 Burnside retreated across the Rappahannock and established his winter camps.

14 Skirmish at *Kinston, North Carolina* (**Union Victory**)

Union troops, in an effort to destroy the 200-foot bridge spanning the Neuse River and disrupt the Wilmington and Weldon Railroad at Goldsborough, were confronted by Confederate forces. Realizing they were outnumbered, Confederate forces fled after burning the bridge to prevent Union troops from following them. The bridge was rebuilt several weeks afterwards.

	U.S.A.				C.S.A.
	John G. Foster				Nathan Evans
	Troops	*Killed*	*Wounded*	*Missing/Captured*	*Total Casualties*
U.S.A.	10,000	40	120		160
C.S.A.	2,000				600

19–20   *Raid on Holly Springs, Mississippi* (**Confederate Victory**)

General Earl Van Dorn led a raiding party on Holly Springs, Mississippi, burning and destroying what supplies he could not carry. He had captured 1,500 Union soldiers in the raid. After destroying the railroad depot, along with two engines and forty-three rail cars, Van Dorn moved north. This raid destroyed many of General Grant's supplies and forced Grant back to Tennessee. At the same time, Grant ordered Sherman to move from Memphis and head toward the Vicksburg area in preparation for an eventual assault.

21   John Hunt Morgan, known as the fearless and quick cavalry guerrilla leader, began to make raids into Kentucky with General Bragg's approval. At the same time, Union General William Rosecrans started for Murfreesboro.

26   Rosecrans arrived at Murfreesboro in pursuit of Bragg.

26–Jan. 1, 1863   *Raid on Dumfries, Virginia*

Stuart's cavalry began to make raids along the Union supply lines. His most daring raid was made during the last week of December at Dumfries, one of the most important Union supply depots. Finding the town heavily defended, Stuart proceeded to raid and harass Union lines in the surrounding countryside. He ended his raid on January 1, 1863, after going all the way to the outskirts of Washington before returning to the Confederate lines near Fredericksburg.

27–29   *Action at Chickasaw Bayou, Mississippi* (**Confederate Victory**)

As Sherman approached the vicinity of Vicksburg, he found the Confederates strongly entrenched at Chickasaw Bayou. After trying various approaches to take the city, he ultimately ordered a frontal assault, only to be fiercely repulsed, losing many men. Sherman was forced to pull back.

	U.S.A.			C.S.A.	
	William T. Sherman			John C. Pemberton, Martin L. Smith	
	Troops	*Killed*	*Wounded*	*Missing/Captured*	*Total Casualties*
U.S.A.	32,000	208	1,005	563	1,776
C.S.A.	14,000	63	134	10	207

30   The USS *Monitor* sank off Cape Hatteras.

31 *Engagement at Parker's Cross Roads* (**Confederate Victory**)
Union troops attempted to cut off Forrest's forays into Tennessee. They confronted Forrest near Parker's Cross Roads as he attempted to cross the Tennessee River. For a brief time, Forrest was trapped between two Union detachments charging from opposite directions.

	U.S.A.				C.S.A.
	Jeremiah C. Sullivan, C.L. Dunham				Nathan B. Forrest
	Troops	*Killed*	*Wounded*	*Missing/Captured*	*Total Casualties*
U.S.A.	3,000	27	140	70	237
C.S.A.	2,000	4	27	122	153

31–Jan. 2, 1863 *Battle of Stone River (Murfreesboro), Tennessee* (**Union Victory**)
After his defeat at Perryville, Bragg took his army to Murfreesboro in anticipation of going into winter quarters. Union troops under Rosecrans followed and, upon finding Bragg's army, launched his attack. Both sides fought back and forth until January 2, when Bragg was forced to pull back. Rosecrans did not pursue.

	U.S.A.				C.S.A.
	Williams S. Rosecrans				Braxton Bragg
	Troops	*Killed*	*Wounded*	*Missing/Captured*	*Total Casualties*
U.S.A.	41,400	1,730	7,802	3,686	13,218
C.S.A.	35,000	1,294	7,945	1,027	10,266

Chapter 8

1863

"Opinion was then expressed that fifteen thousand men who could make successful assault over that field had never been arrayed in battle"[1]

*— James Longstreet, in reference to the
Pickett/Pettigrew Charge of July 3, 1863*

January 1863

1 *Engagement at Galveston, Texas* (**Confederate Victory**)

Four Confederate gunboats slipped down the bay towards Galveston and re-took the city. W.B. Renshaw, the Union commander of the USS *Westfield*, blew up his ship after it had run aground, to prevent its capture by Confederate forces. He was killed in the explosion.

U.S.A.	C.S.A.
I.S. Burell (Killed), W.B. Renshaw (Killed)	J.B. Magruder

	Troops	Killed	Wounded	Missing/Captured	Total Casualties
U.S.A.	350	11			350
C.S.A.	3,000	26	117		143

1 Lincoln signed the Emancipation Proclamation, which freed slaves held in areas "in rebellion against the United States."

2 General Braxton Bragg established his winter quarters near Tullahoma.

8 *Engagement at Springfield, Missouri* (**Union Victory**)

In an attempt to destroy the Union Communications Center and supply depot at Springfield, Confederate forces advanced in battle lines upon the city, only to be met with stiff Union resistance. Fighting continued into the night when the Confederate troops withdrew, leaving the city in Union hands.

	U.S.A.			C.S.A.	
	Egbert G. Brown			J.S. Marmaduke	
	Troops	*Killed*	*Wounded*	*Missing/Captured*	*Total Casualties*
U.S.A.	2,099	14	146	170	330
C.S.A.	5,000				240

9–11 Skirmish *at Hartville, Missouri* (**Confederate Victory**)

Confederate forces assaulted the Union soldiers occupying the city. After a four-hour battle, Union troops left the city. Although the Confederates won the skirmish and captured the city, they were forced to abandon it when they learned of Union presence in the area.

	U.S.A.			C.S.A.	
	S. Merrill			J.C. Porter (Wounded), E. MacDonald (Killed)	
	Troops	*Killed*	*Wounded*	*Missing/Captured*	*Total Casualties*
U.S.A.	700	7	64	7	78
C.S.A.	1,500	15	70	27	112

11 The USS *Hatteras* was sunk by the Confederate raider CSS *Alabama* commanded by Raphael Semmes off the coast near Galveston, Texas.

11 *Battle of Fort Hindman at Arkansas Post* (**Union Victory**)

General Grant directed General McClernand to move north from Vicksburg to attack Fort Hindman located in the village of Arkansas Post on the Arkansas River. The Confederates had been using the fort to disrupt Union shipping on the Mississippi River. Outnumbered 6 to 1, General Churchill was unable to hold on to the fort and it fell to the Union attackers. Because the fort did not add to the Union's control of the Mississippi, McClernand burned it before returning to Vicksburg.

	U.S.A.			C.S.A.	
	D.D. Porter, J.A. McClernand			Thomas J. Churchill	
	Troops	*Killed*	*Wounded*	*Missing/Captured*	*Total Casualties*
U.S.A.	29,000	134	890	29	1,053
C.S.A.	5,000	28	81	4,791	4,900

20–22 Burnside made his "mud march" as he searched for a place to cross the Rappahannock. The march made by the Army of the Potomac along the James River was a futile attempt to cross north of Lee's Army during the rainy season. The move resulted in the loss of wagons and equipment that were trapped in the freezing rain and deep mire along the banks. Many soldiers either drowned or froze to death in the terrible cold weather. Meanwhile, the Confederates relaxed in the relative comfort of their defenses and watched the bedraggled Union troops, cold, disgusted and defeated, return to the Washington area.

26   Major General Joseph Hooker replaced Burnside as commander of the Army of the Potomac.

29   *Attack on Bear River, Idaho* (**Union Victory, Later Termed A Massacre**)
   Union forces under Colonel Patrick E. Conner attacked 300 Shoshoni Indians who had been conducting raids against the military presence in their area. Union troopers killed an estimated 250 Indians warriors along with many women and children. Though the battle was considered a Union victory, it was later called a massacre, as no Confederate soldiers were involved.

February 1863

1   Grant's attempt to capture Vicksburg from the rear by cutting a passage at Yazoo, Mississippi, failed.

1   *Skirmish at Dover, Tennessee* (**Union Victory**)
   Confederate forces, frustrated in their attempts to disrupt Union shipping on the Cumberland River, decided to attack the small city of Dover. The Union troops were able to hold and, by nightfall, both sides were almost out of ammunition. The Confederates pulled back. This failure not only left the Union in firm control of Middle Tennessee but also created a rift between two Confederate generals, Nathan Bedford Forrest and Joseph Wheeler. Forrest denounced Wheeler for his failure to take Dover, stating that he would never serve under him again.

	U.S.A.			*C.S.A.*	
	Abner C. Harding			Joseph Wheeler, Nathan B. Forrest	
	Troops	*Killed*	*Wounded*	*Missing/Captured*	*Total Casualties*
U.S.A.	800	13	51	62	126
C.S.A.	2,500				670

14   The Union ship *Queen of the West* made a run past Vicksburg, capturing several Confederate vessels, but the ship ran aground and was captured.

25   Confederate General James Longstreet assumed command of the Department of Virginia and North Carolina, beginning the Tidewater Operations.

March 1863

3   Federal Congress passed the Conscription Act, which called for the draft of men between 20 and 45. Draft quotas set by the president were based on population and the number of men already in service from each district. A man drafted into the service could hire a substitute to serve in his place, or, he could buy his way out of the service for $300.

3   *Affair at Fort McAllister, Georgia* (**Confederate Victory**)
   A Union naval flotilla consisting of three ironclads was ordered to test its guns by firing them at the Confederate battery at Fort McAllister. The fort was manned by a small three-gun earthwork battery. Though the bombardment lasted eight hours, it failed to destroy the Confederate guns. The flotilla pulled back with minor damage but its crew had gained more skill in the firing and positioning of their guns.

4   *Skirmish at Thompson's Station, Tennessee* (**Confederate Victory**)
   Union forces moved toward Thompson's Station, but were quickly surrounded by Confederate troops. The Union cavalry was able to escape, but the infantry was not as fortunate and the soldiers were taken prisoner.

	U.S.A.			*C.S.A.*	
	John Colburn			E. Van Dorn, William H. Jackson	
	Troops	*Killed*	*Wounded*	*Missing/Captured*	*Total Casualties*
U.S.A.	2,000	48	247	1,151	1,446
C.S.A.	Cav. Corps	150	450		600

8   *Mosby captured Union General E.H. Stoughton* at Fairfax Courthouse, Virginia.
   John S. Mosby, a Confederate guerilla, entered General Stoughton's bedroom as he slept. Mosby awakened him by giving Stoughton slap on his rear with a sword. Mosby informed the general that he was now a prisoner.

13–22   Union forces attempted once more to pass through the Yazoo River to get behind the Confederate forces located at Vicksburg, Mississippi. Again, the attempt failed.

15   *Engagement at Fort Anderson, North Carolina* (**Union Victory**)
   Confederate forces advanced on the Union garrison at New Bern, North Carolina, where they found it well manned. The Confederates, abandoning that idea, decided to move against the forces stationed at Fort Anderson. The Confederates withdrew when several Union gunboats sailed into view of the fort.

	U.S.A.				*C.S.A.*
	Hiram Anderson				D.H. Hill
	Troops	*Killed*	*Wounded*	*Missing/Captured*	*Total Casualties*
U.S.A.	5,000	2	4	1	7
C.S.A.	12,000				

17   *Battle of Kelly's Ford, Virginia* (**Confederate Victory**)
   Union cavalry operating near Culpeper Court House crossed the Rappahannock River and were challenged by Confederate cavalry operating in the vicinity. After a heated

exchange, the Union forces were driven back. In the course of the action, the "gallant" John Pelham was killed. He had come to "only witness" the cavalry fight.

	U.S.A.			C.S.A.	
William Woods Averell			James E.B. Stuart, F. Lee, J. Pelham (Killed)		
	Troops	Killed	Wounded	Missing/Captured	Total Casualties
U.S.A.	2,100	6	50	22	78
C.S.A.	800				170

20   *Engagement at Vaught's Hill, Tennessee* (**Union Victory**)
Union forces leaving Murfreesboro reconnoitered near Milton and came upon Morgan's Confederate cavalry. The Union troops pulled back to Milton but were pursued and encircled. The Confederates broke off the engagement when news was received that reinforcements were en route.

	U.S.A.			C.S.A.	
A.S. Hall				John H. Morgan	
	Troops	Killed	Wounded	Missing/Captured	Total Casualties
U.S.A.	1,300	7	48	7	62
C.S.A.	3,500	63	300	10	373

25   *Skirmish at Brentwood, Tennessee* (**Confederate Victory**)
Nathan Bedford Forrest ordered Confederate forces to seize the railroad station at Brentwood. The day before the attack, they cut the telegraph lines and tore up the tracks. They then moved against the garrison, calling for its surrender. At first, the garrison refused, but when the Confederates moved their artillery into position, they surrendered. The depot was a significant loss to the Union.

	U.S.A.			C.S.A.	
Edward Bloodgood				Nathan B. Forrest	
	Troops	Killed	Wounded	Missing/Captured	Total Casualties
U.S.A.	Division		3	748	751
C.S.A.	5,000	1	5		6

30–April 20   *Siege at Washington, North Carolina* (**Undetermined**)
Longstreet ordered Confederate forces to move against the Union garrison at Washington, North Carolina. After encircling the city, the Confederates were unable to prevent supplies and reinforcements from reaching the city and were forced to withdraw.

April 1863

2   Bread riots took place in Richmond, Virginia, when angry and hungry citizens mobbed a wagon in the heart of the city demanding bread. Some of the crowd broke into neighboring businesses, carrying off what they could. The riot ended peacefully when local militia and police dispersed the crowd without bloodshed after effecting several arrests.

7   *Engagement at Charleston Harbor, South Carolina* (**Confederate Victory**)

Rear Admiral Samuel F. DuPont sailed into Charleston Harbor with nine warships. Confederate batteries positioned at both Fort Sumter and Fort Moultrie confronted him. The Confederates were reported to have fired over 2,200 shells at the ships with good accuracy. At the same time, the Union ships were only able to fire a little over 150 shots. A week later, Lincoln ordered DuPont to hold his position just outside Charleston Harbor. Union ships involved were the USS *Keokuk*, USS *Weehawken*, USS *Passaic*, USS *Montauk*, USS *Patapsco*, USS *New Ironsides*, USS *Nahant*, USS *Catskill* and the USS *Nantucket*.

U.S.A.				C.S.A.	
S.F. DuPont				P.G.T. Beauregard, Roswell Sabine Ripley	
	Troops	*Killed*	*Wounded*	*Missing/Captured*	*Total Casualties*
U.S.A.	9 warships	1	22		23
C.S.A.		4	10		14

10   *Skirmish at Franklin, Tennessee* (**Union Victory**)

Confederate cavalry on reconnaissance came across Union skirmishers outside of Franklin. A fight ensued with reinforcements being brought up on both sides, forcing the Confederates to pull back.

U.S.A.				C.S.A.	
Gordon Granger, David S. Stanley				Earl Van Dorn, N.B. Forrest	
	Troops	*Killed*	*Wounded*	*Missing/Captured*	*Total Casualties*
U.S.A.	5,194	12	21	26	59
C.S.A.	Cav. Corps				137

11–May 4   General Longstreet, in conjunction with General Daniel H. Hill, began a siege of the Union garrison at Suffolk, Virginia, south of the James River. Several attempts were made to dislodge the Union troops from their encampments and, at the same time, mount an attack on Union shipping along the Nansemond River. Over the course of the month, numerous skirmishes occurred. On April 20, the Union troops were successful in capturing Hill's Point. On May 4, Longstreet abandoned the siege when he was ordered to rejoin the Army of Northern Virginia.

U.S.A.				C.S.A.	
John Peck				James Longstreet, Daniel H. Hill	
	Troops	*Killed*	*Wounded*	*Missing/Captured*	*Total Casualties*
U.S.A.	25,000				260
C.S.A.	20,000				900

12–13   *Engagement at Fort Bisland, Louisiana* (**Union Victory**)

Union troops began an expedition up the Bayou Teche toward Alexandria. The Confederates sent troops to stop the Union movement. Numerous skirmishes occurred before heavy artillery bombardment shook both sides. Union soldiers advanced to Fort Bisland as gunboats on the Atchafalaya River sent their shells into the fray. After it was discovered Union troops had managed to secure a landing in their rear, the Confederate troops packed up their supplies and withdrew, leaving Fort Bisland in Union hands.

U.S.A.				C.S.A.
Nathaniel P. Banks				Richard Taylor

	Troops	Killed	Wounded	Missing/Captured	Total Casualties
U.S.A.	4,000	40	184	10	234
C.S.A.	5,000				450

14   *Engagement at Irish Bend, Louisiana* (**Union Victory**)

Union troops moved up the Atchafalaya River to catch the Confederate troops fleeing from Fort Bisland. They met and scattered several Confederate units before becoming involved in heavy fighting. The Confederates pulled back when they realized they were outnumbered. This left the western part of Louisiana in Union hands.

U.S.A.				C.S.A.
Cuvier Grover				Richard Taylor

	Troops	Killed	Wounded	Missing/Captured	Total Casualties
U.S.A.	Division	49	274	30	353
C.S.A.	2 regiments				Not available

16   Admiral David D. Porter's fleet sailed down the Mississippi and passed below the guns of Vicksburg, setting up Grant's new campaign against Vicksburg, which would be concentrated below the city. Eleven of Porter's twelve ships made it past the Confederate batteries.

17   Colonel Benjamin Grierson began his raid through Mississippi hoping to draw or force Pemberton out of Vicksburg to meet him. Meanwhile, Confederate communications to Vicksburg were cut off.

17   *Skirmish at Vermilion Bayou, Louisiana* (**Union Victory**)

General Nathaniel P. Banks, hoping to catch Confederate General Richard Taylor as he fled with his men from Fort Bisland, confronted the Confederate force at Vermilion Bayou. Confederate artillery had been strategically placed and held off the Union advance. Union artillery was later brought up, and the artillery duel continued until dark. During the night, the Confederates made good their escape.

20   Lincoln announced that Congress had approved of West Virginia's admittance to the Union. The western section of Virginia had supported the Union cause and had broken from Virginia. West Virginia officially became a state on June 20, 1863.

26   *Skirmish at Cape Girardeau, Missouri* (**Union Victory**)

Marmaduke, believing Union forces under McNeil were at Cape Girardeau, ordered one of his brigades to make a demonstration against the Union fortifications. This demonstration escalated into a general skirmish. The brigade, realizing the Union force was much larger than suspected, pulled back.

	U.S.A.				C.S.A.
John McNeil					John S. Marmaduke
	Troops	*Killed*	*Wounded*	*Missing/Captured*	*Total Casualties*
U.S.A.	2,000				12
C.S.A.	Brigade				325

28–29   General Hooker marched his troops across the Rappahannock and the Rapidan rivers toward Chancellorsville, in what become known as "Stoneman's Raid." Union General Stoneman led his cavalry deep into the Confederate rear hoping to isolate Confederate troops from their supplies. As Stoneman and his men started, it began to rain and the rivers rose, preventing the Unions troops from crossing.

29   *Engagement at Grand Gulf, Mississippi* (**Confederate Victory**)

Admiral Porter led seven ironclads on the fortifications and batteries at Grand Gulf with the idea of not only silencing the Confederate guns but also securing the area for Union troops. Confederate batteries kept up their barrage on the ironclads. As the Confederate batteries were kept busy, General Grant moved his men below the Confederate strong points on the Mississippi River. Though termed a Confederate victory in that the ironclads withdrew, it was a shallow victory, for Union troops were now in position to control movement above and below Grand Gulf.

	U.S.A.				C.S.A.
David D. Porter					John S. Bowen
	Troops	*Killed*	*Wounded*	*Missing/Captured*	*Total Casualties*
U.S.A.	Regiment	26	54		80
C.S.A.	Division				Unknown

29   Lee ordered Longstreet to abandon his siege of Suffolk and to rejoin the Army of Northern Virginia at Fredericksburg.

29–May 1   *Affair at Snyder's Bluff* (**Confederate Victory**)

To make sure Confederate reinforcements were not sent to Grand Gulf, Union troops under William T. Sherman feigned an attack on Snyder's Bluff. Both land and naval forces were involved. The swampy terrain and heavy artillery from Louis Herbert's men forced the Union troops to withdraw.

30   *Raid on Day's Gap, Alabama* (**Union Victory**)

Union troops made a raid into Alabama to cut the tracks used by the Western and Atlantic Railroad, which carried supplies to the Confederate troops in middle Tennessee.

Near Day's Gap, the Confederate cavalry, which had been tracking the Union's movements, launched their attack. At first, the Confederates were repulsed, but for the next few days, these same troops engaged in numerous skirmishes in the vicinity. This raid was considered a Union victory, for the initial Confederate assault was repulsed within a few days. Ultimately, the exhausted Union troops would be surrounded by Confederate cavalry and would surrender on May 3.

U.S.A.				C.S.A.	
Abel Streight				Nathan Bedford Forrest	
	Troops	Killed	Wounded	Missing/Captured	Total Casualties
U.S.A.	5 regiments				23
C.S.A.	3 regiments				65

30   Grant began to cross the Mississippi below Vicksburg.

May 1863

1   *Battle of Port Gibson, Mississippi* (**Union Victory**)
   Unable to cross the Mississippi River at Grand Gulf, Union troops under Grant moved farther south to make the crossing at Bruinsburg. As they moved north, they ran into Confederate troops under Bowen, who was advancing along Rodney Road towards Port Gibson. After a day's fighting, the Confederates withdrew. This battle showed that the Confederates were unable to hold or defend the Mississippi River.

U.S.A.				C.S.A.	
U.S. Grant, John A. McClernand				John S. Bowen	
	Troops	Killed	Wounded	Missing/Captured	Total Casualties
U.S.A.	2 corps	131	719	25	875
C.S.A.	1 division				787

1   *Raid at Chalk Bluff, Arkansas* (**Confederate Victory**)
   Union troops clashed with Marmaduke in an attempt to prevent the Confederates from crossing the St. Francis River. Despite suffering heavy casualties, Confederate forces were able to get most of their men across the river.

U.S.A.	C.S.A.
John McNeil, William Vandever	John S. Marmaduke

1–4   *Battle of Chancellorsville, Virginia* (**Confederate Victory**)
   Union troops under General Joseph Hooker crossed the Rappahannock and Rapidan Rivers above Fredericksburg, concentrating near Chancellorsville. Lee marched east from Fredericksburg to meet the threat on the Confederates doorstep — Richmond. While making a night reconnaissance on May 2, Jackson was shot by his own men and Stuart assumed temporary command of Jackson's force. Outnumbered, Lee split his army, launching an

attack on both Union wings and breaking their lines. This forced Hooker to retreat. On May 3, Union troops assaulted and carried the Confederate entrenchment on Marye's Heights, forcing the Confederate troops to move west and southwest of Fredericksburg. That evening and the next day, fighting resumed near Salem's Church as Confederate forces held off Union troops under Sedgwick who were attempting to join up with Hooker west of the area.

U.S.A.				C.S.A.	
Joseph Hooker, John Sedgwick, George Meade, George Stoneman				Robert E. Lee, Thomas Jackson (Mortally wounded), A.P. Hill (wounded)	
	Troops	*Killed*	*Wounded*	*Missing/Captured*	*Total Casualties*
U.S.A.	133,868	1,606	9,762	5,919	17,287
C.S.A.	60,000	1,665	9,081	2,018	12,764

2 As Stonewall Jackson was making his way back to his camp after checking his lines, he was wounded by his own men. In the darkness, his men opened fire, believing they were under attack. Jackson was carried to a field hospital where his arm had to be amputated. General Ambrose P. Hill was wounded by enemy fire during the fighting on the 2nd. Hill would be absent for a brief period.

3 General Grierson reached the Union lines at Baton Rouge after devastating the Mississippi-Louisiana territory.

4 Fearing the Union presence near Chancellorsville, Stonewall Jackson was moved to a safer place twenty-five miles away near Guiney's Station. Jackson developed pneumonia, which would result in his death on May 10.

9 General Joseph Johnston received orders to "proceed at once" to Mississippi and take charge of the forces, while Pemberton continued to defend Vicksburg.

10 Thomas Jonathan "Stonewall" Jackson died while being cared for in a small house near Guiney's Station, Virginia.

12 *Battle of Raymond, Mississippi* (**Union Victory**)
Confederate forces moved toward Raymond to intercept Union forces moving toward Vicksburg. The Confederates held off the much larger body of troops and were able to delay their arrival.

U.S.A.				C.S.A.	
James B. McPherson, John Logan				John Gregg	
	Troops	*Killed*	*Wounded*	*Missing/Captured*	*Total Casualties*
U.S.A.	12,000	66	339	37	442
C.S.A.	4,000	72	252	190	514

14   *Engagement at Jackson, Mississippi* (**Union Victory**)

When General Johnston arrived in Jackson, he was informed of the imminent arrival of a heavy Union force, which had been dispatched to destroy the railroad link between Jackson and Vicksburg. Knowing that the Confederates would be overpowered, Johnston ordered the evacuation of Confederate troops from the city, asking General Gregg to try to hold back the Union troops until the evacuation was complete. Once in the city, Union soldiers burned part of the town and cut the railroad link. By evacuating Jackson, Vicksburg was left to fend for itself. As soon as the Union troops left to join in the siege of Vicksburg, Confederate forces re-entered the city.

U.S.A.				C.S.A.
U.S. Grant, William Sherman, James B. McPherson				Joseph Johnston, John Gregg

	Troops	Killed	Wounded	Missing/Captured	Total Casualties
U.S.A.	20,000	42	251	7	300
C.S.A.	6,000				850

16   *Battle of Champion's Hill, Mississippi (Baker's Creek)* (**Union Victory**)

Pemberton, against orders, decided to attack the Union supply wagons moving from Grand Gulf to Raymond. Johnston countermanded this order, instead ordering Pemberton to move toward the Union force gathering at Clinton. As he was turning to obey this order, Pemberton came across Grant's forces moving toward Vicksburg after taking and burning Jackson. Vicksburg was an important rail center that was badly needed by the Confederates. As Grant neared Vicksburg, he decided to cut off his supply lines and live off the Mississippi countryside.

U.S.A.				C.S.A.
John A. McClernand, James B. McPherson				John Pemberton, Lloyd Tilghman (Killed)

	Troops	Killed	Wounded	Missing/Captured	Total Casualties
U.S.A.	29,000	410	1,844	187	2,441
C.S.A.	20,000	381	1,800	1,670	3,851

17   *Battle of Big Black River Bridge, Mississippi* (**Union Victory**)

Confederate forces fleeing from Champion Hill reached Big Black River Bridge on the evening of the 16th, where they built fortifications and breastworks. Union troops, pursuing the fleeing Confederates, made a sudden frontal assault. Many of the Confederate troops fled across the Big Black River, burning the two bridges upon reaching the other side. This stopped the Union advance but many Confederate soldiers were captured. Pemberton, though, was able to make good his escape to Vicksburg.

U.S.A.	C.S.A.
John A. McClernard	John Pemberton, John S. Bowen

	Troops	Killed	Wounded	Missing/Captured	Total Casualties
U.S.A.	10,000	39	237	3	279
C.S.A.	8,000			1,700	1,700

18 *Siege of Vicksburg began.*

Union troops under General Grant converged on Vicksburg, surrounding the city and cutting it off from needed supplies and reinforcements. The city would surrender on July 4, 1863.

21 *Siege of Port Hudson, Louisiana began.*

In conjunction with the siege of Vicksburg, Union forces under General Nathaniel P. Banks moved against Port Hudson. After numerous skirmishes, the city would finally surrender on July 9 after hearing of the fall of Vicksburg.

21 *Skirmish at Plains Store, Louisiana* (**Union Victory**)

In an attempt to secure a landing place for Banks, Union troops advanced toward Plains Store and Bayou Sara Roads. As they approached Plains Store, they ran across Confederate cavalry bringing on a general engagement.

U.S.A.			*C.S.A.*		
Christopher C. Augur			Frank P. Powers, William R. Miles		

	Troops	Killed	Wounded	Missing/Captured	Total Casualties
U.S.A.	Division	15	71	14	100
C.S.A.	Division				

27 *First assault on Port Hudson, Louisiana* (**Confederate Victory**)

With his men in position, Banks attempted to assault and capture Port Hudson. Confederate troops held off the attack, forcing the Union to resume its siege operations against the city.

U.S.A.			*C.S.A.*		
Nathaniel P. Banks			Franklin Gardner		

	Troops	Killed	Wounded	Missing/Captured	Total Casualties
U.S.A.	13,000	239	1,545	157	1,941
C.S.A.	4,500				235

28 The First Negro Unit, 54th Massachusetts, left Boston to join the Union army.

30 General Robert E. Lee revamped his army after the death of Jackson. He divided his army into three corps, promoting both A.P. Hill and R.S. Ewell to the position of lieutenant general.

June 1863

1 General Ambrose Burnside ordered the *Chicago Times* to cease publication because of its anti–Union sentiments.

3 Lee, with the Army of Northern Virginia, left Fredericksburg in a second attempt to take the war northwards. He first moved westward, then turned north upon reaching South Mountain. He left General Hill's Third Corps behind in Fredericksburg temporarily to give the impression the army was still in position. This was the start of the Gettysburg campaign.

5 *Engagement at Franklin's Crossing, Virginia* (**Confederate Victory**)
Receiving news that there was a Confederate force on the move, Union forces under John Sedgwick attempted to cross the Rappahannock River at Franklin's Crossing where Ambrose P. Hill's Third Corps met them. The Union troops pulled back, convinced that Lee's army was still occupying the area near Richmond.

7 *Engagement at Milliken's Bend, Louisiana* (**Union Victory**)
Confederate soldiers attacked Union troops near Milliken's Bend and at first were driven inward. The Union troops, consisting of several African brigades, pursued and became involved in severe hand-to-hand fighting with the Texas brigade commanded by Henry McCullough. The fight seesawed and the Union troops had to pull back to the edge of the river. As they did, two Union ironclads, the *Choctaw* and the *Lexington*, steamed up the river and fired upon the pursing Confederates. By late afternoon, Confederate forces pulled back toward Walnut Bayou.

	U.S.A.				C.S.A.	
	Hermann Lieb				Henry E. McCulloch	
	Troops	*Killed*	*Wounded*	*Missing/Captured*	*Total Casualties*	
U.S.A.	1,061	101	285	266	652	
C.S.A.	2,700	150	300		450	

9 *Battle of Brandy Station, Virginia* (AKA Fleetwood Hill or Beverly's Ford) (**Undetermined**)
Considered by some historians to be the greatest cavalry battle ever fought on American soil. Union cavalry with a few infantry units from the Army of the Potomac crossed the Rappahannock River and surprised the Confederate cavalry of the Army of Northern Virginia. The contest for several low hills resulted in a daylong battle. The battle is considered significant because it was the first time the Union cavalry was able to hold its own against the Confederates. Both sides claimed victory.

	U.S.A.				C.S.A.	
	Alfred Pleasonton				J.E.B. Stuart	
	Troops	*Killed*	*Wounded*	*Missing/Captured*	*Total Casualties*	
U.S.A.	10,000	81	403	382	866	
C.S.A.	10,000				523	

14 *Second assault on Port Hudson, Louisiana* (**Confederate Victory**)
When Confederate forces refused to surrender Port Hudson, as demanded by General

Banks, an assault was begun at dawn by Union troops. After numerous attempts, Banks was forced to retreat after failure to gain any ground.

		U.S.A.			*C.S.A.*
		Nathaniel Banks			Franklin Gardner
	Troops	*Killed*	*Wounded*	*Missing/Captured*	*Total Casualties*
U.S.A.	6,000	203	1,401	188	1,792
C.S.A.	3,750	22	25		47

14–15   Second *Battle of Winchester, Virginia* (**Confederate Victory**)

After Brandy Station, Lee ordered Ewell to clear the Shenandoah Valley of Union troops. Ewell moved on Winchester, forcing Milroy to flee towards Charles Town. The pursuing Confederates soon overtook the fleeing Union troops. This Confederate victory cleared the valley of Union opposition and made way for Lee's invasion of the North.

		U.S.A.			*C.S.A.*
		Robert Milroy			Richard S. Ewell, Edward Johnson
	Troops	*Killed*	*Wounded*	*Missing/Captured*	*Total Casualties*
U.S.A.	6,900	95	348	4,000	4,443
C.S.A.	12,500	47	219	3	269

16   Lee's army started across the Potomac River, using the Blue Ridge Mountains as a screen.

17   *Skirmish at Aldie, Virginia* (**Undetermined**)

Union cavalry, in pursuit of Confederate troops moving behind the Blue Ridge Mountains, came across Thomas Munford's Confederate cavalry near Aldie. The ensuing fight lasted for four hours and, in the end, the Confederates withdrew when Judson Kilpatrick received reinforcements.

17–19   *Skirmish at Middleburg, Virginia* (**Undetermined**)

Union and Confederate cavalry clashed once more as J.E.B. Stuart's Confederate army moved behind the Blue Ridge Mountains toward Pennsylvania. David M. Gregg led Union forces.

20   West Virginia became the 35th state in the Union.

20–21   Engagement *at LaFourche Crossing, Louisiana* (**Union Victory**)

Confederate raiders were disrupting Union activities by conducting raids on not only Union ships and troops but plantations as well. Union troops under Stickney were sent to stop the raids. Confronting the Confederate forces, Union troops were able to drive them from the field after several days of skirmishing. It was considered a Union victory, as the Union was in command of the field at the close of the engagement.

	U.S.A.				C.S.A.
	Albert Stickney				James P. Major

	Troops	Killed	Wounded	Missing/Captured	Total Casualties
U.S.A.	838	8	41		49
C.S.A.	1,200				219

21 *Skirmish at Upperville, Virginia* (**Undetermined**)

As the Confederate army crossed the Potomac into Maryland, Stuart's cavalry once more sparred with Union cavalry sent to locate where the Confederate army had disappeared.

U.S.A.	C.S.A.
Alfred Pleasonton, John Buford	Wade Hampton, Beverly Robertson, William Jones

24–26 *Engagement at Hoover's Gap, Tennessee* (**Union Victory**)

Fearing that Confederate forces under Bragg might try to reinforce Vicksburg, Union officials launched an assault. Fighting extended along the Confederate line near Hoover's Gap as the Confederates were forced to pull back. To prevent them from crossing the Elk River Bridge, the Lighting Brigade was sent to burn the bridge, but arrived too late. Bragg escaped, leaving middle Tennessee in Union hands.

U.S.A.	C.S.A.
George H. Thomas	Alexander P. Stewart

25 J.E.B. Stuart began his third ride around the Army of the Potomac, leaving Lee without a scouting force or the "eyes and ears of his army."

28 Confederates marched in and seized York, Pennsylvania.

28 Major General George G. Meade replaced General Joseph Hooker as commander of the Army of the Potomac.

28 *Skirmish at Donaldsonville, Louisiana* (**Union Victory**)

Confederate forces under Green and Major were ordered to seize Donaldsonville. Before they could take the town, they first had to capture Fort Butler. Unable to clear a ditch, the Confederate force came under fire from a Union gunboat coming down the Mississippi.

U.S.A.	C.S.A.
Joseph D. Bullen	Tom Green, James P. Major

	Troops	Killed	Wounded	Missing/Captured	Total Casualties
U.S.A.	2 companies	9	15		24
C.S.A.	2 brigades				301

29 Lee moved toward Gettysburg. Stuart was still moving around the Union line. At the same time, Union forces concentrated north of the Potomac.

29–30 Engagement *at Goodrick's Landing, Louisiana* (**Undetermined**)

As Union forces began to have success in Louisiana, many slaves ran away from their owners and flocked to the Union lines. Setting up plantations, these now freed slaves worked the plantations to provide the Union with much needed supplies. Confederate forces under William H. Parsons attempted to destroy these plantations, burning them as they went, as Union forces under Alfred W. Ellet moved down the river to confront the invaders. The attacks resulted in minor setbacks for the Union.

30 *Skirmish at Hanover, Pennsylvania* (**Undetermined**)

Confederate cavalry, moving northward, came across the Union cavalry near Hanover and drove it through the city. As soon as they were reinforced, Union troops under H. Judson Kilpatrick forced J.E.B. Stuart to abandon the fight and move eastward. When he discovered that Lee's army had engaged Union troops near Gettysburg on the 1st, Stuart turned northward to rejoin Lee. Stuart's would not rejoin the Army of Northern Virginia until July 2, after the fighting had begun.

July 1863

1–3 *Battle of Gettysburg, Pennsylvania* (**Union Victory**)

One of the most decisive battles in human history, the Battle of Gettysburg was started almost by accident when Union and Confederate cavalry ran into each other on the outskirts of the town on July 1. Hill's corps was moving along the Chambersburg-Gettysburg Pike when they ran into Buford's cavalry. Buford, aware of Confederates in the area, had posted his men along the pike. By the end of the first day, the Union line ran from Spangler's Spring and Culp's Hill on the North along Cemetery Ridge to Little Round Top on the South. The Confederates established a line on Seminary Ridge, facing the Union line. On the second day of the battle, Lee's forces attacked the Union's flanks but failed to drive them in. On the third day, the Confederate attack was made on the center of the Union line and that attack would forever be known as Pickett's Charge, named for the commander — George E. Pickett. The Confederates began the attack with an artillery barrage that rocked the countryside for more than two hours. Afterwards, Pickett's 's division of Virginians stepped out to walk across an open field toward the Union line, where they were greeted by Union cannon filled with double and sometimes triple canister. Pickett's division was almost annihilated in the last major action of the battle. Picket lost 75 percent of his men, including all of his brigade commanders; two were killed and one severely wounded and captured. On the morning of the 4th, Lee took his army back to Virginia. The line was reported to have been in excess of seventeen miles long. Meade was reprimanded for failing to follow or pursue Lee even though he had ordered his cavalry to do so.

U.S.A.	*C.S.A.*
George G. Meade, Winfield Scott Hancock, Daniels Sickles, George Sykes, Henry Slocum, O.O. Howard	Robert E. Lee, James Longstreet, Richard Ewell, A.P. Hill

	Troops	Killed	Wounded	Missing/Captured	Total Casualties
U.S.A.	85,000	3,155	14,529	5,365	23,049
C.S.A.	65,000	3,903	18,735	5,425	28,063

1–2 *Skirmish at Cabin Creek, Oklahoma* (**Union Victory**)

Confederate forces under the command of Colonel Stand Watie attacked the command of Colonel James M. Williams. Williams commanded the colored troops who were moving supplies from Fort Scott, Kansas, to Fort Gibson, Oklahoma. The Union soldiers, using artillery and cavalry charges, were able to drive the Confederates off and continued to make their way to Fort Gibson.

U.S.A.					C.S.A.
James M. Williams					Stand Watie

	Troops	Killed	Wounded	Missing/Captured	Total Casualties
U.S.A.	2,000	1	20	2	23
C.S.A.	1,800				65

4 *Skirmish at Helena, Arkansas* (**Union Victory**)

In an effort to relieve the pressure on Vicksburg, Confederate forces attacked Helena, Arkansas. Instead of drawing the Union men from the Vicksburg siege lines, troops stationed at Helena were able to drive the Confederates off. This opened the door to move against Little Rock.

U.S.A.					C.S.A.
Benjamin Prentiss					Theophilus H. Holmes

	Troops	Killed	Wounded	Missing/Captured	Total Casualties
U.S.A.		57	146	36	239
C.S.A.		37	194	121	352

4 *Vicksburg, Mississippi surrendered* (**Union Victory**)

Pemberton surrendered his army, his men and the city to General Grant, who pardoned the soldiers.

Totals for entire Vicksburg sieges

U.S.A.					C.S.A.
U.S. Grant, W.T. Sherman					John C. Pemberton

	Troops	Killed	Wounded	Missing/Captured	Total Casualties
U.S.A.	45,000	502	2,550	147	3,199
C.S.A.	12,000		500		12,000

6–16 As the Confederate army pulled back from Gettysburg, Stuart's cavalry with Union cavalry in close pursuit screened their movement. By the 7th, Confederate cavalry had moved into Williamsport, Maryland, holding that area for the infantry's arrival. Lee's army arrived on the 8th, but was unable to cross the Potomac River. The river was swollen due to the recent rains and a bridge across the river had been destroyed. Over the next few days, Lee's men constructed a new bridge and, as soon as the flooding subsided, Lee was finally able to cross into Virginia. During the entire time, his army was under heavy skirmishing, resulting in a total casualty loss of over 1,700 men for both sides. The Union army did not pursue into Virginia until days later.

8 *Port Hudson, Louisiana fell under Union control*

The Mississippi River was now completely under Union control. Grant's campaign against Confederate forces in the West had resulted in a siege and numerous assaults, which ultimately resulted in the capture of not only Vicksburg but also Port Hudson, a strategically vital Mississippi River city.

8 A siege was begun of Battery Wagner in Charleston Harbor, South Carolina, by Union forces in preparation for the capture Charleston.

8 *Skirmish at Corydon, Indiana* (**Confederate Victory**)

John Hunt Morgan, despite orders not to leave Kentucky, crossed the Ohio River on the 7th and entered Indiana. The local militia was called out. Near Corydon, about 400 members of the Home Guard challenged Morgan and his raiders. The Confederates captured the majority of the Home Guard before moving toward Ohio, where they burned bridges and supply depots. At the same time, they tore up the railroad track.

		U.S.A.			C.S.A.	
		Lewis Jordan			John Hunt Morgan	
	Troops	*Killed*	*Wounded*	*Missing/Captured*	*Total Casualties*	
U.S.A.	400				360	
C.S.A.	1,800				41	

10–11 *Bombardment of Battery Wagner, South Carolina begins* (**Confederate Victory**)

In an effort to capture Charleston, South Carolina, Union forces under Quincy Gilmore moved on Morris Island, which was guarded by a small Confederate earthen fort known as Battery Wagner. William B. Taliaferro was in command of the fort. A bombardment began as forty-one cannon and seven gunboats blasted away at the fort for over seven hours. By morning, three infantry regiments moved out to make the assault on the fort. When the attack and his frontal charge failed, Gilmore instituted a siege and maintained a constant bombardment of the fort.

12–13 *Engagement at Kock's Plantation, Louisiana* (AKA Bayou LaFourche) (**Confederate Victory**)

With the fall of Port Hudson on the 8th, Union troops were moved inland to control inner Louisiana. As the brigade led by Colonel Nathan A.M. Dudley went down the west side of the bayou, Joseph S. Morgan took his men to the east bank. On July 12th, they ran into several Confederate brigades posted on both sides of the bayou near Kock's Plantation in Ascension Parish. Despite overwhelming numbers, the Union troops had to pull back to Donaldsonville, leaving the Confederates in charge of the interior. Later, a Union investigation of the incident found that Morgan had been drunk during the engagement. He was court-martialed and ultimately dismissed from the army.

		U.S.A.			C.S.A.	
		Godfrey Wietzel, Cuvier Grover			Thomas Green	
	Troops	*Killed*	*Wounded*	*Missing/Captured*	*Total Casualties*	
U.S.A.	6,000	56	223	186	465	
C.S.A.	1,200	3	30		33	

13   John Hunt Morgan, along with 2,400 cavalrymen, crossed the Ohio River and entered Indiana, where they conducted numerous raids across the countryside. In addition to destroying railroad tracks and bridges, they also captured several Union garrisons, burning depots and stealing horses. While they were setting things ablaze, many of Morgan's men also plundered private businesses and residences.

13–16   New York City draft riots occurred and General Meade was ordered to send troops to quell the riots.

14   Lee's army finally made their way across the Potomac River, ending his second and last invasion of the North. Lee's army settled south of Orange Court House.

16   *Engagement at Grimball's Landing, South Carolina* (**Undetermined**)

     To distract Confederate forces from renewing their resistance of Battery Wagner, Terry landed on James Island on the 7th and was immediately attacked by Confederate forces. The attack was disorganized and soon collapsed. Union forces withdrew from the island the next day. Their mission was deemed a success, for no additional Confederate troops were sent to defend Battery Wagner.

		U.S.A.			C.S.A.	
		Alfred H. Terry			Johnson Hagood	
	Troops	*Killed*	*Wounded*	*Missing/Captured*	*Total Casualties*	
U.S.A.	3,800	14	20	12	46	
C.S.A.	3,000	3	12	3	18	

17   *Engagement at Honey Springs, Oklahoma* (**Union Victory**)

     Blunt, anticipating an attack would be launched on Fort Gibson as soon as additional Confederate troops arrived at Honey Springs from Fort Smith, decided to attack Honey Springs before their arrival. The attack was deemed successful, for the Confederates were forced to pull back and abandon any idea of attacking Fort Gibson in the near future. For now, the Union was in control of the Indian Territory north of the Arkansas River.

U.S.A.	C.S.A.
James G. Blunt	Douglas H. Cooper

	Troops	Killed	Wounded	Missing/Captured	Total Casualties
U.S.A. Division		13	62		75
C.S.A. Brigade		150	400	77	627

17 *Abandonment of Jackson, Mississippi* (**Union Victory**)

Upon the surrender of Vicksburg and Port Hudson, Confederate forces under General Joseph Johnston pulled back to Jackson, Mississippi. General Grant ordered Sherman to pursue and, if possible, capture Johnston. Knowing the Confederates were well entrenched at Jackson, Sherman decided on a siege rather than sacrifice his men. Johnston realized that he had but one chance to pull out and took it, leaving the city open to Union devastation. According to one bystander, the city was "one mass of charred ruins."

18 *Assault on Fort Wagner (AKA Morris Island), South Carolina* (**Confederate Victory**)

Confederate artillery aided by the battery at Fort Sumter helped stem the repeated Union assaults on the fort. Nearly half of the assaulting troops of the 54th Massachusetts Colored Infantry were killed in their failed attack on this strong point, near Charleston Harbor. Among the fallen was their commander, Colonel Robert G. Shaw. Though many of the black soldiers were killed, their bravery and determination in the assault convinced Northerners that the blacks could and would fight valiantly, and if needed, would fight to the end and die to win freedom for their race.

U.S.A.	C.S.A.
George Strong, H.S. Putnam, Robert G. Shaw (all killed)	William Taliaferro, P.G.T. Beauregard

	Troops	Killed	Wounded	Missing/Captured	Total Casualties
U.S.A.	6,000	246	880	389	1,515
C.S.A.	1,785	36	133	5	174

19 Union troops believed they had trapped John Hunt Morgan near Buffington, Ohio. Morgan and 400 of his men avoided capture when Union Commander General Edward H. Hobson's brigade captured half of Morgan's raiders. Morgan was now trapped in northern Ohio.

21–23 Pursuing Lee into Virginia, Union troops under General William H. French tried to cut off the retreat at Front Royal by forcing the Confederates to move through Manassas Gap. Part of Richard Anderson's division was trapped but, by evening, additional troops from Robert Rodes' division arrived to help Anderson's men. During the night, the Confederates were able to withdraw to the Luray Valley, leaving the Union in command of Front Royal.

24–28 *General Henry H. Sibley put down an uprising of the Santee and Teton Sioux Indians under Chief Inkpaduta in the North Dakota Territory.*

Numerous skirmishes took place at Big Mound, Dead Buffalo Lake and Stony Lake. The Santee Sioux had initiated an Indian uprising the previous year and now had joined forces with the Teton Sioux. Members of the tribe had feigned friendship with the Union troops and when their guard was down, the Indians launched an attack on the 24th. Bringing up his artillery, Sibley was able to drive the Indians off but they renewed the skirmish on the following days. On the 28th, the Sioux prepared to make another attack, but after probing the Union positions, decided to abandon it. The Indians left at "great speed, preventing pursuit, " Sibley later remarked. He said it was "the greatest conflict between our troops and the Indians, so far as numbers are concerned."[2]

26   *Union troops capture John Hunt Morgan in Ohio*
      Morgan and his men had tried to find a safe place to cross back into Kentucky. He was spotted on the 26th and pursued by Union cavalry who finally caught him near Salineville, Ohio. In the course of his raids in Indiana and Ohio, Morgan had destroyed thirty-four bridges, tore up railroad tracks in sixty different places, and captured approximately 6,000 Union troops and local militia. At the same time, Morgan and his raiders burned and destroyed tons of Union supplies.

August 1863

5   Union cavalry commander William W. Averell began to make raids in western Virginia to destroy gunpowder mills scattered throughout the Allegheny Mountains.

16   Union forces began moving toward Tennessee in what would become known as the Chickamauga Campaign.

17–23   Union batteries on Morris Island opened fire on not only Fort Sumter but also on Charleston Harbor. The Confederates, stationed at Fort Wagner, turned their guns upon the Union batteries positioned on Morris Island.

21–September 8   Union General William S. Rosecrans moved the Army of the Cumberland toward Chattanooga with intentions of taking the city. In the meantime, Confederate commander Braxton Bragg concentrated his forces northeast of the city, believing the attack would come from that direction. Over the course of the next few weeks, sporadic shelling of the city occurred.

21   Confederate raider William C. Quantrill with 450 guerillas sacked Lawrence, Kansas, killing 140 civilians. It is suspected that the raid was in retaliation for the death of four women who had been held prisoner in a dilapidated building in Kansas City. That building had collapsed on August 14, killing the four women and injuring many others. Union General Thomas Ewing had arrested the women, suspecting them of aiding Quantrill. Members of Quantrill's raiders would later gain their own fame after the war: Jesse James, his brother Frank, and the Younger Brothers were all members of Quantrill's raiders.

26   *Engagement at Rocky Gap, West Virginia* (**Confederate Victory**)
      General Averell's cavalry moved to attack a gunpowder mill near White Sulphur Springs, West Virginia. Two miles from the location, they came across Confederate troops near Rocky Gap who were ordered to defend the gunpowder mill. After several unsuccessful attempts to dislodge the Confederate force, Averell pulled his men back.

	Troops	Killed	Wounded	Missing/Captured	Total Casualties
U.S.A.	2,000	20	125	67	212
C.S.A.	1,900	26	129	13	168

William W. Averell (U.S.A.) — *George S. Patton* (C.S.A.)

September 1863

1 *Action at Devil's Backbone, Arkansas* (**Union Victory**)
Ordered to pursue the Confederate soldiers fleeing Fort Smith, Colonel Cloud was ambushed by General Cabell near Devil's Backbone. Cabell was gaining ground until Cloud, with the assistance of artillery, made a charge that routed the Confederates.

Colonel William F. Cloud (U.S.A.) — *General William L. Cabell* (C.S.A.)

	Troops	Killed	Wounded	Missing/Captured	Total Casualties
U.S.A.	2 regiments	4	12		16
C.S.A.	1 brigade				65

2 Union troops commanded by Ambrose E. Burnside occupied Knoxville, Tennessee.

3–5 *Skirmish at Whitestone Hill, North Dakota* (**Union Victory**)
After General Sibley defeated the Sioux Indians, the Indians decided to return to their old lands and not the reservation. General Sully took it upon himself to pursue the Indians and punish them. When he ran across the tribe near Whitestone Hill, many were killed and many Indian women and children were taken prisoner. Historians believe the military action weakened but did not destroy resistance on the part of the Indians in the area.

Alfred Sully (U.S.A.) — *Chief Inkpaduta* (C.S.A.)

	Troops	Killed	Wounded	Missing/Captured	Total Casualties
U.S.A.	700				72
Indians	1,500				750

4 General William S. Rosecrans chased Confederate commander Braxton Bragg across the Tennessee River as he moved toward Chattanooga.

5 The British were building ships for the Confederacy and, by early September, had two rams ready for delivery. United States Minister Charles Francis Adams informed Lord Russell that if the two rams were delivered, it would amount to declaring war on the United States. The British stopped shipbuilding for the Confederacy.

6–7   The Confederates evacuated Battery Wagner during the night. As soon as it was discovered that the fort was empty, Union commander General Quincy Gillmore ordered his 11,000-man force to occupy it. Now, Union forces occupied all of Morris Island.

8   *Attack on Fort Sumter, South Carolina* (**Confederate Victory**)
     With the Union in command of Morris Island, Gillmore decided it was now time to capture Fort Sumter. He was aware that only a small contingent of soldiers guarded it. At the same time, Admiral John A. Dahlgren believed it was the Navy's responsibility to capture of the fort. On the evening of the 8th, several boats carrying soldiers were launched to take the fort but the Confederates were ready and opened fire when the Union boats were less than 50 yards away. At the same time, Confederate batteries from Sullivan and Johnson Island opened fire, damaging every boat. The majority of Union soldiers were either killed or taken prisoner.

U.S.A.			C.S.A.	
Admiral John A. Dahlgren, Quincy Gillmore			Major Stephen Elliott	

	Troops	Killed	Wounded	Missing/Captured	Total Casualties
U.S.A.	Unknown	3		114	117
C.S.A.	320				0

8   *Action at Telford (AKA Limestone Station), Tennessee* (**Confederate Victory**)
     Confederates under Lt. Col. Love were ordered to guard the various railroad bridges in the Telford area. As the 100th Ohio Infantry Regiment attempted to cross a bridge, Love's men assaulted them. As the Union troops tried to escape the onslaught, they ran down the tracks to a limestone blockhouse where they entrenched. The blockhouse was attacked on all sides as the assault continued, forcing the soldiers inside to surrender or perish.

U.S.A.			C.S.A.	
Lt. Col. Edwin L. Hayes			Lt. Col. James R. Love	

	Troops	Killed	Wounded	Missing/Captured	Total Casualties
U.S.A.	300	12	20	240	272
C.S.A.	1,800				20

8   *Action at Sabine Pass, Texas* (**Confederate Victory**)
     Union ships sailed up the Sabine River intending to take Fort Griffin and, at the same time, land Union soldiers on Texas soil. They wanted to not only capture Houston but also the state. The Confederates in the fort had been spending their spare time in target practice and as Union ships sailed up the river, they were struck by accurate artillery firing, destroying or damaging the ships. The Union sailed back down the river and returned to Louisiana. (The 44-man Davis Guard, defending the fort, had been confined at Fort Griffin for punishment. Their crime was listed as "riotous and mutinous conduct.")

U.S.A.	C.S.A.
William B. Franklin, Frederick Cooper	Lt. Richard Dowling

	Troops	Killed	Wounded	Missing/Captured	Total Casualties
U.S.A.	5,000 men				230
	4 gunboats				
	7 transports				
C.S.A.	44 men				Unknown

8   Bragg left Chattanooga. Longstreet, with his First Corps, would soon join him.

9   Union troops entered and now occupied Chattanooga, Tennessee.

9   *Surrender of Cumberland Gap, Tennessee* (**Union Victory**)
   Confederate troops left Knoxville to aid Bragg at Chattanooga, leaving behind a small contingent of soldiers with orders to hold Cumberland Gap at all costs. With Burnside now in Knoxville and another Union force on the other side, Cumberland Gap was virtually surrounded. The Union demanded the surrender of the small southern force there. Twice the Confederates refused but when a stronger force came out of Knoxville, Frazier and his men surrendered, turning the gap over to the Union. Frazier was condemned by President Davis for his "cowardly action" and would spend the rest of the war as a prisoner of the United States government.

9   Confederate General James Longstreet, detached from the Army of Northern Virginia, began moving toward Tennessee, where he and his men would assist General Braxton Bragg. Due to the surrender of Cumberland Gap, Longstreet was forced to travel first east to Richmond and then south to North Carolina and Georgia before heading on to Tennessee. He used the railroad to move his troops, which took about ten days.

9   *Engagement at Bayou Forche, Arkansas* (**Union Victory**)
   While trying to advance on Little Rock, Union cavalry ran into a small contingent of Confederates near Bayou Forche. With the use of artillery, the Union drove the Confederates from the location, opening the door for the Union to take possession of Little Rock.

U.S.A.				*C.S.A.*	
John W. Davidson				John S. Marmaduke	

	Troops	Killed	Wounded	Missing/Captured	Total Casualties
U.S.A.	Cav. Division	7	64	1	72
C.S.A.	1,200	6	18	13	37

14   President Lincoln suspended the writ of habeas corpus throughout the nation, affecting how military or civil authorities held persons or suspects in custody.

19–20   *Battle of Chickamauga, Georgia* (**Confederate Victory**)
   The encounter between two large enemy armies resulted in equally enormous casualties for both. Longstreet broke through the Union lines, but Thomas delayed him long enough to allow Rosecrans and his battered army to evacuate safely to Chattanooga. Bragg did not follow and lost a great opportunity to finish off Rosecrans' army.

	U.S.A.			C.S.A.	
William S. Rosecrans, George H. Thomas, Thomas J. Wood, Gordon Granger			Braxton Bragg, James Longstreet, Leonidas Polk, Nathan B. Forrest		

	Troops	Killed	Wounded	Missing/Captured	Total Casualties
U.S.A.	58,000	1,657	9,756	4,757	16,170
C.S.A.	66,000	2,312	14,674	1,468	18,454

22 *Engagement at Blountville, Tennessee* (**Union Victory**)

Union troops, in an effort to clear the roads from eastern Tennessee to Virginia, ran into a small Confederate force near Blountville. After four hours of fighting, the Confederates withdrew. According to some historians, this was the initial step to securing East Tennessee.

	U.S.A.			C.S.A.	
Colonel John W. Foster			James C. Carter		

	Troops	Killed	Wounded	Missing/Captured	Total Casualties
U.S.A.	Brigade	5	22		27
C.S.A.	1,200				165

22 *Skirmish at Jack's Shop (AKA Madison Court House, Rochelle, Liberty Mills), Virginia* (**Undetermined**)

Union cavalry under Buford entered Madison Court House intending to join up with Kilpatrick's Cavalry near Liberty Mills. They were to conduct reconnaissance of Lee's army encamped near Orange Court House. Lee, aware of Union movement, had Stuart's cavalry on the alert when they came across Union cavalry near Rochelle. Buford's cavalry attacked from one end and Kilpatrick from the other in an attempt to cut off Stuart's escape route. With the use of his horse artillery, Stuart charged in both directions, preventing his capture. Union claimed victory as Buford reported the Confederate cavalry was dispersed and the reconnaissance made. The Confederacy claimed victory in that Buford pulled back to Madison Court House.

23 *Confederates begin to lay siege to Chattanooga, Tennessee.*

Bragg did not follow the Union forces as they fled from Chickamauga, but instead entrenched at Missionary Ridge and Lookout Mountain, where he laid siege to Chattanooga. In Chattanooga, the Union troops eagerly awaited food supplies believed to be en route by wagon trains. The men had been on half rations for several weeks following their defeat at the Battle of Chickamauga.

29 *Action at Stirling's (Sterling's) Plantation, Louisiana* (**Confederate Victory**)

General Banks ordered Major General Napoleon J.T. Dana to keep Confederate troops from operating on the Atchafalaya River, for Banks intended to use the river to launch attacks on various outposts in Texas. Confederate troops in the area, at the same time, decided to remove the Union presence in the area. Green and Moulton launched their attacks and drove the Union men from their posts.

	U.S.A.			C.S.A.	
	Napoleon J.T. Dana, Colonel J.B. Leake			Tom Green, Alfred Moulton	

	Troops	Killed	Wounded	Missing/Captured	Total Casualties
U.S.A.	1,000	16	45	454	515
C.S.A.	unknown				unknown

October 1863

1   General Braxton Bragg ordered Confederate General Joseph Wheeler to disrupt the Union supply lines. With 4,000 cavalrymen, Wheeler crossed the Tennessee River near Washington, Tennessee, to begin a very successful and damaging raid. In the course of the weeklong raid, Wheeler destroyed over a thousand wagons carrying supplies, burned Union supply depots at McMinnville and Shelbyville, ripped up miles of railroad tracks and destroyed five critical bridges.

1   On the first day of his raid, Wheeler, dividing his force, took 1,500 men and descended on Walden Ridge, Tennessee, where they captured and destroyed thirty-two wagons. When Union officials heard that their wagon trains had been destroyed, they placed the troops at Chattanooga on quarter rations.

5   *Naval Engagement between CSS* David *and USS* New Ironsides (**Confederate Victory**)
    Intent on sinking the *New Ironsides*, the most powerful boat in the Union fleet blockading Charleston Harbor, the CSS *David*, a torpedo boat under Lt. William T. Glassel, sailed out of the harbor making its way through the Union fleet. It was spotted only after it had rammed the *New Ironsides*. Some of the crew were forced to abandon the ship, but it was able to limp back into the Charleston Harbor. The *New Ironsides*, under Admiral John A. Dahlgren, received severe damage and was forced to return to its home port for needed repairs.

6   *Action at Baxter Springs, Kansas* (**Confederate Victory**)
    William Quantrill, moving toward his winter quarters, came upon a Union wagon train moving supplies from Fort Scott to Fort Smith. The majority of the wagon train was captured and many of the soldiers were either killed or captured. Union commander James G. Blunt, who was leading the train, was able to make good his escape. Blunt was removed from command for failing to protect his men but was later restored.

	U.S.A.			C.S.A.	
	Gen. James G. Blunt,			William C. Quantrill,	
	Lt. James B. Pond			David Poole	

	Troops	Killed	Wounded	Missing/Captured	Total Casualties
U.S.A.	3 regiments				103
C.S.A.	400				3

7 *Action at Farmington, Tennessee* (**Undetermined**)

After doing all the damage they could to disrupt Union supplies headed for the besieged troops in Chattanooga, Wheeler and his cavalry attempted to re-cross the Tennessee River. Union Commander General George Crook's cavalry, sent to capture Wheeler, found him near Farmington. In a desperate attempt to escape, Wheeler was forced to sacrifice General George B. Hodge's brigade. After reaching safety, Wheeler provided support, allowing the remaining portion of Hodge's brigade to escape and make their way to safety.

	U.S.A.			*C.S.A.*	
	George Crook			Joseph Wheeler, George B. Hodges	
	Troops	*Killed*	*Wounded*	*Missing/Captured*	*Total Casualties*
U.S.A.	25,000	15	60	0	75
C.S.A.	4,000	10	60	240	310

9 *Bristoe, Virginia, campaign begins*

Upon learning that General Lee had detached two divisions of Longstreet's corps, Meade put his army in motion, moving them into Culpeper County and keeping Lee below the Rapidan River. Lee at the same time learned Meade had also detached several corps to Tennessee. Lee decided now was the time to move his army northward, hoping to drive the Union from southern soil. He wanted to get in the Union rear to force a fight of his choosing while Meade was looking for a place to do battle. On the 9th, Lee moved his men around the right flank of the Union army as Meade withdrew toward Washington.

9 *Engagement at Blue Springs, Tennessee* (**Union Victory**)

With the Union in control of the Cumberland Gap, Confederate forces attempted to disrupt Union activities in the area. Confederate commander General John Williams wanted to capture the East Tennessee and Virginia Railroad. From the 3rd of the month, Union and Confederate forces skirmished almost daily until an overwhelming number of Union troops had almost completely encircled the Confederates on the 10th. With well-placed artillery, Williams was able to break out of the net as he and his small band made good their escape and returned to Virginia. A few weeks later, General Williams asked to be relieved of his command.

	U.S.A.			*C.S.A.*	
	Ambrose E. Burnside, Samuel P. Carter			John S. Williams	
	Troops	*Killed*	*Wounded*	*Missing/Captured*	*Total Casualties*
U.S.A.	4,500	13	115	2	130
C.S.A.	1,700				250

13–14 *Engagement at Auburn, Virginia* (**Undetermined**)

Stuart, on a scouting expedition, came across a long line of Union troops moving along the railroad toward Manassas. As he was about to send word to Lee to hasten to catch the Union troops, another Union column was discovered moving northward on the other side of Stuart. Stuart discovered that he and his men were now caught between two huge Union lines. Spending the night in concealment with orders to maintain strict silence, Stuart camped within yards of the Union camp. The next morning, Union troops fired on a relief column which was coming to assist Stuart. Stuart, riding in a large arc around the Union column, managed to reach the safety of his lines.

U.S.A.				C.S.A.
William H. French, G.K. Warren				J.E.B. Stuart

	Troops	Killed	Wounded	Missing/Captured	Total Casualties
U.S.A.	Unknown	11	42		53
C.S.A.	3,000				

14 *Engagement at Bristoe Station, Virginia* (**Union Victory**)

A.P. Hill, without proper reconnaissance, attacked a Union column unaware there were additional Union soldiers nearby who had been observing the Confederates. When Hill's men were in range, the Union opened fire. Hill ordered a frontal charge, believing he was going against a small contingent instead of a corps. Hill lost a great many men. It is believed that it was here that Lee lost confidence in Hill. When Hill met with General Lee after the fight, it was reported that Hill was instructed to bury his dead and to say no more about the incident.

U.S.A.				C.S.A.
Gouverneur K. Warren				Ambrose P. Hill

	Troops	Killed	Wounded	Missing/Captured	Total Casualties
U.S.A.	Corps	50	335	161	546
C.S.A.	Corps	136	797	445	1,378

16–18 *Engagement at Fort Brooke, Florida* (**Union Victory**)

Union ships bombarded Fort Brooke as a diversion while a landing party was sent to capture several steamers located on the Hillsborough River. They were able to capture two of the Confederates' blockade running ships, the *Scottish Chief* and the *Kate Dale*. To prevent her capture, the Confederates destroyed the *A.B. Noyes*.

U.S.A.	C.S.A.
A.A. Semmes, T.R. Harris	Captain John Westcott

16 General Ulysses S. Grant assumed command of the newly created Military District of Mississippi, composed of the Departments of the Cumberland, the Ohio and Tennessee.

19 *Action at Buckland Mills, Virginia* (**Confederate Victory**)

Stuart purposely let a portion of his cavalry be discovered by Union cavalry and led them on a five-mile chase into a trap. When the concealed Confederates opened fire on the Union cavalry, Stuart turned his men about and chased the Union back over the same five miles they earlier had chased Stuart. Stuart captured several of the Union's wagons, including one belonging to General George Custer that Stuart used for himself. This skirmish became known as the "Buckland Races."

	U.S.A.				*C.S.A.*
H. Judson Kilpatrick					J.E.B. Stuart

	Troops	*Killed*	*Wounded*	*Missing/Captured*	*Total Casualties*
U.S.A.	Cav. Division	20	60	100	180
C.S.A.	Cav. Division	50			

22   The Bristoe Campaign, started on the 9th, ended with Union casualties exceeding 2,292. (Killed: 136. Wounded: 733. Missing: 1,423.)

22   Grant arrived in Chattanooga and initiated a plan to get supplies to the besieged troops stationed there.

24   General William T. Sherman replaced Grant as commander of the Army of Tennessee.

25   *Scout expedition at Pine Bluff, Arkansas* (**Union Victory**)
Union cavalry, moving toward Princeton, Arkansas, ran into Confederate cavalry, resulting in a skirmish where the Confederates demanded the Union's surrender. They were met with a resounding "no" as the Union troops pulled back into Pine Bluff. Soldiers established a breastworks made of cotton bales near the town square. The Confederate cavalry pulled back when they could not force the surrender of the soldiers nor capture the town square.

	U.S.A.				*C.S.A.*
Powell Clayton					John S. Marmaduke

	Troops	*Killed*	*Wounded*	*Missing/Captured*	*Total Casualties*
U.S.A.	Garrison	16	39	1	56
C.S.A.	Division				Unknown

26–27   *Action at Brown's Ferry, Tennessee* (**Union Victory**)
Grant was able to lift the siege of Chattanooga when he sent troops down the Tennessee River toward Brown's Ferry to confront Confederates blockading the Tennessee River. He had another group move across land toward the same objective. A small contingent of Confederate soldiers decided it best to retreat and move toward Lookout Mountain, leaving the river open. Grant had opened the river. Now, supplies began to pour into Chattanooga, first by rail to Bridgeport, Alabama, then by boat to Kelly's Ferry, then by wagon to a bridge at Brown's Ferry and across a second bridge into Chattanooga.

	U.S.A.				*C.S.A.*
U.S. Grant, John B. Turchin					William C. Oates

	Troops	*Killed*	*Wounded*	*Missing/Captured*	*Total Casualties*
U.S.A.	5,000	10	38	9	57
C.S.A.	1,000	8	14	6	28

28–29 *Engagement at Wauhatchie (Lookout Valley), Tennessee (**Union Victory**)*

Longstreet, ordered by Braxton Bragg to reestablish the Confederate siege of Chattanooga, attacked Geary's troops, who had been ordered to guard the lines of communications and supplies to Chattanooga now that they were open. Two divisions sent from Brown's Ferry assisted Geary's division in holding off the Confederate attack. This battle was one of the few night engagements during the war. The line to Chattanooga was safe for the rest of the campaign.

	U.S.A.				*C.S.A.*
	John Geary				James Longstreet
	Troops	*Killed*	*Wounded*	*Missing/Captured*	*Total Casualties*
U.S.A.	3 divisions	78	327	15	420
C.S.A.	4,000	34	305	69	408

November 1863

1 *Engagement at Collierville, Tennessee (**Union Victory**)*

Chalmers intended to disrupt the Memphis and Charleston Railroad supplying Sherman's army. When he came upon what he thought was a small contingent of Union soldiers near Collierville, he launched his attack. Hatch, the Union commander, learned of the planned attack and was prepared. Realizing the surprise was off and additional troops were a possibility, Chalmers withdrew to Mississippi.

	U.S.A.				*C.S.A.*
	Edward Hatch				James R. Chalmers
	Troops	*Killed*	*Wounded*	*Missing/Captured*	*Total Casualties*
U.S.A.	850				60
C.S.A.	2,500				95

3 *Engagement at Bayou Bourbeau, Louisiana (**Undetermined**)*

General Banks departed southern Louisiana and began to march up the Bayou Teche, with the intention of going into Texas. At Grand Coteau on Bayou Bourbeau, a strong Confederate force led by Thomas Green suddenly attacked the Union forces. Union troops, suddenly surprised, became disorganized and fled to the rear and to the safety of the additional troops moving up to assist. Confederate forces withdrew.

	U.S.A.				*C.S.A.*
	Nathaniel Banks, Stephen G. Burbridge				Thomas Green
	Troops	*Killed*	*Wounded*	*Missing/Captured*	*Total Casualties*
U.S.A.	19,500				716
C.S.A.					125

4 General Bragg sent Longstreet from Chattanooga to assault Burnside in east Tennessee near Knoxville.

6 *Engagement at Droop Mountain, West Virginia* (**Union Victory**)
    Averell, who was determined to disrupt Confederate rail operations, came upon a Confederate brigade that had withdrawn to Droop Mountain. The Confederates, joined by additional troops, put up stiff resistance as the Union tried a frontal assault. That failing, the Union brought up additional artillery and began an artillery barrage while blue-clad troops circled the mountain. When in place, they attacked both front and rear. The Confederates withdrew down another side of the mountain that was unguarded and made good their escape. Averell's raid on the railroad ended.

	U.S.A.			*C.S.A.*	
	William W. Averell			John Echols, William L. Jackson	
	Troops	*Killed*	*Wounded*	*Missing/Captured*	*Total Casualties*
U.S.A.	5,000				119
C.S.A.	1,700				275

7 *Engagement at Rappahannock Station, Virginia* (**Undetermined**)
    Lee, after the failure at Bristoe Station, fell back to the south side of the Rappahannock where the river intersected with the Rapidan. He placed a portion of his army near Kelly's Ford, believing the Union would cross there, and the other portion of his army was positioned near Rappahannock Station. The Union troops made the crossing and drove the Confederates in, capturing 349 prisoners. Lee regrouped his men intending to make an attack the following day, but Meade launched a night assault. Only 600 of Early's men escaped, the rest being either killed or captured. Consequently, Lee pulled farther back into Virginia, making his winter camp south of Orange instead of Culpeper, where he wanted to establish his winter quarters. Meade, the following month, established his camp near Culpeper.

	U.S.A.			*C.S.A.*	
	George G. Meade			Robert E. Lee, Jubal Early	
	Troops	*Killed*	*Wounded*	*Missing/Captured*	*Total Casualties*
U.S.A.	5 corps				514
C.S.A.	2 corps			1,949	2,023

9 President Abraham Lincoln attended the theater and saw John Wilkes Booth in the play *The Marble Heart*.

16 General Banks finally achieved his objective of entering Texas. His troops established a base near Corpus Christi, Texas.

16 *Engagement at Campbell's Station, Tennessee* (**Union Victory**)
    Both Union and Confederate commanders raced to secure the strategic hamlet of

Campbell's Station, as it was the key route to Knoxville. If Union forces could get there first, they would be able to make their way safely to Knoxville, but if the Confederate forces got there first, they could block reinforcements from reaching Knoxville. This would cut the Union's line of retreat and force them out of their fortifications. The Union got there first and deployed by the time of Longstreet's arrival. Longstreet decided on a double envelopment; one wing struck hard and fast but the other was slow and ineffective. The Union was able to make its way to Knoxville while the Confederates had to pull back.

	U.S.A.				*C.S.A.*
	Ambrose E. Burnside				James Longstreet
	Troops	*Killed*	*Wounded*	*Missing/Captured*	*Total Casualties*
U.S.A.	5,000				318
C.S.A.	16,000				570

17   Reinforcing their position on the Texas coast, Union troops captured a Confederate battery at Aransas Pass, Texas.

19   Lincoln delivered his "Gettysburg Address" as a National Cemetery was established on the Gettysburg battlefield.

20   Sherman arrived at Chattanooga with reinforcements.

22   General Banks captured Fort Esperazza and Matagorda Island on the Texas coast.

23–25   *Battle of Chattanooga, Tennessee* (**Union Victory**)

The Union Army had been pinned up in Chattanooga since losing the Battle of Chickamauga. For two months, Confederate forces under General Bragg had besieged the Union. Bragg, believing his position impregnable, had sent Longstreet with his two divisions to Knoxville. The Union forces under Grant, after obtaining supplies and reinforcements, decided to oust the Confederates from their entrenchments. A three-day battle ensued with terrible fighting and carnage at Orchard Knob, Lookout Mountain, and Missionary Ridge. The fight at Lookout Mountain would, for years to come, be popularized as the "Battle above the Clouds," because of the patches of fog that shrouded areas of Lookout Mountain's slopes. The battle began when General Thomas overran the Orchard Knob in front of Missionary Ridge. Bragg evacuated Lookout Mountain under pressure from Hooker while Sherman struck Missionary Ridge from across the Tennessee River. A Union victory opened up the Confederacy's heartland to invasion from the West while Bragg retreated to Georgia.

	U.S.A.				*C.S.A.*
	Ulysses S. Grant, George Thomas,				Braxton Bragg, Patrick Cleburne,
	William T. Sherman, Philip Sheridan				William J. Hardee
	Troops	*Killed*	*Wounded*	*Missing/Captured*	*Total Casualties*
U.S.A.	56,000	753	4,722	349	5,824
C.S.A.	46,000	361	2,160	4,146	6,667

27   *Engagement at Ringgold Gap, Georgia* (**Confederate Victory**)

In order to buy time for Bragg to get his men and guns from Missionary Ridge, Confederate leader Patrick Cleburne positioned his troops near Ringgold Gap to either stop or delay the Union troops pursuing the fleeing army. When Hooker appeared with his men, the Confederates held their fire until the Union soldiers were in range and then opened fire with everything they had. The Union was thrown back as Cleburne accomplished his mission.

	U.S.A.				C.S.A.
	Joseph Hooker				Patrick Cleburne
	Troops	Killed	Wounded	Missing/Captured	Total Casualties
U.S.A.	12,000				432
C.S.A.	4,100				480

26–December 1   Mine *Run Campaign, Virginia* (**Confederate Victory**)

Meade began what would be his first major offensive since his victory in Gettysburg. He moved his men across the Rapidan River with the intention of attacking Lee in several swift assaults. Union General Gouverneur Warren had convinced Meade that there was a way to break through the Confederate Army on the east bank of the Mine Run west of Chancellorsville. Having checked the area, Meade discovered that the Confederate positions were impregnable. As Lee prepared to launch an attack on the Union lines, Meade took his army back across the Rapidan and into winter camp.

	U.S.A.				C.S.A.
	George G. Meade, Gouverneur Warren				Robert E. Lee
	Troops	Killed	Wounded	Missing/Captured	Total Casualties
U.S.A.	69,643	173	718	381	1,272
C.S.A.	44,426				680

27   John Hunt Morgan escaped from the Ohio State Penitentiary.

29   *Engagement at Fort Sanders, Tennessee* (**Union Victory**)

In an effort to launch an assault on Knoxville, the Confederates first made an assault on Fort Sanders just northwest of the city. They were unaware that the Union defenders had placed telegraph wire knee high around the fort and, in addition, had dug a ditch 12 feet wide and 4 to 8 feet deep. When the Confederates attempted to cross, they had no ladders, and once they were in the ditch the Union artillery dropped 50 cannon shells loaded with three-second fuses, killing many of the invaders.

	U.S.A.				C.S.A.
	Ambrose E. Burnside				James Longstreet
	Troops	Killed	Wounded	Missing/Captured	Total Casualties
U.S.A.	500	8	5		13
C.S.A.	3,000				813

30 President Jefferson Davis accepted Braxton Bragg's resignation. Bragg would later become a military adviser to President Davis.

December 1863

1 Upon finding the Confederates firmly entrenched near Mine Run, Meade ended his campaign in Virginia for the winter. Lee moved his army back to Orange Court House, where he went into winter quarters.

14 *Engagement at Bean's Station, Tennessee* (**Confederate Victory**)
After the disaster at Fort Sanders, the Confederates moved northward pursued by Union cavalry. The Confederate cavalry had been directed to destroy the pursuing army. Near Bean's Station, they came upon a portion of the Union cavalry and chased them into and through the town. The Union cavalry gave ground and by nightfall had retreated.

U.S.A.				*C.S.A.*	
James M. Shackelford				James Longstreet, Bushrod Johnson	
	Troops	*Killed*	*Wounded*	*Missing/Captured*	*Total Casualties*
U.S.A.	4,000				115
C.S.A.	4,000				290

16 General Joseph Johnston replaced General Braxton Bragg as commander of Confederate Army of Tennessee.

29 *Action at Mossy Creek, Tennessee* (**Union Victory**)
Union Commander General Sturgis, learning that there was a brigade of Confederate cavalry near Dandridge, sent most of his men to capture them. This left Mossy Creek without adequate coverage and vulnerable to attack. This is exactly what Martin did. The Confederate cavalry attacked and drove the defenders from the fort. As the Union men fled from Mossy Creek, they ran into the returning Union cavalry coming from Dandridge, after not being able to locate the Confederate force. The combined Union forces turned and retook Mossy Creek.

U.S.A.				*C.S.A.*	
Samuel D. Sturgis				William T. Martin	
	Troops	*Killed*	*Wounded*	*Missing/Captured*	*Total Casualties*
U.S.A.	4,000	18	86	6	110
C.S.A.	2,000				300

Chapter 9

1864

"I beg to present you, as a Christmas gift, the city of Savannah, with 150 heavy guns and plenty of ammunition, and also about 25,000 bales of cotton."

— Letter to President Abraham Lincoln
from General William T. Sherman
on December 22, 1864

January 1864

8–9   The Union began bombardment of the Confederate works at the mouth of Caney Bayou, Texas.

17   *Action at Dandridge, Tennessee* (**Confederate Victory**)
    Three days earlier Union troops had moved into Dandridge, forcing the Confederates to fall back. The Confederates had been in the vicinity with orders to threaten the Union base at New Market, but decided to attack the troops at Dandridge after being reinforced with artillery. They were able to force the Union troops to withdraw from the area, retreating toward their secure base at New Market. Because of equipment problems, the Confederates were unable to follow.

	U.S.A.			C.S.A.	
	Samuel D. Sturgis				James Longstreet
	Troops	*Killed*	*Wounded*	*Missing/Captured*	*Total Casualties*
U.S.A.		8	58	17	83
C.S.A.					

19 Arkansas adopted a new constitution which outlawed slavery.

21 Distillation of whiskey was forbidden in the Department of Ohio due to the scarcity of grain.

25 Union forces evacuated Corinth, Mississippi, to consolidate their western occupation points.

26 *Engagement at Athens, Alabama* (**Union Victory**)
The 1st Alabama Cavalry attacked Athens, which was held by a small contingent of Union troops. After fighting for about two hours, the Confederate force withdrew without dislodging the Union troops who were not only outnumbered but also were without fortifications.

	U.S.A.			*C.S.A.*	
Captain Emil Adams			Lt. Col. Moses W. Hannon		
	Troops	*Killed*	*Wounded*	*Missing/Captured*	*Total Casualties*
U.S.A.	100				20
C.S.A.	600				30

27 *Engagement at Fair Garden, Tennessee* (**Union Victory**)
Ever since Dandridge, Union forces had been disrupting Confederate foraging activities. Longstreet ordered his men to do something to stop these activities. After learning that the Confederates were concentrating near Fair Garden, the Union forces attacked. The infantry attack, combined with a cavalry charge, drove the Confederates back. The Union did not pursue and soon left the area.

	U.S.A.			*C.S.A.*	
Samuel D. Sturgis, Edward M. McCook			Major William T. Martin		
	Troops	*Killed*	*Wounded*	*Missing/Captured*	*Total Casualties*
U.S.A.		4	27	3	34
C.S.A.	Cavalry Div.				165

February 1864

1 The Federal conscription began calling for 500,000 men to serve 3 years or for the duration of the war.

1–2 *Skirmish at New Bern, North Carolina* (**Union Victory**)
During the winter, North Carolina was the source of supplies for the Army of Northern Virginia. Union forces had been fortifying the coastal areas of North Carolina as well as conducting raids on the countryside. Many towns were put to the torch and crops destroyed. Confederate forces under General Pickett were sent to curtail the destruction and to capture the town of New Bern, which was considered a large supply depot under

Union control. Pickett was forced to call off the planned attack when two sides of his three-prong attack failed. (Three hundred Union soldiers were taken prisoner and among them were twenty-two former North Carolina soldiers who had taken up the uniform of the North. Pickett had them court-martialed and hung as traitors.)

	U.S.A.			*C.S.A.*	
	General Innis N. Palmer			George E. Pickett, Robert F. Hoke	
	Troops	*Killed*	*Wounded*	*Missing/Captured*	*Total Casualties*
U.S.A.	7,000				400
C.S.A.	13,000				45

2 *Destruction of the USS* Underwriter

In the attempt to take New Bern, North Carolina, Confederate forces under John T. Wood converged on the USS *Underwriter* as it was docked near New Bern. The Confederate raiders were spotted and fired upon, but they were able to board the Union gunboat and burn it before making good their escape.

	U.S.A.			*C.S.A.*	
	Jacob Westervelt (killed)			John T. Wood	
	Troops	*Killed*	*Wounded*	*Missing/Captured*	*Total Casualties*
U.S.A.		9	20	26	55
C.S.A.	255	5	15	4	24

3–March 4 *Sherman began the Meridian Campaign in Mississippi*

In preparation for the spring campaign, Sherman stated he would burn towns, if he had to, in order to eliminate any resistance in Mississippi that would affect his supply lines. It would not matter if the women and children were present in the towns or not. Sherman planned to destroy railroad tracks all across the state, including the rail lines leading to Meridian, the rail center in the state. He also planned to lay waste to the surrounding countryside. By the end of his campaign, Sherman would burn ten thousand bales of cotton and two million bushels of corn, and carry off eight thousand slaves.

6–7 *Skirmish at Morton Ford, Virginia* (**Confederate Victory**)

Union forces planned to create a diversion while a surprise attack was to be made on Richmond. Union forces made threatening moves along the Rapidan River at Raccoon Ford, Robertson Ford and Morton's Ford. With the buildup of Confederate forces at Morton's Ford, the Union troops pulled back. The planned Union assault on Richmond proved to be a failure, as Richmond officials were aware of it.

	U.S.A.			*C.S.A.*	
	John C. Caldwell			Richard S. Ewell	
	Troops	*Killed*	*Wounded*	*Missing/Captured*	*Total Casualties*
U.S.A.		11	204	40	255
C.S.A.					60

7   Troops commanded by Union Major General Quincy A. Gillmore, Department of the South, occupied Jacksonville, Florida. He was to secure Union territory in Florida, disrupt Confederate supply routes and recruit black soldiers. President Lincoln believed the state could easily be taken since only a small state militia defended Florida.

9   *Escape of Union officers from Libby Prison in Richmond, Virginia*
    The largest and most sensational escape of the war occurred as 109 Union officers made their way from Libby Prison. The escape was engineered and led by Colonel Thomas E. Rose, who was taken prisoner during the Battle of Chickamauga in September 1863. Rose and a few others had dug a tunnel from the cellar of the old Libby and Son Ship Chandlers and Grocers, which had been converted into a prison for prisoners of war. Only fifty-nine of the men reached the Union lines, two drowned and forty-eight were recaptured.

10   The CSS *Florida*, a Confederate raider, sailed from Brest, France. The ship had been laid up since August 1863.

14–20   Campaign *at Meridian, Mississippi* (**Union Victory**)
    Union officials launched a campaign to take the important rail center at Meridian. Confederate forces under Lieutenant General Leonidas Polk were ordered to the area but retreated with the arrival of William T. Sherman and his 20,000 men. Union troops destroyed the rail lines servicing the area by bending the rails and burning the ties. They also put the torch to numerous buildings in the city.

17   The Confederate submarine CSS *Hunley* sank the USS *Housatonic* off Charleston Harbor, becoming the first submarine in history to sink an enemy vessel in combat. The *Hunley* also sank after driving a torpedo spar into the *Housatonic*.

20   *Battle of Olustee, Florida* (**Confederate Victory**)
    A Union expedition of white and Negro troops attempted to take a section of Florida but met with defeat at the hands of the Confederates. Some historians believe it was a hollow victory, as the area was of no major importance to the Union and had no valid strategic importance. According to some historians, the fight was simply a waste of manpower.

	U.S.A.			*C.S.A.*	
	Brig. Gen. Truman Seymour			Brig. Gen. Joseph Finegan	
	Troops	*Killed*	*Wounded*	*Missing/Captured*	*Total Casualties*
U.S.A.	5,500	203	1,152	506	1,861
C.S.A.	5,000	93	841	9	943

22   *Engagement of Okolona (Ivey's Farm or Hill), Mississippi* (**Confederate Victory**)
    Smith had been ordered to capture Meridian with not only his cavalry force but also with several infantry regiments. In addition, he was to destroy the Confederate communication lines. Smith delayed his departure by ten days, and once on the road, conducted numerous raids destroying crops and railroad tracks and occasionally skirmishing with Confederate cavalry units. As he neared West Point, Tennessee, he became engaged in a

brief skirmish with Nathan Bedford Forrest. After the skirmish, Smith retreated to Okolona, where he was assaulted once more by Forrest. The engagement of Okolona was one of Forrest's greatest victories and an immense loss for Smith. Colonel Jeffrey Forrest, the younger brother of Nathan, was killed in the struggle. The elder Forrest was reported to have mourned for a minute before he resumed the fight.

U.S.A.				C.S.A.	
William Sooy Smith				Nathan B. Forrest, Colonel	
				Jeffrey Forrest (Killed)	

	Troops	Killed	Wounded	Missing/Captured	Total Casualties
U.S.A.	6,000	54	179	155	388
C.S.A.	2,500	25	75	9	109

22–27   *Demonstration at Dalton, Georgia* (**Confederate Victory**)
    With Confederates forces sent to aid General Polk in Mississippi, Union officials believed that Joseph E. Johnston would be vulnerable to attack. George H. Thomas made a demonstration against Johnston but found that the Confederate force was strong and on the defensive.

29   *Skirmish at Rio Mills (Charlottesville), Virginia* (**Confederate Victory**)
    George A. Custer was to make a diversionary raid toward Charlottesville to destroy the communication links, while at the same time, a raid was to be made on Libby Prison in Richmond to rescue Union soldiers. Custer attacked the Confederate battery under Marcelleus Moorman at Rio Mills, but withdrew when he believed additional Confederate soldiers had arrived. Custer destroyed bridges and flour mills and burned numerous buildings in surrounding cities as he made his way back to Madison Court House.

March 1864

1   H. Judson Kilpatrick and Ulric Dahlgren led a raid on Richmond's Libby Prison in an abortive attempt to release Union prisoners. Kilpatrick found Confederate forces aware of his presence and fled, leaving Dahlgren to fend for himself. Dahlgren was killed in a trap as he fled Richmond. Papers found on his body implicated him in a plot to assassinate Jefferson Davis. President Lincoln, General Meade, Kilpatrick and Dahlgren's father, Rear Admiral John Dahlgren, denied it.

4   Sherman's troops returned to Vicksburg after staging a month long raid on the countryside near Meridian, Mississippi.

9   General Ulysses S. Grant was promoted to lieutenant general.

10   Federals forces under Admiral David D. Porter, with a 20,000-man infantry force under General Nathaniel P. Banks, began the Red River Campaign in Louisiana. Porter was to sail his fleet up the Red River to capture the town of Shreveport.

12 Grant was named general in chief of all Union armies.

14 *Capture of Fort DeRussy, Louisiana* (**Union Victory**)
Union forces under Smith moved to eliminate the threat from Fort DeRussey, an earthen fortification, which was in a position where the Confederates could take direct aim at Porter's flotilla as it came up the river.

	U.S.A.			*C.S.A.*	
A.J. Smith, Joseph Mower				William Boyd	
	Troops	*Killed*	*Wounded*	*Missing/Captured*	*Total Casualties*
U.S.A. Division	3	35			38
C.S.A. 350					269

15 Porter's fleet reached Alexandria, Louisiana.

16 Union troops under General Banks occupied Alexandria, Louisiana.

18 Grant placed General William T. Sherman in command of the Union forces in the West.

23 General Frederick Steele, receiving orders from General Grant, moved south from Little Rock toward Shreveport. Despite making numerous protests, Steele was ordered to assist Banks in capturing the city.

24 *Action at Union City, Tennessee* (**Confederate Victory**)
While Nathan Bedford Forrest was in Kentucky, other Confederate forces were ordered to capture the Union garrison at Union City. Using deception, Duckworth was able to convince Union officials that Forrest was nearby and ready to launch an attack on the city. The bluff worked, and the Union garrison surrendered.

	U.S.A.			*C.S.A.*	
Colonel Isaac R. Hawkins				Colonel W.L. Duckworth	
	Troops	*Killed*	*Wounded*	*Missing/Captured*	*Total Casualties*
U.S.A.	500	1		450	451
C.S.A.	500				0

25 General Banks was named commander for the Red River Campaign.

25 *Action at Paducah (AKA Fort Anderson), Kentucky* (**Confederate Victory**)
Forrest rode into Paducah and ordered the Union garrison, located at the town's west end, to surrender. With assistance from two Union gunboats on the Ohio River, Union forces refused to surrender and opened fire. The Confederate cavalry did not take the garrison but did destroy various supplies. Some historians believe that though the raid failed, it put the Ohio Valley on notice of possible future cavalry raids.

	U.S.A.				*C.S.A.*
	Colonel Stephen G. Hicks, Lt. Cdr. James W. Shirk				Nathan Bedford Forrest

	Troops	*Killed*	*Wounded*	*Missing/Captured*	*Total Casualties*
U.S.A.	650				90
C.S.A.	3,000				50

April 1864

3–4   *Engagement at Elkin's Ferry, Arkansas* (**Union Victory**)
    As Union forces attempted to ford the Little Missouri River, Confederate cavalry assaulted them. Steele managed to make his way across and was not pursued.

	U.S.A.				*C.S.A.*
	Maj. Gen. Frederick Steele				Brig. Gen. John S. Marmaduke

	Troops	*Killed*	*Wounded*	*Missing/Captured*	*Total Casualties*
U.S.A.	10,400	5	33		38
C.S.A.	5,000				54

4   General Philip Sheridan assumed command of the cavalry in the Army of the Potomac.

8   *Battle of Sabine Crossroads (AKA Mansfield), Louisiana* (**Confederate Victory**)
    Confederates under General Taylor established a defensive position near Sabine Crossroads, an important communications center. Union troops under Banks approached but were driven back. Banks reconsidered his Red River Campaign and abandoned the idea of moving on Shreveport. He retreated toward Alexandria. (Nathaniel P. Banks was relieved of his command after the end of the Red River Campaign due to his military ineptitude.)

	U.S.A.				*C.S.A.*
	Nathaniel Banks				Richard Taylor

	Troops	*Killed*	*Wounded*	*Missing/Captured*	*Total Casualties*
U.S.A.	12,000	113	581	1,541	2,235
C.S.A.	8,800				11,500

8   U.S. Senate passed a joint resolution 38–6 abolishing slavery and approving the 13th Amendment. It would later be ratified by three-fourths of the state legislatures and become law on December 6, 1865.

9   *Engagement of Pleasant Hill, Louisiana* (**Union Victory**)
    Banks, after his defeat at Sabine Crossroads, moved his men to Pleasant Hill where he could receive support. Confederate forces followed and, spotting the Union troops, launched an immediate attack. Banks, on the verge of defeat once more, received the

expected support and assistance from Pleasant Hill when A.J. Smith's men charged the Confederate position and drove them from the area. (Though the Union forces won the battle, Banks continued his retreat, leaving behind many of his dead and wounded on the field.)

		U.S.A.		*C.S.A.*	
		Nathaniel P. Banks, A.J. Smith		E. Kirby Smith, Richard Taylor	
	Troops	*Killed*	*Wounded*	*Missing/Captured*	*Total Casualties*
U.S.A.	12,000	150	844	375	1,369
C.S.A.	12,500			426	1,626

9   General Grant issued orders for the new campaign: (a.) Meade was to follow Lee wherever he went; (b.) Banks was to move against Mobile, Alabama; (c.) Sherman was to head to Georgia and pursue Joseph Johnston; (d.) Sigel was ordered to move into the Shenandoah; and (e.) Butler was to move toward Richmond from the south.

9   *Attack on the USS* Minnesota *by the CSS* Squib

The USS *Minnesota*, a warship bearing forty-seven guns, was part of a fleet of ships blockading southern ports. The CSS *Squib* was a tugboat that had been converted into a Confederate warship. Lt. Hunter Davidson, formally of the CSS *Virginia*, set out to destroy the *Minnesota*. Attached to the front of the *Squib* was a long pole carrying a bomb filled with 53 pounds of powder. In the early morning hours, the *Squib* maneuvered near the *Minnesota* and exploded the bomb-torpedo, damaging the *Minnesota*. The *Minnesota* remained afloat and, after repairs were made, returned to service.

10–13   *Action at Prairie D'Ane, Arkansas* (**Union Victory**)

Union forces marching south from the Cornelius Farm came across a Confederate detachment under Maj. Gen. Sterling Price. Skirmishing between the two units continued for most of the day, each driving the other back and forth. On the 13th, Confederate forces withdrew and Maj. Gen. Frederick Steele continued on to Camden, where he occupied the town. Steele suffered twenty killed, forty-two wounded.

12   *Battle (Massacre) at Fort Pillow, Tennessee* (**Confederate Victory**)

Fort Pillow was manned by the 11th U.S. Colored Troops (265 black soldiers) along with the 13th Tennessee Cavalry (295 white soldiers) when it was surrounded by Confederate troops commanded by Nathan Bedford Forrest. Forrest made demands for the surrender of the fort. Twenty minutes later, after Bradford's refusal, Forrest ordered the fort to be taken, driving many of the soldiers from the fort down to the river banks where, when they tried to surrender, they were reportedly shot down. Opinions varied then and now as to whether this attack on Fort Pillow was simply a successful attack on a military objective or a massacre of Negro and white soldiers after the surrender. According to extensive testimony taken afterwards by the U.S. military officials, the Union troops surrendered almost at once, but the soldiers were shot down afterward in what amounted to a "massacre," especially of Negro soldiers. Confederate military and civil authorities hotly denied these charges and called them hysterical propaganda.

	U.S.A.			C.S.A.	
	Major Lionel F. Booth (Killed), Major William F. Bradford			Nathan Bedford Forrest	
	Troops	Killed	Wounded	Missing/Captured	Total Casualties
U.S.A.	560	231	100	226	557
C.S.A.	1,500	14	86		100

12–13 *Action at Blair's Landing (AKA Pleasant Hill Landing), Louisiana* (**Union Victory**)

The water level was falling on the Red River, making it difficult for Porter to get his boats clear. General Green discovered Porter's fleet and charged the boats. The boatmen were able to hold off the assault as additional gunboats appeared on the scene. With the arrival of additional support, the Confederates withdrew.

U.S.A.	C.S.A.
Brig. Gen. Thomas K. Smith, Rear Admiral David D. Porter	Brig. Gen. Thomas Green (Killed)

15 Major General Frederick Steele, after a severe fight with the Confederates at Prairie D'Ane, managed to make it to Camden, Arkansas, where he was able to hold on despite being low on ammunition and supplies. Steele ordered his men on half rations until supplies could be obtained.

17 Grant halted prisoner exchanges, which increased the strain on Confederate manpower.

17–20 *Siege of Plymouth, North Carolina* (**Confederate Victory**)

Confederate forces were ordered to seize the port at Plymouth, North Carolina, now held by Union forces. Hoke, along with the CSS *Albemarle*, attacked the Union garrison at Plymouth, destroying several Union ships (the USS *Southfield* and the USS *Miami*) and driving off other ships. On the 20th, the garrison surrendered.

	U.S.A.			C.S.A.	
	Colonel Henry W. Wessells			Maj. Gen. R.F. Hoke, Commander James W. Cook	
	Troops	Killed	Wounded	Missing/Captured	Total Casualties
U.S.A.	3,000	20	82	2,732	2,834
C.S.A.	13,000				

17 *Engagement at Poison Springs, Arkansas* (**Confederate Victory**)

With his supplies dwindling, General Steele sent out a foraging party. Finding supplies near White Oak Creek, the troopers under Williams loaded their wagons full of corn and began their return. As the wagons were returning, Confederate forces, which had arrived near Lee Plantation, attacked both front and rear. Williams was forced to abandon the wagons. The Confederates captured 198 wagons full of supplies.

	U.S.A.			C.S.A.	
	Colonel James M. Williams			Brig. Gen. John S. Marmaduke, Brig. Gen. Samuel Bell Maxey	

	Troops	*Killed*	*Wounded*	*Missing/Captured*	*Total Casualties*
U.S.A.	1,170	92	97	106	295
C.S.A.	3,335				114

22   The motto "In God We Trust" was first stamped on coins under an act of the federal Congress.

23   *Engagement at Monett's Ferry, Louisiana* (**Union Victory**)
    In pulling back to Alexandria, Banks came across Confederate troops commanded by General Bee near Monett's Ferry. Bee had been ordered to defend the crossing at Cane River. General Emory, hesitant to charge directly into the Confederate line, instead made demonstrations while searching for another crossing. After one of his brigades discovered a crossing, Emory assaulted the Confederates from the rear, forcing Bee to withdraw.

	U.S.A.			C.S.A.	
	Nathaniel P. Banks, William H. Emory			Brig. Gen. Hamilton P. Bee	

	Troops	*Killed*	*Wounded*	*Missing/Captured*	*Total Casualties*
U.S.A.		40	160		200
C.S.A.	Cavalry Div.				400

25   Porter's gunboats were trapped by low water in the Red River.

25   *Engagement at Marks' Mill, Arkansas* (**Confederate Victory**)
    With General Steele's men at Camden without rations, Lt. Col. Drake was sent to fetch supplies. As he was returning with 240 wagons full of supplies, Confederate forces quickly overtook the trains and captured all the wagons and men. Accompanying the supply wagons were three hundred runaway slaves, of which over half were killed.

	U.S.A.			C.S.A.	
	Lt. Col. Francis Drake (wounded)			Brig. Gen. James B. Fagan	

	Troops	*Killed*	*Wounded*	*Missing/Captured*	*Total Casualties*
U.S.A.	1,500	100	250	1150	1,500
C.S.A.	2 divisions	41	108	149	

26   Major General Frederick Steele decided he could no longer hold out. In the middle of the night, he moved his men from Camden crossing the Ouachita River and began the long trip back to Little Rock.

30   Joe Davis, the 5-year-old son of Confederate President Jefferson Davis, died after falling off a high veranda at the Confederate White House in Richmond.

30   *Engagement at Jenkins Ferry, Arkansas* (**Union Victory**)

Steele's forces, pulling back from Camden, reached the vicinity of Jenkins Ferry when Confederate forces pursuing them began to make made numerous attacks. Union troops were able to hold back the Confederates until the majority of the Union soldiers made it across the Saline River, burning their pontoon bridge behind them. The Confederates did not pursue.

	U.S.A.		*C.S.A.*	
	Maj. Gen. Frederick Steele		Gen. Sterling Price, Gen. E. Kirby Smith	

	Troops	*Killed*	*Wounded*	*Missing/Captured*	*Total Casualties*
U.S.A.		64	378	86	528
C.S.A.					443

May 1864

4   General Grant ordered the Army of the Potomac to cross the Rapidan River into Virginia, beginning of the start of Grant's new campaign. At the same time, General Benjamin Butler was ordered by Grant to make a simultaneous assault against Petersburg and move on Richmond. This was later referred to as the Bermuda Hundred Campaign. General Franz Sigel was directed to secure the Shenandoah Valley.

5   General William T. Sherman, named as commander of the western front by General Grant, began the Atlanta Campaign. Sherman moved southward from Chattanooga toward Atlanta, Georgia, on Grant's order "to move against Johnston's army, to break it up, and get into the interior of the enemy's country as far as you can, inflicting all the damage you can against their war resources."[1] Sherman's army consisted of a hundred thousand men made up of the Army of the Cumberland, the Army of the Tennessee and the Army of the Ohio.

5   *Naval Engagement at Albemarle Sound, North Carolina* (**Undetermined**)

The Confederate ram CSS *Albemarle*, under Commander J.W. Cooke, fought against seven Union ships that were blockading the Roanoke River. The naval battle was considered a draw in that the Confederate ram left the area while the USS *Sassacus* was damaged. The Union, under Captain Melancton Smith, continued their blockade of the river.

5–7   *Battle of the Wilderness, Virginia* (**Confederate Victory**)

In his march toward the heart of the Confederacy, Grant encountered one of his few setbacks. In a tangled maze of brush and woods, the Union army became bogged down and was attacked by Longstreet. Lee's other forces in that area were bunched near the Rapidan River, but Grant (leading Meade's army) slid around Lee's right flank before the heavy fighting began. The Army of the Potomac was at its greatest strength at this time, and almost doubled Lee's force. After minor skirmishing, the forces came face to face at a point chosen by Lee near the tangled terrain of the Wilderness, so foreign to the Union forces, and so familiar to the Confederates. Soon, the area was covered with smoke from guns of the two armies as soldiers fired more by instinct than by aiming. Chaos reigned in the smoke-filled woods as soldiers fought each other hand to hand. Many of the wounded perished where they fell after brush fires broke out and they were burned to death. Grant made one of his rare tactical errors—he allowed Meade's army to be caught between the Confederates at the Wilderness and those at Richmond. However, the Union made a relentless advance through the woods until stopped by a terrific concentration of fire from Brigadier General John Gregg's Texans. Gregg's force of 800 hit in such concentrated force that the advance stopped long enough to allow the Confederates to regroup. The battle seesawed all day from that point. However, on the seventh, Longstreet turned the Union flank while Lee moved around the right flank. This was the first show of tactics. Confusion spread through the Union ranks with the troops falling back. On the following day, Grant took his men out of line and ordered them to prepare for a march. To the surprise of most, the order was given to advance southward, bypassing the Wilderness. This was the first time that the Army of the Potomac had suffered a defeat without returning directly to Washington with its "tail between its legs." Longstreet was wounded by his own men during the fighting, and Grant was criticized for his callous use of manpower. The Wilderness, because of its terrain, was a series of individual and group conflicts rather than one concerted battle.

U.S.A.	C.S.A.
Ulysses S. Grant, George G. Meade, Philip H. Sheridan, John Sedgwick, Winfield S. Hancock	Robert E. Lee, Richard S. Ewell, A.P. Hill, James Longstreet (Wounded), J.E.B. Stuart

	Troops	Killed	Wounded	Missing/Captured	Total Casualties
U.S.A.	101,895	2,246	12,037	3,383	17,666
C.S.A.	61,025	1,495	7,690	1,940	11,125

6 Confederate forces, operating on the James River, sank the USS *Commodore Jones* by exploding a submerged 2,000 pound torpedo. Admiral David D. Porter reported later, "Scarcely had she gathered stern-way, when suddenly and without any apparent cause she appeared to be lifted bodily, her wheels rapidly revolving in the air, and persons declared they could see the green grass of the river-bank beneath her keel. An immense fountain of foaming water shot to a great height, followed by a denser column thick with mud. The vessel absolutely crumbled to pieces, dissolved as it were in mid-air, enveloped by the falling spray, mud, water, and smoke. When the excitement of the explosion subsided, not a vestige of the vessel remained in sight, except small fragments of her frame which came shooting to the surface. Nearly every one on board was killed or wounded."[2]

6–7 *Action at Port Walthall Junction, Virginia* (**Union Victory**)

General Butler sent troops to break the railroad line connecting Richmond to Petersburg. Unable to dislodge the Confederates from the rail center, the Union troops tore up a quarter mile of track before departing. The next day, Union troops returned with additional manpower and overran the station, taking command of Port Walthall Junction.

U.S.A.	C.S.A.
Benjamin Butler	Daniel H. Hill, Johnson Hagood

	Troops	Killed	Wounded	Missing/Captured	Total Casualties
U.S.A.	6,000	48	256	70	374
C.S.A.	3,000				

7   *Battle of Todd's Tavern, Virginia* (**Union Victory**)

Instead of retreating as previous Union commanders had done, Grant advanced toward Spotsylvania Court House, leaving his dead and wounded on the field. Grant ordered his cavalry to cut the route he believed Lee would take. At the same time, Lee ordered his cavalry chief to delay the Union advance. The two cavalries met with the ensuing cavalry battle at Todd's Tavern. The Confederates delayed the Union movement but were pushed back toward Spotsylvania as they retired from the field.

U.S.A.			C.S.A.	
Philip H. Sheridan			J.E.B. Stuart	

	Troops	Killed	Wounded	Missing/Captured	Total Casualties
U.S.A.	4 brigades	40	150		190
C.S.A.	2 brigades				

7–13   *Demonstration at Rocky Face Ridge, Georgia* (**Union Victory**)

Confederate forces had entrenched on the mountain known as Rocky Face Ridge in Georgia when Union forces under Sherman approached. Sherman, realizing that it would be almost impossible to dislodge the Confederates from their strong position, decided to see if he could force them to withdraw. He feigned attacks on the northern and western sides of the mountain as a third force moved south to Snake Creek Gap and there cut the rail line to Resaca. With their supply lines destroyed, the Confederates would have to withdraw. The Union made numerous demonstrations against the Confederate positions, suffering high casualties. On the 10th, General Sherman pulled his army back and decided to put it between the mountain and Resaca. Discovering this, Confederate forces moved down the south face of the mountain and made a quick march to Resaca, beating the slow moving Union force. This was considered a Union victory, as the mission of removing the Confederates from Rocky Face Ridge had been accomplished.

U.S.A.			C.S.A.	
William T. Sherman			Joseph E. Johnston	

	Troops	Killed	Wounded	Missing/Captured	Total Casualties
U.S.A.	100,000	200	460	240	900
C.S.A.	45,000				unknown

8   The USS *Connecticut* captured the blockade-running ship *Greyhound*. General Benjamin Butler took possession of the ship and made it his private transport. The inside of the ship, lavishly decorated, became the floating headquarters for Butler.

8–21   *Battle of Spotsylvania Court House, Virginia* (Includes Corbin's Bridge, Alsop's Farm, Laurel Hill, Harris Farm) (**Undetermined**)

After Grant pulled his troops from the Wilderness, a race began to see who could reach Spotsylvania, forty miles north of Richmond, first. Grant forced Lee to push his exhausted troops to protect the Confederate capital. Lee won the race and had his men entrenched after his cavalry had defeated a small Union cavalry force that had reached Spotsylvania Court House far ahead of the Grant's army. On the 9th, both sides dug in, resulting in several small skirmishes. A Confederate sharpshooter killed Union commander General Sedgwick in one of these minor engagements. The Union began a swinging movement in an attempt either to bypass the Confederates or to cut them off. The Confederates followed each move with a countermove from the 12th to the 18th, which caused the battle line to take on the appearance of a huge pendulum. However, on the 19th, the Confederate line moved a bit too much, allowing Grant to bypass Spotsylvania and move toward Richmond. A running battle followed, with losses continuing to pile up. The heavy losses incurred in these two major battles, the Wilderness and Spotsylvania, were a source of great concern for North and South alike. Because of the huge number of Union casualties, Grant was being called "Butcher Grant" in the newspapers. Despite this, Grant continued his movement south, refusing to fight Lee on ground of Lee's choosing, as previous commanders had done.

U.S.A.	*C.S.A.*
Ulysses Grant, Philip Sheridan, George G. Meade, John Sedgwick (Killed)	Robert E. Lee, Richard S. Ewell, Edward Johnson, George Steuart (Captured), Abner Perrin (Killed)

	Troops	*Killed*	*Wounded*	*Missing/Captured*	*Total Casualties*
U.S.A.	100,000	2,725	13,416	2,258	18,399
C.S.A.	52,000	1,467	4,783	6,201	12,451

9 *Engagement at Swift Creek (AKA Arrowfield Church), Virginia* (**Undetermined**)

Union forces moving toward Petersburg ran into Confederate contingents under Johnson, which they drove off. The Union did not pursue the Confederates, but instead tore up railroad tracks leading to and from the area.

U.S.A.	*C.S.A.*
Benjamin Butler	P.G.T. Beauregard, Bushrod Johnson

	Troops	*Killed*	*Wounded*	*Missing/Captured*	*Total Casualties*
U.S.A.	division	36	188	19	243
C.S.A.	division				747

9 While Grant was involved with Lee at Spotsylvania, his cavalry commander, General Philip H. Sheridan, launched a raid on Richmond via the James River. Sheridan was to break up Lee's communication and supplies line. By the time he concluded his raid on the 24th and rejoined the Army of the Potomac, Sheridan had lost 424 troopers (50 killed, 174 wounded and 200 missing or captured).

9 *Combat at Snake Gap, Georgia* (**Confederate Victory**)

General James B. McPherson, pushing toward Resaca, moved through Snake Gap where a brief fight occurred. McPherson, in his attempt to get to the rear of Joseph E. Johnston's army, decided the Confederates were too strong to assault. He thus pulled back and made his report to Sherman. This caused a rift between the two, for Sherman was disappointed in McPherson's actions.

9 *Engagement at Cloyd's Mountain, Virginia* (**Union Victory**)
Confederate troops positioned across Cloyd's Mountain hoped to trap Union forces that were preparing to raid the rail junction at Dublin, Virginia. However, the Confederates instead were surprised when Union officials made an early morning attack. Many Union soldiers were burned to death when brush fires broke out.

		U.S.A.			C.S.A.	
	George Crook, Rutherford B. Hayes			John McCausland, Albert Jenkins (mortally wounded)		
	Troops	*Killed*	*Wounded*	*Missing/Captured*	*Total Casualties*	
U.S.A.	6,500	108	508	72	688	
C.S.A.	2,400				538	

10 *Engagement at Cove Mountain, Virginia* (**Undetermined**)
Union raiders, on their way to destroy the New River Bridge on the Virginia and Tennessee Rail line, came upon Confederate cavalry. The Confederates were able to delay the Union advance but were later forced to withdraw.

		U.S.A.			C.S.A.	
	William W. Averell			William E. Jones		
	Troops	*Killed*	*Wounded*	*Missing/Captured*	*Total Casualties*	
U.S.A.	Brigade				140	
C.S.A.	Brigade				160	

9 *Action at Chester Station, Virginia* (**Undetermined**)
Confederate forces under Robert Ransom assaulted a Union division near Chester Station as they were attempting to destroy the railroad station. A short time later, Benjamin Butler withdrew his forces after the unsuccessful strike leading to Petersburg.

11 Union raiders, under General William W. Averell, accomplished their mission when they were able to burn the New River Bridge over the Virginia and Tennessee Railroad in Wythe County, Virginia.

11 *Battle of Yellow Tavern, Virginia* (**Union Victory**)
Union cavalry, under Sheridan, had been tearing up and destroying rail lines near Richmond when Stuart's Confederate cavalry confronted them. Stuart had been ordered to get between the Union line and Richmond. The two forces met six miles north of Richmond near Yellow Tavern, an abandoned inn. Stuart was mortally wounded in the fight. The fatal shot is believed to have been fired by Private John A. Huff, Company E, 5th

Michigan Cavalry. The struggle continued but the Confederates were forced to pull back. Sheridan continued toward Richmond being pursued by additional Confederate troops. J.E.B. Stuart died the following day. Fitzhugh Lee assumed command of the Confederate cavalry. (Before Stuart reached Yellow Tavern, he had stopped off to see his wife and children. It was reported that he did not dismount but rode up to his wife, gave her a kiss and went off toward Yellow Tavern.)

U.S.A.			C.S.A.	
Philip H. Sheridan, George A. Custer			J.E.B. Stuart (Mortally wounded), Fitzhugh Lee	

	Troops	Killed	Wounded	Missing/Captured	Total Casualties
U.S.A.	10,000	35	142	82	259
C.S.A.	3,000	54	244	168	466

12–16 *Battle of Drewry's Bluff (AKA Proctor's Creek or Fort Darling), Virginia* (**Confederate Victory**)

General Butler advanced from his position at the Bermuda Hundred towards Richmond, but was blocked by a strong Confederate entrenchment at Drewry's Bluff overlooking the James River, nine miles below Richmond. The Confederates under Beauregard defeated Butler's troops, forcing them to retreat to their base at the Bermuda Hundred. The battle had seesawed back and forth for a span of four days. Butler pulled back his offensive actions against Richmond and, with that Southern forces were able to re-establish communications and supply lines west of Richmond. This delayed Grant's action against Richmond.

U.S.A.			C.S.A.	
Benjamin Butler, Quincy A. Gillmore			P.G.T. Beauregard, Robert Ransom	

	Troops	Killed	Wounded	Missing/Captured	Total Casualties
U.S.A.	30,000	390	2,380	1,390	4,160
C.S.A.	18,000	355	1,941	210	2,506

13–15 *Battle of Resaca, Georgia* (**Undetermined**)

After abandoning his lines on Rocky Face Ridge, Johnston advanced toward Resaca via the Western and Atlantic Railroad, where he would wait for the Union advance. For the next two days, the two armies collided as the Union experienced difficulty in forcing the Confederates out of their strong entrenchment. When additional Union soldiers crossed the Oostanaula River six miles below Resaca, Johnston, feeling his line of retreat might be blocked, ordered his men to abandon their position during the middle of the night. Using green cornstalks to muffle the sounds of wagons and artillery, Johnston's army crossed the bridge. The next morning, Union officials discovered the Confederates were gone.

U.S.A.	C.S.A.
William T. Sherman, Joseph Hooker	Joseph E. Johnston, John B. Hood, Leonidas Polk

	Troops	Killed	Wounded	Missing/Captured	Total Casualties
U.S.A.	100,000	600	2,147	253	3,000
C.S.A.	70,000				2,600

15 *Battle of New Market, Virginia* (**Confederate Victory**)

At the time that Grant gave orders for Meade to move on Lee in the Wilderness, he also ordered Sigel to secure the Shenandoah Valley. Sigel was to destroy the rail lines bringing needed supplies to Lee. As he marched from Winchester toward the valley, Sigel was confronted near New Market by Confederate forces. Breckinridge was able to prevent the Union advance, eventually forcing Sigel to withdraw. This essentially ended the Union's Shenandoah Valley campaign. Breckinridge used 247 cadets from VMI in the battle. Of those cadets, 10 were killed and 47 were wounded. (These figures are included in the Confederate totals.) Sigel was relieved of his command and was replaced by General David Hunter.

U.S.A.				C.S.A.	
Franz Sigel				John C. Breckinridge	

	Troops	Killed	Wounded	Missing/Captured	Total Casualties
U.S.A.	6,275	96	520	225	841
C.S.A.	4,090	43	474	3	520

16 *Engagement at Mansura, Louisiana* (**Union Victory**)

General Nathaniel P. Banks retreated down the Red River with the Confederates close behind him. General Richard Taylor wanted to destroy the Union presence in Louisiana and, if he could not do that, he at least hoped to lessen their numbers. Taylor waylaid Banks near Mansura by opening with artillery and following with an infantry assault. Banks kept the upper hand, driving Taylor off. Taylor continued to harass Banks since he could neither stop nor destroy him.

17 *Engagement at Adairsville, Georgia* (**Confederate Victory**)

As the Confederates fled from Resaca, William T. Sherman pursued them. Joseph Johnston divided his forces, ordering General Leonidas Polk to delay Sherman and George H. Thomas while Johnston took the army toward Cassville.

18–19 *Engagement at Harris Farm, Virginia* (**Undetermined**)

After the Battle of Spotsylvania, Lee instructed General Ewell to scout Grant's strengths and weaknesses and to locate his right flank. Instead, the Confederates discovered a Union picket line and fighting broke out. Additional Union regiments were called up and the fight lasted most of the day and well into the night. Richard O. Tyler's heavy artillery battalion became involved and at times was reported to have fired into their own lines. The Union troops fell back to the Alsop House, where they were pursued all the way by General Stephen Ramseur. Ewell, instead of determining Grant's strength, brought on a general engagement. He was able to delay Grant's advance movement by one day but after the fight at Harris Farm, Ewell was discharged from the army. At the time, it was reported he resigned due to poor health after being been "knocked from his mount." Other reports indicate it was because of his poor judgment.

18 *Engagement at Yellow Bayou, Louisiana* (**Union Victory**)

In his retreat, General Banks made it to the Atchafalaya River but had to wait as his engineers built a bridge across the river. Banks, aware of General Taylor's presence nearby, ordered Mower to attack Taylor's camp. General Mower attacked Taylor at Yellow Bayou, where both two armies skirmished for most of the day. The ground cover and brush caught fire, compelling both sides to withdraw. Banks' Red River campaign was finally over.

U.S.A.				C.S.A.	
Joseph A. Mower				Richard Taylor	
	Troops	Killed	Wounded	Missing/Captured	Total Casualties
U.S.A.		54	261		315
C.S.A.					500

20 *Action at Ware Bottom Church, Virginia* (**Confederate Victory**)

Confederate forces were able to bottle up Gen. Benjamin Butler's line at Ware Bottom, allowing Gen. P.G.T. Beauregard to send additional troops to help Lee in central Virginia.

23–26 *Battle of North Anna, Virginia* (**Undetermined**)

After Spotsylvania, Grant continued his pursuit of Lee, who likewise hastened his men to North Anna where he believed he had one more chance to attack Grant. As Grant neared the North Anna River, he found the Confederates heavily entrenched and guarding the three crossings of the river: the ford at Jericho Mills on the left, Ox Ford in the center and Chesterfield Bridge on the right. Grant was forced to divide his army. By evening, Grant's men had crossed the two fords on the flanks. Lee pulled his men back into a V-shape and waited to receive Grant the next morning. Grant realized before launching his attack that his men would be divided into three groups with a river between each one. The Confederate army would be in the middle. To support either flank would require Grant's men to make a long, arduous march and to cross the river twice. Grant pulled his men back and once again swept around Lee's flank.

U.S.A.				C.S.A.	
Ulysses S. Grant, Winfield S. Hancock, Gouverneur K. Warren				Robert E. Lee, A.P. Hill, Cadmus Wilcox	
	Troops	Killed	Wounded	Missing/Captured	Total Casualties
U.S.A.		186	942	165	1,293
C.S.A.		126	680	752	1,558

24 *Action at Wilson's Wharf, Virginia* (**Union Victory**)

Confederate cavalry attacked the Union supply depot at Wilson's Wharf without success.

U.S.A.	C.S.A.
Edward Wild	Fitzhugh Lee

	Troops	Killed	Wounded	Missing/Captured	Total Casualties
U.S.A.	1,800	2	24		26
C.S.A.	3,000				139

25–27 *Campaign at New Hope Church and Pickett's Mill, Georgia* (**Confederate Victory**)

Union troops under Hooker were moving toward Dallas, Georgia, when they came upon a Confederate detachment blocking the way. The Confederates were heavily entrenched at New Hope Church. Sherman ordered Hooker to attack. The Confederates opened with 16 cannon in the midst of a driving rainstorm. Unable to penetrate the Confederate line, additional troops under Howard attacked the flank located near Pickett's Mill. General Johnston, anticipating this move, had Cleburne's division entrenched there. When Cleburne opened fire, Howard was driven backward. Hood ordered a night attack, capturing some of the fleeing Union soldiers.

U.S.A.	C.S.A.
Joseph Hooker, Oliver O. Howard	Joseph E. Johnston, John B. Hood, Patrick Cleburne

	Troops	Killed	Wounded	Missing/Captured	Total Casualties
U.S.A.	20,000	385	2,233	282	2,900
C.S.A.	4,700				1,400

26 General Grant ordered David Hunter, who had replaced Sigel, to move into the Shenandoah Valley and destroy the Virginia Central Railroad at Lynchburg, which brought needed supplies and ammunition to General Lee in central Virginia.

28 *Engagement at Dallas, Georgia* (**Union Victory**)

Confederate troops under Hardee probed the Union lines to determine the weak point. Fighting broke out when they came across Union troops commanded by General John Logan. Logan was able to force the Confederates back with great loss.

U.S.A.	C.S.A.
John A. Logan	William J. Hardee

	Troops	Killed	Wounded	Missing/Captured	Total Casualties
U.S.A.	Division	240	1,400	160	1,800
C.S.A.	Division				3,000

28 *Engagement at Haw's Shop, Virginia* (**Undetermined**)

Union cavalry, covering the infantry's advance, came across a portion of Confederate cavalry at Enon Church near Haw's Shop. Both sides fought dismounted over the next several hours, which temporarily halted the Union advance. Both sides brought up their armies in anticipation of additional fighting.

U.S.A.	C.S.A.
David M. Gregg	Fitzhugh Lee, Wade Hampton

	Troops	Killed	Wounded	Missing/Captured	Total Casualties
U.S.A. Division					344
C.S.A. Division		120	412	224	756

28–30   *Engagement at Totopotomoy Creek, Virginia* (**Undetermined**)
After the fight at Haw's Shop, infantry from both sides were rushed to the area with the Confederates entrenching behind Totopotomoy Creek. The Union probed the Confederate positions, finding they were able to push the Confederates from their first line of trenches. The battle seesawed over the next several days with neither side achieving the advantage. The Union advance was stopped and was driven backwards.

U.S.A.	C.S.A.
U.S. Grant, George G. Meade	Robert E. Lee, General George Doles (Killed)

	Troops	Killed	Wounded	Missing/Captured	Total Casualties
U.S.A.	100,000	101	578	52	731
C.S.A.	75,000	137	473	225	835

30   A four-day series of battles began between the forces of Lee and Grant in a move against Richmond. The fighting began along the banks of the creek and ended with Lee entrenching at Cold Harbor.

30   *Engagement at Old Church, Virginia* (**Union Victory**)
With the skirmish at Totopotomoy at a stalemate, Union cavalry attempted to go around the Confederate line but ran in Confederate cavalry en route to Cold Harbor.

U.S.A.	C.S.A.
General Alfred Torbert	General Matthew C. Butler

	Troops	Killed	Wounded	Missing/Captured	Total Casualties
U.S.A.	Brigade	16	74		90
C.S.A.	Brigade				100

30   John Hunt Morgan renewed his attacks in Kentucky.

31   Promoted to lieutenant general, General Jubal Early assumed command of Ewell's Second Corps. Lee believed Ewell was unfit for field duty due to illness that had affected his competency. Lee recommended that instead of being discharged from the military, Ewell should be sent to Richmond where his services would be of value.

31   John C. Fremont was nominated for president by a dissident group of Radical Republicans. Fremont named John Cochran as his vice presidential nominee.

June 1864

1 Federal cavalry under General George Stoneman captured Allatoona Pass, Georgia, where the important rail lines leading to Chattanooga ran. Now Sherman could advance his supplies closer to the fighting lines by rail.

1–3 *Battle of Cold Harbor, Virginia* (**Confederate Victory**)

After moving around Lee's troops at the North Anna River, Grant marched toward Mechanicsville where he found Lee once more firmly entrenched. Rather than risk further losses for an unimportant location, he bypassed Lee for the fourth time during the campaign. Lee, aware that the Union movement would bring them to the vicinity of Cold Harbor, a vital crossroads, ordered his cavalry to secure it until he could arrive. At the same time, Grant also ordered his cavalry to secure Cold Harbor until the infantry could be brought up. The Confederates were driven from the position but retook it with the arrival of Lee. Immediately entrenching, the Confederate soldiers were able to not only protect themselves but also deliver a murderous firepower upon the Union troops. Grant had been reinforced with additional manpower, as had Lee. Without accurate reconnaissance, Grant threw three charges against the Confederate front but heavy musket fire and artillery stopped each. Grant was forced to settle for trench warfare. In his memoir, Grant remarked that he regretted ordering the assault on the 3rd that resulted in additional loss of life. Grant abandoned the trenches on the 15th and quietly moved toward Petersburg.

U.S.A.			C.S.A.	
U.S. Grant, Philip Sheridan, Horatio Wright, George G. Meade, G.K. Warren, Ambrose Burnside, William F. Smith			Robert E. Lee, Jubal Early, Richard H. Anderson, A.P. Hill, G.P. Doles (Killed)	

	Troops	Killed	Wounded	Missing/Captured	Total Casualties
U.S.A.	108,000	1,905	10,570	2,456	14,931
C.S.A.	62,000	782	3,313	1,199	5,294

2 Union General David Hunter, who had replaced Franz Sigel, was ordered by Grant to move to the Shenandoah Valley and destroy the Virginia Central Railroad located at Lynchburg. He began this campaign as he moved into Covington, Virginia.

3 *Capture of the USS* Water Witch

The 378-ton steamer USS *Water Witch* had been on blockade duty at the mouth of the Mississippi River since the beginning of the war. By late spring 1864, the ship was off the coast of Georgia assisting in the blockade of Savannah. On May 31, the CSS *Firefly* towed several small boats down the Savannah River to the Isle of Hope with the intention of capturing the USS *Water Witch* moored in Ossabaw Sound. On the June 2, the Confederates located the ship and five small boats silently rowed toward it, all reaching the Union ship at the same time. The men boarded and quickly subdued the crew, capturing the ship. It was taken to the Georgia mainland.

4 General Joseph Johnston moved to check Sherman's advance at Lost Mountain, Pine Mountain and Brush Mountain.

5 *Occupation of Staunton, Virginia (AKA Piedmont)* (**Union Victory**)
Hunter, in his Lynchburg campaign, moved against Staunton, Virginia, where intense fighting resulted in heavy casualties on both sides. Hunter remained in Staunton overnight awaiting the arrival of General George Crooke before moving toward Lynchburg.

U.S.A.				C.S.A.	
David Hunter				W.E. "Grumble" Jones (killed)	
	Troops	*Killed*	*Wounded*	*Missing/Captured*	*Total Casualties*
U.S.A.	8,500	130	650		780
C.S.A.	5,500	60	440	1,000	1,500

6 Union soldiers under General Hunter occupied Staunton, Virginia, where they commenced to destroy and burn private residences, granaries and military stores before departing for Lynchburg.

6 *Engagement at Old River Lake, Arkansas* (**Union Victory**)
Union forces under Mower, in an effort to get to Lake Village, came up against a portion of General Marmaduke's division. The Confederates fell back to Ditch Bayou with the Union troops in pursuit. After skirmishing once more, the Confederates fled to Parker's Landing while the Union forces continued on to Lake Village. The Confederates were able to delay but not prevent the Union advance.

U.S.A.				C.S.A.	
Joseph A. Mower				Colonel Colton Greene	
	Troops	*Killed*	*Wounded*	*Missing/Captured*	*Total Casualties*
U.S.A.	2 brigades				180
C.S.A.	Brigade				100

8 John Hunt Morgan entered and captured Mount Sterling, Kentucky.

8 Lincoln was nominated to serve a second term as president of the United States.

9 Union officials drove Morgan out of Mount Sterling, Kentucky.

9 *Engagement at Petersburg, Virginia* (**Confederate Victory**)
Union infantry under Gillmore demonstrated against a smaller Confederate contingent on the outskirts of Petersburg. At the same time, Union cavalry, commanded by Colonel August V. Kautz, entered the city but was driven back by the Home Guards. This skirmish has often been referred to as the "battle of old men and young boys."

U.S.A.				C.S.A.	
Quincy Gillmore, August V. Kautz				P.G.T. Beauregard	
	Troops	*Killed*	*Wounded*	*Missing/Captured*	*Total Casualties*
U.S.A.	4,500	20	67		87
C.S.A.	2,500				33

10 *Battle of Brice's Crossroads, Mississippi* (**Confederate Victory**)

Confederate forces under Forrest moved into middle Tennessee intent on destroying the Nashville and Chattanooga Railroad, which carried men and supplies to Sherman in Georgia. Union General Sturgis was sent to protect the railroad and engaged the Confederate cavalry. After a long pursuit, Forrest turned on his pursuers and soundly overcame them. The defeat was considered one of the most degrading to the Union in the Tennessee-Mississippi campaign and one of Forrest's most outstanding victories. The Union troops, originally stationed at Memphis, were forced to retreat to the safety of that base in order to escape annihilation.

U.S.A.				C.S.A.	
Samuel Sturgis				Nathan Bedford Forrest	
	Troops	*Killed*	*Wounded*	*Missing/Captured*	*Total Casualties*
U.S.A.	8,000	223	394	1,623	2,240
C.S.A.	3,500	96	396		492

10 Confederate Congress authorized men ages 17 to 50 for military service.

11 *Raid on Lexington, Virginia* (**Union Victory**)

David Hunter, along with William Averell's cavalry and General George Crook's infantry, deviated from the plan to attack Lynchburg and instead raided Lexington. They spent three days plundering the city. The VMI cadets who had returned from New Market retreated with the small Confederate force under McCausland. Libraries, laboratories and dormitories at both VMI and Washington College were looted and destroyed. Hunter gave the order to burn the barracks and other buildings at VMI, stating the school was a place "where treason was systemically taught." A bronze statue of George Washington was removed from the VMI barracks area and sent to Wheeling, West Virginia. Hunter's chief of staff, David Hunter Strother, a distant relative, stated, "I felt indignant that this effigy should be left to adorn a country whose inhabitants were striving to destroy a government he founded."[3] The statue was returned to VMI after the war thanks to Strother.

U.S.A.				C.S.A.	
David Hunter, William Averell				John McCausland	
	Troops	*Killed*	*Wounded*	*Missing/Captured*	*Total Casualties*
U.S.A.		6	18		24
C.S.A.	1,500				

11–12 *Action at Cynthiana, Kentucky* (**Union Victory**)

After being driven from Mount Sterling, Morgan moved toward Cynthiana and, as he did, he divided his men into three groups to secure the town, but was met with resistance from an infantry regiment. The Confederates were able to push the small force back. Morgan ordered the town burned. As the town burned, another Union force commanded by General Hobson arrived and attacked Morgan, who was able to quickly overwhelm Hobson, capturing him and approximately 1,500 officers and men. The following day at dawn,

General Burbridge, with a combined force of infantry and cavalry, assaulted the town and drove Morgan from the area. Morgan could not carry his prisoners with him and, as a result, Burbridge was able to free all the Union prisoners.

		U.S.A.			C.S.A.	
	Edward H. Hobson, Stephen Gano Burbridge			John Hunt Morgan		
	Troops	*Killed*	*Wounded*	*Missing/Captured*	*Total Casualties*	
U.S.A.	5,200	8	17	280	305	
C.S.A.	2,500	80	125	400	605	

12 *Battle of Trevilian Station, Virginia* (**Confederate Victory**)

In an effort to shield the army's movement toward Petersburg, General Grant ordered his cavalry commander to create a diversion. By moving westward, Sheridan hoped Lee's cavalry would follow, depriving Lee of his "eyes and ears." Sheridan was also to link up with Hunter to destroy the Confederate rail system from central Virginia. His first movement was toward Trevilian Station and there Confederate cavalry met him. The fight between the two cavalry units was described by some as "a wild melee of saber strokes and pistol shots." With his defeat at Trevilian Station, Sheridan's planned cavalry raids into the Shenandoah were stopped.

		U.S.A.			C.S.A.	
	Philip Sheridan, George Custer			Wade Hampton, Fitzhugh Lee		
	Troops	*Killed*	*Wounded*	*Missing/Captured*	*Total Casualties*	
U.S.A.	8,000	150	738	624	1,512	
C.S.A.	5,000				612	

11 General Lee ordered General Early, now commander of the Second Corps, to take his men to the Shenandoah Valley and stop the Union raids being conducted by General Hunter. Early was advised that if he stopped Hunter in the valley, he would be free to raid Maryland and Washington.

14 While watching the Union artillery from a position atop Pine Mountain, Confederate General Leonidas Polk was killed when he was hit by Union artillery shell.

15–18 *Assault on Petersburg, Virginia* (**Confederate Victory**)

After Cold Harbor, Grant made a swift march, crossing the James and heading toward Petersburg, just south of Richmond. Approaching Petersburg, Grant discovered that a ten-mile line of fortifications and trenches protected the city. On the 15th, Union forces assaulted a few of the fortifications and were able to capture a one mile wide section of the line. Confederate forces quickly moved down from Bermuda Hundred, a defensive line protecting Richmond, to fortify Petersburg. Up until this time, Lee had no idea where Grant had disappeared to until word came from General Beauregard requesting his assistance. Lee quickly dispatched additional troops to assist Beauregard, which allowed Beauregard to hold his defensive lines from the Union's numerous assaults. Grant also received another fifty thousand men. On the 17th, when the Union forces overran one of the defensive positions, they found another one behind it. On the 18th, Grant ordered an attack against the Confederate line. In what later was identified as a suicidal charge, the 1st Maine Artillery lost over two-thirds of their number in the first ten minutes of the assault. In four days of fighting, the Union lost more than ten thousand men. Grant realized that he would not be able to take the city by direct assault and thus could not enter Richmond by the back door. He would have to switch from an active assault to a siege operation. He would surround the city and, at the same time, cut all the supply routes to and from the city. The Union casualty rates were rising sharply, especially after the last four battles. Newspapers referred to the general as "Bloody Grant" or "the Butcher." The last four battles, the Wilderness, Spotsylvania, Cold Harbor and Petersburg, resulted in over fifty thousand Union casualties.

U.S.A.			C.S.A.	
U.S. Grant, W.F. Smith, G.K. Warren, George G. Meade, Winfield S. Hancock (wounded)			Robert E. Lee, P.G.T. Beauregard, Richard Anderson, A.P. Hill	

	Troops	Killed	Wounded	Missing/Captured	Total Casualties
U.S.A.	62,000	1,127	4,874	2,277	8,278
C.S.A.	42,000				3,236

17–18 *Engagement at Lynchburg, Virginia* (**Confederate Victory**)

Union troops, after ransacking and burning Lexington, moved toward Lynchburg. They were to destroy the rail lines furnishing supplies to Lee's army. However, as they approached the town, Confederate forces from Charlottesville had arrived. Their timely arrival prevented the destruction, for Hunter believed that he was now outnumbered. He pulled his troops back and made his retreat through West Virginia, delaying his arrival in the Shenandoah Valley. While Hunter was gone for almost a month, he had left the Shenandoah Valley in Confederate hands, which allowed General Early to make a move on Washington during the following month. This action ultimately resulted in Hunter being replaced.

U.S.A.			C.S.A.	
David Hunter			Jubal A. Early, John C. Breckinridge	

	Troops	Killed	Wounded	Missing/Captured	Total Casualties
U.S.A.	Corps	103	564	271	938
C.S.A.	15,000				

18 The Union siege of Petersburg began after the initial assault failed.

19 *Sea Battle between USS* Kearsarge *and the CSS* Alabama (**Union Victory**)

The CSS *Alabama*, in Cherbourg, France, for repairs, prepared for battle after her commander learned the USS *Kearsarge* had taken a position off the French coast waiting for the ship to depart. On the morning of the 19th, the CSS *Alabama* escorted by a French warship sailed into international waters. Once clear of the three-mile limit, the two ships opened fire with their guns and each began to circle the other. After ninety minutes, the *Alabama* "struck her colors" when she went down. Her crew was rescued by the English ship HMS *Deerhound* and taken to an English port, thus preventing their capture by Union officials. Had they had been rescued by Union officials, they would have been treated as prisoners of war. Some historians have decreed this sea battle under officers John A. Winslow and Raphael Semmes to have been the greatest ship-to-ship combat of the war in open waters.

22 *Engagement at Weldon Railroad (AKA Jerusalem Plank Road), Virginia* (**Confederate Victory**)

Union cavalry under General James H. Wilson, along with General August V. Kautz's infantry division, were ordered to cut the rail line from Petersburg southward to North Carolina. At the same time, they were to cause as much destruction as they could. They moved west of Petersburg toward the Weldon Railroad that entered the city from the south. In addition, they were to destroy the rail lines at Southside Railroad, which ran from Richmond to Lynchburg. To prevent any type of interference from the Confederate cavalry, a demonstration was to be made against Richmond. Union troops tore up several miles of track and set fire to the rail station before moving on to destroy the Southside Railroad. They were challenged by Confederate troops under William H.F. Lee and William H. Mahone sent to protect the rail line and to keep the supply and communication lines open. Buildings were burned and some bridges destroyed before the arriving Confederate troops forced the Union troops from the area. The Union troops continued southwest, raiding as they went.

22 *Combat at Kolb's Farm, Georgia* (**Union Victory**)

Union troops under Schofield and Hooker moved to menace the rail line protected by Confederate troops under Joseph Johnston. Upon hearing of the Union's movement, Johnston dispatched Hood to cover that portion of the territory. Hood decided to launch his own attack against orders. The Union troops, aware of Hood's intentions, were firmly entrenched and had their artillery guns in a position. Hood suffered many casualties before he withdrew.

	U.S.A.				*C.S.A.*
	John M. Schofield, Joseph Hooker				John B. Hood
	Troops	*Killed*	*Wounded*	*Missing/Captured*	*Total Casualties*
U.S.A.	2 corps	80	450	160	690
C.S.A.	1 corps				1,000

23 Confederate General Jubal Early, fresh from his decisive victory over the Union forces in the valley, began a movement northward that would carry him into Maryland.

23 Union commander Lieutenant William B. Cushing was sent to determine the status of the Confederate ironclad CSS *Raleigh*, reported stranded on a sandbar near Wilmington, North Carolina. Cushing became involved in numerous skirmishes as he and his men scouted the defenses of Wilmington, but they did verify that the vessel was stranded on the sandbar and it was nothing but a rusted and useless ship.

24 *Engagement at Saint Mary's Church, Virginia* (**Undetermined**)

Union and Confederate cavalry clashed as the Confederates attempted to cut off the Union's retreat from Trevilian Station. After fighting a delaying action, Sheridan managed to rejoin the Union lines at Bermuda Hundred.

	U.S.A.				*C.S.A.*
	Philip Sheridan				Wade Hampton
	Troops	*Killed*	*Wounded*	*Missing/Captured*	*Total Casualties*
U.S.A.		29	188	122	339
C.S.A.					291

25 *Action at Staunton River Bridge, Virginia* (**Confederate Victory**)

Union troops commanded by August V. Kautz discovered the bridge which they had been ordered to burn defended by Confederate militia. Using the cavalry under General James Wilson to hold off a Confederate brigade moving up on his rear, Kautz's infantry moved toward the bridge, but were held at bay by the Virginia Home Guard until Lee's cavalry arrived. Upon the arrival of the Confederate cavalry, the Union attackers pulled back. By then they were far behind their lines and decided to break off their mission and return to the safety of the Union lines, abandoning their artillery and supply wagons. Many Union soldiers were captured and taken prisoner.

27 *Battle of Kennesaw Mountain, Georgia* (**Confederate Victory**)

General Johnston had withdrawn his men to Kennesaw Mountain and had entrenched in an arc-shaped line. With the defeat of General Hood at Kolb's Farm, Union commanders believed Johnston now had stretched his line too far and would be vulnerable to a frontal assault. Also by now, Sherman had grown tired of the flanking marches and did not want to become engaged in a siege operation. He opened the attack with an artillery barrage followed by an infantry charge uphill. Within two and a half hours, the fighting was over and Sherman was forced to withdraw.

	U.S.A.				*C.S.A.*
	William T. Sherman				Joseph Johnston
	Troops	*Killed*	*Wounded*	*Missing/Captured*	*Total Casualties*
U.S.A.	12,000	1,068	3,484	1,558	6,110
C.S.A.	17,733				442

28 *Engagement at Sappony Church, Virginia* (**Confederate Victory**)

Confederates pursued James Wilson and August Kautz as they attempted to make it to their lines, especially after the fighting at the Staunton River Bridge. They caught up with the retreating line as they crossed the Nottoway River near Stony Creek. When the additional troops of W.H. "Rooney" Lee's cavalry arrived to join Wade Hampton, the Union force disengaged and headed toward Reams Station, where they thought they might find support and reinforcements.

29 *Engagement at Reams Station, Virginia* (**Confederate Victory**)

Union commanders, fleeing from the Stony Creek area, approached Reams Station, believing it to be in Union hands. They soon discovered that Confederate infantry stood in their way and was soon joined by cavalry. After a brief skirmish, Union commanders set their wagons on fire and extricated themselves. Wilson fled southward on the Stage Road to cross the Nottoway River, while General Kautz made his way cross-country, as both commands attempted to reach the Petersburg lines.

U.S.A.	C.S.A.
James H. Wilson, August V. Kautz	William Mahone, W.H.F. "Rooney" Lee

	Troops	Killed	Wounded	Missing/Captured	Total Casualties
U.S.A.	5,000	142	654	2,166	2,962
C.S.A.	Division				1,038

This chart includes the totals from the Wilson-Kautz raid (June 22–29).

July 1864

2 Marietta, Georgia, was evacuated as news of the Union presence in the area was received.

3 General William T. Sherman began a drive toward Atlanta, forcing General Joseph E. Johnston to move his army from the vicinity of Kennesaw Mountain. He moved to the Chattahoochee River to avoid being flanked.

5 The Confederate Army moved through Hagerstown, Maryland, toward Washington.

6 Confederate Lieutenant General Jubal A. Early entered Frederick City, Maryland, meeting with very little resistance. As a diversion, he sent a cavalry brigade toward Baltimore in an attempt to free Confederate prisoners at Point Lookout while the rest of his men moved toward Washington. In the meantime, Washington officials requested additional militia from New York and Pennsylvania to help defend the nation's capital. General Grant, encamped near Petersburg, sent troops from the Petersburg area.

8 General Schofield crossed the Chattahoochee River, forcing General Joseph Johnston into his last defenses before Atlanta.

9 *Battle of Monocacy, Maryland* (**Confederate Victory**)

General Lew Wallace prepared for the defense of the capital when news was received that the Confederate Army was within ninety miles of Washington. Wallace established a defensive line across the Monocacy River at a spot where he could keep an eye on the three bridges that crossed the river. Upon the arrival of General Early and his army, Wallace's pickets were at first driven in, but the Confederate advancement was temporarily halted. General Early called for an all-out assault on the Union line. With the arrival of additional Confederate troops, fierce fighting commenced in earnest. Just when it looked as if the Union line was about to break, Wallace called for a retreat, which turned into a rout by the inexperienced Union defenders. Historians credit Wallace with saving Washington by delaying the Confederate charge long enough for additional troops to arrive from Petersburg and set up defensive positions.

		U.S.A.		C.S.A.	
		General Lew Wallace		Jubal Early, John B. Gordon	
	Troops	Killed	Wounded	Missing/Captured	Total Casualties
U.S.A.	6,000	123	603	568	1,294
C.S.A.	10,000				700

11–12 *Attack on Washington, D.C.* (**Union Victory**)

On the 11th, Confederate forces under General Jubal A. Early approached Silver Springs, Maryland, on the outskirts of Washington. Here, they came across the first line of the Washington defenders, which were members of the Home Guard, clerks and members of the Invalid Corps. The Confederate army pushed them aside but decided to rest for the night, as they were exhausted from the fight at Monocracy and the hasty march to the Washington outskirts. This allowed the troops coming from Petersburg to arrive and position themselves at Fort Stevens. When the Confederate army reached the fort on the 12th, they found it heavily guarded by the experienced troops of General Grant's army under Horatio G. Wright and Alexander McCook. President Lincoln also arrived to view the battle. Aware that he was out-manned, General Early withdrew. He later stated, "I had therefore, reluctantly to give up all hopes of capturing Washington, after I had arrived in sight of the dome of the Capitol."[4]

11 President Lincoln paid a visit to Fort Stevens near Washington and witnessed the attack by Confederates. While in the fort watching the skirmishing out front, President Lincoln was told by Lieutenant Colonel Oliver Wendell Holmes, Jr., to "get down, you damn fool, before you get shot."[5] Apparently, Holmes did not know at the time that he was yelling at the president of the United States.

12 Confederates withdrew from Washington area.

14 *Engagement at Tupelo, Mississippi* (**Union Victory**)

General Sherman ordered Smith to keep General Forrest from breaking the Union supply lines. As Smith left La Grange, Tennessee, he burned and destroyed crops and the countryside as he moved toward the rail line that he was to protect. Stephen D. Lee proposed that an all-out attack be made on the Union line, whereas Forrest suggested that they instead use hit and run tactics as they moved southward along the rail line. Lee won out and the attack was made near Tupelo. They were quickly driven back. Lee called off the assault, as he was outmanned and the Union troops were firmly entrenched. These Union troops had defeated Forrest, some of the few who did in actual combat. Because of his precarious position and because he was low on ammunition, Smith withdrew. Smith had accomplished his mission to protect the Chattanooga to Nashville line of Sherman's Georgia force. Sherman later criticized Smith for not destroying Forrest when he had the chance. Smith was ordered to "follow Forrest to the death."

		U.S.A.		C.S.A.	
	General Andrew J. Smith		Nathan Bedford Forrest, Stephen D. Lee		
	Troops	*Killed*	*Wounded*	*Missing/Captured*	*Total Casualties*
U.S.A.	14,200	77	559	38	674
C.S.A.	9,500				1,347

17 President Jefferson Davis, dissatisfied with General Joseph Johnston due to his strategic withdrawal earlier in the month, replaced him with General John B. Hood. Hood, upon taking command of the Army of Tennessee, stated the army would not retreat anymore.

17–18 *Engagement at Cool Spring, Virginia (AKA Snicker's Ferry)* (**Confederate Victory**)
General Early, as he departed the Washington area, was pursued by Union troops under General Wright. At the same time, Union cavalry had moved to prevent Early from crossing the fords of the Shenandoah River near Snicker's Gap, but came across several Confederate infantry units sent forth to secure the fords. The Union cavalry had to withdraw.

		U.S.A.		C.S.A.	
	General Horatio Wright, Colonel Joseph Thoburn		General Jubal Early, General Robert Rodes		
	Troops	*Killed*	*Wounded*	*Missing/Captured*	*Total Casualties*
U.S.A.	5,000	65	301	56	422
C.S.A.	8,000				397

18 Lincoln issued a call for an additional five hundred thousand volunteers to serve in the armed forces.

18 New York businessman J.R. Gilmore, hoping to bring an end to the hostilities, met with President Lincoln in Washington suggesting that the president recognize the Confederacy. Gilmore had numerous contacts in both the North and the South. At the same time, Horace Greeley traveled to Niagara Falls, New York, to speak to several men who said they represented the Confederacy and wished to discuss possible peace negotiations based on the independence of the Confederate states. Both discussions ended in failure, as Lincoln insisted the only way to end the war was the restoration of the Union and the abolition of slavery.

20 *Skirmish at Rutherford's Farm, Virginia* (**Union Victory**)
Union troops discovered General Stephen D. Ramseur's division near Rutherford's Farm. A brief skirmish occurred as Union forces under General William W. Averell were able to drive the Confederates from the area toward Winchester. As a result, it was reported, Early withdrew to Fisher Hill.

20 *Battle of Peachtree, Georgia* (**Union Victory**)
Prior to General Hood assuming command of the Army of Tennessee, Johnston had withdrawn south of Peachtree Creek, about three miles north of Atlanta. He had made

plans to attack Sherman, but now the command fell to General Hood. Hood made an attack on one wing of Sherman's army (Army of the Cumberland) commanded by General Thomas. Hood's men made continuous assaults into heavy artillery charges and within three hours had suffered heavy casualties. Hood was forced to pull back.

	U.S.A.			C.S.A.	
	General George H. Thomas			General John B. Hood, General William Hardee	

	Troops	Killed	Wounded	Missing/Captured	Total Casualties
U.S.A.	20,000	310	1,254	215	1,779
C.S.A.	19,000				4,796

20 General Sherman began shelling the City of Atlanta with long-range guns. The first shell reportedly traveled 2.5 miles, landing at the intersection of Ivy and Ellis streets, where a small girl and her dog were killed.

22 *Battle of Atlanta, Georgia* (**Union Victory**)
   Confederate commander John B. Hood was determined to attack a portion of Sherman's troops under the command of General McPherson (Army of the Tennessee). Hood split his army, sending them in several directions to launch attacks on the various wings of the Union army. Hood had miscalculated the time it would take for all elements to get into position. Two of his divisions ran into the reserve force of McPherson and were forced to retreat. As Commander General James B. McPherson rode out to inspect the lines, he accidentally rode into the Confederate line and was shot when he refused to surrender. Hood's third division ran up against heavy artillery fire and was also forced to pull back. In the meantime, Sherman cut the supply lines to Atlanta and settled into a siege operation around the city.

	U.S.A.			C.S.A.	
	James B. McPherson (Killed), John A. Logan			John B. Hood, Benjamin F. Cheatham, General William H.T. Walker (killed)	

	Troops	Killed	Wounded	Missing/Captured	Total Casualties
U.S.A.	30,000	430	1,559	1,733	3,722
C.S.A.	40,000				8,500

24 *Engagement at Kernstown, Virginia* (**Confederate Victory**)
   General Early, coming from the attack on Washington, was ordered to prevent reinforcements from supporting Grant in Petersburg. Coming across a Union detachment moving from Winchester, Early attacked, forcing the Union troops to retreat back to Winchester, where they crossed the Potomac near Williamsport.

	U.S.A.			C.S.A.	
	George Crook, James Mulligan (mortally wounded)			Jubal Early, Stephen Ramseur, John Breckinridge	

	Troops	Killed	Wounded	Missing/Captured	Total Casualties
U.S.A.	10,000	100	606	479	1,185
C.S.A.	13,000				600

27–29 *Engagement at Deep Bottom, Virginia* (**Confederate Victory**)

Sheridan launched an extensive cavalry raid north of the James River to threaten Richmond. Confederate cavalry, reinforced by infantry, was able to force the Union to call off the raid and to return to the other side of the river.

U.S.A.	C.S.A.
General Winfield S. Hancock, General Philip Sheridan	General Charles Field

	Troops	Killed	Wounded	Missing/Captured	Total Casualties
U.S.A.		62	340	86	488
C.S.A.					Unknown

28 *Battle of Erza Church, Georgia* (*part of the battle for Atlanta*) (**Union Victory**)

In a move to encircle Atlanta and cut off its communications to the west and south, Sherman moved the Army of Tennessee from the far left to the extreme right of the battle line. General O.O. Howard was ordered to cut the rail lines between East Point and the city itself. Hood, at the same time, moved the greater part of his force to this area during the night of the 27th with instructions to destroy the Union force. Fighting began the next morning and lasted until late afternoon. Union forces had entrenched and inflicted severe casualties on the Confederates, forcing Hood to withdraw to the inner confines of the works surrounding the city. Howard was unable to cut the rail lines.

U.S.A.	C.S.A.
General Oliver O. Howard	General John B. Hood, Stephen D. Lee, Alexander P. Stewart

	Troops	Killed	Wounded	Missing/Captured	Total Casualties
U.S.A.	13,000				650
C.S.A.	18,000				2,800

28 *Engagement at Killdeer Mountain, North Dakota* (**Union Victory**)

General Alfred Sully had been sent to the Northwest Territory to deal with the Indian situation. Indian uprisings and raids were spreading as more and more tribes became involved. During July 1864, Sully was in the North Dakota area when he learned that several different tribes that had gone on the war path. Sully formed a large, hollow square, placed the horses and artillery inside and advanced on the Indian camp. The Indians turned out to meet the Union force but the artillery guns were too much for the Indians. They called off the fight and left the area.

U.S.A.	C.S.A.
General Alfred Sully	Indian Chief Inkpaduta (Sioux)

	Troops	Killed	Wounded	Missing/Captured	Total Casualties
U.S.A.	2,200	5	10		15
Indians	1,600	31			unknown

29   Confederates under Jubal Early and John McCausland crossed the Potomac, west of Williamsport near Cave Spring, to enter Maryland and Pennsylvania. Word spread to the citizens of Chambersburg of the imminent arrival of a portion of the Confederate army.

30   *Confederates enter and burn Chambersburg, Pennsylvania.*
General John McCausland had been ordered by General Jubal Early to raid Chambersburg for the third time during the war. This raid was to be in retribution for General Hunter's destruction in the Shenandoah Valley and the burning of Staunton and Lexington. The citizens of Chambersburg had been aware of the Confederates moving in their direction and, by the time of their arrival, had sent most of the supplies, animals and bank funds to the state capital. McCausland demanded $100,000 or he would set fire to the town. At 9 a.m., he set fire to the city; over 400 buildings, including 274 private residences, were set ablaze. By 11 a.m., the Confederates were on their way back to Virginia. (The State of Pennsylvania granted emergency relief funds to rebuild the city but some of the claims were not settled until 130 years later.) After this incident, General Grant appointed Philip Sheridan as commander of all Union forces in the Shenandoah Valley.

30   *Assault on the Crater, Virginia (AKA Petersburg Mine Fiasco)* (**Confederate Victory**)
Just 130 yards from the Confederate trenches at Petersburg, the 48th Pennsylvania under Colonel Henry Pleasants began to dig a tunnel towards the Confederate lines. The unit, made up mainly of coal miners, took 28 days to dig the tunnel, and placed four tons of powder inside the tunnel. During the digging operations, the Confederates, who were aware of the tunneling operation, dug numerous counter tunnels hoping to either break through or cave in the Union's efforts. On July 30, the charge was exploded. Due to ineffective preparations for the attack through the tunnel, disaster struck the Union force. The charge, as planned, ripped a gaping hole 500 yards wide in the very center of Lee's lines. The explosion created a hole 30 feet deep, 60 feet wide and 170 feet long. A heavy Union artillery barrage coming from 114 artillery pieces accompanied the explosion. Although fresh Negro troops were standing by to lead the assault, Union officials felt there would be repercussions if the move failed and the Negro soldiers were killed, so battle-weary white soldiers were sent into the tunnel. In addition to this fiasco, no scaling ladders were provided for the troops, and the crater walls were inaccessible. This allowed the Confederates time to rally from the initial shock of the explosion and slaughter the Union forces in the deep crater. The Union soldiers were crowded so tight in the crater that only those on the fringes could actually fire their weapons. The Confederate assault on the Union line had been termed "a turkey shoot."

U.S.A.	C.S.A.
General Ambrose Burnside,	General William Mahone,
General James H. Ledlie,	General Stephen Elliott
Colonel Henry Pleasants	

	Troops	Killed	Wounded	Missing/Captured	Total Casualties
U.S.A.	15,000	504	1,881	1,413	3,798
C.S.A.	Unknown				1,500

28 Union cavalry under General George Stoneman attempted to liberate the Union prisoners at Andersonville, Georgia, but Stoneman was captured and taken prisoner at Macon, Georgia, by forces under Joseph Wheeler.

August 1864

1 *Action at Folck's Mill, Maryland* (**Undetermined**)

After leaving Chambersburg, Pennsylvania, in flames, Confederate cavalrymen moved toward Cumberland, Maryland, where they intended to destroy the B and O Rail line. Warned of the Confederate marauders, a small Union contingent ambushed them as they approached Folck's Mill near Cumberland. Taken by surprise, the Confederates withdrew after several hours of fighting. By evening, the Confederates had left the area.

U.S.A.				C.S.A.	
General Benjamin F. Kelley, Lt. T.W. Kelley				General John McCausland, General Bradley T. Johnson	

	Troops	Killed	Wounded	Missing/Captured	Total Casualties
U.S.A.	Divisions	1	1		2
C.S.A.	2600	8	30		38

5 *Battle of Mobile Bay, Alabama* (**Union Victory**)

Combined naval and land forces moved to close Mobile Bay to Confederate blockade raiders. Mobile Bay had been fortified by the Confederates and this was the only port open on the Gulf Coast. Union naval commander David G. Farragut, with a fleet of 14 wooden ships and 4 ironclads, moved to secure the entrance to the bay strongly guarded by three Confederate gunboats and one ironclad. Three garrisons also guarded the harbor — Fort Morgan, the strongest of the forts, Fort Gaines and Fort Powell. During the attack, one of Farragut's commanders informed Farragut that the harbor was full of torpedoes. Farragut replied, "Damn the torpedoes! Full speed ahead."[6] The port was closed, but the city remained in Confederate hands. Union officials began to consider siege operations as the way to take the city.

U.S.A.				C.S.A.	
David G. Farragut				Benjamin Buchanan (Wounded)	

	Troops	Killed	Wounded	Missing/Captured	Total Casualties
U.S.A.	18 ships	145	170	4	319
C.S.A.	4 ships	12	20	270	302

5 Representative Henry Winter Davis of Maryland and Senator Benjamin Wade of Ohio issued the Wade-Davis Manifesto in the *New York Tribune*, which stated, "It is their right and duty to check the encroachments of the Executive on the authority of Congress." They had accused Lincoln of personal ambition in refusing to sign the Wade-Davis bill.

5–7   *Combat at Utoy Creek, Georgia* (**Undetermined**)
Sherman directed General John M. Schofield to extend his line to the north bank of the Utoy Creek. He had been trying to get into a position where he could destroy the rail line between East Point and Atlanta. On the 5th, Union troops met General John B. Hood's Army of Tennessee and became engaged in several skirmishes. Because of delays in forming the Union lines, the Confederates were able to take advantage of the situation by creating several abatis from fallen trees. This slowed the Union assault and, by the 7th, the Union troops had entrenched. For the rest of the month, there existed a standoff between the two sides.

7   Major General Philip Sheridan assumed command of all Union troops in the Shenandoah Valley. General Grant instructed him to follow General Early "to the death."

7   *Engagement at Moorefield, West Virginia* (**Union Victory**)
As the Confederates were returning to the Shenandoah Valley from their mission to Pennsylvania and Maryland, Union cavalry surprised them. After a brief skirmish, the Confederates withdrew and their effectiveness in the valley diminished.

U.S.A.			C.S.A.	
General William W. Averell			General John McCausland	
	Troops	*Killed*	*Wounded*	*Missing/Captured*	*Total Casualties*
U.S.A. Division					60
C.S.A. Division					470

8   Fort Gaines in Mobile Bay, Alabama, surrendered to the Union army.

9   Union troops surrounded Fort Morgan in Mobile Bay, Alabama, and laid a siege line to prevent ships and supplies from reaching the city.

9   *Explosion at City Point, Virginia*
Union commander Ulysses S. Grant had established his headquarters at City Point, Virginia. Captain John Maxwell, a Confederate spy, managed to penetrate the Union lines making his way to the river's edge. There he placed a time bomb made with 12 pounds of gunpowder on an ammunition barge containing between 20,000 and 30,000 artillery shells and 75,000 rounds of small arms ammunition. Shortly before noon, the bomb exploded, destroying two million dollars worth of property and supplies. The bomb narrowly missed General Grant, who had been sitting outside his headquarters above the harbor. Ten men were killed and 130 officers and men were injured.

10   General Benjamin F. Butler suggested to General Grant that a large canal be built through a 174-foot wide section of the James River. Butler said this canal, later called the Dutch Gap Canal, would allow gunboats to circumvent the Confederate artillery. Grant, preoccupied with Petersburg, gave his approval, not so much for what could be made of the canal, but rather to keep General Butler busy and out of his hair. After the war, the canal was used for commercial navigation that trimmed almost five miles off the trip up the James River.

10 General Joseph Wheeler began an extended cavalry raid in an effort to destroy Union communications lines between Atlanta and Nashville.

13–20 *Engagement at Deep Bottom (AKA Fussell's Mill or Strawberry Plains), Virginia* (**Confederate Victory**)

While involved with the siege operations in Petersburg, General Grant issued orders for Generals Kautz and Wilson to make attacks along the Weldon Railroad line while Hancock made an attack on Richmond. Hancock split his forces—one to demonstrate near New Market Heights while the other went toward Fussell's Mill, which they were to capture. This would open a route to Richmond. Hancock's troops encountered resistance before they reached Fussell's Mill. The battle seesawed back and forth until Hancock realized he could not take the position. He pulled his men back after suffering severe casualties. Union forces retreated while holding their position at Deep Bottom.

	U.S.A.			C.S.A.	
General Winfield S. Hancock			General Robert E. Lee, General Charles Field, General John R. Chambliss (killed)		

	Troops	Killed	Wounded	Missing/Captured	Total Casualties
U.S.A.	28,000	328	1,852	721	2,901
C.S.A.	20,000				1,600

14–15 *Combat at Dalton, Georgia* (**Union Victory**)

Wheeler's Confederate cavalry approached Dalton and demanded the surrender of the garrison. When the garrison commander refused, fighting began immediately. Outnumbered, the garrison retired to fortifications outside of the town. The Confederates kept up their assault but the small Union contingent was able to hold out until Union reinforcements came to assist. Wheeler withdrew his forces.

	U.S.A.			C.S.A.	
General James B. Steedman, Colonel Bernard Laibolt			General Joseph Wheeler		

	Troops	Killed	Wounded	Missing/Captured	Total Casualties
U.S.A.	3,000	9	24	24	57
C.S.A.	5,000	33	57	110	200

16 *Engagement at Guard Hill (AKA Front Royal, Cedarville), Virginia* (**Confederate Victory**)

General Richard Anderson, with divisions of Confederate infantry and cavalry from Petersburg, arrived in the Shenandoah Valley to assist General Early. Near Front Royal,

Union cavalry surprised them as they crossed the Shenandoah River. After a brief skirmish, the Confederates were able to push back the Union cavalry and join up with Early.

U.S.A.			C.S.A.	
General Wesley Merritt			General Richard Anderson	
Troops	Killed	Wounded	Missing/Captured	Total Casualties
U.S.A. Division	13	58		71
C.S.A. Division				479

18–21 *Battle of Weldon Railroad (AKA Globe Tavern), Virginia* (**Union Victory**)

In conjunction with Hancock's attempted raid on Richmond, Grant ordered General Warren to capture the Weldon Railroad running south from Petersburg. Warren managed to seize a portion of the rail line around Globe Tavern. Confederate forces attempted to regain this vital rail line. After several days of hard fighting, General Lee ordered his forces to pull back. The Union now extended the siege lines around Petersburg and, at the same time, had cut the rail line from Petersburg to Wilmington, North Carolina.

	U.S.A.			C.S.A.	
	General Gouverneur K. Warren, Samuel Crawford			General Henry Heth, A.P. Hill, William Mahone, John C.C. Sanders (killed)	
	Troops	Killed	Wounded	Missing/Captured	Total Casualties
U.S.A.	20,000	198	1,105	3,152	4,455
C.S.A.	14,000				2,300

18–22 Sherman conducted a wheeling movement to strike at Jonesboro, southeast of Atlanta. At the same time, in conjunction with the movement, he sent his cavalry to raid the Confederate supply depots. This was in retaliation for the earlier Confederate cavalry raid on the Union supply wagons.

18 Union cavalry under General H. Judson Kilpatrick conducted raids along the Atlanta and West Point Railroad, where they tore up tracks, burned ties, and bent the rails.

19 General Kilpatrick reached Jonesboro, Georgia, where his troops destroyed whatever they could locate near the Macon and Western Railroad.

20 *Action at Lovejoy's Station, Georgia* (**Confederate Victory**)

As the Union cavalry under General H. Judson Kilpatrick reached Lovejoy's Station with the intention of destroying it, a small Confederate cavalry under William H. Jackson confronted them. The Confederates were able to drive the Union back, but not before they had destroyed some of the track.

21 *Skirmish at Summit Point, West Virginia* (**Undetermined**)

As the Confederate cavalry moved toward Charlestown, where Sheridan's Union cavalry was concentrated, they ran into a cavalry patrol under Wilson near Summit Point.

At the same time, Fitzhugh Lee's cavalry became involved in a small skirmish at nearby Berryville. Both engagements broke off when it turned dark. Historians state that the Union fought more of a delaying action before withdrawing to Charlestown the next morning.

U.S.A.			C.S.A.	
General Philip Sheridan,			General Jubal Early,	
General James H. Wilson			General Richard Anderson	

	Troops	Killed	Wounded	Missing/Captured	Total Casualties
U.S.A.	Division				600
C.S.A.	Division				400

21 *Raid on Memphis, Tennessee* (**Confederate Victory**)

General Nathan Bedford Forrest made a raid on Memphis, Tennessee, with the idea of capturing several of the leading commanders. At the same time, he hoped to release Confederate prisoners held at the Irving Block Prison. Forrest hoped by these actions, he could force the recall of Union troops from Mississippi. The raid was termed a Confederate success, though Forrest failed to achieve his first two objectives. The third objective was met; his raid through Memphis revealed a weakness and additional Union troops were pulled from Mississippi to provide protection for Memphis.

23 Fort Morgan, in Mobile Bay, Alabama fell to the Union. With the fort in Union hands, they now controlled the port, although the Confederates still held the city.

25 *Battle of Reams Station, Virginia* (**Confederate Victory**)

Confederates under A.P. Hill were ordered by General Lee to retake the Weldon Railroad captured earlier by Union troops. After a fierce attack that stunned the Union troops, the Confederates swept through, capturing nine guns, twelve flags and over 2,100 Union soldiers.

U.S.A.			C.S.A.	
General Winfield S. Hancock,			General Ambrose P. Hill,	
General Nelson A. Miles			General Henry Heth	

	Troops	Killed	Wounded	Missing/Captured	Total Casualties
U.S.A.	Corps	140	529	2,073	2,742
C.S.A.	Corps				720

28 General Edmund Kirby Smith, commander of the Trans-Mississippi, ordered General Sterling Price to make diversionary raids into Missouri, causing the Union to release its hold on Atlanta. In addition, it was also hoped the Union's hold on the Mississippi would be reduced. Price left Camden, Arkansas, with 12,000 soldiers. It would take him three weeks to reach the Arkansas-Missouri border.

29 *Engagement at Smithfield Crossing* (**Undetermined**)

Confederate cavalry came upon Union troops, forcing them back toward Charlestown.

U.S.A.				C.S.A.
General Wesley Merritt				General Jubal Early

	Troops	Killed	Wounded	Missing/Captured	Total Casualties
U.S.A. Division		10	90		100
C.S.A. Division					Unknown

31   George McClellan received the Democratic Party nomination for president, picking George H. Pendleton as his vice president.

31   Union forces cut the Macon and Western Railroad connection into Atlanta.

31–Sept. 1   *Battle of Jonesboro, Georgia* (**Union Victory**)
   During the extensive maneuver around the city, Sherman moved his force to East Point, Georgia, six miles southwest of Atlanta, to cut off the communications to that sector. Troops under General Thomas were busy destroying thirteen miles of track and were in the process of establishing a battle line in conjunction with Couch and Schofield when forces under Hardee and Stephen D. Lee struck General Howard's line. Howard's line was to the right of Thomas. Because Hardee's attack was a feeble one, the effort failed. The fighting left Hardee entrenched near Jonesboro. After a hard-fought battle between his forces and those of Union commander Jeff Davis, Hardee retreated under cover of darkness to Lovejoy, Georgia, leaving Jonesboro and the surrounding terrain to the Union. The Confederate loss eventually resulted in the fall of Atlanta.

U.S.A.				C.S.A.
General Oliver O. Howard, General John Schofield				General William J. Hardee, General Stephen D. Lee

	Troops	Killed	Wounded	Missing/Captured	Total Casualties
U.S.A.	60,000				1,149
C.S.A.	24,000				1,725

September 1864

1   With the fall of Jonesboro, Georgia, the Confederates evacuated Atlanta. General John B. Hood set up a line of defense at Lovejoy's Station south of Jonesboro.

2   *Atlanta, Georgia falls* (**Union Victory**)
   The fall of Atlanta was a long, drawn out affair. The Union had established a siege line to the city, as occasional skirmishes occurred from the time Sherman left Chattanooga. The fights seesawed back and forth, ranging from Kennesaw Mountain to New Hope to Adairsville to Resaca, and finally to the defeat of the Confederates at Jonesboro. The Confederate commander, John B. Hood, strategically fought with and retreated from the relentless oncoming armies sent forth by Sherman under various commanders. As the skirmishes took place, Sherman continued his march through the South. Sherman, an advocate of

total war, pressed on to Atlanta in a systematic drive that followed a format laid down by Grant — divide the weakened enemy, defeat each segment individually and push on regardless of the cost of lives and equipment. Sherman settled down to a siege operation that lasted over a month. The siege ended when Sherman began another encircling movement toward Jonesboro and was met by Confederate Generals Hardee, S.D. Lee, and Chatham. When the trio failed to dislodge the Union force below the city, Hood abandoned the city and united with Hardee at Lovejoy Station near Jonesboro, leaving Atlanta open for the Union. Upon his arrival in the city, Sherman sent the following message to President Lincoln: "Atlanta is ours, and fairly won."[7]

3–4 *Skirmish at Berryville, Virginia* (**Undetermined**)
 As General Philip Sheridan moved his army toward Berryville to pursue General Jubal Early, he skirmished with R.H. Anderson's division as it moved from Winchester towards Richmond. When General Early brought up additional manpower, he found the Union's position strongly defended by Sheridan and General George Crook. He pulled his men back to Opequon Creek near Winchester, Virginia.

4 Confederate raider John Hunt Morgan was killed near Greenville, Tennessee.

5 Sergeant George Shedburne, a notorious Confederate guerilla or scout from the Jeff Davis legion, reported to General Hampton there was a large supply of beef cattle near City Point, Virginia. He reported that a small contingent of Union troops guarded the cattle, and he made a suggestion as to how the Confederate cavalry could strike and take the cattle to feed the starving Confederate soldiers manning the siege lines around Petersburg.

7 Evacuation of Atlanta was ordered as Sherman decided to put the city to the torch. Between September 11 and 20, 446 families, totaling 1,600 people, evacuated the city. Sherman reported: "If the people raise a howl against my barbarity and cruelty, I will answer that war is war and not popularity seeking."[8]

16 *The Great Beefsteak Raid, Coggins Point, Virginia* (**Confederate Victory**)
 Confederates under General Thomas L. Rosser made a raid on City Point with the idea of capturing several thousand head of cattle. Before departing on the raid, Confederate cavalry made a diversionary ride on the 14th in the opposite direction. They then swung around the Union lines to Coggins Point and swept down on the small force guarding the cattle, capturing 219 soldiers of the 1st District of Columbia Cavalry and 85 members of the 13th Pennsylvania Cavalry. In addition, they drove 2,468 cows back to the Confederate lines along with 11 wagons of supplies.

17 John C. Fremont withdrew his name from the presidential contest and threw his support to Lincoln.

17 *Third Battle of Winchester, Virginia (AKA Opequon Creek)* (**Union Victory**)
 Six weeks into his campaign to clear the Shenandoah Valley, Sheridan believed he had the Confederates bottled up near Winchester. Confederate troops, taking advantage of the Union's delay, moved up additional soldiers. The southern troops fought a fierce fight but

the large Union numbers overpowered them and drove them back. Sheridan ordered his cavalry to pursue and they drove the Confederates through the town and into the surrounding countryside. Darkness stopped the pursuit. The victory was widely celebrated in the North, as it was beneficial to the political aspirations of Lincoln seeking reelection in November.

	U.S.A.				C.S.A.	
	General Philip Sheridan, George Crook, David A. Russell (Killed)				General Jubal Early, Stephen Ramseur, John Breckinridge, Robert Rodes (Killed)	

	Troops	Killed	Wounded	Missing/Captured	Total Casualties
U.S.A.	39,240	697	2,983	338	4,018
C.S.A.	15,200	276	1,827	1,818	3,921

19   General Sterling Price entered Missouri from Arkansas with twelve thousand Confederate soldiers.

22   *Battle of Fisher's Hill, Virginia* (**Union Victory**)
   Taking up a strong defensive position, the Confederates awaited further pursuit by Union troopers. They did not have long to wait. Soon they were faced with a Union assault on all sides. Early and his men were able to retreat southward toward Rockfish Gap near Waynesboro, Virginia. It is believed that this action on the part of Early and his men subjected the Valley to the Union's "scorched earth policy."

	U.S.A.			C.S.A.
	General Philip Sheridan, General George Crook			General Jubal Early

	Troops	Killed	Wounded	Missing/Captured	Total Casualties
U.S.A.	29,444	52	457	19	528
C.S.A.	9,500				1,235

26–27   *Engagement at Pilot Knob (AKA Fort Davidson), Missouri* (**Union Victory**)
   General Sterling Price approached Pilot Knob, where General Thomas Ewing, Jr., was defending Fort Davidson, a six-sided earthwork fort protected by a 12 by 9 foot moat. Price could have bypassed the fort, but when he heard that Ewing was present, he decided to attack. Price disliked Ewing and the cruel manner in which he treated Confederate supporters. On the third attempt to take the fort, Price's men were able to reach the moat, but were slaughtered by rifle fire and hand-thrown grenades. Price called off the attack and Ewing withdrew during the night. It was considered a Union victory for though Price continued the raid, he did not try to take the city of St. Louis.

	U.S.A.			C.S.A.
	General Thomas Ewing			General Sterling Price

	Troops	Killed	Wounded	Missing/Captured	Total Casualties
U.S.A.	6,000	28	56	100	184
C.S.A.	9,000				unknown

26 *Guerilla raid on Centralia, Missouri* (**Guerilla Massacre**)

Confederate guerilla William "Bloody Bill" Anderson, along with 30 of his raiders, rode into Centralia, Missouri, where they terrorized the citizens. The incoming stage was held up and its occupants robbed of their belongings as was a train coming into the town. The raiders executed twenty-four soldiers accompanying the train. Union soldiers, believing Anderson's band consisted of only 30 soldiers, swept into the guerillas' camp and were ambushed. Of the 158 men of the 39th Missouri Infantry, only 19 survived and they did so by taking refuge in a blockhouse five miles from the city. In one day, Anderson killed 142 men. When the bodies of the Union soldiers were found, it was discovered the men had been "shot through the head, then scalped, bayonets thrust through them, ears and noses cut off, and privates torn off and thrust in the mouths of the dying."[9] William Anderson truly earned the nickname of "Bloody Bill."

U.S.A.				C.S.A.	
Major A.V.E. Johnson				William Anderson	
	Troops	*Killed*	*Wounded*	*Missing/Captured*	*Total Casualties*
U.S.A.	158	116	2	6	124
C.S.A.	225				

28 General John B. Hood attacked Sherman's supply lines across the Chattahoochee River.

29–30 *Engagement at Fort Harrison (AKA Fort Gilmer, Chaffin's Farm or New Market Heights), Virginia* (**Union Victory**)

General Grant, hoping to draw Confederate defenders from Petersburg, ordered Butler to assault the Richmond defense lines along the James River. This was to be a two prong Union assault — one north of the James against the Richmond defenses and the other west of Petersburg — seeking to extend the lines and penetrate to the South Side Railroad and the Appomattox River. On the morning of the 29th, Union forces took Fort Harrison and New Market Heights. The Confederate defenders fled to Fort Gilmer about one mile away. It was necessary to cross a small ditch to reach the fort and here many Union troops fell as they were shot down. The Confederates held firm to Gilmer as Lee on the 30th ordered Confederate forces to re-take Fort Harrison. This was deadly for the Confederates, as the attack was reported to have been "disjointed."

U.S.A.				C.S.A.	
General Benjamin Butler, General Edward Ord				General Robert E. Lee, Richard S. Ewell	
	Troops	*Killed*	*Wounded*	*Missing/Captured*	*Total Casualties*
U.S.A.	20,000	383	2,299	645	3,327
C.S.A.	10,000				2,000+

29–30 *Battle of Peeble's Farm (AKA Poplar Spring or Jones' Farm), Virginia* (**Union Victory**)

At the same time that Butler was making his movement against Richmond, Grant pushed his lines west of Petersburg to cut the communication line. The initial Union attack overtook Fort Archer, but Confederate reinforcements soon came up, slowing the Union advance. The Union did capture Fort MacRae, extending its line to Pebble's Farms. Upon taking this area, Meade suspended the drive and established a new trench line. The Union now was entrenched from the Weldon railroad to the Pegram Farm.

		U.S.A.			C.S.A.	
General George G. Meade,				General A.P. Hill,		
General Gouverneur Warren,				General Wade Hampton		
General John G. Parke						

	Troops	Killed	Wounded	Missing/Captured	Total Casualties
U.S.A.	Corps	187	900	1,802	2,889
C.S.A.	Corps				1,300

October 1864

2–3 *Action at Saltville, Virginia* (**Confederate Victory**)

Union raiders en route to destroy the salt works at Saltville were delayed at Clinch Mountain and Laurel Gap by Confederates sent to intercept them. Salt was a very valuable commodity for the Confederates, who desperately needed it to preserve meat. At the same time of the delaying action, another Confederate contingent led by Jackson reached Saltville. When the Union raiders reached the city, they became involved in a daylong skirmish and were prevented from destroying the salt works. By nightfall, the Union withdrew. (It was reported that Confederate Captain Champ Ferguson led a group of Confederate soldiers in the killing of black and wounded Union soldiers left on the field after the fight. Confederate General John C. Breckinridge, angered over the incident, placed Ferguson under arrest and reported the incident to his superiors. Before they could bring Ferguson to trial, he was taken prisoner by Union authorities. Ferguson was convicted of murder and hung on October 20, 1865.)

		U.S.A.			C.S.A.	
General Stephen Burbridge				General Alfred E. Jackson		

	Troops	Killed	Wounded	Missing/Captured	Total Casualties
U.S.A.	4,200	54	190	104	348
C.S.A.	8,000				Unknown

5 *Battle of Allatoona, Georgia* (**Union Victory**)

With the fall of Atlanta, Confederates under General Hood moved north destroying several miles of rail track belonging to the Western and Atlanta Railroad, which served Sherman's supply lines. In addition, Confederates raided several Union garrisons. Sherman sent troops to Allatoona to stop the destruction. Upon arrival at Allatoona, the Confederates demanded the surrender of the Union detachment. According to resources, they received a "a nasty negative reply." The Confederates attacked but were repulsed after a two-hour fight. They soon regrouped, launching another attack, and again were repulsed and forced to pull back. When their ammunition ran low, they called off the attack and departed the area.

	Troops	Killed	Wounded	Missing/Captured	Total Casualties
U.S.A. General John M. Corse			C.S.A. General Samuel G. French		
U.S.A.	3,944	142	352	212	706
C.S.A.	2,000	122	443	234	799

6   General Sheridan began a path of destruction in the Shenandoah Valley as he put the torch to fields, barns and other supplies. Afterward, he withdrew to Winchester, Virginia.

7   *Engagement at Darbytown/New Market Roads (AKA Johnson Farm), Virginia* (**Union Victory**)

With the fall of Fort Harrison, Lee ordered an attack on the Union's right flank, which was located near the New Market Road. Confederate cavalry were able to rout the Union troops at Darbytown Road but when they went against the main Union line, they were forced to pull back.

	Troops	Killed	Wounded	Missing/Captured	Total Casualties
U.S.A. General August V. Kautz, General David Birney			C.S.A. General Robert E. Lee, General John Gregg (killed)		
U.S.A.	Corps	49	253	156	458
C.S.A.	Corps				1,000 est.

7   The CSS *Florida*, a Confederate raider ship, was fired upon by the USS *Wachusett* off the coast of Bahia, Brazil, after an attempt to ram her failed. The Confederate ship soon surrendered and was taken as a prize of war. Her crew was left in Brazil. Prior to this, the CSS *Florida* had set sail in March 1862 from England and, in the previous two years, had captured thirty-seven ships and their cargoes.

7   Confederate General Sterling Price entered Jefferson City, the state capital of Missouri, creating alarm and spreading panic.

9   *Engagement at Tom's Brook, Virginia* (**Union Victory**)

As Union cavalry under Sheridan withdrew from the Shenandoah Valley, they burned everything that could be of support to the Confederacy. General Early and Confederate cavalry under Rosser pursued the Union troops as they left the area. One report stated Rosser and his men kept snapping at the heels of the Union detachment. General Torbert ordered Custer and Merritt to protect the rear. Union cavalry waited and attacked the Confederate pursuers near Tom's Brook and quickly overwhelmed them. With this action, the Union exerted control over the valley as Confederate presence dwindled.

	U.S.A. General Alfred Torbert			C.S.A. General Thomas Rosser	
	Troops	Killed	Wounded	Missing/Captured	Total Casualties
U.S.A.	6,300	9	48		57
C.S.A.	3,500				350

13 *Engagement at Darbytown Road, Virginia* (**Confederate Victory**)

The Confederates made numerous attempts to retake Fort Harrison and all had failed. With the last defeat, the Confederate high command ordered new defensive lines formed around Richmond. When Grant learned of the new defensive positions, he ordered a reconnaissance "to drive the enemy from the work." As they approached the Darbytown Road, Union troops were lured into a small area that in essence was a narrow gap. As they filed through the gap, firing came at them from three sides. Numerous skirmishes broke out between the various units, causing the Union to suffer heavy losses, and forcing them back to their lines along the New Market Road.

	U.S.A. General Alfred Terry			C.S.A. General Richard Anderson	
	Troops	Killed	Wounded	Missing/Captured	Total Casualties
U.S.A.	Corps	36	358	43	437
C.S.A.	Corps				40

13 General John B. Hood destroyed Sherman's communication and supply lines, forcing Sherman to move his troops from Atlanta to Resaca.

15 *Action at Glasgow, Missouri* (**Confederate Victory**)

As Price made his way westward across Missouri, he sent a small detachment toward Glasgow to liberate rifles and supplies stored there at the garrison. The garrison surrendered after suffering Confederate infantry and artillery fire for most of the day. The Confederates remained in the area for three days before leaving with supplies and rifles to rejoin Price's army.

	U.S.A. Colonel Chester Harding			C.S.A. General Joseph Shelby, General John B. Clark	
	Troops	Killed	Wounded	Missing/Captured	Total Casualties
U.S.A.	800	11	32	469	512
C.S.A.	unknown				50

15 As Confederate troops assailed Glasgow, General Price captured the cities of Sedalia and Paris, Missouri.

19 *Battle of Cedar Creek, Virginia* (**Union Victory**)

The Confederates made a surprise attack on Sheridan's cavalry while he was away.

Upon hearing of the attack, Sheridan raced back to his unit, winning lasting fame for his miraculous ride. He arrived in time to turn the tide and he launched a counterattack later in the afternoon. The attack was a victory for the Union and drove the Confederates from the valley. The Battle of Cedar Creek marked the last major battle of the war in the Shenandoah Valley.

	U.S.A.			*C.S.A.*	
	General Philip Sheridan, General Horatio Wright			General Jubal Early, Joseph Kershaw, Stephen Ramseur (Mortally wounded)	
	Troops	*Killed*	*Wounded*	*Missing/Captured*	*Total Casualties*
U.S.A.	31,945	644	3,430	1,591	5,665
C.S.A.	21,000	320	1,540	1,050	2,910

19   *Action at Lexington, Missouri* (**Confederate Victory**)

Union forces hoped to trap General Sterling Price as he moved along the Missouri River. Unable to co-ordinate plans between several Union contingents, General James G. Blunt set out for Lexington, where he ran into Price. Price's force was able to drive the Union troops back, pushing them through the town. Many historians believe Blunt's action not only delayed Price's movement but also allowed Blunt to determine Price's strength.

19   *Confederate raid on St. Albans, Vermont*

A Confederate force of guerillas and ex-cavalrymen from Canada made a raid on St. Albans, Vermont, that created fear in the northern section of the United States. On June 16, 1864, Confederate Secretary of State James A. Seddon directed Lieutenant Bennett H. Young, a graduate of Center College in Danville, Kentucky, to "organize for special service a company not to exceed twenty in number from those who belong to the service and are at this time beyond Confederate states."[10] The Confederate raiders, coming from Canada, were to strike St. Albans to create fear and panic and take money desperately needed by the Confederacy. Confederate raiders held up the three banks and escaped with $201,522 in currency and negotiable bonds.

The raid began October 15, 1864, when the raiders arrived in small groups of two to three, all registering at the American House Hotel located on the main street. By the 19th, all twenty-one raiders were present. At 3:30 p.m. on that day, the raiders struck the banks simultaneously, taking $58,000 from the First National Bank, $73,522 from the St. Albans Bank, and $70,000 from the Franklin County Bank. While no more than four men robbed each bank, the remaining raiders rounded up citizens who were walking or riding on the main street near the bank. One of the prisoners was Union Captain George P. Conger of the 1st Vermont Cavalry who was home on leave. He escaped from his captors and was able to spread the alarm as the raiders were firing upon him. While Conger alerted the town authorities, the raiders set time-delayed incendiary devices in various sections along the main street. The raiders fled, immediately pursued by the townsfolk. Believing the chase would end when they reached the border, the raiders hastily "crashed the border check." The townsfolk, now commanded by Captain Conger, also "crashed the border check" and immigration station. As they approached the outskirts of Montreal, they managed to capture ten of the raiders, recovering only $86,000. When they townsfolk attempted to cross the border into the States with their prisoners, Canadian authorities detained them. The Confederate raiders were taken into protective custody. Damage to the town was excessive when the bombs exploded. While in Canadian custody, the raiders taunted the citizens of St. Albans by sending them humorous cards. Finally, the Canadian authorities released the raiders, deeming them belligerents of a foreign nation at war. This was the northernmost raid made during the war by the Confederates.

21 *Action at Big Blue River, Missouri* (**Confederate Victory**)

Union cavalry had been pressing the Confederates under Price as he tried to make his way toward Kansas. Union troops commanded by General James Blunt, en route to Lexington, arrived at Little Blue River and prepared to meet the large Confederate force on the west bank. Blunt blocked Price's westward movement at Westport while Alfred Pleasonton pursued from the rear. General Joseph Shelby's Confederates made a frontal assault on the west bank, where Union troops held the position. This assault was an attempt to buy time to allow the remaining Confederate forces to make a flanking attack. When the attack began, the Union was forced to pull back to Westport.

U.S.A.			*C.S.A.*	
General James G. Blunt, Colonel Thomas Moonlight			General Sterling Price, General Joseph Shelby	

	Troops	*Killed*	*Wounded*	*Missing/Captured*	*Total Casualties*
U.S.A.		18	83	14	115
C.S.A.					Unknown

22 *Action at Independence, Missouri* (**Confederate Victory**)

The Union troops stationed at Independence was forced from the city when Price, on his way to Kansas, attacked. The fighting at times was house to house. When Pleasonton's cavalry arrived, they found the Union entrenchments occupied by Price's men. In the meantime, Blunt decided he would try to hold out until additional Union support could arrive. He still hoped to catch Price in a pincher movement between the two forces, one on the east and the other on the west. If the movement could be completed, Price would be defeated and eliminated.

U.S.A.			*C.S.A.*	
General James G. Blunt			General Sterling Price	

	Troops	*Killed*	*Wounded*	*Missing/Captured*	*Total Casualties*
U.S.A.		14	58	11	83
C.S.A.					

22–23 *Skirmish at Byram's Ford, Missouri* (**Union Victory**)

General John Marmaduke made a stand at Byram's Ford, trying to buy time for Price to move his wagon trains across the river at the ford to head south toward Little Sante Fe and safety. General Alfred Pleasonton's cavalry was on Price's rear. After about three hours of fighting between Union forces under Pleasonton and James G. Blunt and Confederates under Marmaduke and General Joseph Shelby, the Confederates pulled back, also toward Westport.

22 General Hood began his Tennessee campaign, first by moving his troops into Alabama. He left Gadsden for Guntersville and found the Tennessee River high and his supplies short. Despite this, Hood continued on his way across Alabama.

23 *Engagement at Westport, Missouri* (**Union Victory**)

Price found himself between two large Union contingents—one under Blunt and the other under Pleasonton. Encouraged by Shelby, Price decided to make a stand against one and then move against the second one. Price would take on Blunt while Marmaduke would hold off Pleasonton. After defeating Blunt, Price and Shelby would join Marmaduke in finishing off Pleasonton. Price and Shelby moved against Blunt at Westport, but after trying numerous times to break the Union lines, Price was forced to call off the attack and move south. Price took his wagons and left Missouri. The last Confederate effort in Missouri of any consequence was over, as was most fighting west of the Mississippi.

	U.S.A.			C.S.A.	
	General James G. Blunt, General Alfred Pleasonton			General Sterling Price, Joseph O. Shelby, James F. Fagan, John Marmaduke	

	Troops	*Killed*	*Wounded*	*Missing/Captured*	*Total Casualties*
U.S.A.	20,000				1,500
C.S.A.	8,000				1,500

25 *Skirmish at Marais des Cygnes (pronounced Mary de Zene), Missouri* (**Union Victory**)

As Price was retreating from Westport, Pleasonton pursued him, following him into Kansas, where he confronted Price near Marais des Cynes. Price ordered the vast majority of his wagons burned to hasten his retreat. Troops under Marmaduke and General James F. Fagan were involved.

25 *Skirmish at Mine Creek (AKA Osage), Missouri* (**Union Victory**)

Following Marais des Cygnes, Union cavalry overtook the fleeing Confederates as they crossed Mine Creek. Delayed because of the wagons, the Confederates formed on the north bank of the creek and held back the Union attack. However, by morning additional troops ordered up by Pleasonton arrived, resulting in the capture of both General John S. Marmaduke and General William L. Cabell. Six hundred men, wagons and other supplies were also captured. Lieutenant Colonel Lauchlan A. MacLean, Price's A.A.G, called "the morale of the army ruined." (Private James Dunlavey captured Marmaduke single-handedly and was awarded with the general's sword as a prize. He was also given an eight-month furlough, the time left on his enlistment.)

U.S.A.	C.S.A.
Colonel Frederick W. Benteen, Colonel John F. Phillips	General John S. Marmaduke, General James F. Fagan

	Troops	Killed	Wounded	Missing/Captured	Total Casualties
U.S.A.					100
C.S.A.					1,200

25 *Engagement at Marmiton River, Missouri* (**Union Victory**)

Retreating from Mine Creek, General Sterling Price continued towards Fort Scott but his wagon trains had trouble navigating the Marmiton River. Once again, Union cavalry attacked him. The cavalry commander, John McNeil, believing he was outnumbered and unaware that most of the Confederates were unarmed, withheld an all-out attack. This permitted many of the Confederates to slip away.

26–29 *Engagement at Decatur, Alabama* (**Union Victory**)

Confederate forces under General Hood attempted to cross the Tennessee River at Decatur. A small Union contingent challenged them, preventing the Confederates from crossing the river.

U.S.A.	C.S.A.
General Robert S. Granger	General John B. Hood

	Troops	Killed	Wounded	Missing/Captured	Total Casualties
U.S.A.	5,000				155
C.S.A.					450

26 Confederate guerilla William "Bloody Bill" Anderson was killed in an ambush near Richmond, Missouri. Experts describe Anderson as a psychotic cold-blooded killer. He was at one time a member of William Quantrill's band of guerillas but had made a split with him in the summer of 1864 after an argument. Taking some of the band with him, Anderson attacked various Union detachments and sympathizers. Anderson and his band of outlaws would scalp and slit the throats of those who were unfortunate enough to come within his path. Anderson died when he was shot in the back of the head. His body was placed on display. His head then was cut off and placed on a telegraph pole for all to see.

27–28 *Engagement at Hatcher's Run (AKA Boydton Plank Road or Burgess Mill), Virginia* (**Confederate Victory**)

Union troops commanded by General Hancock moved against the Boydton Plank Railroad, where they intended to control the communication lines into Petersburg. With initial success, they captured the position. Having regrouped, the Confederates counterattacked in the afternoon, driving the Union from the position.

U.S.A.	C.S.A.
General Winfield S. Hancock	General Henry Heth, William Mahone

	Troops	Killed	Wounded	Missing/Captured	Total Casualties
U.S.A.	17,500	166	1,028	564	1,758
C.S.A.	8,500				

27–28 *Engagement at Darbytown Road (AKA Second Fair Oaks), Virginia* (**Confederate Victory**)

General Butler, in conjunction with a Union attack on Hatcher's Run (Boydton Plank Road), assaulted the Confederate defense line from Darbytown Road to Fair Oaks. Butler's troops were met with stiff resistance, suffering heavy casualties, and were forced to pull back.

	U.S.A.			*C.S.A.*	
	General Benjamin Butler			General James Longstreet, General Charles W. Field	
	Troops	*Killed*	*Wounded*	*Missing/Captured*	*Total Casualties*
U.S.A.		118	787	698	1,603
C.S.A.					

27 Protected by the rear guard fighting of General Joseph O. Shelby, Confederate General Sterling Price retreated southward from Carthrage, Missouri. His one thousand mile raid through the state had turned into a desperate attempt to escape his Union pursuers.

28 *Engagement at Newtonia, Missouri* (**Union Victory**)

In his effort to retreat from the Union pursuers, Price rested two miles south of Newtonia, twenty miles south of Carthage. Union troops surprised him and forced him back. In the meantime, General Shelby arrived with his cavalry. Shelby rode to the front of his men and dismounted. There they held off the Union, as many of Price's soldiers escaped toward the Indian Territory. As more Union troops under Sanborn arrived, Shelby withdrew. This was the last military action between regular Union and Confederate forces west of the Mississippi River.

	U.S.A.			*C.S.A.*	
	General James G. Blunt, Samuel R. Curtis, John B. Sanborn			General Sterling Price, General Joseph Shelby	
	Troops	*Killed*	*Wounded*	*Missing/Captured*	*Total Casualties*
U.S.A.					400
C.S.A.					250

31 Nevada became the 36th state in the Union by proclamation of President Lincoln.

November 1864

4–5 *Skirmish at Johnsonville, Tennessee* (**Confederate Victory**)

With Sherman advancing through Georgia, the Confederates would have to do something to pull the Union troops from that state. In an effort to do so, Confederate forces, under General Nathan Bedford Forrest, began a raid into Tennessee with the intention of creating as much destruction of Union property as possible, hoping Sherman would send some of his men after Forrest. As Forrest entered Tennessee, he temporarily blocked the

Tennessee River at Fort Herman. As he moved his men and supplies across the river, he took possession of several Union gunboats. On the 4th, when Union officials discovered that the Confederates were preparing their artillery to fire on a Union supply depot at Johnsonville, Union gunboats opened on the Confederates. Because of their positions, the Union was unable to inflict any damage. The Confederates, though, were able to disable the Union gunboats. A fire broke out at the supply depot and Confederate gunfire prevented Union soldiers from extinguishing the fires. Forrest withdrew during the night as the soldiers fought the fire. Later Forrest would team up with General Hood. Union forces in this engagement were led by Colonel C.R. Thompson and Lt. Col. Edward M. King.

7   General Sterling Price and his men retreated westward, crossing the Arkansas River and entering the Indian Territory. Union commander General Samuel Curtis arrived the next day and, upon learning that Price had escaped, called off his pursuit. Price continued raiding as he made his way through the Indian Territory. He ended his raid at Laynesport, Arkansas, having "marched 1,434 miles, fought 43 battles and skirmishes, captured and paroled over 3000 federal officers and men."[11]

8   Abraham Lincoln was reelected as president of the United States with Andrew Johnson as his vice president.

11–13   *Action at Bull's Gap, Tennessee* (**Confederate Victory**)
      General Breckinridge went into Tennessee in hopes of encouraging Confederate sympathizers in the state to join him in an effort to clear the state of Union troops. Finding a small contingent of Union soldiers at Bull's Gap, Breckinridge attacked. At first, the Confederates were driven back, but by the next day, they assaulted the Union line on several fronts. The Union line held. On the 13th, Confederates prepared to make a flanking attack but found that the Union soldiers had withdrawn.

	U.S.A.			*C.S.A.*	
	General Alvan C. Gillem			General John C. Breckinridge	
	Troops	*Killed*	*Wounded*	*Missing/Captured*	*Total Casualties*
U.S.A.		13	36	200	249
C.S.A.					

15   After putting Atlanta to the torch, General Sherman began his march to the sea. Before starting on the march, he reportedly stated: "The utter destruction of its roads, houses and people will cripple their military resources.... I can make this march, and make Georgia howl!"[12]

19   Forrest's cavalry reinforced General Hood. Hood's army now stood at 39,000 men.

21   With Forrest's cavalry present, Confederate General John B. Hood split his army into three columns and marched northward into Tennessee from Alabama. This was the start of Hood's Tennessee Campaign, which was an attempt to draw Sherman out of Georgia. However, Sherman had begun his "March to the Sea" five days previously.

22   *Engagement at Griswoldville, Georgia* (**Union Victory**)

In order to determine the position and strength of the Confederate troops in the area, General Charles Walcutt was to march toward Macon, Georgia. Shortly after he had begun his march, he came across a small portion of Confederate cavalry and drove them toward Griswoldville. Walcutt took up a position near Duncan's Farm expecting to be attacked and had his men prepare fortifications. In the meantime, part of the Georgia militia, consisting of both old men and young schoolboys inexperienced in the task of the soldier, were ordered from Macon to Augusta to help in the fight against Sherman. They unexpectedly ran across Walcutt and his entrenched troops. Phillips, who had orders not to get involved in any fighting until his forces reached Augusta, instead ordered an attack. The Georgia militia made the attack but was driven off when Walcutt was reinforced by another Union regiment.

	U.S.A.			*C.S.A.*	
	General Charles Walcutt			General Pleasant J. Phillips, General Joseph Wheeler	

	Troops	*Killed*	*Wounded*	*Missing/Captured*	*Total Casualties*
U.S.A.	1,513	14	79	2	95
C.S.A.	3,000				650

22   Sherman's troops enter Milledgeville, the state capital of Georgia. The U.S. flag was quickly flown. The day before, city officials fled the city aware that Sherman was close. After two days, Union troops pulled out, moving toward Savannah. The city was left intact without any damage. Some historians reported that Sherman had slowed his march in an effort to give his men time to destroy anything useful to the Confederacy. Finding the bodies of some of Sherman's marauding foragers, it was said that Sherman's men increased their violence toward civilians.

24–26   *Skirmish at Columbia, Tennessee* (**Confederate Victory**)

Aware that General John Bell Hood was advancing into Tennessee, Union commander John Schofield also moved into Tennessee, arriving at Columbia just hours before Hood's cavalry. Schofield skirmished with Forrest's cavalry, as Schofield tried to prevent them from crossing the Duck River. Union troops burned two bridges over the river before retreating toward Nashville. Hood's three columns arrived the next day. As Hood made demonstrations against the Union line, he advanced two of the columns to Davis Ford, five miles east of the location where they were able to cross the river. The Union had not stopped Hood, only delayed him.

25   Colonel Robert M. Martin, having obtained permission from the Confederate Secret Service, along with eight co-conspirators checked into various hotels in New York City. Once they checked in, they prepared 402 bottles of "Greek fire," a highly flammable substance. They intended to set the hotels on fire and create as much damage as they could in retaliation for the actions of Generals Hunter and Sheridan in the Shenandoah Valley. Fires were set in ten hotels and in the Barnum's Museum. Many of the bottles fizzled out while hotel staff and visitors extinguished the other fires. The raiders quickly departed toward Canada. Only one man, Robert Cobb Kennedy, was caught and he was sentenced to death by General John A. Dix. The sentence was carried out at Fort Lafayette, New York Harbor, on March 25, 1865.

27   General Butler with a few Union commanders sailed down the Atlantic coast toward North Carolina aboard the *Greyhound*, a Confederate blockade runner that had been captured on May 8 and converted into Butler's floating headquarters. As the ship left Bermuda Hundred, it exploded. Before the explosion, Admiral David D. Porter, who was aboard, had spotted several "rascals" on board and had ordered the ship to pull into Bermuda Hundred, where he put the "rascals" off. It is believed one of them had left behind a time bomb. All on board were able to escape unhurt but the ship was destroyed.

28   *Raid on New Creek, West Virginia* (**Confederate Victory**)
    The Confederates were in desperate need of supplies since Sheridan and his men had burned most of the crops in the Shenandoah. General Rosser led a raid on a Union supply depot near Fort Kelly, located at the intersection of the New Creek and Potomac valleys. As they moved on the depot, they had a brief skirmish with a few pickets who quickly spread the alarm. The Union commander of the fort did not heed the alarm. The Confederates were able to quickly capture the fort, taking prisoners and supplies that helped Rosser and his men survive to the end of the year.

	U.S.A.			*C.S.A.*	
	Colonel George R. Latham			General Thomas L. Rosser	
	Troops	*Killed*	*Wounded*	*Missing/Captured*	*Total Casualties*
U.S.A.	800				700
C.S.A.	600				5

28   *Skirmish at Buck Head Creek, Georgia* (**Union Victory**)
    The Union cavalry under Kilpatrick was ordered to destroy the railroad between Augusta and Macon and to burn the trestle near Briar Creek. If it was possible, Kilpatrick was also to free Union prisoners believed held near Camp Lawton. In the meantime, the Confederate cavalry concentrated close to Augusta, waiting for a chance to attack Kilpatrick. When Kilpatrick did not appear, Wheeler went in search of him. He found his Union counterpart and prevented the burning of the Briar Creek trestle, but Kilpatrick was able to destroy a mile of track leading to the trestle. When Kilpatrick went into camp on the evening on the 27th, Wheeler learned of his position. He was almost able to capture the Union commander, as the two units clashed with musketry and sabers over the next few hours. Wheeler chased the Union men across Buck Head Creek. After getting across the creek, Union soldiers set up their artillery guns and unleashed their fury as the Confederates pursued. Soon Wheeler was forced to retire.

	U.S.A.			*C.S.A.*	
	General H. Judson Kilpatrick			General Joseph Wheeler	
	Troops	*Killed*	*Wounded*	*Missing/Captured*	*Total Casualties*
U.S.A.					46
C.S.A.	3,500				600

29   *Engagement at Spring Hill, Tennessee* (**Union Victory**)

Hood made his way across Tennessee with the hope of taking Nashville. He felt if he could take the city, Sherman would have to call off his raid to the sea and pursue him. Hood, who had previously divided his army into three units, kept one column on one side of the river blasting away at a Union detachment with artillery. The other two columns crossed the Duck River and moved 12 miles to Spring Hill where they could block Schofield's escape route to Nashville. Once in Spring Hill, the Confederates came across a Union contingent protecting the road and, as they tried to move them out of the way, were repulsed pulling back to await reinforcements. As night fell, the Confederates went into camp as the Union army quietly moved from Columbia, around the position at Spring Hill, and were well on their way to Franklin by morning. The "Spring Hill Affair" has become one of the most controversial non-fighting events of the entire war, for participants and historians were never able to determine what did happen or did not happen —charges and counter-charges were many.

	U.S.A.			*C.S.A.*	
	General John M. Schofield			General John B. Hood	
	Troops	*Killed*	*Wounded*	*Missing/Captured*	*Total Casualties*
U.S.A.		16	64	20	100
C.S.A.					

29   *Engagement at Sand Creek, Colorado Territory* (**Termed a Union Massacre**)

An uneasy peace existed in the Colorado Territory. In the fall of 1864, amnesty was offered to the Indians if they would report to the army forts. Chief Black Kettle, who believed he and his people were safe and protected, established his camp about forty miles from Fort Lyon. Union General J.M. Chivington, believing the only good Indian was a dead Indian, took 900 volunteers and moved to attack the Indian camp on Sand Creek. The Indians not only flew a white flag above their camp but also an American flag. Chivington and his men attacked the Indian village without warning, massacring between 500 and 600 Cheyenne and a few Arapaho warriors, women and children. Among the dead was Black Kettle, a major chief of the tribe.

30   *Battle of Franklin, Tennessee* (**Union Victory**)

Twenty-two thousand Union troops under General Schofield had reached Franklin and had dug in. Schofield wanted to regroup and replenish his supplies. He had no intention of fighting at this time but instead wanted to hold Franklin until he could repair the bridges to get his trains across. On the other hand, General Hood, having been humiliated with the Union troops slipping past him at Spring Hill, raced toward Franklin, where he intended to have a showdown. Hood ordered his troops to cross an open field of nearly 2 miles to make a frontal attack on the strongly entrenched Union soldiers. Despite arguments by his generals, the attack came off as ordered and it was a battle that saw much bloody hand-to-hand fighting and the death of no less than six Confederate generals. Hood would also lose the use of 54 of his regimental commanders.

U.S.A.	C.S.A.
General John M. Schofield, General Jacob D. Cox	General John B. Hood. The following generals were killed: Patrick Cleburne, States Right Gist, Hiram Granbury, John Adams, Otho Strahl, and John C. Carter

	Troops	Killed	Wounded	Missing/Captured	Total Casualties
U.S.A.	22,000	189	1,033	1,104	2,326
C.S.A.	20,000	1,750	3,800	702	6,252

30   *Battle of Honey Hill, South Carolina* (**Confederate Victory**)

A Union force left Hilton Head and steamed up the Broad River with orders to cut the Charleston and Savannah Railroad near Pocotaligo. They disembarked at Boyd's Landing and moved inward, where they encountered a small Confederate force at Honey Hill, which appeared to be waiting for them. After hours of fighting, the Union attempted a flanking maneuver but found the fields on fire, preventing such action. By night, the Union departed the area and returned to their ships on the Broad River. (This battle was fought with Georgia militiamen. The governor of Georgia, Joseph Brown, had forbidden the militia to leave the state. General Gustavus W. Smith had the militia put on trains that carried them to South Carolina, telling them that "they were going to South Carolina ... and that they ... would be engaged in a big fight before 12 o'clock — must win it — and would be brought back to Georgia within forty-eight hours."[13])

U.S.A.	C.S.A.
General John Hatch	Colonel Charles Colcock

	Troops	Killed	Wounded	Missing/Captured	Total Casualties
U.S.A.	5,000	88	623	44	755
C.S.A.	1,400	8	42		50

December 1864

1   General Hood declared victory at Franklin after he discovered the Union had pulled out during the night. Hood pursued them to Nashville. There, General Hood established a defensive line to await the Union attack. Hood still believed that Sherman would be pulled from Georgia if the Confederates destroyed the Nashville and Chattanooga Railroad, disrupting the Union supply depot at Murfreesboro.

4   *Skirmish at Overall Creek, Tennessee* (**Union Victory**)

General Hood directed Forrest and General William Bate to destroy the rail lines and supply depots in and around Nashville. On this day, Bate's division attacked Blockhouse Number 7, which protected the railroad crossing at Overall Creek, but Union forces drove Bate from Nashville. The Union suffered a total of 53 casualties (4 killed, 49 wounded).

4 *Engagement at Waynesborough, Georgia* (**Union Victory**)

As Sherman marched through Georgia, he ordered his cavalry commander to move north and attack Wheeler's cavalry at every opportunity. Wheeler awaited the attack at Waynesborough and, after some severe fighting, was forced to pull back into the town. Union infantry came up in support of Kilpatrick, which forced the Confederates to withdraw.

	U.S.A.				C.S.A.	
	General H. Judson Kilpatrick				General Joseph Wheeler	
	Troops	*Killed*	*Wounded*	*Missing/Captured*	*Total Casualties*	
U.S.A.	Cav. Division				190	
C.S.A.	3,500				250	

5–7 *Engagement at Murfreesboro, Tennessee* (**Union Victory**)

Confederate cavalry, under Forrest, managed to team up with Bate's infantry division and advance on the union supply depot at Murfreesboro. On the 7th, Union troops emerged from the fort to "feel the enemy" and engaged with a small contingent of Forrest's cavalry. When it appeared that the Union was getting the upper hand, many of the southern cavalrymen fled, causing a rout of Forrest's men. Neither Forrest nor Bate were able to stop it. Forest attempted to re-organize his men to effect an organized withdrawal. Though termed a Union victory, Forrest was able to accomplish his mission, the destruction of the railroad and blockhouses, and, to a minor degree, he disrupted the Union supply operations.

	U.S.A.			C.S.A.	
	General Lovell H. Rousseau, General Robert Milroy			General Nathan Bedford Forrest, General William Bate	
	Troops	*Killed*	*Wounded*	*Missing/Captured*	*Total Casualties*
U.S.A.		30	175	20	225
C.S.A.					197

6 General George H. Thomas, in command of the Union troops at Nashville, had been ordered by General Grant to "attack Hood at once and await no longer the remount of your cavalry."[14] Thomas had delayed making the attack on Hood's entrenchments, as he needed horses for his cavalrymen, whom he felt were needed to deal with Forrest's cavalry. Thomas responded to Grant's order by writing to General Halleck, "I can only say I have done everything in my power to prepare, and if you should deem it necessary to relieve me I shall submit without a murmur."[15]

9 Union forces under General Gouverneur K. Warren, en route to destroy the Weldon Railroad, discovered a small Confederate contingent under General Wade Hampton. The Confederates held off the Union attack. Upon learning that additional Confederate infantry were en route, the Union troops pulled out. As they were making their way back to Petersburg, the soldiers came across a supply of applejack. Drunk on applejack, they began destroying civilian property. Citizens began to waylay and kill some of the Union stragglers. As punishment, Union troops burned and destroyed homes of the civilians, including slave quarters.

10   Sherman's army arrived on the outskirts of Savannah, Georgia, and found it defended by 10,000 Confederate soldiers.

11   Once more General Grant ordered Thomas to move against Hood, saying "delay no longer for weather." The day before, Nashville had received over an inch of ice as a severe winter storm rushed through the area. Thomas replied, "I will obey the order as promptly as possible."[16]

13   General Grant ordered General John A. Logan to Nashville to take command from General Thomas, but rescinded the order and set out himself to take charge of the situation, but went to Washington first.

13   *Engagement at Fort McAllister, Georgia* (**Union Victory**)
      Sherman needed supplies as his men made their move toward Savannah. If his men could take Fort McAllister, he would be able to receive what he needed by ship. Fort McAllister was on the Ogeechee River just south of Savannah. Sherman contacted Admiral Dahlgren, whose forces were blocking the port.

U.S.A.			C.S.A.	
General William B. Hazen			Major George A. Anderson	

	Troops	Killed	Wounded	Missing/Captured	Total Casualties
U.S.A.	Division	24	110		134
C.S.A.	120				71

14   Supplies and manpower from Port Royal, South Carolina, set sail to join Sherman twenty miles below in Savannah. The supplies would go through Fort McAllister.

15–16   *Battle of Nashville, Tennessee* (**Union Victory**)
      Hood, with his numbers dwindling, awaited the attack he knew was coming. Since his arrival on December 2, General Thomas had been preparing to attack the Confederate position. The attack began in earnest on the 15th, with heavy fighting occurring on both of Hood's flanks. By nightfall, the fighting stopped as Hood moved his defensive lines two miles south of his former position. Additional Union troops were brought up. Another attack was made on the Confederate line. Hood's small army fled through Franklin Pike, an area left unmanned. Then the Union took up the pursuit and followed the fleeing Confederate force for the next ten days. Hood managed to reach Tupelo, Mississippi, where he resigned his command. Some historians have credited this as the last battle in the west.

U.S.A.	C.S.A.
General George H. Thomas	General John B. Hood, General Stephen D. Lee

	Troops	Killed	Wounded	Missing/Captured	Total Casualties
U.S.A.	54,000	387	2,562	112	3,061
C.S.A.	24,000			4,500	6,000

15   General Grant, while in Washington, received the news that Thomas finally had begun the attack on Nashville and was winning. Grant responded: "Well, I guess we won't go to Nashville."

17–18   *Engagement at Marion, Virginia* (**Union Victory**)
    General Stoneman led his men on a raiding expedition with the intention of destroying or damaging the important lead mines near Marion, after driving off the small Confederate force.

U.S.A.	C.S.A.
General George Stoneman	General John C. Breckinridge

	Troops	Killed	Wounded	Missing/Captured	Total Casualties
U.S.A.					58
C.S.A.					216

18   Hood, with his defeated Confederate army, crossed Rutherford Creek as he pulled out of Nashville. He burned the bridges behind him, buying time for his retreat.

20   General Hardee, with his 10,000 Confederate troops, left Savannah, Georgia.

20–21   *Skirmish at Saltville, Virginia* (**Union Victory**)
    After destroying the lead mines at Marion, Stoneman moved on to Saltville, where he destroyed the Confederate salt works.

21   Union troops occupied Savannah, Georgia, as Sherman completed his "March to the Sea." Sherman's march to the sea had cut through the middle of Georgia almost unhindered and had caused over $100 million in damage. His men had killed many who resisted and had burned and devastated towns and farms. It was also widely reported that Sherman's men had raped and pillaged as they went. Sherman sent the following message to President Lincoln: "I beg to present you, as a Christmas gift, the city of Savannah, with 150 heavy guns and plenty of ammunition, and also about 25,000 bales of cotton."[17]

23–27   *Attack on Fort Fisher, North Carolina* (**Confederate Victory**)
    Union forces were assigned to capture Fort Fisher, the last major port partially open for the Confederacy. Fort Fisher had long been effective in helping vessels run the blockade off Wilmington, North Carolina. When learning of a large contingent of Union troops leaving Hampton Roads, General Lee ordered General Robert Hoke to protect Fort Fisher. By the time of Hoke's arrival, the fort was already under attack by both naval and land forces under General Benjamin Butler and Admiral David D. Porter. Soon General Butler called off the Union assault and pulled his forces back to Fort Monroe.

Chapter 10

1865

"With an unceasing admiration of your constancy and devotion to your country and a grateful remembrance of your kind and generous consideration for myself, I bid you all an affectionate farewell."
— *Robert E. Lee, General Order No. 9,*
April 10, 1865

January 1865

7   General Benjamin Butler was removed from command due to his failure to capture Fort Fisher. His replacement was General E.O.C. Ord. General Grant, the day before, had wired President Lincoln requesting that Butler be replaced as commander of the Army of the James, citing his many levels of incompetence.

9   General John Bell Hood and what was left of his Army of the Tennessee arrived at Tupelo, Mississippi.

11   Confederate General Thomas L. Rosser, along with 300 volunteers, rode in the snow from Staunton, Virginia, to Beverly, West Virginia, to make a raid on the supply depot in Beverly. A small contingent of Union soldiers, who offered little resistance, guarded the depot. The Confederate raid netted 100 horses, 600 rifles plus over 10,000 rations, enough to feed Rosser and his men for the winter. The raid also netted Rosser the title of "Savior of the Valley."

13   General Hood resigned as commander of the Army of Tennessee and turned his command over to General Richard Taylor, who would take his orders from General P.G.T. Beauregard.

13–15 *Battle of Fort Fisher, North Carolina* (**Union Victory**)

After General Butler's removal, orders were again issued to his successor to take Fort Fisher. Operations against the fort were renewed. Naval bombardment by Porter's 44-ship flotilla pounded the fort for two days and nights before the infantry assault was made on the 15th. Previously, Union forces had established a beachhead five miles from the fort and this was of value to the final assault. The initial attack, made by Union soldiers and sailors on the northeast section of the fort, was repulsed, but the Union attack on the rear was a success. Hand-to-hand fighting took place and, by nightfall, the fort was in Union hands. The capture of Fort Fisher closed off the last port for supplies to reach the Confederacy. Fort Fisher at Wilmington, North Carolina, had been the primary destination of blockade raiders who attempted to supply the Confederacy with food and ammunition.

U.S.A.	C.S.A.
General Alfred H. Terry, Admiral David D. Porter	General Braxton Bragg, General Robert Hoke, Colonel Charles Lamb (Wounded)

	Troops	Killed	Wounded	Missing/Captured	Total Casualties
U.S.A.	11,300	266	1,018	57	1,341
C.S.A.	1,900				1,900

18 Grant ordered General E.R.S Canby to move against and capture Mobile, Alabama.

19 Sherman left Savannah, Georgia, to begin his march northward to South Carolina.

23–24 *Engagement at Trent's Reach, Virginia* (**Union Victory**)

The Confederates planned to make a naval assault on the Union supply depot located at City Point, Virginia. When the Confederates reached Trent's Reach, a few miles from City Point, they ran into obstacles placed in the river to prevent such an attack. The CSS *Fredericksburg*, along with two smaller ships, attempted to remove the barriers. Union batteries fired at the Confederate ship to no avail. In the meantime, low tide had stranded two other Confederate ships, CSS *Virginia II* and the CSS *Richmond*. Each of the Confederate ships had been equipped with spar torpedoes intended to be used against the USS *Onondage*, the only ironclad operating on the James. As daylight broke, the Union gunners could see their targets and they took deliberate aim, causing the magazine abroad the CSS *Drewry* to explode. Finally, the USS *Onondage* made its appearance but the stranded Confederate ships were once more afloat and were retreating. The captain of the USS *Onondage* was court-martialed for not arriving sooner and the commander of the Confederate fleet was relieved of his command for failure to attempt to destroy the supply depot.

24 The Congress of the Confederate States again made an offer to Union Officials to exchange prisoners. This offer was declined, as were many other previous requests for the return of captured soldiers.

28 Confederate President Jefferson Davis appointed a committee to hold unofficial and informal talks with Union officials about possible peace negotiations. The committee consisted of Alexander Stephens, his vice president; John A. Campbell, former U.S. Supreme Court justice who now was assistant secretary of war; and former secretary of state R.M.T. Hunter.

30   President Lincoln issued a pass for the three named Confederate commissioners to travel through military lines from Richmond to Fort Monroe in an effort to discuss peace negotiations.

31   The United States Congress submitted the 13th Amendment to the states for ratification. This amendment called for the abolition of and the end of slavery. It had passed in the House by a vote of 119 to 56.

31   Robert E. Lee was named as general in chief of all Confederate armies. He was now in command of all military forces for the Confederacy. His rank remained the same but he was now on the same footing as General Ulysses S. Grant.

31   Lincoln ordered Secretary of State Seward to meet with the Confederate commissioners at Fort Monroe.

February 1865

1   Sherman's army left Savannah, Georgia, with 2,500 wagons, 600 ambulances and 68 guns. They made their way through South Carolina to the state's capital at Columbia. The army constructed corduroyed (crossed log) roads as they moved through swamps and built pontoon bridges to cross rivers and streams. At that time Sherman said, "The whole army is burning with an insatiable desire to wreak vengeance upon South Carolina. I almost tremble at her fate, but feel she deserves all that seems in store for her."[1]

3   *Hampton Roads Conference*
    Aboard the *River Queen* off Fort Monroe, President Lincoln and Secretary of War Seward met with the Confederate delegation seeking peace negotiations. Lincoln insisted that the national authority of the United States be recognized within the states of the Confederacy before anything else was discussed, for Lincoln did not recognize the Confederate States as a nation. The Confederate delegation asked what action would be taken toward the southern states if the Union were restored. Lincoln explained that only the unconditional surrender would be considered and that the Confederate army would have to be disbanded and national authority established over the states. The meeting failed to reach any terms and was disbanded.

3   *Skirmish at Rivers' Bridge, South Carolina* (**Union Victory**)
    A small Confederate force, in control of the river crossing on the Salkehatchie River, was charged with the responsibility of preventing the Union from crossing it. As Sherman's army marched toward Charleston, a detachment was sent to remove the Confederate threat. Two Union brigades managed to get on the flanks and rear of the Confederate force and, after a brief skirmish, forced them to withdraw, leaving the crossing open for Sherman's army.

	U.S.A.			C.S.A.	
	General Francis P. Blair			General Lafayette McLaws	
	Troops	*Killed*	*Wounded*	*Missing/Captured*	*Total Casualties*
U.S.A.	5,000				92
C.S.A.	1,200				170

5–7 *Battle of Hatcher's Run (AKA Dabney's Mill), Virginia* (**Confederate Victory**)

For the last several months, the two armies had been involved in a siege operation at Petersburg but General Grant decided to lengthen it, ordering some of his divisions to move southward from Petersburg to the Boydton Plank Road. When informed of the Union movement, Lee believed it was an attempt to destroy his supply lines and sent several divisions to protect the Southside Railroad. His troops ran into the Union force near Hatcher's Run. Several charges and countercharges were made as the Union troops erected breastworks. By evening, the Confederates were also entrenched. Additional manpower was brought up on both sides. Again, charges and countercharges were made as each side charged and fell back. Grant sent more troops but the Confederates held firm and stopped the Union advance. This was termed a Confederate victory even though Grant's line was extended. This was the last time Grant extended his lines prior to the final push he would make in March.

	U.S.A.			C.S.A.	
	General A.A. Humphreys, General Gouverneur Warren			General John B. Gordon, General John Pegram (Killed)	
	Troops	*Killed*	*Wounded*	*Missing*	*Total Casualties*
U.S.A.	34,517	170	1,160	182	1,512
C.S.A.	13,835				1,188

12–22 Engagement *at Wilmington, North Carolina* (**Union Victory**)

With Fort Fisher now in Union hands, the next step was to move on Wilmington. Several Confederate forts in the area had defended the gateway to Wilmington. On the 16th, a Union division, under the cover of Union gunboats, moved against Fort Anderson, forcing the Confederates to flee on the 18th. They retreated to Town Creek to form a new defensive line. The Union under General John Schofield maintained steady pressure on the Confederates and it was apparent they could no longer hold out or protect Wilmington. On the 22nd, General Braxton Bragg ordered the city to be evacuated and, at the same time, ordered the destruction of all supplies to keep them from falling into Union hands.

13 *Skirmish at Levyville, Florida* (**Confederate Victory**)

Much of the supplies needed to feed the Confederate troops came from south central Florida, which furnished over 600,000 head of cattle and hogs. In an effort to stem the flow of livestock to the Confederacy, 400 Union troops landed at Cedar Key, Florida, on February 8 and marched toward Gainesville. The Confederate commander, Captain John "Dixie" Dickison, with 90 men, moved to confront them. The two forces met near Levyville, where Union troops were forced to pull back into the swamps. There they formed a strong line and the fighting resumed. As darkness descended, the Union pulled back to Cedar Key and left the state. They believed the way to Gainesville was strongly defended, unaware that the Confederate soldiers were almost out of ammunition.

16   Union artillery opened on Columbia, South Carolina.

17   *Confederates Abandoned Columbia, South Carolina*
    Hearing that Sherman and his army were about to enter the city, Confederate soldiers abandoned Columbia, South Carolina. As the Union soldiers approached, city officials met them and surrendered the city, hoping to prevent its destruction. It was to no avail. As the Union troops entered the city, they plundered homes and businesses. The city was set ablaze and it is believed General Sherman ordered it. After the war, an argument arose as to who actually set fire to the city of Columbia. Sherman placed the blame on General Wade Hampton's cavalry, saying the cavalrymen set fire to bales of cotton and the fire spread as strong winds fanned the flames. Hampton placed the blame on Sherman and his scorched earth policy, for Sherman had been quoted as wanting to punish South Carolina. Sherman viewed the state as the "cradle of secession." Other officials placed the blame on drunken soldiers, freed blacks, slaves and prisoners recently released from jails.

17   With the Union army in Columbia, Confederates in nearby Charleston abandoned the city.

18   Fort Sumter was also abandoned.

18   The Confederate garrison at Charleston, in danger of being cut off as Sherman and his army approached, was abandoned. The Confederate soldiers marched out of the city and moved toward Cheraw, South Carolina, near the North Carolina border, where they would make a stand. In the meantime, Union troops entered and occupied Charleston, South Carolina.

18   Union naval guns began bombarding Fort Anderson, six miles upstream from Wilmington, North Carolina. Wilmington had served as a major supply depot for the Confederacy. At the same time the big guns opened on the fort, Union infantry approached the fort from the rear.

19   Confederates evacuated Fort Anderson, leaving the way open for Union troops to move against Wilmington, North Carolina.

20   Sherman and his army leave Columbia and resume their march northward.

21   Confederate guerilla leader Lieutenant Jesse McNeill led a raid into Cumberland, Maryland. He had long held a grudge against Union General Benjamin F. Kelley, who had arrested McNeill's mother, sister and 4-year-old brother and had imprisoned them at Camp Chase in Columbus, Ohio. Union soldiers had killed McNeill's father, John Hanson McNeill, in October 1864. On this day, McNeill learned of Kelley's whereabouts and that of General George Crook. When he entered Cumberland, McNeill's raiders found General Kelley at the Barnum House while another unit located General Crook at the Revere House. Both generals were taken prisoner and escorted out of town. They were turned over to General

Thomas L. Rosser in Moorefield, West Virginia. Escorted to Richmond, the generals were confined in Libby Prison before being exchanged weeks later.

22 Union troops entered Wilmington from the south as Confederates left the city via the north roads. The Union army now occupied Wilmington, North Carolina, the last major Confederate port.

22 General Joseph Johnston was reinstated as commander of the Confederate Army of Tennessee, now operating in North Carolina.

23 General Joseph E. Johnston arrived in Cheraw to take command of the remaining portion of the Army of the Tennessee. In order to have a line of defense, Johnston ordered cavalry commander General Hardee to delay a column of Union troops led by General Slocum near Averasborough, North Carolina.

March 1865

2 *Engagement at Waynesboro, Virginia* (**Union Victory**)

On February 27, Union cavalry moved down the Shenandoah Valley from Winchester toward Staunton, Virginia. Reaching Staunton, Sheridan ordered General Custer to pursue the small remaining Confederate force in the Shenandoah Valley. Custer ran into the remaining Confederate forces in the valley near Waynesboro. After a brief skirmish, most of the Confederates surrendered. General Early and his staff evaded capture. With the Shenandoah Valley now under Union control, General Sheridan and his cavalry made their way toward Petersburg. Sheridan reported that the Shenandoah Valley was so devastated by the effects of war that "a crow would have to carry its rations if it had flown across the valley."[2] (General Early met with Lee and explained what had happened. Lee expressed confidence in Early, but when the press vilified Early for losing the Shenandoah, Lee was forced to relieve him of his command.)

	U.S.A.				*C.S.A.*
	General Philip Sheridan, General George Custer				General Jubal Early
	Troops	*Killed*	*Wounded*	*Missing/Captured*	*Total Casualties*
U.S.A.	5,000				30
C.S.A.	1,600				1,500

2 General Robert E. Lee wrote a note to General Grant proposing a meeting in which an attempt to arrive "at a satisfactory adjustment of the present unhappy difficulties by means of a military convention."[3] Grant sent word he had no authority to hold such a conference.

3 General Grant received word from the Secretary of War Edwin Stanton informing him that he was to have "no conference with General Lee, unless it be for the capitulation of General Lee's army or on some minor and purely military matter. He instructs me to say that you are not to decide, discuss, or confer upon any political question. Such questions the President holds in his own hands, and will submit them to no military conferences or conventions. Meantime you are to press to the utmost your military advantages."[4]

3   The Bureau for the Relief of Freedmen and Refugees (The Freedmen's Bureau) was established by the 38th Congress of the United States to provide temporary subsistence, clothing and fuel for freed slaves.

4   Lincoln took the oath of office for his second term. In his Second Inaugural Address, Lincoln stated, "With malice toward none, with charity for all, with firmness in the right, as God gives us to see the right, let us strive on to finish the work we are in, to bind up the nation's wounds, to care for him who shall have borne the battle, and for his widow, and his orphan, to do all which may achieve and cherish a just and a lasting peace, among ourselves, and with all nations."[5]

6   *Battle of Natural Bridge, Florida* (**Confederate Victory**)
    Between the 1st and the 3rd, Union troops along with a Union flotilla prepared to make a move to capture the state capital of Florida at Tallahassee. It was planned for the Union flotilla to sail up the St. Marks River to Port Leon, but they found could not due to shallow waters. The infantry continued their advancement but the Confederates in the city were warned of the imminent arrival of the Union army. A group of local militia held up one part of the Union infantry at Newport Bridge, while the other contingent ran into the larger Union force at Natural Bridge over the St. Marks River. The fighting at the bridge lasted more than ten hours but the Confederates held the bridge, which prevented the capture of the city. The Union was forced to pull back, sailing back to Key West.

	U.S.A.			C.S.A.	
	General John Newton			General Sam Jones	
	Troops	*Killed*	*Wounded*	*Missing/Captured*	*Total Casualties*
U.S.A.		21	89	38	148
C.S.A.	1,000	3	22	1	26

7   Sherman reached the North Carolina border and ordered the scorched earth policy to be discontinued. His men, though, had other ideas and continued to plunder.

7–10   Battle *of Kingston (AKA Wise's or Wyse Forks), North Carolina* (**Union Victory**)
    General John Schofield had been ordered to capture Goldsborough and to repair the rail lines into the town. He was also commanded to stockpile supplies that would be needed for Sherman's army. As Union troops commanded by General Jacob D. Cox moved toward Goldsborough, they ran into a Confederate contingent at Wise's Forks near Kingston. The Confederates were part of General Bragg's army. Bragg earlier had refused to send troops in defense of Fort Fisher. Many of his officers despised Bragg, for on numerous occasions he failed to follow up on an attack that would have, some believed, turned defeat into a victory. At Kingston, Bragg won the first contest between the two forces and, on the next day, ordered General Robert F. Hoke to locate the Union's weakness. Hoke reported Union troops were firmly entrenched and any attack would be difficult. Bragg ordered it anyway.

General D. H. Hill carried out an attack on the opposite flank, but both attacks failed. The Confederates had to pull back. Bragg would take what was left of his men and team up with General Joseph Johnston to try to stop Sherman.

	U.S.A.			C.S.A.	
	General John Schofield,			General Braxton Bragg,	
	General Jacob D. Cox			General Robert F. Hoke,	
				General D.H. Hill	

	Troops	Killed	Wounded	Missing/Captured	Total Casualties
U.S.A.	12,000	65	319	782	1,166
C.S.A.	8,500				1,500

10 *Battle of Monroe's Cross Roads, North Carolina* (**Undetermined**)

Union cavalry, coming from South Carolina, encamped near Solemn Grove and Monroe Cross Roads on the Fayetteville Road near Cumberland, North Carolina. Confederate cavalry commanded by Wade Hampton surprised them and were able to capture several wagons and artillery pieces, but had to withdraw when news of Union reinforcements en route reached them. The assault by the Confederates did break the hold that the Union held on the Fayetteville Road. (General H. Judson Kilpatrick, aware of the Confederate presence, laid a trap to surprise the Confederate cavalry. While waiting for the trap to be sprung, he spent some time with a young maiden by the name of Mary Boozer. When the attack occurred, Kilpatrick was said to have rushed out of the young lady's home with only his nightshirt, boots and sword, leaving his trousers behind.)

	U.S.A.			C.S.A.	
	General H. Judson Kilpatrick			General Wade Hampton,	
				General Joseph Wheeler	

	Troops	Killed	Wounded	Missing/Captured	Total Casualties
U.S.A.	1,850				183
C.S.A.	3,000				86

11 General Sherman and his vast army entered Fayetteville, North Carolina.

12 After entering Fayetteville, Sherman made contact with General Schofield, whose forces occupied Wilmington, North Carolina. They agreed to meet in Goldsborough, North Carolina.

13 Confederate Congress authorized the use of slaves as troops. President Davis asked slave owners to volunteer their slaves to the Confederacy. It was understood, although not specifically stated, that any slave who fought for the Confederacy would be freed after the war.

16 *Battle of Averasborough, North Carolina* (**Undetermined**)

The left wing of Sherman's army, coming from South Carolina, made a march toward Raleigh, North Carolina. This was a ruse, for the plan was to have them join with the right wing and move toward Goldsborough. From there they would move on to Virginia. Confederates believed there was a chance to beat Sherman if they could attack one section at a time. General Joseph Johnston ordered Hardee to delay Slocum and hopefully cut him off from the right wing. Sherman was with Slocum's wing when the Confederates made their surprise attack. The fighting lasted most of the evening with both sides pushing and retreating. Knowing they were overwhelmed, Confederate forces pulled back, having accomplished their mission of delaying the Union advance by two days.

	U.S.A.			C.S.A.	
	General Henry Slocum			*General William Hardee*	
	Troops	*Killed*	*Wounded*	*Missing/Captured*	*Total Casualties*
U.S.A.	25,992	95	533	54	682
C.S.A.	5,400				865

17   General E.R.S. Canby was near Mobile, Alabama.

18   The Confederate Congress adjourned for what would be the last time.

19–21   *Battle of Bentonville, North Carolina* (**Union Victory**)
      This would be the last major battle of the East. General Johnston gathered the troops he thought would be necessary to battle Sherman. His attack on Sherman would be one of divide and conquer. It was well planned and executed, but Johnston realized he did not have the necessary manpower to carry it out. After the battle, Johnston sent General Lee the following message in reference to Sherman: "I can do no more than annoy him."[6]

	U.S.A.			C.S.A.	
	William T. Sherman, Henry Slocum, Otis Howard, J.C. Davis			*Joseph Johnston, William Hardee, A.P. Stewart, D.H. Hill, Joseph Wheeler*	
	Troops	*Killed*	*Wounded*	*Missing/Captured*	*Total Casualties*
U.S.A.	30,000	478	1,168		1,646
C.S.A.	21,000	912	1,694	486	3,092

22   Union commander General John Schofield entered Wilmington, North Carolina.

23   Goldsborough, North Carolina, fell to the Union when Sherman's army routed the Confederates at Bentonville.

25   After taking command of Goldsborough, Sherman took a steamer to City Point, Virginia. At that time Sherman made reference to the fact that Grant had been "so long behind fortification that he had gotten fossilized." He stated that he was "going to stir him up."[7]

25   *Battle of Fort Stedman, Virginia* (**Union Victory**)
      In a last ditch effort, Lee decided to see if he could destroy the Union's supply depot at City Point and, at the same time, break the Union's siege line. As the Confederates under

General Gordon began the attack, they quickly captured Fort Stedman, near Petersburg, turning the fort's guns on nearby forts. By now, the Union had regrouped and, with additional infantry, were able to catch the Confederate soldiers in a crossfire that devastated their line. Lee called off the assault and the Confederates fell back, leaving many of their wounded on the field and in Union hands.

	U.S.A.			*C.S.A.*	
	General John G. Parke			General John B. Gordon	
	Troops	*Killed*	*Wounded*	*Missing/Captured*	*Total Casualties*
U.S.A.		72	450	522	1,044
C.S.A.	12,000				2,900

25 With Sherman issuing orders to cease the "scorched earth policy," others had different ideas. General George Stoneman took 6,000 men and headed east from Mossy Creek, Tennessee, giving orders to "destroy but not to fight battles."[8]

25–April 12   *Siege of Mobile, Alabama*
The Union navy had assumed command of Mobile Bay, but had not moved on the city located thirty miles upstream. Union infantry, commanded by General Canby, approached Mobile, Alabama. Two days later in conjunction with naval forces, a siege of the city began. Two weeks after the fall of Mobile Bay, the Union began bombardment of Mobile, which was guarded by numerous forts surrounding the city. Mines and piles driven into the sand protected the harbor.

26 General Robert E. Lee advised President Jefferson Davis that he could no longer defend and protect Richmond. Lee explained he was preparing to take his 57,000 soldiers south to North Carolina where he hoped to join with General Joseph Johnston.

27 President Lincoln met with Grant, Sherman and Admiral Porter aboard the *River Queen* at City Point, Virginia. There they discussed the status of the war as the generals outlined their plans. Lincoln was told that it would take only one more major campaign to end the war. According to Admiral Porter, Lincoln told them, "I want submission and no more bloodshed.... We want those people to return to their allegiance to the Union and submit to the laws."[9]

27–April 8   Siege *of Spanish Fort, Alabama* (**Union Victory**)
Union troops gathered at Danley's Ferry and laid siege to Spanish Fort. By April 1, they had surrounded the fort, which surrendered on April 8.

	U.S.A.			*C.S.A.*	
	General E.R.S. Canby			General Randall L. Gibson	
	Troops	*Killed*	*Wounded*	*Missing/Captured*	*Total Casualties*
U.S.A.	2 corps	52	575	30	657
C.S.A.	Garrison				744

28   General Stoneman and his raiders moved into Boone, North Carolina, where they plundered and burned. The following day, they moved on to Wilkesboro.

28   The USS *Milwaukee*, stationed in Mobile Bay, sank after striking a Confederate mine.

29   *Engagement at Lewis' Farm, Virginia* (**Union Victory**)
The final campaign of the war began as Union cavalry combined with infantry moved toward Dinwiddie Court House in an attempt to turn the flank of Lee's army, which was defending Petersburg. To prevent the action, Confederate cavalry under Johnson left their entrenchments to engage the Union forces. Outmanned and overpowered, the Confederates retreated to their entrenchments.

	U.S.A.			*C.S.A.*	
	General G. K. Warren			General Bushrod R. Johnson	
	Troops	*Killed*	*Wounded*	*Missing/Captured*	*Total Casualties*
U.S.A.		55	306	22	383
C.S.A.					370

30   *Skirmish at Dinwiddie Court House, Virginia* (**Confederate Victory**)
In an another attempt to turn the Confederate flank at Petersburg, Union cavalry and infantry advanced on Dinwiddie Court House, but were met by Fitzhugh Lee and his cavalry as well as infantry under General Pickett. Confederates were able to drive back the Union advance. This would only be temporary, for additional troops were rushed up and Confederate forces had to withdraw. They withdrew and entrenched at Five Forks. General Lee ordered them to hold that crossroads "at all hazards."

	U.S.A.			*C.S.A.*	
	General Philip Sheridan		General George Pickett, General Fitzhugh Lee		
	Troops	*Killed*	*Wounded*	*Missing/Captured*	*Total Casualties*
U.S.A.	13,000	67	354		421
C.S.A.	20,030				400

31   *Engagement at White Oak Road (AKA Hatcher's Run), Virginia* (**Union Victory**)
With the Union making advances on his flank, General Lee shifted some of his troops to meet the threat. As the engagement was taking place at Dinwiddie Court House, additional Union troops were sent to White Oak Road to cut communications between the main Confederate line and those at the Five Forks crossroads.

	U.S.A.			*C.S.A.*	
	General Gouverneur K. Warren			General Richard H. Anderson, General Samuel McGowan	
	Troops	*Killed*	*Wounded*	*Missing/Captured*	*Total Casualties*
U.S.A.	Corps	177	1,134	556	1,867
C.S.A.	Corps				800

April 1865

1 *Battle of Five Forks, Virginia* (**Union Victory**)

Confederate General Pickett had been ordered to hold the crossroads at Five Forks "at all hazards," which would keep the Confederate supply lines open. On the 1st, Union cavalry under General Sheridan approached and attacked Confederates in a holding engagement. In the meantime, General Warren brought up the infantry and attacked the Confederate rear, forcing Pickett out of his trenches. The Confederates were overwhelmed and many surrendered. With the capture of the crossroad, communication and the supply lines to the Confederate troops in Petersburg were cut off. (It was reported the reason for the success of the Union assault was that Generals Pickett, Fitzhugh Lee and Thomas Rosser were all at Rosser's headquarters enjoying a "shad bake" when the Union attack began.)

	U.S.A.			C.S.A.	
	General Philip Sheridan			General George Pickett, General W.H.F. "Rooney" Lee	
	Troops	*Killed*	*Wounded*	*Missing/Captured*	*Total Casualties*
U.S.A.	53,000	124	706	54	884
C.S.A.	19,000				5,000

1 *Battle of Ebenezer Church, Alabama* (**Union Victory**)

Union troops under General James H. Wilson overran a portion of General Nathan B. Forrest's cavalry, causing them to fall back toward Selma, Alabama.

2 *Skirmish at Sutherland's Station, Virginia* (**Union Victory**)

Union forces overran four Confederate brigades on the White Oak Road and took possession of the South Side Rail line. Lee's last supply line feeding Petersburg was now in Union hands.

	U.S.A.			C.S.A.	
	General Nelson A. Miles			General Henry Heth, General Cadmus Wilcox	
	Troops	*Killed*	*Wounded*	*Missing/Captured*	*Total Casualties*
U.S.A.	Division	33	236	97	366
C.S.A.	Division				600

2 *Battle of Fort Gregg, Petersburg, Virginia* (**Union Victory**)

Encouraged by the victory at Five Forks, General Grant ordered an all-out assault along the lines protecting Petersburg. Efforts were concentrated on Fort Gregg, an unfinished earthwork defending the southwestern approach to Petersburg. After three successive attacks, the fort was taken and now the door to Petersburg was open. As the fighting took place, Lee decided if his army was to survive, he would have to abandon the trenches. In the confusion of the battle, General A.P. Hill was killed after he had become separated from his men and had tried to rejoin them. That evening, Lee led his men out of Petersburg in the direction of Amelia Court House. The ten-month siege of the city was over.

	U.S.A.			*C.S.A.*	
	General U.S. Grant			General Robert E. Lee, General A.P. Hill (Killed)	

	Troops	*Killed*	*Wounded*	*Missing/Captured*	*Total Casualties*
U.S.A.	63,000	296	2,565	500	3,361
C.S.A.	18,500				4,250

2 Lee led his men out of Petersburg westward towards Amelia Court House, as General John B. Gordon staged a charge against the Union lines. This allowed Lee and his men time to make their departure, abandoning Petersburg for good. Before departing, he sent President Jefferson Davis a wire advising him that he could no longer defend Petersburg or Richmond and advised him to evacuate Richmond.

2 Jefferson Davis summoned his cabinet, and by 11 p.m., Davis, with most of his cabinet, was on a special train headed for Danville, Virginia. Government records either were destroyed to prevent them falling into Union hands or, in some cases, boxed up and carried away by various officials as they fled the city.

2 General Stoneman crossed into Virginia, where he spent a week destroying 150 miles of the Virginia and Tennessee Railroad track.

2 *Battle of Selma, Alabama* (**Union Victory**)

Selma had become one of the few munitions and manufacturing areas of the Confederacy. Union troops under General Wilson left Tennessee in mid–March to capture the area and deny another source of assistance to the failing Confederacy. After his defeat at Ebenezer Church, Forrest, with his small cavalry, retreated to the city and set up a defensive position in which to protect the city. The assault began in the late afternoon, but as darkness settled in, the city was in the hands of the Union. Forrest and a few of his men managed to slip away, making their way to freedom while leaving behind 2,700 men in Union hands.

	U.S.A.			*C.S.A.*	
	General James H. Wilson			General Nathan B. Forrest	

	Troops	*Killed*	*Wounded*	*Missing/Captured*	*Total Casualties*
U.S.A.	13,500	42	270	7	319
C.S.A.	8,000				2,700

3 *Skirmish at Namozine Church, Virginia* (**Undetermined**)

As the Army of Northern Virginia moved eastward, General Grant ordered Union cavalry to pursue, which resulted in numerous small skirmishes with the Confederate cavalry guarding Lee's rear. In action near the Namozine Church, Union troops almost devastated the brigade of General Rufus Barringer, capturing the general.

	Troops	Killed	Wounded	Missing/Captured	Total Casualties

U.S.A. — General George Custer
C.S.A. — General Fitzhugh Lee

	Troops	Killed	Wounded	Missing/Captured	Total Casualties
U.S.A.		10	85		95
C.S.A.					75

3 *Union troops marched in and occupied Richmond and Petersburg.*

Major Atherton H. Stevens Jr. with the 4th Massachusetts Cavalry raised the United States flag over the Confederate White House in Richmond.

4 *Engagement at Jetersville, Virginia (**Union Victory**)*

Union commanders realized General Fitzhugh Lee was heading toward Danville in an effort to slip around Union forces and join General Joseph Johnston in the Carolinas. General Phil Sheridan followed Lee via parallel roads, preventing Lee from turning south. At Jetersville, Union troops under General George Crook secured the rail line and forced Lee to seek another route to North Carolina.

4 President Lincoln visited Richmond after traveling up the James River. His ship docked not far from Libby Prison, where many Union soldiers had been confined as prisoners of war. Sailors and marines escorted Lincoln to the Confederate White House.

5 General Lee managed to get his army to Amelia Court House, where he hoped to find the needed supplies to feed his starving army. Before leaving Petersburg, Lee had instructed the Commissary Department to deliver 350,000 rations to Amelia Court House. From there, he intended to push south toward North Carolina. Upon his arrival at Amelia Court House, Lee found no food supplies and his forage wagons empty. By now, Union infantry and cavalry had moved parallel to Lee, and, had in effect blocked his passage south. Lee had only one alternative left and that was to move northward towards Lynchburg, Virginia.

6 *Battle of Sayler's Creek (Sailor's Creek), Virginia (**Union Victory**)*

As the Confederate army was making its way toward Lynchburg, Union cavalry kept nipping at their heels. The men were exhausted. Soon, a gap developed between the fast moving front line and the slower moving baggage wagons near the rear. When the rear column approached Sayler's Creek, they were discovered by Sheridan's cavalry. Union cavalrymen entered the gap and secured the road, prohibiting the Confederates from crossing. General Ewell, according to some reports, had directed the wagons to take a different route but had neglected to inform General Gordon of his orders. The rear column was now trapped between Union cavalry and the infantry. A portion of General Gordon's troops, having followed the slower moving wagon trains, became engaged in a severe fight before retreating to the southwest to link up with General Lee and the rest of the army. Eight Confederate generals (Ewell, Barton, Simms, Kershaw, Curtis Lee, Dubose, Hunton and Corse) were captured by Union troops. Over 6,000 Confederate soldiers were taken prisoner. This was the last major engagement between the Army of Northern Virginia and the Army of the Potomac.

	U.S.A.			C.S.A.	
	General Philip Sheridan, General A.A. Humphreys			General Richard Ewell, General John B. Gordon	

	Troops	Killed	Wounded	Missing/Captured	Total Casualties
U.S.A.	18,000	166	1,014		1,180
C.S.A.	9,000				9,000

6 *Engagement at Rice's Station, Virginia* (**Union Victory**)

A portion of the Confederate army (Longstreet's corps) was attempting to move southward, making it to Rice's Station before they discovered the Union's 24th Corps had blocked the route. The Confederates pulled back and withdrew over the High Bridge to Farmville.

6–7 *Skirmish at High Bridge, Virginia* (**Undetermined**)

Confederate forces engaged in a brief skirmish as they attempted to make their way across the High Bridge before arrival of their Union pursuers. The following day as the Confederates attempted to burn the bridge, additional Union troops confronted them. After a brief skirmish, the Confederates were forced to withdraw toward Farmville. The way was now clear for the final pursuit.

	U.S.A.			C.S.A.	
	Colonel T. Read, General A.A. Humphreys			General Thomas Rosser, General William Mahone	

	Troops	Killed	Wounded	Missing/Captured	Total Casualties
U.S.A.		10	31	1,000	1,041
C.S.A.					159

7 *Skirmish at Cumberland Church, Virginia* (**Confederate Victory**)

As the Union troops advanced toward Farmville, they came upon Confederates entrenched near Cumberland Church. The fighting, which was intense, came to a halt as darkness moved in.

	U.S.A.			C.S.A.	
	General A.A. Humphreys, General J.I. Gregg (captured)			General Robert E. Lee	

	Troops	Killed	Wounded	Missing/Captured	Total Casualties
U.S.A.	Corps				655
C.S.A.	Corps				255

7 *Encounter at Farmville, Virginia*

Ever since leaving Petersburg, Lee's army had been on the move trying to find a way around the Union army. Their path to North Carolina was now blocked. Lee's men were starving and he ordered foodstuffs be sent from Lynchburg by rail. The supplies awaited Lee at Farmville. While his men ate, Lee was advised the Union army was approaching.

The men left their uneaten food to take up their rifles once more in defense of their position. Confederate defenders held back the Union advance temporarily, as the army pulled back.

7 That evening, General Grant sent the following message to Lee: "The result of the last week must convince you of the hopelessness of further resistance on the part of the Army of Northern Virginia in this struggle. I feel that it is so, and regard it as my duty to shift from myself the responsibility of any further effusion of blood, by asking of you the surrender of that portion of the Confederate States Army known as the Army of Northern Virginia."[10] Lee reportedly showed the note to General Longstreet, who is reported to have responded, "Not yet." Lee sent his response to General Grant saying that he did not have the "opinion you express of the hopelessness of further resistance on the part of the Army of Northern Virginia, I reciprocate your desire to avoid useless effusion of blood, and therefore, before considering your proposition ask the terms you will offer on condition of its surrender."[11]

8 *Battle of Appomattox, Virginia* (**Union Victory**)
After a meeting among Lee's commanders, it was decided to first see if his forces could break the stranglehold on their line. If they could not, then it was time to consider Grant's offer. However, as Confederate infantry charged the Union line and forced their cavalry backwards, they found themselves surrounded by one line after another. Union cavalry under General George Custer captured some of the supply wagons bringing food to Lee's starving army. Confederate artillery under General Lindsay Walker attempted to battle the cavalry, but with no infantry in support, the guns were captured. Custer burned the supply wagons. The Union suffered a total loss of 118, including 32 killed and 86 wounded.

8 Lee's army was near Appomattox Court House now surrounded. Meade, with the Army of the Potomac, was behind him, and, in front was the Fifth Corps commanded by Charles Griffin along with the Army of the James. In addition, Union cavalry under Sheridan was everywhere. There was no place for them to go and fighting their way out would result in needless deaths. Lee took all of this and his supply needs under advisement. In the meantime, General Grant sent the terms of surrender he would consider. In his note, Grant stated, "Peace being my greatest desire, there is but one condition I would insist upon, namely that the men and officers surrendered shall be disqualified from taking up arms again against the Government of the United States until properly exchanged."[12]

8 *Spanish Fort, Alabama fell* (**Union Victory**)
Union forces under General E.R.S. Canby took possession of Spanish Fort, Alabama, after a ten-day siege.

U.S.A.			*C.S.A.*		
General E.R.S. Canby			General Randall L. Gibson		
	Troops	*Killed*	*Wounded*	*Missing/Captured*	*Total Casualties*
U.S.A.	2 Corps	52	575	3	630
C.S.A.	3,500				744

9 *Surrender of the Army of Northern Virginia at Appomattox Court House, Virginia* Appomattox Court House was a small village located ninety miles west of Richmond and 180 miles south of Washington. At dawn, near Appomattox Station, Confederates attacked there, hoping to force a passage through the Union lines. After learning that escape was impossible, Lee turned to his adjutant and friend Colonel Walter H. Taylor and stated, "It would be useless and cruel to provoke the further effusion of blood and I have arranged to meet with General Grant with a view to surrender."[13] Lee sent the following note to General Grant: "I ask a suspension of hostilities pending the adjustment of the terms of the surrender of the army."[14] That afternoon, General Lee, with his aide Charles Marshall, met with General Grant and his staff in the parlor of the Wilmer McLean house at Appomattox Court House. After a brief conversation, both men got down to business. Grant showed great compassion and leniency when he offered the terms he would accept. Officers and men, upon their surrender, would be paroled and allowed to return to their homes if they promised not to take up arms; guns, ammunition, and military supplies were to be confiscated and turned in as captured property. Grant, knowing that the soldiers of the Confederacy were in need of food, made arrangements to feed Lee's army from Union supplies. In the evening, General Grant sent the following note to Edwin Stanton, Lincoln's secretary of war: "Gen. Lee surrendered the Army of Northern Va. this afternoon on terms proposed by myself. The accompanying additions and responses will show the conditions fully."[15]

9 General Stoneman's raiders re-entered North Carolina to wreak whatever havoc they could and, this time, their intention was focused on Salem and Winston. The Union raiders burned all the factories, bridges and over 1,700 bales of cotton in High Point.

9 *Capture of Fort Blakely, Alabama* (**Union Victory**)
With the fall of Spanish Fort on the 8th, Union troops were able to concentrate their efforts on Fort Blakely, which defended the city of Mobile. Overpowered and outmanned, the fort was taken. Now the way was clear for the movement to secure Mobile, Alabama.

	U.S.A.				*C.S.A.*	
	General Frederick Steele				General John R. Liddell	
	Troops	*Killed*	*Wounded*	*Missing/Captured*	*Total Casualties*	
U.S.A.	16,000	116	685	4	805	
C.S.A.	4,000	250			2,900	

10 Three commissioners from each army (Generals James Longstreet, John B. Gordon and William Pendleton representing Lee and the Army of Northern Virginia and Generals John Gibbon, Charles W. Griffin and Wesley Merritt representing Grant and the Union) met at the Clover Hill Tavern at Appomattox Court House to work out the details for the surrender. The commissioners later adjourned to the McLean House to complete their discussions. The terms did not include the surrender of officers' sidearms or their private horses or baggage. Each officer and man would be allowed to return to their home and not be disturbed as long as the parole was observed. After several discussions with Lee and Grant, it was decided to allow Confederate cavalrymen and artillerymen to take their own horses with them since they would be needed for spring planting. Both Grant and Lee accepted the surrender terms. The six officers signed the final surrender in the McLean's parlor at 8:30 a.m. on April 10, 1865. Lee and Grant met only one time after leaving Appomattox and that was when Lee visited President Grant in the White House in 1869.

10   After learning that Lee had surrendered the Army of Northern Virginia to General Grant, Confederate government officials left Danville, Virginia, and headed toward Greensboro, North Carolina.

10   General Sherman's army arrived at Goldsborough, North Carolina, where they began the last leg of its devastating march through the Carolinians.

11   Confederate General D.H. Maury began the evacuation of Mobile, Alabama.

12   *The Collection of Arms*
A ceremony took place at Appomattox Court House where the Union troops formed a line along the principal street in the small town and saluted as Confederates soldiers marched in to lay down their battle flags and rifles. General Joshua Chamberlain said as he viewed this highly emotional occurrence: "Before us in proud humiliation stood the embodiment of manhood, men whom neither toils and sufferings, nor the fact of death, nor disaster, nor hopelessness could bend from their resolve; standing before us now, thin, worn and famished, but erect and with eyes looking level into ours, waking memories that bound us together as no other bond."[16] As the bugle sounded, the Union soldiers presented a military salute to the Confederate troops as they passed. According to historians, the Union soldiers were called to attention when each Confederate regiment marched in and came to a halt. The order was given and the men laid down their guns and flags. As the Union blue rendered a salute, the Confederate regiment, once more called to attention, was marched out. The Union troops then gathered the arms and flags and removed them to be stacked elsewhere. They returned to line the road in time to receive the next Confederate regiment.

12   Union cavalry under James H. Wilson entered and occupied Montgomery, Alabama.

12   The Confederate government met at Greensboro, North Carolina, and held meetings with Generals Johnston and Beauregard. At that time, President Jefferson Davis requested additional armies be raised to continue the fight. Johnston was reported to have tried to point out the futility of the situation.

12   *Union forces take Mobile, Alabama* (**Union Victory**)
After a long siege in which numerous skirmishes were fought around the many forts in the area, Union troops entered the city only to find the Confederates had withdrawn during the night.

Losses during the siege of Mobile, Alabama

U.S.A.	C.S.A.
General E.R.S. Canby	General Dabney H. Maury

	Troops	Killed	Wounded	Missing/Captured	Total Casualties
U.S.A.	45,000	232	1,303	43	1,578
C.S.A.	10,000				5,500

12 General Stoneman with his band of raiders entered Salisbury, an important railroad hub and military depot and a known prison for captured Union soldiers. The Union prisoners had been evacuated earlier, but that did not stop Stoneman from setting fire to the prison. They then continued westward, burning and destroying as they went through Statesville, Lincoln, Taylorsville and Asheville. Confederate troops, consisting 100 Virginia troops plus junior reserves and the Old Men of the Home Guard commanded by General William M. Gardner, took up a stand along Grant's Creek on the road from Mocksville. They posed no threat to the Union troops who swiftly captured the town.

13 Secretary of War Stanton issued orders calling for a stop to the draft and suspending the purchase of war supplies.

13 The Union army occupied Raleigh, North Carolina, as General Sherman entered the city.

13 General Alvan C. Gillem, one of Stoneman's commanders, was a brutal and vindictive man. He, like some of his men, were born and raised in the mountains of North Carolina and had enlisted in the Union army, for they supported the Union cause. Now as they traveled through North Carolina, they pillaged the homes of innocent, defenseless women and children. When Gillem and his band of terrorists approached Asheville, Confederate General James G. Martin assembled every Confederate partisan he could find to defend the area.

14 *Lincoln assassinated*
President Lincoln, accompanied by his wife, along with Miss Clara Harris and Major H.R. Rathbone, attended Ford's Theatre to see the play *Our American Cousin*. A little after 10 p.m., actor John Wilkes Booth sneaked up the back stairs and entered the president's box. Once inside the box, Booth shot the president in the back of the head with a small gun and proceeded to jump to the stage, injuring his leg as he landed. The crowd heard him yell as he ran across the stage: "sic semper tyrannis" (thus always to tyrants). President Lincoln was carried across the street to the home of William Peterson and placed in a rear bedroom where various doctors attended him. The doctors discovered the bullet fired by Booth had entered the rear of the president's head and had lodged near his right eye.

14 At approximately the same time as the incident at Ford's Theatre, Lewis Payne (Paine) entered the home of Secretary of State William Seward, who was recovering from a recent carriage accident. Payne (Paine) entered Seward's bedroom and stabbed him, causing minor injuries, before fleeing from the scene.

14 General Joseph Johnston wrote to General Sherman in Raleigh asking if he was "willing to make a temporary suspension of active operations." Sherman suggested the same terms that Grant offered to Lee.

14 *The United States flag was raised again over Fort Sumter*
General Robert Anderson returned to Fort Sumter to raise the same flag he had removed from Fort Sumter four years earlier.

15 *Lincoln died at 7:22 a.m.*
Secretary of War Stanton remarked, "Now he belongs to the ages."

15 At 11 a.m. in the Kirkwood Hotel, Andrew Johnson took the oath of office administered by Chief Justice Samuel P. Chase.

15 John Wilkes Booth and a confederate, David Herold, stopped at the home of Dr. Samuel Mudd in Bryantown, Maryland, where Dr. Mudd set Booth's injured leg.

16 Union troops under General James H. Wilson entered Columbus, Georgia, unaware of the surrender of Lee's army. When they entered the city, approximately 3,000 old men, young boys plus various factory workers challenged them with whatever weapons they had. Columbus was a large manufacturing city that not only made war equipment but also possessed large cotton mills. Upon entering the city, the Union troops burned two of the three bridges leading into it. They then mounted a night attack, driving off the defenders within an hour, capturing the city. Union troops set fire to the city the next day in retaliation for the resistance. Afterwards, General Wilson stated, "Had we but known what had taken place in Virginia ... we should certainly have not ... participated in the injury which was inflicted upon [Columbus'] industries."[17] The damage, according to witnesses, was so complete that the city almost ceased to exist. It was reported that Wilson burned approximately 125,000 bales of cotton worth an estimated 62.5 million dollars.

17 Sherman and Johnston met at the Bennett House near Durham Station, North Carolina. In their talks, the two generals went further than just discussing the surrender of Johnston's army. They discussed terms of an armistice for the remaining armies.

17 Jefferson Davis and the fleeing Confederate government left Greensboro en route to Charlotte, North Carolina.

18 Confederate General Joseph E. Johnston and Sherman signed the "Memorandum or Basis for Agreement" that called for an armistice by all armies in the field. Under the agreement, Confederate forces were to be disbanded and would deposit their arms in the state arsenals; each man would agree not to take up arms and to obey all state and federal authority; the president of the United States would recognize the existing state governments when their officers took an oath to the United States; and the re-establishment of federal courts would take place and the people would be guaranteed their rights. In addition, it was agreed upon that the United States government would not disturb the people of the South as long as they lived in peace; and a general amnesty for Confederates would be issued. Sherman sent the terms to General Grant and Secretary of War Henry Halleck asking the president to approve the terms.

19   President Johnson, the cabinet, Supreme Court justices, the Congress, military figures and the diplomatic corps filed into the East Room of the White House for the funeral services of President Lincoln. Robert Lincoln represented the family as Mrs. Lincoln and son Tad remained sequestered. General Grant was reported to have stood alone at the head of the president's coffin. After a brief service, the funeral carriage was escorted by the various military units, all with their banners draped and all playing sorrowful tunes, as it passed throngs of people on the way to the rotunda of the Capitol.

19   Davis and his entourage arrived in Charlotte, North Carolina.

21   The body of Lincoln left Washington for Springfield, Illinois.

21   At Millwood, Virginia, John Singleton Mosby disbanded his Confederate raiders.

21   President Johnson and his cabinet disapproved of the Johnston-Sherman armistice, and they sent Grant to inform Sherman of the refusal.

22   Union forces under General Alvan C. Gillem approached Asheville. Confederate General Martin, aware that General Lee and Grant had signed an armistice, sent an officer to meet with Gillem under a flag of truce to arrange a cease-fire. After he was given 9,000 rations, Gillem and his men left the area, promising not to destroy the town. However, four days later, on the 26th, Gillem and his men returned and looted the town. One of Gillem's fellow officers sent a letter of apology to General Martin, calling the destruction and sacking of Asheville "unbecoming to the Honor of the United States."

22   John Wilkes Booth and Herold crossed the Potomac to Gumbo Creek on the Virginia side of the river.

23–24   The CSS *William H. Webb*, a 190 foot long, 31 foot wide side-wheeler, was considered one of the fastest steamships at the time. Having been outfitted as a ram, the CSS *Webb* was bottled up on the Red River near Shreveport, Louisiana. Secretary of the Confederate Navy Stephen R. Malloy had ordered the ship's commander, Lt. Charles W. Read, to slip past the Union defenders and to get to the open sea. Once in the open, Lt. Read was to sell the valuable crop of cotton stored in her cargo hold, as the Confederacy was in dire need of cash and other supplies. Lt. Read disguised the ship as a Yankee transport and attempted to slip past Union gunboats unnoticed. After passing several gunboats, the CSS *Webb* was challenged by the USS *Richmond*. Rather than risk the death of his crew, Lt. Read, after running up her "colors," ran the ship aground and then set her on fire as he and his crew escaped into the nearby swamps.

24   Grant informed General Sherman that President Johnson disapproved of Sherman's agreement with Johnston. Grant gave Sherman forty-eight hours to secure another agreement or hostilities against Johnston and his men would be renewed.

24   Booth and Herold crossed the Rappahannock at Port Conway, Virginia.

26 At approximately 7 a.m., Federal troops, under the command of Lt. Colonel Everton Conger, surrounded the barn of Richard H. Garrett near Bowling Green, Virginia. Inside the barn, Booth and Herold lay hidden. The suspects were ordered to come out. Herold surrendered but Booth refused. The barn was set on fire. A shot, later attributed to Sgt. Boston Corbett, killed Booth as he tried to exit the barn in a futile escape attempt.

26 Sherman and Johnston met once more at the Bennett House in Durham Station during the afternoon hours. Johnston accepted Sherman's new terms, which were the same as those offered Lee. Johnston surrendered his army to General Sherman.

26 The Confederate cabinet met for the last time in Charlotte, North Carolina. They agreed to leave that day in an attempt to put the Mississippi River between them and Union pursuers.

26 General Stoneman and his men entered Tennessee.

27 *The* Sultana *Disaster*
The *Sultana*, a ship overcrowded with Union soldiers, many of them former prisoners of war on their way home from Vicksburg, exploded just north of Memphis on the Mississippi River. Of the 2,021 people on board, 1,238 were killed.

30 A few miles north of Mobile, Alabama, Union commander General E.R.S. Canby and Confederate General Richard Taylor agreed to a truce prior to the Confederate surrender.

May 1865

1 President Johnson ordered a military commission formed to try the conspirators identified as David E. Herold, George A. Atzerodt, Samuel Arnold, Lewis Payne (Paine), Michael O'Laughlin, Edward Spangler, Mrs. Mary E. Surratt and Dr. Samuel A. Mudd. The commission would be made up of nine Army officers and one congressional representative. They were General David A. Hunter, Judge Joseph Holt, General Henry L. Burnett, General James A. Elkin, General Robert S. Foster, General T.M. Harris, General A.P. Howe, General A.V. Kautz, General Lew Wallace, Colonel D.R. Clendenin, Colonel C.H. Tompkins and Ohio Congressman John A. Bingham.

2 President Johnson issued a proclamation accusing Confederate President Jefferson Davis and others of inciting the murder of President Lincoln. He proclaimed they had procured the assassins. A one hundred thousand dollar reward was offered for Jefferson Davis' arrest.

4 President Lincoln was buried in Springfield, Illinois.

4 General Richard Taylor surrendered the remaining troops to Union commander General E.R.S. Canby at Citronelle, just north of Mobile, Alabama. The surrender terms were most "generous," according to General Taylor. The terms not only allowed mounted soldiers to keep their horses and officers their sidearms, but also allowed Taylor to maintain control of the railroads and riverboats so paroled Confederate soldiers could reach their homes.

5   Jefferson Davis arrived in Sandersville, Georgia, seeking a way to avoid Union officials who were searching the countryside for him.

6   The War Department issued orders establishing the military commission to try the Lincoln conspirators. Major General David Hunter was named president and would serve as the head of the commission; Brigadier General Joseph Holt would act as the judge advocate. Ohio Congressman John A. Bingham and General Henry L. Burnett would serve as the prosecuting officers.

9   The trial of the Lincoln conspirators began under tight security in Washington, D.C.

10   Early in the morning, the Fourth Michigan Cavalry captured Jefferson Davis near Irwinville, Georgia. Davis, along with his wife, presidential secretary Burton Harrison and others were taken into custody. When captured, Davis, wearing a raincoat with a shawl over his head to protect him from the rain, was but a few yards from his tent. Davis was at first taken to Macon, Georgia, and then transported to Fort Monroe in Virginia. While confined in prison, he was kept in chains. After a while, prison life improved and he was able to receive family visits. He remained a prisoner until May 13, 1867, when he was released without charges. It was reported that throughout his capture and imprisonment, Davis maintained a quiet and dignified manner.

10   President Johnson issued a proclamation declaring the rebellion over. In this proclamation, Johnson stated that "armed resistance to the authority of the Government in the said insurrectionary States may be regarded as virtually at an end."[18]

10   Union soldiers fatally wounded William Clarke Quantrill, a twenty-seven year old Confederate raider, near Taylorsville, Kentucky. He died of his wounds on June 6, 1865, in Louisville, Kentucky.

12–13   *Battle of Palmito Ranch, near Brownsville, Texas* (**Confederate Victory**)
       The last engagement of the war occurred when Union troops from Brazos Santiago Post, Texas, marched inland toward Brownsville. Earlier in March, forces in Texas had agreed to an informal truce. According to many historians, Colonel Barrett, an ambitious man, had been ordered not to engage in any military action, but he decided to capture the remaining Confederate force located near the Mexican border. After an initial success, Union forces were driven off by "Rip" Ford's forces.

	U.S.A.			*C.S.A.*	
	Colonel Theodore H. Barrett, Lt. Col. David Branson			Colonel John S. Ford	
	Troops	*Killed*	*Wounded*	*Missing/Captured*	*Total Casualties*
U.S.A.	800				143
C.S.A.	350	5			5

12   The Lincoln conspirators pleaded not guilty at their trial before the military commission.

12   President Johnson appointed General O.O. Howard to head the Freedman's Bureau.

23–24   The Grand Armies of the Republic passed in review from the Capitol to the White House in Washington, D.C. The crowds roared with approval and fell silent only when the ambulances with bloodstained stretchers rolled by. Sherman stated: "On the whole, the grand review was a splendid success, and was a fitting conclusion to the campaign and the war."[19]

25   The Confederates evacuated Sabine Pass, Texas.

26   Lieutenant General Edmond Kirby Smith surrendered additional Confederate troops to General E.R.S. Canby in New Orleans, Louisiana.

29   President Johnson proclaimed amnesty for all citizens of the South who pledged allegiance to the United States. All property rights were to be restored except slaves. An oath was required to fully support, protect and defend the Constitution of the United States. Persons who participated in the rebellion and had taxable property of over $20,000 were excluded from the amnesty. Others excluded from the amnesty were those who held civil or diplomatic offices; those who left United States judicial posts; officers above the rank of colonel in the Army or lieutenant in the Navy; all who left Congress to join the South; all who resigned from the U.S. Army or Navy "to evade duty in resisting the rebellion"; all those who mistreated prisoners of war; all who were educated in the U.S. military or naval academies; governors of states in insurrection; those who left homes in the North to go South; those who engaged in destroying commerce; and those who had violated previous oaths. Any person under those exceptions could apply to the president where "such clemency will be liberally extended as may be consistent with the facts of the case and the peace and dignity of the United States."[20]

June 1865

6   Confederate prisoners who were confined in Union prisons and willing to take the oath of allegiance were released to return to their homes.

13   William L. Sharkey was named as provisional governor of Mississippi.

17   James Johnson was named as provisional governor of Georgia and Andrew J. Hamilton as the provisional governor of Texas.

21   Lewis E. Parsons was named as provisional governor of Alabama.

23   President Johnson declared the Union blockade of the Southern states would end.

23   Stand Watie surrendered his Indian force to Union commander Lieutenant Colonel Asa Mathews at Doaksville, located near Fort Towson in the Indian Territory.

30   *The Lincoln conspirators are convicted*
After a lengthy trial, the military commissioners found all eight conspirators guilty. Dr. Samuel Mudd, Samuel Arnold, and Michael O'Laughlin were sentenced to life in prison at hard labor while Edward Spangler was given six years. Condemned to death and ordered to be hanged were David Herold, Lewis Payne (Paine), George Atzerodt and Mary E. Surrett, "by proper military authority under the direction of the Secretary of War on the 7th of July between 10 o'clock a.m. and 2 o'clock p.m. of that day."[21]

July 1865

6   The accused conspirators were advised of the sentence of the military court and were given one day to prepare for their execution the following morning.

7   The Lincoln conspirators were executed in a public hanging at the Old Penitentiary Building's arsenal grounds after being brought to the courtyard shortly before 2 p.m.

7   William Marvin was named as provisional governor of Florida.

October 1865

12   President Johnson paroled Confederate Vice President Alexander H. Stephens as well as cabinet members John H. Reagan, George A. Trenholm, Governor Charles Clark of Mississippi and Assistant Secretary of War John A. Campbell, all of whom had been confined in prison.

6   The Confederate cruiser CSS *Shenandoah* was surrendered by its commander, Lieutenant James Waddell, at Liverpool, England, when he finally learned that the war was over.

December 1865

18   The Thirteenth Amendment to the Constitution abolishing slavery was declared to "be in effect" after being ratified by 27 of the 36 states.

MILITARY DISTRICTS ESTABLISHED AFTER THE WAR

At the end of the war, there were five military jurisdictions created to govern the "occupied states of the Confederacy" prior to their re-admission to the Union.

District #	Consisted of	Military Governor
First Military	Virginia	General John Schofield
Second Military	North and South Carolina	General Daniel Sickles
Third Military	Florida, Georgia, Alabama	General John Pope
Fourth Military	Arkansas, Mississippi	General Edward Ord
Fifth Military	Texas, Louisiana	General Philip Sheridan

DATES OF SECESSION AND RE-ADMISSION OF CONFEDERATE STATES

	Seceded from the Union	Re-Admitted to the Union
Alabama	January 11, 1861	July 13, 1868
Arkansas	May 6, 1861	June 22, 1868
Florida	January 10, 1861	June 25, 1868
Georgia	January 19, 1861	July 15, 1870
Louisiana	January 26, 1861	July 9, 1868
Mississippi	January 9, 1861	February 23, 1870
North Carolina	May 20, 1861	July 4, 1868
South Carolina	December 20, 1860	July 9, 1868
Tennessee	May 6, 1861	July 24, 1866
Texas	February 1, 1861	March 30, 1870
Virginia	April 17, 1861	January 26, 1870

Chapter 11

Casualties

Many of the men who fought during those four awful years of war fell in battle. Many more suffered horrible wounds that affected them all their lives. Some men carried not only external scars but internal ones as well.

In 1888, Lieutenant Colonel William F. Fox gathered all the statistical records he could find on strengths of every unit that fought for the Union. He published the results in *Regimental Losses in the American Civil War 1861–1865: A Treatise on the Extent and Nature of the Mortuary Losses in the Union Regiments, with Full and Exhaustive Statistics Compiled from the Official Records on File in the State Military Bureaus and at Washington.* Fox's book is recognized as one of the most accurate sources of information on losses that occurred during the Civil War. "The history of a battle or a war should always be studied in connection with the figures which show the losses. By overlooking them an indefinite, and often erroneous, idea is obtained. By neglecting them, many historians fail to develop the important points of the contest,"[1] wrote Fox when he published his findings. It's as true today as it was when he wrote it.

In any war or conflict, there will always be casualties and the figures never can measure the true loss. In the Civil War, exact totals are impossible. The North kept good records and, for the most part, the records are complete and accurate. Unfortunately, the records for the South are mostly guesswork. Many Confederate records either were destroyed in the final days of the war or were lost. There are many arguments and controversies involving the casualty figures for the South, as various historians and researchers have come up with different numbers. Exact accountings of the totals were difficult at the time and are all but impossible today. When mentioning casualties, it should be remembered that they not only represent those killed, but also the wounded, the injured, and the missing in action.

What crossed these soldiers' minds as they stepped out to face the enemy is a question often asked but never answered. Men lined up shoulder to shoulder as they went forward into the onslaught of bullets and shells. At times, men fought from behind breastworks or in trenches while shells flew overhead or shots sped in their direction. No matter where men fought, shells and bullets found their mark, creating huge gaps in the lines. Up to this time, armies fought in what has often been referred to as the Napoleonic style. Men formed two ranks, one right behind the other, as they went forth to confront the enemy. At the command all would load their weapons, and when the order was given to fire, all would fire at the same time, creating a volley. Then came the order to reload. There were several variations to this procedure depending on the circumstances and the commander.

When a man fell, the ranks closed up, filling his space as they moved forward to continue the fight. The wounded were left to fend for themselves. Some soldiers were detailed to assist the wounded from the field, but in the heat of battle it was often difficult to find all the wounded, especially if the fighting was still going on. If possible, the wounded were taken to a medical facility or regimental hospital set up behind the fighting, where his wound might be addressed. From there, the wounded were sent by wagon to a field hospital. The poor wounded soldier, if he was fortunate enough to make it this far, might have to wait hours or even days before receiving medical attention, depending on how busy the surgeons were with others.

Field hospitals were established behind the lines and ambulances transported those they could. From there the wounded were transported further from the field to division or corps hospitals and then on to general hospitals miles from the fighting. Sometimes, though, an army had to leave the area quickly and the wounded were left behind to be cared for by others. Sometimes the wounded were left in the fields and were not discovered until days later in a weak and dehydrated condition. Some soldiers were so badly wounded they could not move or call out for help and, as they lay dying on the field, vultures circled above. Ghost stories from many battlefields tell of vultures not waiting for the soldier to die before starting their grisly deeds.

Conditions on the field also contributed to the death of the soldier. In the Battle of the Wilderness, the fighting took place in heavy, thick, dry underbrush that caught fire from the sparks of the guns which had been fired fast and so furiously. Many of the wounded could not escape the flames and were burned to death. This happened on many fields, not just during the Battle of the Wilderness.

Both Union and Confederate soldiers died of drowning during the Battle of the Crater as water filled the low-lying areas. Some soldiers fell as they crossed Antietam Creek and, though their wounds might have been minor, they died, drowning in several inches of water. Many soldiers who made Burnside's infamous "mud-march" also died from drowning. During the war, 4,944 Union soldiers died from water deaths. Records are unavailable as to the exact number of Confederates who perished this way.

It is estimated the total casualty figure for both the North and the South was 1,094,453 (623,026 deaths, 471,427 wounded). The wounded figures are questionable because the definition of wounded varied as much as the men who recorded the figures. What was considered wounded? If a soldier went to the hospital from the field, was he considered wounded? What about the soldier who was shot and, instead of going to the hospital for treatment, went back to camp to recover? Was he considered wounded? Many men were wounded more than once and some were hit a second or a third time in the same battle. In this case, was the soldier considered being wounded, once, twice or three times? During the Battle of Gettysburg, there were soldiers who suffered minor wounds on the first day, rested on the second day's fight, and were wounded again on the third.

A wound might be bandaged and the soldier sent to fight again the following day. We do not know whether these men and every incident mentioned of a soldier being wounded were recorded.

Although many officers and cavalrymen carried sabers, fewer than a thousand deaths were attributed to this weapon. During the Battle of Brandy Station on June 9, 1863, fierce fighting on horseback occurred as two thundering armies advanced on one another. Men fought with sabers drawn, slashing as they rode. Some pulled their revolvers, while others who had been toppled from their mounts used tree limbs to knock down their opponents. Sabers rose and fell, horses wheeled as men fought hand to hand. Units became intermingled as dust and smoke filled the battlefield and the fight lasted for hours. Even though sabers were raised, the majority of the men who died that day died of bullet wounds. In *Regimental Losses*, Fox reported, "The number of wounded treated at the hospitals during the war was 246,712, which, according to the Surgeon-General's estimate, embraced nine-tenths of all the wounded. Of these hospital cases, only 922 were wounded by sabers or bayonets, and a large proportion of these originated in private quarrels, or were inflicted by camp-guards in the discharge of their duty."[2]

The war was indeed harsh, especially for the enlisted ranks. The officer ranks also suffered, and because they were in command, their loss was felt more. While it is the duty of the soldier to fight, it is the duty of the commander to lead, and some led by staying in front of their men. It was expected for company and regimental commanders to lead and direct from the front, where they could encourage or inspire their men. Brigade and division commanders often were in the front lines for the same reason, although they did not have to be there. Many commanders led from the rear and did a fine job from that position.

One of these was General Robert E. Lee. During the Battle of the Wilderness, Lee, charged with adrenaline from the fight, rode to the front lines to direct the action in person. When members of the Texas Brigade spotted him, one grabbed the reins of the general's horse and begged him to go to the rear. Upon his refusal, the men told Lee they would not fight until he did and soon a chant went up among members of the brigade, "Lee to the rear." He acknowledged his men, turned his horse about and went to the rear. After he was out of sight, the men went forward into the fray.

Both North and South experienced a great loss in leadership with the deaths or injuries of many of its senior commanders. The Union army had 583 men in its officer corps and lost forty-seven of them in combat, eighteen from disease or accident, and one from murder. General Jefferson C. Davis (no relationship to the president of the Confederacy) shot and killed General William Nelson on September 29, 1862. It was said that Davis provoked an argument with Nelson in the lobby of the Galt House in Louisville, Kentucky. When Nelson slapped him across the face, Davis shot him. No legal action was taken against Davis, even though witnesses at the time stated it was cold-blooded murder.

Some of the Union's brightest stars died in battle. Major General James B. McPherson, commander of the Army of Tennessee, died when in the heat of battle he mistakenly rode into a Confederate camp on July 22, 1864, and was shot down. Major General John F. Reynolds died during the opening hours of the Battle of Gettysburg, when a Confederate sharpshooter shot him in the head shortly after his arrival on the battlefield to take charge. During the Battle of Spotsylvania, Major General John Sedgwick fell just after being told by another to get to a place of safety as the Confederates were shooting everywhere. It was reported that no sooner had he stated that the Confederates could not hit the side of a barn than he was shot and instantly killed.

Of the 425 officers serving the Confederacy, seventy-seven of them were either killed or mortally wounded while another fifteen died from accidents or illness. One died in a duel. At dawn on September 6, 1863, General John S. Marmaduke and General Lucius M. Walker met in an open field near Little Rock, Arkansas, to "have pistols at ten paces to fire and advance." General Walker fell mortally wounded, dying the following day. On May 7, 1863, Doctor George B. Peters walked into General Earl Van Dorn's headquarters at Spring Hill, Tennessee, and shot the general in the head. He suspected Van Dorn was having an affair with his wife.

According to many, the South lost its brightest star when Lieutenant General Thomas Jonathan "Stonewall" Jackson was mortally during the Battle of Chancellsorsville, shot by friendly fire. After his arm was amputated, Jackson developed pneumonia and died ten days later. President Jefferson Davis had great hopes for the war effort in the guise of Major General Albert Sidney Johnston, for he thought Johnston a capable and experienced commander. Johnston was killed during the Battle of Shiloh/Pittsburg Landing. The flamboyant cavalry commander James Ewell Brown Stuart died during the Battle for Yellow Tavern in 1864. Six Confederate generals were killed in one day during the Battle of Franklin: Patrick Cleburne, States Right Gist, Hiram Granbury, John Adams, Otho Strahl, and John C. Carter.

The tragic loss of life was experienced on both sides, yet, surprisingly, the chance of surviving the war was good. Statisticians have calculated that in the Union army, one in every sixty-five men would be killed outright in battle, while one out of fifty-six would later die of their wounds. One in ten would be wounded in action, while one in every fifteen would either be listed as missing or reported captured by the enemy. Of those who were captured, one in ten would die as a prisoner of war. Close to one in thirteen would die of some type of disease. Of those who were wounded and returned to fight again, one in six would suffer another wound.

When talking about losses in a battle or a skirmish, it is important to know how many men were actually involved in the fight to get a better perspective of the loss. Some regiments fought with a full contingent of men and were considered at full strength. A loss of fifty was considered negligible when compared to a regiment who entered a fight with fewer than a hundred men. Then the loss of fifty would be considered significant.

During the Battle of Gettysburg, which was a battle fought over a three-day period, Fox's *Regimental Losses* revealed that the 26th North Carolina suffered the greatest regimental loss in a single battle. It went into battle with 800 men and suffered a total loss of 687 (172 killed, 443 wounded and 72 unaccounted) for an 85 percent loss. The majority of the casualties occurred on the first day as the regiment tangled with the 151st Pennsylvania. That evening, there were fewer than 200 men fit for duty. The 26th North Carolina also played a part in the Pickett-Pettigrew charge and could only muster 80 men the following morning. In the same battle, on the second day's fighting, the 1st Minnesota suffered almost the same loss (85 percent) when it sustained a total loss of 224 (50 killed, 174 wounded) out of 262 men available for duty, or as they were often referred to, "effectives." The 1st Minnesota lost seventeen of its officers, including the colonel, the lieutenant colonel, its major and the adjutant.

During the infamous Pickett-Pettigrew charge made on the afternoon of July 3, 1863, Scales' Brigade stepped out with approximately 800 men. These men marched shoulder to shoulder, across a mile long open field, toward the center of the Union line and into the face of cannons firing double and sometimes triple canister. By the end of the day, 708 of them were dead, wounded or missing. In one company of 84 men, everyone, including the officers, had been injured. In another company, after the charge, the highest-ranking person left standing was a corporal. Sixteen of General Pickett's seventeen regimental and field officers were lost while the one surviving officer was severely wounded.

During the four years of fighting, the 5th New Hampshire Infantry lost more men than any Union regiment, according to Fox's *Regimental Losses.* It lost 295 (18 officers, 277 men) killed or mortally wounded in action. This regiment was in the thickest of the fights, those which "occurred entirely in aggressive, hard, stand-up fighting; none of it happened in routs or through blunders."[3] The 83rd Pennsylvania came in second with the highest killed in action over the course of the war, losing 282 (11 officers and 271men).

Did the casualties include those who died of accidents or those who came down with illness and disease while serving in the war? Disease claimed more lives in this war than bullets ever did on the battlefield. Many men answering their nation's call had never been more that twenty miles from the place of their birth and were now exposed to camp life for the first time, where they were required to share space with thousands of men all jammed together. Sanitation was poor, to say the least. Latrines, commonly called "sinks," were often open pits, usually located a short distance from camp. At times, the same water that flowed through the latrines or the open pits also flowed into the rivers and creeks, from which water was pulled for drinking and cooking. There were times when the weather was so bad that the men did not go to the latrines but rather used the nearest shrub or tree to conduct their business. There were some also who were not used to conducting their private business in public, while others were just plain lazy.

It was known at the time that poor sanitary conditions could lead to illness, but enforcement of the rules and regulations in some camps was almost impossible. In the beginning of the war, many officers were elected to positions of command by the same men they were to supervise. Strict enforcement of camp cleanliness was not high on the agenda or priorities of these officers. As the war progressed, military men were appointed as commanders, replacing those who were incompetent. Strict and sometimes harsh discipline was employed, not only for drill, but also for camp cleanliness. Inspection officers were employed to inspect the camps each day to ensure cleanliness. The commander of the camp would and could be "gigged" or disciplined for maintaining a dirty camp.

In the inspection report forwarded to General John B. Hood by R.H. Chilton on November 14, 1862, Chilton reported the following on one of the regiments: "The First Texas, Lieutenant-Colonel (P. A.) Work: Arms mixed and in very bad order; two-thirds badly clad and shod, 60 barefooted; camp in bad order, and the regiment showing inexcusable neglect on the part of its officers."[4] It is not recorded anywhere what action General Hood took, but the inspection reports the following year revealed the camp to be in better order.

With the cramped and crowded conditions, colds and infectious diseases quickly engulfed a camp. Men marched in all types of weather, under the hot sun, in the pouring rain and foot deep snow. They went without sleep, and often their resistance to disease was low. Records indicate 19,971 Union soldiers died of pneumonia, while 44,558 died from diarrhea and dysentery. Another 40,656 men died of typhoid, typhus and various other fevers. Smallpox, measles, and consumption, all highly contagious diseases, claimed many more lives. In addition to those who died from these diseases, 20,995 Union soldiers were discharged from the service due to the lingering effects of disease.

Figures for the Confederacy are non-existent. No one really knows how many hospitals existed in the South during the war. In situations where a skirmish or a battle took place, homes and churches were converted into makeshift hospitals. When soldiers were in camp or in winter quarters, homes, churches and businesses in the vicinity were converted into hospitals. Many of the southern hospitals kept records as to the ailments and treatment of the soldiers entering their doors. Of those that did maintain good records, many were either burnt or destroyed during or immediately following the war's end. After the war, if the building was still intact, the records were boxed up, and some sent off to Richmond for safekeeping. Others have disappeared. Some may remain in cellars or in attics and are yet to be discovered. If the Confederate figures for the killed and wounded in battle are in question today, so must be the figures for those who died of disease. However, many historians have estimated that for every soldier killed in battle, three to five men died from disease.

Desertion must also be considered when discussing casualties. In every war desertion happens and this war was no different. Many who deserted did so not so much out of fear of battle or death, but out of homesickness and loneliness. Having seen so much death and destruction on the battlefield and being a witness to man's inhumanity to man, some soldiers did not want to see anymore. Some of the men were receiving letters from loved ones begging them to come home and take care of the family, or informing them of the death of a child, a mother or a wife. Some wives wrote saying they could not handle things and needed their husbands and fathers at home. Some complained of being cheated or bullied by the Home Guard or a neighbor. Other letters told of being threatened with the loss of home and hearth. Some women did not know where their next meal was coming from and needed their husbands' guidance.

Some deserters were opportunists. They would enlist under one name only to desert and then re-enlist in another regiment under a different name. This was profitable, especially when a bounty or a reward was offered for enlisting. However, most deserters were men who simply wanted to go home and made the attempt. A few deserters were caught and were tried and punished for leaving their comrades in arms, which was considered a most heinous crime. Punishments ranged from imprisonment at hard labor to death. Many of the executions were carried out in front of the offender's division with hopes it would thwart others from the same offensive behavior. It did not.

In Fox's *Regimental Losses*, the Union recorded 268,530 desertions. This number was later reduced to 201,397 as stragglers returned to camp. Approximately 75,000 soldiers were arrested and punished in some form or another for desertion, or being absent without leave. The Union army executed 267 men for various offenses; of these, 147 were for actual desertion. Records are unavailable at this time for the Confederacy.

Many, when the war was over, could not put it behind them. They were casualties just as much as those who were left on the field. The idea of treating a soldier for the effects of trauma or mental fatigue was never considered. There was no R and R. It was difficult to get a break from the carnage and destruction witnessed by the soldiers. There was no time to grieve for a friend or comrade lost in battle. The soldier was expected to carry on, doing his duty. When the war was over, he was expected to return home, pick up the pieces where he left off and get on with his life. His wife and children were expected to do the same. Many could not. Some men continued to crave the excitement or the adrenaline that charged through their veins. They were always looking for a new adventure, a new thrill. Some of these men turned to crime. Others held it all inside and never discussed their experiences, while still others became involved in fraternal orders making pilgrimages to Civil War battles or reunions. Some of those who withdrew into themselves later committed suicide.

The Civil War took a terrible toll on all Americans, both North and South. For years afterwards, the hostility generated by those long four years of fighting and arguing continued, especially during the reconstruction era, a story in itself. Today, over one hundred and forty years later, this war has become the most researched and the most studied of any war fought in the last five hundred years. Many people spend their vacations touring Civil War battlefields. Some are seeking information on their ancestors who may have served during the war, while others are trying to study the various battles. The popularity of Civil War reenactments continues to increase. With the popularity of the Civil War increasing, one thing should never be forgotten — the men who marched across open fields into the face of guns and cannons and died for their beliefs. Despite their hardships and their losses, they continued to do their duty and it must be remembered that no matter what side they fought on, they were Americans. They were Americans before the war and Americans after the war. They lived, breathed, and were real. Some say we should recognize their sacrifices, but in reality, we should recognize them and cherish their memories.

UNION AND CONFEDERATE CASUALTY FIGURES

Category	Union	Confederacy
Total battle deaths	68,892	54,000
Total mortally wounded	43,012	40,000
Died from disease	227,580	164,000
Died while prisoners of war	30,192	26,000
Died as result of accidents	4,114	unavailable
Drowned	4,944	unavailable
Murdered	520	unavailable
Killed after capture	104	unavailable
Committed suicide	391	unavailable
Executed by Federal authority		
Desertion	147	unavailable
Murder	67	unavailable
Mutiny	19	unavailable
Rape	23	unavailable
Miscellaneous	11	unavailable
Executed by the enemy	64	unavailable
Died of sunstroke	313	unavailable
Other	2,043	unavailable
Causes not stated	12,121	unavailable
Total deaths from all causes	360,222	284,000
Wounded	277,401	226,000
Total casualties	637,623	510,000

Appendix I. Glossary

Abatis A defensive obstacle formed by felled trees. A sharpened end, made of branches, pointed toward the enemy.

Action Widely used term for an engagement between enemy forces, often used interchangeably for the word "battle."

Adjutant A staff officer assisting the commanding officer, usually with his correspondence.

Affair An engagement of minor size.

Aft The back of a ship. (See also stern.)

Aide-de-camp A confidential officer, appointed by general officers to their staffs. An aide-de-camp reported directly to his commander and took orders only from him. He was able to modify orders on the battlefield if the commanding general was not available to issue the new orders. In wartime, a lieutenant general was permitted to appoint four aides, a major general could have two and a brigadier general usually had only one.

Artillery Called cannons, guns or howitzers. Field artillery was usually taken to the battlefield with the infantry forces during a battle. A gun was a long barreled weapon designed to throw a solid shot with a heavy charge of powder at long range using a low angle of elevation. A howitzer had a shorter barrel and fired shells or other type of ammunition with lower charges than guns and at higher elevation. They were lighter than guns of the same caliber and had less range.

Assault An all-out attack.

Battalion A unit composed of two or more, but fewer than ten, companies. During the latter stages of the war, a battalion consisted of three to six companies. Battalions sometimes were increased to regimental strength and re- designated; in other cases, regiments were consolidated down to battalion size and re-designated. The battalion was usually commanded by a lieutenant-colonel or major.

Battery The basic unit of artillery, consisting of 4 to 6 guns in either two or three sections, with each section comprising two artillery pieces. Usually commanded by a captain, and each section by a lieutenant. For each artillery piece in the battery, 15 to 25 men were required for support and to service the piece during battle. Teams of horses were also required to pull both the artillery piece and ammunition caissons. Usual strength of a battery was one captain, four lieutenants, two staff sergeants, six sergeants, twelve corporals, six artificers, two buglers, fifty-two drivers and seventy cannoneers. Standard supply of ammunition varied from 1,218 to 1,344 rounds.

Battery Positions In battle, a lieutenant commanded the section of two guns, each gun under a sergeant known as the chief of the caisson. Besides the gunner (usually a corporal), who sighted the gun, seven men serviced a piece and each was designated with a number.

No. 1—at the right of the muzzle, sponged and rammed;

No. 2—at the left, inserted either fixed ammunition or powder bag and projectile;

No. 3—at right of the breech, kept his left thumb (in a leather thumbstall) over the vent during sponging and loading, and pricked the cartridge through the vent;

No. 4—at the left of the breech, inserted friction primer in the vent, hooked his lanyard to it, and jerked the lanyard on command to fire;

No. 5—carried ammunition from the limber located five yards behind the gun, to No. 2;

No. 6—at the limber, cut fuses when necessary, and issued ammunition to No. 7;

No. 7—collected the ammunition from No. 6 and carried it to No. 5.

Battle A wide scale encounter between major elements of independent commands usually directed by general officers.

Battle Flag *see* **Regimental Flag**

Bayonet Detachable blade mounted to the end of a musket or rifle musket and used in close-order combat. Bayonets rarely inflicted wounds during the Civil War because the longer range of the musket generally prevented enemy infantry from getting close enough for an effective bayonet charge. A sword bayonet was usually used with rifles, an angular bayonet with muskets.

Beam The breadth of a ship at its widest point.

Bivouac A temporary encampment, or to camp out or sleep in the open for the night. Defined by the U.S. Army as, "When an army passes the night without shelter, except such as can be hastily made of plants, branches, it is said to bivouac."

Blockade The isolation of a nation, an area, a city, or a harbor by ships or forces to prevent supplies and manpower from entering or exiting the port. Over the course of the war, the northern blockade of southern ports proved to be effective. (On land, a blockade was usually referred to as a siege.)

Blockade-runner A ship or vessel carrying needed supplies that attempted to run or avoid the blockade of a ports. These ships were usually manned by civilians or mercenaries.

Bow Front end of ship, usually pointed or streamlined.

Breastwork A temporary fortification, usually of earth, stone or whatever was available, and about chest high, over which a soldier could fire at the enemy.

Breech The "closed" end of a cannon.

Breechloader A gun loaded from the rear by opening the breech and placing the projectile and charge directly in the firing chamber. Few Civil War cannons were of this type.

Brevet An honorary title given for exceptional bravery or merit in time of war. It carries none of the authority or pay of the real rank. Many officers held brevet commissions higher than their ordinary rank, which was usually granted for gallant action or meritorious service or combat. It allowed the man to serve in a staff position. The rank also allowed volunteers to be eligible for promotion. The brevet ranking position has not been used since World War I.

Brigade Composed of two or more regiments (generally three to seven). A brigadier general usually commanded a Confederate brigade, while a colonel usually commanded a Union brigade.

Broadside The firing of guns simultaneously from one side of a ship.

Caisson A four-wheel cart with two or three large chests for carrying artillery ammunition and a spare wheel. It was connected to a horse-drawn limber when moved.

Camp The name applied to places where an army came to rest. When the army was at rest, cavalry was often posted nearby while pickets were posted and skirmishers sent forth for protection.

Campaign A series of military operations undertaken to accomplish a purpose or objective.

Canister (Also called case shot) A tin can containing lead or iron balls that scatter when fired from a cannon. Consisted of a canister (cylindrical container) filled with small iron or lead balls (in an emergency, just about any kind of scrap metal available). The artillery piece then became a giant shotgun, spraying death over a wide swath. Although both rifled guns and smoothbores could fire canister, the rifling made it somewhat less effective. It was fired at close range against advancing enemy infantry or cavalry (usually within 300 yards). When the enemy approached to a very close range, the canister would sometimes be doubled or tripled for an even deadlier effect. Charging enemy troops were usually badly hurt and, in some cases, virtually annihilated.

Cascabel The large, round knob at the base of a cannon breech.

Case Shot *see* **Canister** and **Shrapnel**

Cavalry Units that utilized horses or mules as a primary means of transportation, whether the units actually fought mounted or dismounted. When cavalry units fought dismounted, one man in four, or sometimes one man in five, had to act as horse holders, proportionally reducing the effective strength of the unit. Sometimes cavalry units were without horses for long periods and were pressed into service as infantry, although still carrying the cavalry designation in their unit names.

Change Front To alter the direction troops faced to deliver or defend against attack.

Colors *see* **Regimental Flag**

Commissary A store in which supplies are drawn.

Commutation A legalized form of evading the draft during the war. The commutation fee, normally about $500, allowed one to avoid the draft or military service. Military records indicated 86,724 draftees bought their way out of military service. This figure does not include substitutes, men paid for serving for another.

Company At the beginning of the war, the company was usually made up of eighty to one hundred privates, four corporals, four sergeants, three lieutenants and one captain. It may have also contained a few musicians. Each company was subdivided into four squads commanded by a sergeant or corporal and each company in a regiment was required to have an official letter designation for purpose of record. The letter "J" was not used, as when sounded in the field, it sounded like "A" and could be misinterpreted. The company was generally recruited within a limited geographic area. Neat the end of the war, these figures changed and some companies were down to under thirty officers and men.

Conscription Similar to today's draft. Enacted first by the Confederacy in 1862 and the following year by the Union, men were called into service. Voluntary enlistment had fallen off and the need for manpower was great. Failure to report often resulted in arrest and detention. Conscripts in the South accounted for approximately a fourth to a half of troops in the last year of the war.

Corps Composed of two or more divisions. The informal term "wing" is sometimes used to denote the same organization. A lieutenant general usually commanded a Confederate corps, while in the Union army, a major general usually commanded a corps.

Cottonclad A ship whose deck was protected by bales of cotton instead of iron plating.

Deflection The horizontal (left-right) portion for aiming an artillery piece.

Demonstration A detached unit from the main force ordered to make a show of strength on a portion of the enemy's line not actually targeted for attack. Used to distract the enemy while the main attack was made elsewhere.

Division Comprised of two or more brigades. For the Confederates, it was commanded by a major general and for the Union, a brigadier general.

Double Ender A shallow-draft paddle boat that is tapered on both ends. The ship was able to change direction without having to make a turn.

Double Quick Pace at which the troops moved in battle. A double-quick pace was 165 steps per minute with the average step being thirty-three inches. In a normal march, the pace was 90 steps per minute with the average step being twenty-eight inches.

Draft (Naval) The amount of a ship's hull that was under water, usually measured in feet.

Dragoons Men who were trained to fight from the saddle, which was very effective in the frontier against the Indians. At the start of the war, the dragoons were brought east. The 1st Dragoon became the 1st U.S. Cavalry and the 2nd Dragoons was split to form the 4th and 5th U.S. Cavalry.

Dress by the Colors To arrange troops into lines according to placement of the unit's flag.

Earthworks Mounds of dirt piled high or trenches dug to afford soldiers some form of protection from incoming missiles or shots.

Effective(s) The actual number of men actively involved in or ready for combat.

Elevation The vertical component in aiming a cannon that was used for ranging purposes. Elevation was expressed in degrees above horizontal.

En Echelon A staggered or stair-step-like formation of parallel units of troops. A line or movement that involves a formation in which the brigade or division takes its cue from a preceding one, occupying a parallel line in advance on the one it holds. The first unit in line would deliver the attack initially, and then once the momentum of the attack had taken effect, the next unit up attacked, and so on. The idea was to continue the shock effect of successive attacks to prevent enemy forces from having time to reorganize their defensive dispositions. Such attacks were successive rather than simultaneous and often broke down if just one unit in the sequence failed to advance in the proper order.

Enfield Rifle Fired a .577 caliber projectile similar to the minie ball. It was accurate at 1,100 yards.

Enfilade Gunfire that rakes an enemy line lengthwise, or the position allowing such fire. To bring an enemy position under fire from the side or end instead of direct or obliquely from the front. The advantage of enfilading fire was twofold: shots that missed the initial target could hit men further down the line; and the enemy had difficulty returning the fire effectively without risk of hitting their own men.

Engagement Denotes a combat of limited scope, involving subordinate units or detachments of main armies.

Envelopment The object of this offensive, directed against a flank of a fixed position, was to pour an enfilading fire along the enemy's line. A double envelopment, usually a risky operation, involved an attack against both flanks simultaneously with the hope of surrounding the enemy.

Feint A means of distraction to ensure the commitment of enemy troops away from the point of the primary assault.

Field Officer Any officer who operated in the field rather than at a command post. They were usually officers at the regimental level in charge of multiple companies. Fields officers held the rank of colonel, lieutenant colonel, or major.

15–20 second shell An artillery projectile containing an explosive charge. Its fuse detonated the charge in the air near the enemy 15 to 20 seconds after the round was fired.

File Closer A soldier marching in the rear of a line of battle to make sure that the formation stayed in order.

Firing a Gun *see* **Battery Positions**

Flag Officer In the Navy, a rank above captain but below rear admiral.

Flagship A ship that carried the fleet or squadron commander and bore the commander's flag.

Flank The right or left end of a military formation. Usually applies to the end of a line of battle. The flanks were usually anchored on a natural obstacle such as a dense forest or river to prevent the enemy from "turning" the flank. Therefore, to flank is to attack or go around the enemy's position on one end or the other. A natural fear at all levels was being "flanked" by a large body of enemy troops.

Flanking March Movement of troops to get on the enemy's flank or rear.

Flanking Position To arrange battle lines so that one or more lines thrust forward at an angle from the main lines. These roughly perpendicular defensive lines brought fire to bear on the enemy's flank. Troops in this position were placed to bring down a crossfire on the enemy or charge forward and hit undefended sides of his assault or communications lines.

Forage Live off the land.

Forced March A long march of troops at a fast pace made necessary by an impending battle or emergency.

Friction Primer Device for igniting the gunpowder charges in a cannon.

Frigate The "eyes of the fleet." Usually served as a reconnaissance vehicle, protecting the other ships in the convoy and usually carrying anywhere from 28 to 44 guns. In battle, the frigate would usually stand away from the other ships in order to relay signals from the flagship to the other ships that could not see the flagship because of smoke from the guns.

Frontal Attack Troops charged the enemy directly and engaged one another with the bayonet. In the face of an entrenched enemy, troops wielding rifled firearms leveled tragic consequences with frontal attacks.

Furlough A leave of absence granted to an enlisted man. The soldier's company or regimental commander granted furloughs. Officers were granted leaves. When granted a furlough, the soldier left his equipment, including arms, in camp and carried papers that outlined the dates of his furlough, the unit to which he was assigned and the date he was to return to duty. In many cases, the papers carried a description of the soldier.

General Officer An officer with the rank above colonel. Usually in command of multiple regiments. Rank included general, lieutenant general, major general or brigadier general.

Grapeshot Iron balls (usually 9) bound together and fired from a cannon. It resembled a cluster of grapes; the balls broke apart and scattered upon impact. Had an effective range of 300 to 600 yards.

Handspike A wooden bar that attached to the rear of the gun trail, which allowed for easier maneuvering of the cannon.

Hardtack A durable cracker or biscuit made of plain flour and water. Normally about three inches square and a half to a quarter inch thick.

Haversack A white canvas shoulder bag, about a foot square, that was usually strapped over the right shoulder and rested on the left hip. Used for carrying personal items and rations. It had a waterproof lining and a flap that buckled over the top. In addition, the term applied to the large leather bag used by artillerymen to carry rounds to the guns in order to protect the gunpowder from errant sparks.

High Ground An elevated piece of ground or small hill where troops were placed to command a clear view of the field.

Hors de Combat Out of combat.

Howitzer A short, squat piece with a tapered breech interior; lobbed a heavy shell a short distance with a light charge. Fired shells or other types of ammunition with lower charges than guns and at higher elevations, lighter than guns of the same caliber and had less range. (This gun often exploded during firing.)

In the Air Not anchored to any natural feature. In essence, unprotected.

Independent Command High ranking commanders on their own charged with the

responsibility of not only developing the strategy but also formulating the plans to carry out the assignment.

Ironclad A warship with a wooden hull covered with iron for protection. Ironclads were generally plated with four inch or more sheets of iron that protected the ship from cannon fire. Some ships were covered with iron just above the main deck.

Knapsack Backpack, usually painted canvas, though some were made of rubber. Soldiers carried necessities in it, but soon discarded it as cumbersome. Soldiers instead preferred to carry all their belongings wrapped in a blanket slung over their shoulder.

Lanyard An artillerist's cord with a handle on one end and a clip connector for a friction primer on the other. The friction primer was inserted into the touchhole on an artillery piece and, when the gunner jerked the lanyard, friction in the touchhole ignited powder in the breech, firing the weapon.

Legion Must consist of elements of all three branches of the army (infantry, cavalry and artillery). For example, the typical legion might consist of eight companies of infantry, six companies of cavalry battalions and an attached six-gun artillery battery. Legions rarely served for long, for the combined units were later re-assigned, the infantry being combined with more infantry to make up a complete regiment. The cavalry battalion was usually assigned to other cavalry commands and the artillery was usually detached.

Lie in the Line of Battle Ships consisting of sixty guns or more were considered "fit to lie in the line of battle" or assume position to take or make an attack. These ships were often referred to as vessels of the line.

Limber A 2-wheel, horse-drawn vehicle in which a gun carriage or a caisson was attached. The term also applied to the act of attaching a canon to a limber for transport. Six horses were usually used to pull the limber.

Line of Battle A formation of a regiment(s) into a prescribed order of two ranks for engaging in combat. The line of battle could refer either to a single regiment "in line of battle," or to the whole army arrayed in such a manner.

Line Officers Field officers who were charged with the responsibility of carrying out the commanders' orders but seldom issued their own. Usually in command of companies of men and held the rank usually of captain or lieutenants.

Lunette (a.) A work consisting of a salient angle with two flanks open to the rear. (b.) A metal ring at the end of a gun trail. The lunette was dropped over the upright pivot pin of the limber, which enabled the gun to be connected to a limber or caisson.

Mess A group of soldiers who prepared and ate their meals together. The place where a meal was prepared and eaten.

Minie Ball The standard bullet-shaped projectile fired from either a Springfield musket or a .577 Enfield. Minie balls were wrapped in a paper cartridge containing powder, which had to be bitten off before being stuffed into the weapon. The ball was a conical bullet with a hollow base made of soft lead. The bullet's hollow base expanded, forcing the sides into the grooves of the musket's barrel. This caused the bullet to spiral in flight, giving it greater range and accuracy and the ability to cause a large, ragged wound. The Minie was approximately one inch long and differed in caliber. The North used a .58 caliber Minie, while the South used the 577.

Monitors A heavily ironclad warship with a low, flat deck and a shallow draft. May have had one or more gun turrets and usually operated on rivers. In addition, some monitors had fixed gun ports instead of turrets. During the Civil War, the hulls of the monitors were subject to swamping and their slow speed was a disadvantage.

Mortar A large caliber gun capable of sending or lobbing a heavy projectile or shell over a short distance using a small powder charge. Mortars were classified by the diameter of their bore, which ranged from 6 to 16 inches.

Mortar Boats Ships or barges, capable of carrying over 25,000 pounds, on which a large gun or mortar was mounted. This mobile gun platform was towed by steamship to its location, which was usually out of sight and out of range of the shore batteries. Once in position, the gun would open fire, sending up to a 220 pound bomb toward the enemy's position.

Musket A smoothbore shoulder type weapon. Typically, these used round lead balls of .69 caliber.

Muster To assemble. The process of taking roll and determining fitness for service. The muster roll also served for payroll purposes.

Muster In First muster of a regiment as it was accepted into the service and came under military rules and regulations.

Muster Out Last muster for a regiment before the soldiers were released from the army.

Muzzle The "opening" end of a cannon.

Muzzleloader A gun that loaded from the front by placing the charge followed by the projectile into the muzzle of the piece and ramming them back to the firing chamber at the rear of the gun.

Napoleon A smoothbore muzzleloading field artillery piece with a fairly accurate scope, usually made of bronze. It fired a 12-pound projectile (sometimes called a 12-pounder). The weapon was capable of firing more than one kind of shot and could be used according to the tactical situation. Comparatively light and portable, it could be used equally well as an offensive or defensive weapon. Had an effective range of 1,619 yards at a 5-degree elevation, and was deadly with canister at short range.

Oblique At an angle. Units would be ordered to fire or move in a direction other than straight ahead.

Operation A military campaign or mission to achieve an objective that usually involved various campaigns.

Order Arms The position for holding a shoulder arm in which the weapon had its butt resting on the ground, as it is held vertically along the soldier's right side.

Order of Battle A particular disposition of troops and other military resources in preparation for battle. Used by the military to describe the organization of military units beginning with the regiment units and working up to the army. Basic structure was the army, corps, division, brigade and regiment, and finally, company.

Orderly A soldier assigned to a superior officer for various duties, such as carrying messages.

Ordnance Gun *see* **Three-inch Ordnance**

Paddle Boat A steamboat driven by a paddle wheel usually located amidships, and some had a pair of wheels placed on either side of the hull. Their maneuverability was poor.

Parole Pledge of a soldier, released after being captured by the enemy, that he would not take up arms again until he had been properly exchanged for one of the captor's soldiers.

Parrott Gun Muzzleloading, rifled artillery piece. Parrott guns of various caliber were made of cast iron with a unique iron reinforcing band around the breech. The guns were accurate at longer range than smoothbore artillery pieces. A 20-pound Parrott had a maximum range of 3,500 yards. In the field, both the 10 and 20-pound Parrott were used, while the heavier 50 to 500 pound Parrotts were usually used as siege guns. The large siege gun, used mainly by the Confederate forces, was capable of hurling a 100-pound projectile four miles. Frequently this gun blew up when fired at long range over a long period of time without rest.

Picket An advance outpost or guard for a large force. Pickets were usually ordered to form a scattered line far in advance of the main army's encampment, but within supporting distance. A picket guard was made up of a lieutenant, two sergeants, four corporals and forty privates from each regiment. Picket duty constituted the most hazardous work of infantrymen in the field. Being the first to feel the enemy, they were also liable to be the first killed, wounded or captured, and most likely the target of snipers. Picket duty, by regulation, was rotated regularly in a regiment.

Picket Line Outer perimeter of a camp patrolled by pickets or sentries.

Pincer Movement To attack from opposite directions, effectively squeezing the enemy between the two.

Pook Turtles Designed by Samuel M. Pook, these ships were round-nosed, flat-bottomed boats, 175 feet long and 51.5 feet wide, and they drew only six feet of water. They were plated with 2.5-inch thick iron and had flat sides with front and rear casements sloping at a 35-degree angle. The ships each had 13 heavy guns and were propelled by a stern paddle completely covered by a rear casement. They were underpowered and very cumbersome, but were the backbone of the Union's river fleet. There were only seven built and all were named after cities on the western rivers: *Cairo, Carondelet, Cincinnati, Louisville, Mound City, Pittsburgh* and *St. Louis.*

Port Facing the front or the left side of a ship.

Prime To pour gunpowder into the touch hole or vent of a cannon or musket.

Privateer A ship that preyed upon the ships, both military and civilian, of its adversary. The Union regarded privateers as pirates and the usual sentence, upon conviction, was death.

Prolonge An 18-foot length of hemp rope 3.5 inch in diameter. It had an iron hook on one end, a metal eye in the center, and three chains and a toggle on the other end. The prolonge was wound between two hooks on a gun carriage trail and kept there to use in maneuvering an unlimbered gun.

Provost Guard A detail of soldiers acting as police under the supervision of an officer.

Prow The portion of the ship's bow or hull ahead of the water line.

Quaker Gun A log positioned to look like a cannon barrel.

Raid A swift and usually fast moving strike behind an enemy's lines to destroy, burn or wreck strategic targets or supplies. Cavalry units usually conducted the raids.

Rammer An artillerist's tool used to force the powder charge and projectile down the barrel of a gun and seat them firmly in the breech.

Ramrod A metal rod used to "ram" a musket or Minie ball down the muzzle to its proper location before firing the weapon.

Rams A ship equipped with a massive iron arm projecting from its prow or bow and usually placed below the water line to do the most damage. When the ship was rapidly propelled through the water, it could ram and cause a hole in the side of an enemy ship so it would take on water.

Ration A specified allotment of food for one person (or animal) per day. The amount varied by time and place.

Reconnaissance Small parties of either cavalry or infantry (or both) would venture out to examine the terrain, or to locate enemy positions, and to discover any indication of movement. A reconnaissance was usually conducted daily when near an opposing force.

Redan Earthworks or breastworks thrown up in front of a cannon in the form of an inverted "V" to protect the gun and its crew from enemy fire.

Redoubt Small field fortification often hastily constructed that was enclosed on all sides.

Refuse the Line Drawing back to the end of the battle line to prevent the line from being overlapped or flanked. Also, anchoring the end of the line on some physical feature to provide a relatively secure flank defense.

Regiment Composed of men mostly from the same area who were acquainted with each other in civilian life, the regiment became their home away from home. A regiment, at full strength, consisted of 10 companies, and was made up of 97 men with three officers. Heavy artillery and cavalry regiments were composed of twelve companies, all lettered in alphabetical order with the letter J omitted. A colonel commanded a regiment, assisted by a lieutenant-colonel and a major. State governments were responsible for recruiting, organizing, and often providing the rudimentary training.

Regimental Flag The flag carried at the front of the regiment in battle. It became a matter of regimental pride not to lose its "colors" to the enemy. In the same way, it was considered a great honor to capture the "colors" of an enemy unit.

Retrograde A backward movement or retreat.

Rout Withdraw in a panic or in disorder.

Saber A sword with a curved blade. Most sabers had a 3-branch brass guard and were carried in steel scabbards.

Sabot A wooden disk attached between the projectile and charge bag in fixed ammunition for smoothbores. In rifled muzzleloaders, a deformable attachment at the rear of a projectile. Upon firing, the sabot would expand and contact the grooves, causing the projectile to spin.

Salient An area of a defensive line or fortification that protruded beyond the main works. It extended closest to an enemy's position and usually invited an attack. Commanding officers erected a salient primarily to cover dominating ground beyond their entrenchments.

Section (of artillery) Part of an artillery battery consisting of two guns, the soldiers who manned them, and their supporting horses and equipment. Normally under the command of a lieutenant.

Sharpshooters Applied to several units; the best known was Berdan's Sharpshooters. Of the units that carried the sharpshooter designation, some were equipped with special rifles and others simply employed marksmen who had standard Springfield or Enfield rifle muskets. Sharpshooters typically targeted high ranking officers and artillery crew members or their horse teams. They were also used on the skirmish line.

Shell Type of ammunition; a hollow iron container filled with gunpowder and a fuse. It could be a percussion fuse type, designed to explode on striking the ground or designed to explode in the air.

Shrapnel An artillery projectile in the form of a hollow sphere filled with metal balls packed around an explosive charge. A fuse ignited the charge at a set distance from the gun, raining balls down on the enemy.

Siege Surrounding or blocking a position for a prolonged period of time in an attempt to gain possession or control of it. Usually this was accomplished by refusing supplies or manpower to re-supply or reinforce an area. (At sea, a siege was usually referred to as a blockade.)

Skedaddle Act of fleeing under fire.

Skirmish Denoted a clash of the smallest scope. In general, a skirmish was a limited combat involving troops other than those of the main body; when the latter participated, the fight was known as an engagement, affair, or battle, depending on the scale. More specifically, a skirmish denoted an encounter between opposing skirmish lines, composed of troops assigned to protect the head or flanks of an army in motion.

Skirmish Line While a regiment would deploy with the men shoulder to shoulder, the skirmish line was made up of an irregular line of men deployed in more open order (with many feet between each man) in front of the main battle line. These troops drew the enemy's fire, developed his position, and warned comrades of an imminent clash. The purpose of the skirmish line was to "feel-out" the dispositions of the enemy troops, screen their own formations from enemy skirmishers, and generally harass the enemy forces as they would attempt to deploy into battle formation.

Skirmisher A soldier sent out in advance of the main body of troops to scout out and probe the enemy's position.

Sloop-of-war A rigged single-mast warship, smaller than a frigate, carrying eight to twenty guns. Its speed and maneuverability was of great advantage.

Smoothbore A cannon without rifling. Smoothbores were less accurate at long ranges, but canister was better dispersed from a smoothbore. They could be loaded, fired and cared for with relative ease.

Solid Shot A solid artillery projectile, oblong for rifled pieces and spherical for smoothbore. This ammunition could be used effectively by smoothbore guns against both artillery and infantry or cavalry formations. The solid shot did not bury itself in the ground as a rifled gun shell would do, but bounced and skipped along the ground. It would cause injuries to many troops before coming to rest. This was especially true if the artillery could put itself in a position to enfilade the enemy formation.

Spar Torpedo An explosive device attached to a long pole extending from the bow of a ship.

It was detonated either by pulling on a rope which acted as a trigger or by contact with an enemy ship.

Spencer Rifle A seven shot lever action repeater. It was shorter than the old musket, and much lighter. The Spencer could be fired five to seven times as fast as the .58 caliber muzzleloading rifle. It used a metal, self-contained cartridge. Invented by Christopher Miner Spencer for use by the Union troops.

Sponge An artillerist's tool used to clear a cannon barrel of the grime, smoldering cloth, and other material between rounds.

Stack Arms To set aside weapons, usually three or more in a pyramid, interlocking at the end of the barrel with the butts on the ground.

Staff Officer A person on the command staff of a high-ranking officer, usually charged with the responsibility of making sure orders were conveyed to the line or field officers. Usually responsible for logistics and administrative duties rather than command responsibilities. Staff officers were adjutants, quartermasters, chaplains, etc.

Stand of Arms A soldier's rifle or musket and cartridge belt or his complete set of equipment: rifle or musket, bayonet, cartridge belt and box.

Stand of Colors A stand of colors was a single color or flag. A Union infantry regiment carried two silken flags, or two stands of colors. The first was the national banner, with the regiment's number or name embroidered in silver thread in the center stripe. The second, or regimental, color had a blue field with the arms of the U.S. embroidered in silk on the center. A typical Confederate infantry regiment possessed only one stand of colors.

Starboard Right side of ship.

Steamboats Boats used for transportation of cargo, supplies and troops. Capable of carrying approximately 500 tons of supplies. Because of the way they were built, they were able to pull alongside a riverbank almost anywhere, however, they were hampered by low tides. River streamers, no matter what their size, were referred to as boats and never called ships.

Stern Rear end of the ship.

Straggler A soldier who lagged or fell behind while on a march. They usually rejoined their companies after the army stopped to make camp.

Substitute One who served in place of another, especially after the implementation of the draft. Men would pay substitutes a certain amount of money to fill in for them so they could avoid military service.

Sutler A peddler with a permit to remain with troops in camp or in the field to sell food, drink, and other supplies to the soldiers.

Tattoo Drum or bugle call signaling the time to return to quarters in the evening.

Three-inch Ordnance Rifled gun with a range of about 1,830 yards at a 5-degree elevation. It had a lighter tube that made it ideal for cavalry's horse artillery.

Timberclad Wooden ships covered with layers of wood rather than iron plating.

Tinclad Wooden ships covered with iron plating less than an inch thick. They were usually stern-wheel or steamers with a shallow drafts, which allowed them to go almost anywhere, and were usually mounted with lightweight guns ranging from 12 to 30 pounders.

Torpedo An underwater explosive device launched from the surface of ships. Also called a mine. The mine floated in the water and would explode when struck by a passing ship or detonated by lookouts on the shore.

Torpedo Boat A cigar shaped 50-foot-long vessel, steam powered and designed to float with only its top and smoke stack above the water. It had on its bow a 10-foot-long spar mounted with percussion caps that would explode as the spar was rammed against the side of an enemy ship.

Traverse Trench or other defensive barrier that ran obliquely to the enemy's guns to protect against enfilading fire.

Turret A low, heavily armored structure, usually rotating horizontally, containing mounted guns and their gunners or crew.

Unlimber The act of unlatching a cannon from its limber preparatory to firing.

Vedette/Vidette Mounted sentry on picket or guard duty.

Vent A small tube from the top of the gun to the firing chamber, used in firing the cannon piece.

Volley The simultaneous firing of guns by an entire unit of soldiers.

Warship A ship outfitted and designed for combat.

Zouave Known for their colorful uniforms and bravery. First organized in Chicago in 1861 by Ephriam Ellsworth, a friend of President Lincoln. Ellsworth was the first officer to die in the war when he was shot in Alexandria on May 24, 1861, while trying to remove a Confederate flag from atop a hotel.

Appendix II. The Armies

Many of the armies were in existence for a short period of time. When the army was merged with another or disbanded, its commanders were reassigned to other supervisory duties. When a commander had to be away from his post for an extended period, whether ill, on furlough, or summoned to either Washington or Richmond, an interim commander was named to handle command of the army, the district or the department. The interim commander would relinquish this command when his superior returned to duty.

United States of America

Army of the Cumberland (Department of Kentucky was merged with the Cumberland)
Major General Don Carlos Buell
Major General William Rosecrans
Major General George H. Thomas

Army of the Frontier—Composed of the Departments of Missouri and Kansas, created in October 12, 1862, and went out of existence on June 5, 1863, when its forces were transferred to the Departments of Tennessee and Missouri.
Major General Francis J. Herron, October 12, 1862–December 7, 1862.
Major General James G. Blunt, December 7, 1862–June 5, 1863.

Army of Georgia—Created March 28, 1865, and was composed of the 14th and 20th Army Corps.
Major General Henry W. Slocum, March 28, 1865–June 1, 1865.

Army of the Gulf—Created February 23, 1862, comprising most of the units operating along the Gulf Coast, including the Department of the Gulf. On May 7, 1864, the Department of the Gulf was merged into the Military District of West Mississippi. The remaining forces retained a separate existence.
Major General Benjamin F. Butler, March 20, 1862–December 17, 1862.
Major General Nathaniel P. Banks, December 17, 1862–September 23, 1864.

Major General S.A. Hurlbut, September 23, 1864–January 1865.
Major General Gordon Granger, January 1865–June 1865.

Army of the James— Created from the Departments of Virginia and North Carolina in April 1864.
Major General Benjamin F. Butler, April 1864–August 27, 1864.
Major General Edward O. Ord, August 27, 1864–September 7, 1864.
Major General Benjamin F. Butler, September 7, 1864–December 14, 1864.
Major General Edward O. Ord, December 14, 1864–December 24, 1864.
Major General Benjamin F. Butler, December 24, 1864–January 8, 1865.
Major General Edward O. Ord, January 8, 1865–January 31, 1865.

Army of the Mississippi— Organized February 23, 1862, and disbanded October 26, 1862.
Major General John Pope, February 23, 1862–June 26, 1862.
Major General William S. Rosecrans, June 26, 1862–October 26, 1862.

Army of the Mountain— Created March 11, 1862, from the Departments of Western Virginia.
Later became the First Corps in the Army of Virginia in June 26, 1862.
Brigadier General William S. Rosecrans, March 11, 1862–March 29, 1862.
Major General John C. Fremont, March 29, 1862–June 26, 1862.

Army of the Ohio— The Department of the Ohio had been merged with the Department of the Mississippi on March 11, 1862, but was re-created August 19, 1862. It was to consist of the States of Ohio, Michigan, Indiana, Illinois, Wisconsin and areas of Kentucky east of the Tennessee River. Many of the troops in this were scattered and some had been combined into the Army of Kentucky. Shortly after March 25, 1863, the department was re-organized and became the 23rd Army Corps. This corps was the beginning of the Army of the Ohio. Soon the 9th Corps was added along with a cavalry division.
Major General H.G. Wright, August 25, 1862–March 25, 1863.
Major General Ambrose E. Burnside, March 25, 1863–December 11, 1863.
Major General J.G. Foster, December 11, 1863–February 9, 1864.
Major General John M. Schofield, February 9, 1864–November 17, 1864.
Major General George Stoneman, November 17, 1864–January 17, 1865.

Army of the Potomac— In July 1861, the Military District of the Potomac was formed consisting of the Department of Washington and the Department of Northeastern Virginia and placed under the command of Major General George B. McClellan. On August 15, 1861, the Army of the Potomac came into existence with fourteen brigades, and later artillery and cavalry were added. A cavalry division was formed in July 1862. Later this cavalry division would form the nucleus of a cavalry corps. The Army of the Potomac was disbanded on June 28, 1865.
Major General George B. McClellan, August 15, 1861–November 9, 1862.
Major General Ambrose E. Burnside, November 9, 1862–January 26, 1863.
Major General Joseph Hooker, January 26, 1863–June 28, 1863.
Major General George G. Meade, June 28, 1863–December 30, 1864.
Major General John G. Parke, December 30, 1864–January 11, 1865.
Major General George G. Meade, January 11, 1865–June 28, 1865.

Army of the Shenandoah— When Major General Philip Sheridan was named commander of the Cavalry Corps, he was placed in command of all Union forces in the Shenandoah on August 7, 1864. Sheridan was directed by General Grant to clear the Shenandoah Valley of Confederates. He created the Army of the Shenandoah in August 1864 by combining the Army of West Virginia with other elements.
Major General Philip H. Sheridan, August 7, 1864–April 22, 1865.
Major General T.A. Tolbert, April 22, 1865–July 12, 1865.

Army of the Southwest— Created December 25, 1861, from the Departments of Missouri. It was merged in the District of Eastern Arkansas and Department of Tennessee on December 13, 1862.

Major General Samuel R. Curtis, December 25, 1861–August 1862.

Major General Frederick Steele, August–December 13, 1862.

Army of Tennessee— Came into existence on October 16, 1862, when the Military District of Cairo was combined with the District of West Tennessee, Western Kentucky and the Department of Mississippi. The Military District of Cairo had been under the command of Brigadier General Ulysses S. Grant when it was combined with the District of West Tennessee on February 17, 1862. In October, this unit was joined by the Districts of Western Kentucky and Mississippi and renamed the Army of the Tennessee. Later, additional elements would be added to this army.

Major General Ulysses S. Grant, August 1, 1861–October 24, 1863.

Major General William T. Sherman, October 24, 1863–March 26, 1864.

Major General James B. McPherson, March 12, 1864–July 22, 1864 when he was killed during the battle of Atlanta.

Major General John A. Logan, July 22, 1864–July 27, 1864.

Major General O.O. Howard, July 27, 1864–May 19, 1865.

Major General John A. Logan, May 19, 1865–August 1, 1865.

Army of Virginia— Created June 26, 1862, and it would be comprised of the forces of the Mountain Department, commanded by General Fremont, the Department of the Rappahannock commanded by General McDowell, the Department of the Shenandoah commanded by General Banks and the Military District of Washington under the command of General Sturgis. This army was later merged into the Army of the Potomac on September 2, 1862.

Major General John Pope, June 26, 1862–September 2, 1862.

Army of West Virginia— The Department of West Virginia was created in June 1863, when West Virginia was admitted into the Union. In the campaign against General Early (June through October), was known as the Army of West Virginia.

Brigadier General B.F. Kelly, June 28, 1863–March 10, 1864.

Major General Franz Sigel, March 10, 1864–May 21, 1864.

Major General David Hunter, May 21, 1864–August 9, 1864.

Major General George Crook, August 9, 1864–February 22, 1865.

Brigadier General J.D. Stevenson, February 22, 1865–February 28, 1865.

Major General W.S. Hancock, February 28, 1865–March 1, 1865.

Major General S.S. Carroll, March 1, 1865–March 7, 1865.

Major General W.S. Hancock, March 7, 1865–March 20, 1865.

Major General George Crook, March 20, 1865–March 22, 1865.

Major General W.S. Hancock, March 22, 1865–June 27, 1865.

Military District of the James— Created April 19, 1865, to consist of the Department of Virginia and such areas of North Carolina as not occupied by the command of General William T. Sherman.

Major General Henry W. Halleck, April 19, 1865–June 27, 1865.

Military District of the Mississippi— Created October 18, 1863, and was to be composed of the Departments of Ohio, Department of Tennessee, Department of the Cumberland and Arkansas. The Department of Arkansas was transferred to the Military District of West Mississippi on May 7, 1864.

Major General Ulysses S. Grant, October 18, 1863–March 18, 1864.

Major General William T. Sherman, March 18, 1864–June 27, 1865.

Military District of the Potomac— Created July 25, 1861, when it was consolidated with the Department of Washington and the Department of Northeast Virginia. Became the Army of the Potomac on August 15, 1861.

 Major General George B. McClellan, July 25, 1861–August 15, 1861.

Military District of West Mississippi— Created May 7, 1864, and composed of elements of the Departments of Arkansas and the Department of the Gulf. Arkansas was later transferred to the Military District of Missouri on March 21, 1865. Disbanded May 1865.

 Major General E.R.S. Canby, May 11, 1864–May 1865.

Department of Annapolis— Created April 27, 1861. It was to include the counties for twenty miles each side of the railroad from Annapolis to Bladensburg. Later became the Department of Maryland on July 19, 1861, and merged into the Department of Pennsylvania on July 25, 1861.

 Brigadier General Benjamin F. Butler, April 27, 1861–May 15, 1861.

 Major General George Cadwallader, May 15, 1861–June 11, 1861.

 Major General N.P. Banks, June 11, 1861–July 19, 1861.

 Major General John A. Dix, July 19, 1861–July 25, 1861.

Department of Arkansas— Created January 6, 1864, to consist of Arkansas except for Fort Smith. Fort Smith and the Indian Territory were added on April 17, 1864. Merged into the Military District of West Mississippi on May 7, 1864.

 Major General Frederick Steele, January 6, 1864–December 22, 1864.

 Major General John J. Reynolds, December 22, 1864–August 1865.

Department of the Cumberland— Created August 15, 1861, and was composed of Kentucky and Tennessee. Was later merged into the Departments of Missouri and Ohio on November 9, 1861, but was later re-created on October 24, 1862, and this time was made up of Tennessee east of the Tennessee River and parts of Alabama and Georgia under Union control.

 Brigadier General Robert Anderson, September 24, 1861–October 8, 1861.

 Brigadier General William T. Sherman, October 8, 1861–November 9, 1861.

 Major General William S. Rosecrans, October 30, 1862–October 20, 1863.

 Major General George H. Thomas, October 20, 1863–June 27, 1865.

Department of Florida— In existence at the start of hostilities but was merged into the Department of the South on March 15, 1861.

Department of Kansas— Created November 9, 1861, and composed of the State of Kansas, the Indian Territory west of Arkansas and the territories of Nebraska, Colorado and the Dakotas. Merged into the Department of Mississippi on March 11, 1862. Was re-created on May 2, 1862, to be merged once more into the Department of Missouri on September 19, 1862. Re-created once again on January1, 1864, only to be once again merged into the Department of Missouri on January 3, 1865.

 Major General David Hunter, November 20, 1861–March 11, 1862.

 Brigadier General J.G. Blunt, May 5, 1862–September 19, 1862.

 Major General S.R. Curtis, January 16, 1864–January 1865.

Department of Kentucky— Created May 28, 1861, to consist of the area in Kentucky lying within one hundred miles of the Ohio River. Merged into the Department of the Cumberland on August 15, 1861.

 Colonel Robert Anderson, May 28, 1861–August 15, 1861.

Department of the Mississippi— Created March 15, 1862, from the Department of Missouri, Ohio and Kansas and merged into the Department of Missouri on September 19, 1862.

 Major General Henry W. Halleck, March 13, 1862–September 19, 1862.

Department of Missouri— Created November 9, 1861, and composed of the states of Missouri, Iowa, Minnesota, Wisconsin, Arkansas and portions of Kentucky west of the Cumberland River. Was merged into the Department of the Mississippi on March 11, 1862, but was re-created September 19, 1862, and this time was composed of Missouri, Arkansas, Kansas and bordering the Indian Territory, Colorado and Nebraska territories.

Major General H.W. Halleck, November 19, 1861–March 11, 1862.
Major General S.R. Curtis, September 24, 1862–May 24, 1863.
Major General John M. Schofield, May 24, 1863–January 30, 1864.
Major General William S. Rosecrans, January 30, 1864–December 9, 1864.
Major General G.M. Dodge, December 9, 1864–June 27, 1865.

Mountain Department— Created March 11, 1862, from the Department of Western Virginia and merged into the Army of Virginia on June 26, 1862.

Brigadier General William S. Rosecrans, March 14, 1862–March 29, 1862.
Major General John C. Fremont, March 29, 1862–June 26, 1862.

Department of North Carolina— Created January 7, 1862, and composed of the State of North Carolina. Merged into the Department of Virginia–North Carolina on July 15, 1863. Was re-created on January 31, 1865.

Brigadier General Ambrose E. Burnside, January 13, 1862–July 10, 1862.
Major General J.G. Foster, July 10, 1862–July 15, 1863.
Major General John M. Schofield, January 31, 1865–June 27, 1865.

Department of the Ohio— Created May 3, 1861, to be composed of the areas of Ohio, Indiana, Illinois and portions of West Virginia and Pennsylvania lying north of the Great Kanawha, north and west of the Greenbriar. The state of Missouri was added to this department on June 6, 1861. Illinois was transferred to the Department of the West on July 3, 1861. The boundaries of the department were changed on September 19, 1861, to encompass Ohio, Indiana and fifteen miles south of Cincinnati into Kentucky. Michigan was added on November 9, 1861. Merged into the Mountain District and the Department of Mississippi on March 11, 1862.

Major General George B. McClellan, May 13, 1861–July 23, 1861.
Brigadier General William S. Rosecrans, July 23, 1861–September 21, 1861.
Brigadier General O.M. Mitchell, September 21, 1861–November 15, 1861.
Brigadier General Don Carlos Buell, November 15, 1861–March 11, 1862.

Department of Pennsylvania— Created April 27, 1861, and composed of Pennsylvania, Delaware and all of Maryland except Annapolis and Washington. Merged into the Department of the Potomac on August 24, 1861. Re-created December 1, 1864.

Major General Robert Patterson, April 29, 1861–July 25, 1861.
Major General John A. Dix, July 25, 1861–August 24, 1861.
Major General George Cadwallader, December 1, 1864–June 27, 1865.

Department of the Potomac— Became the Army of the Potomac on August 15, 1861. (See Army of the Potomac)

Department of the Rappahannock— Created April 4, 1862, to be made up of an area of Virginia east of the Blue Ridge and west of the Potomac. Included the areas of Fredericksburg and Richmond and a portion of Washington, D.C., and the country between the Potomac and the Patuxant River. On June 26, 1862, was merged into the Army of Virginia.

Brigadier General Irvin McDowell, April 4–June 26, 1862.

Department of the Shenandoah— Created July 19, 1861, to consist of the Valley of Virginia, counties of Washington and Allegany in Maryland, and areas in Virginia under Union control.

Was merged into the Department of the Potomac on August 17, 1861, and eventually merged into the Army of the Potomac on June 26, 1862.

    Major General Nathaniel P. Banks, July 25, 1861–August 17, 1861.

Department of the Susquehanna— Created June 9, 1863, to be composed of the portion of Pennsylvania east of Johnstown and the Laurel Hill Mountains. Became the Department of Pennsylvania on December 1, 1864.

    Major General D.N. Couch, June 11, 1863–December 1, 1864.

Department of Virginia— Created May 22, 1861, and later merged into the Department of Virginia–North Carolina on July 15, 1863. Recreated January 31, 1865, and known as the Army of the James.

    Major General Benjamin F. Butler, May 22, 1861–August 17, 1861.

    Major General John W. Wool, August 17, 1861–June 17, 1862.

    Major General John A. Dix, June 17, 1862–July 15, 1863.

    Major General E.O.C. Ord, January 31, 1865–May 1865.

    Major General A.H. Terry, May, 1865–June 27, 1865.

Department of Virginia–North Carolina— Created July 15, 1863, by the consolidation of Virginia and North Carolina. Became the Army of the James in April 1864.

    Major General J.G. Foster, July 18, 1863–November 11, 1863.

    Major General Benjamin F. Butler, November 11, 1863–April 1864.

Department of Washington— Created April 9, 1861, to consist of the District of Columbia to its original boundaries and Maryland as far as Bladensburg. Merged into the Military District of the Potomac on July 25, 1861. Recreated February 2, 1863.

    Lt. Colonel C.F. Smith, April 10, 1861–April 28, 1861.

    Colonel J.K.F. Mansfield, April 28, 1861–March 15, 1862.

    Major General S.P. Heintzelman, February 7, 1863–October 14, 1863.

    Major General C.C. Augur, October 14, 1863–June 27, 1865.

Confederate States of America

Army of the Kanawha— The Kanawha Valley is located in the western part of Virginia, a wild, remote area in which many of its residents wanted to remain in the Union. Two contingents of troops, one under General Wise and the other commanded by General Floyd, were ordered to operate in the valley as of June 6, 1861. They would be designated as the Army of the Kanawha. At first Wise was placed in command but a disagreement arose between him and Floyd. Both had been political appointees and both and been former governors of Virginia. On September 25, Wise was ordered to turn complete command over to Floyd and to report to Richmond for further assignment. Robert E. Lee was sent to see if stability could be brought but it was soon discovered the best alternative was to dissolve the army and transfer the men and the responsibility to other commands. In early 1862, some of the troops were sent, along with General Floyd, to the Central Army of Kentucky.

    Colonel Christopher Q. Tompkins, May 23, 1861–June 6, 1861.

    Major General Henry A. Wise, June 6, 1861–September 25, 1861.

    Major General John B. Floyd, September 25, 1861–December 1861.

Central Army of Kentucky— Originally a subsection of Department Number Two. Organized December 1, 1861, and merged into the Army of Mississippi on March 29, 1862.

    General Albert S. Johnston, October 28, 1861–December 4, 1861.

Major General William J. Hardee, December 4, 1861–February 23, 1862.
General Albert S. Johnston, February 23, 1862–March 29, 1862.

Army of Eastern Kentucky— Formed in November 1861 consisting of the militia of Wise, Scott and Lee counties, a small force of approximately fifteen hundred men. Ceased to exist after the Engagement of Middle Creek on January 10, 1862, when Brigadier General James A. Garfield drove Brigadier General Humphrey Marshall's forces from Kentucky.
Brigadier General Humphrey Marshall, November 1861–January 1862.

Army of Louisiana— When the war broke out, the Louisiana State Troops called themselves the Army of Louisiana. They were merged into the Military District of Louisiana on April 17, 1861.
Major General Braxton Bragg, (State Militia) February 22, 1861–March 7, 1861.
Colonel Paul O. Hebert, April 16, 1861–April 17, 1861.

Army of Middle Tennessee— Was a subsection of Department Number Two before the army was created October 28, 1862. On November 20, 1862, it was merged with the First Corps of the Army of Tennessee.
Major General John C. Beckinridge, October 28, 1862–November 20, 1862.

Army of Mississippi— Organized March 6, 1862, from a subsection of Department Number Two and with portions of the Central Army of Kentucky. On November 20, 1862, was reorganized into the Army of Tennessee.
General P.G.T. Beauregard, March 5, 1862–March 29, 1862.
General Albert S. Johnston, March 29, 1862–April 6, 1862.
General P.G.T. Beauregard, April 6, 1862–May 7, 1862.
General Braxton Bragg, May 7, 1862–July 5, 1862.
Major General William J. Hardee, July 5, 1862–August 15, 1862.
General Braxton Bragg, August 15, 1862–September 28, 1862.
Major General Leonidas Polk, September 28, 1862–November 7, 1862.
General Braxton Bragg, November 7, 1862–November 20, 1862.

Army of the Department of Mississippi and East Louisiana (AKA Army of Mississippi and Department of Mississippi and East Louisiana, not used after January 2, 1863)— Organized December 7, 1862. Title changed to the Department of Mississippi and East Louisiana.
Lieutenant General John C. Pemberton, December 7, 1862–January 2, 1863.
Lieutenant General William J. Hardee, July 24, 1863–October 1863.

Army of Missouri— In August 1864, Major General Sterling Price was ordered to form an independent command and to go on a recruiting drive in Missouri. It was hoped he could add an additional twenty thousand men to the Confederate armies. This force was also known as Price's Expeditionary Corps of the Army in the Field. In November 1864, Price, with his small army, was driven from the state, retreating into Arkansas. His men were transferred to the Army of the Trans-Mississippi.
Major General Sterling Price, August–November 1864.

Army of Mobile— Created January 27, 1862. On June 29, 1862, it was merged with Department Number Two.
Brigadier General Jones M. Withers, January 27, 1862–February 5, 1862.
Major General Braxton Bragg, February 5, 1862–February 28, 1862.
Colonel John B. Villepigue, February 28, 1862–March 14, 1862.
Major General Samuel Jones, March 14, 1862–March 25, 1862.
Colonel William L. Powell, March 25, 1862–April 2, 1862.

Major General Samuel Jones, April 2, 1862–April 28, 1862.

Major General John H. Forney, April 28, 1862–June 29, 1862.

Army of New Mexico— Organized December 14, 1862, with forces on the Rio Grande and in the New Mexico and Arizona territories. Disbanded May 4, 1862, when troops withdrew to Texas.

Brigadier General Henry H. Sibley, December 14, 1861–May 4, 1862.

Army of Northern Virginia— See Department of Northern Virginia. When Lee assumed command of the Department of Northern Virginia, he started calling it the Army of Northern Virginia, creating two corps headed by Thomas J. "Stonewall" Jackson and James Longstreet. After the death of Jackson, Lee revamped the Army of Northern Virginia into three corps consisting of approximately seventy-five thousand men.

General Robert E. Lee, June 1, 1862–April 9, 1865.

Army of the Northwest— Created February 9, 1862, from various units which operated in the western part of Virginia. After the death of General Garnett, Loring was placed in command but when dissension arose between him and General Thomas J. Jackson, commanding the Valley District, the secretary of war divided the army on February 9, 1862. On that day, the majority of the troops were transferred into Jackson's Valley District.

Brigadier General Richard S. Garnett, June 8, 1861–July 13, 1861.

Brigadier General H.R. Jackson, July 13, 1861–July 20, 1861.

Brigadier General William W. Loring, July 20, 1861–February 9, 1862.

Army of the Peninsula— Established May 21, 1861. Merged with the Army of Northern Virginia on April 12, 1862.

Major General John B. Magruder, May 21, 1861–April 12, 1862.

Army of Pensacola— Created October 22, 1861. It was discontinued when troops were placed under the command of Colonel Thomas M. Jones until May 12, 1862, as the city of Pensacola was evacuated.

Brigadier General Adley H. Gladden, October 22, 1861–October 27, 1861.

Major General Braxton Bragg, October 27, 1861–January 27, 1862.

Brigadier General Samuel Jones, January 27, 1862–March 13, 1862.

Colonel Thomas M. Jones, March 13, 1862–May 12, 1862.

Army of the Potomac— In the spring of 1861, men stationed in northern Virginia on the Alexandria were often called the Department of Alexandria. Since it was close to the Potomac, they were also often called the Department of the Potomac. On May 21, 1861, the troops were organized and designated the Army of the Potomac on June 20, 1861. On July 20, 1861, the Army of the Shenandoah was merged with the Army of the Potomac in preparation for the first Battle of Bull Run. On October 22, 1861, it was merged into the Department of Northern Virginia.

Brigadier General Milledge L. Bonham, May 24, 1861–May 31, 1861.

Brigadier General P.G.T. Beauregard, June 20, 1861–July 20, 1861.

Major General Joseph E. Johnston, July 20, 1861–October 22, 1861.

Army of the Shenandoah— Created June 20, from Virginia state troops gathered near Harper's Ferry. After the Battle of First Bull Run, this army formed the nucleus of the Army of the Potomac in July 1861 when Johnston was named commander of the newly formed Army of the Potomac.

Major General Kenton Harper, April 21, 1861–April 28, 1861.

Major General Thomas J. Jackson, April 28, 1861–May 24, 1861.

Major General Joseph E. Johnston, May 24, 1861–July 21, 1861.

Army of the Southwest (AKA Department of the Trans-Mississippi)— Created May 26, 1862, and composed of Arkansas, Missouri, Texas and the Indian Territory and that part of Louisiana west of the Mississippi River.

Joint command of Major General Paul O. Hebert (June 18, 1862–July 30, 1862) and Major General Thomas C. Hindman (May 31, 1862–July 30, 1862)

Major General Theophilus H. Holmes, July 30, 1862–March 7, 1863.

Lieutenant General Edmund K. Smith, March 7, 1863–April 19, 1865.

Lieutenant General Simon B. Buckner, April 19, 1865–April 22, 1865.

Lieutenant General Edmund K. Smith, April 22, 1865–May 26, 1865.

Army of Tennessee— At first was a subsection of Department Number Two. The army was originally organized on November 20, 1862, with three corps made up of armies from Kentucky and Mississippi. Became the Department of Tennessee and Georgia on August 15, 1864.

General Braxton Bragg, November 10, 1862–December 2, 1863.

Lieutenant General William J. Hardee, December 2, 1863–December 27, 1863.

General Joseph E. Johnston, December 27, 1863–July 18, 1864.

Lieutenant General John B. Hood, July 18, 1864–August 15, 1864.

Army of the West— Formed March 17, 1862, was a subsection of Department Number Two. On October 12, 1862, it was merged into the Army of West Tennessee.

Major General Earl Van Dorn, March 17, 1862–June 20, 1862.

Major General John P. McCown, June 20, 1862–June 27, 1862.

Brigadier General Dabney H. Maury, June 27, 1862–July 3, 1862.

Major General Sterling Price, July 3, 1862–October 12, 1862.

Army of West Tennessee— Formed October 12, 1862, and reorganized December 7, 1862, into the Army of the Departments of Mississippi and East Tennessee.

Major General Earl Van Dorn, October 12, 1862–December 7, 1862.

The military districts and departments listed below were fighting units. Departments were often referred to as armies and armies were sometimes referred to as departments. In reviewing the various information sources on the Confederate military organization, it is often confusing to figure out which was which. Below is a list of some of the familiar districts and departments and the various commanders who led them.

Military District of Georgia— Created November 5, 1861, and at first, was a subsection of the Departments of South Carolina, Georgia and Florida.

Brigadier General Alexander R. Lawton, November 5, 1861–June 6, 1862.

Brigadier General Hugh W. Mercer, June 6, 1862–December 24, 1863.

Major General Jeremy F. Gilmer, December 24, 1863–May 25, 1864.

Major General Lafayette McLaws, May 25, 1864–December 21, 1864.

Major General Daniel H. Hill, January 19, 1865–February 24, 1865. (Hill had been ordered to take the army and combine it with the Army of Tennessee in North Carolina, was returned to Georgia after Lee's surrender at Appomattox.)

Major General Lafayette McLaws, April 10, 1865–April 26, 1865.

Military District of Louisiana— Created April 17, 1861, from the various militia forces in and near New Orleans, including the Department of Louisiana. On May 27, 1861, it was merged into Department Number One.

Major General David E. Twiggs, April 17, 1861–May 27, 1861.

Department of East Tennessee/Kentucky— Created March 21, 1862, it was to encompass troops in and near Chattanooga and the vicinity. Later incorporated East Tennessee from the Virginia line to Chattanooga and then the western part of North Carolina from the Blue Ridge Mountains. On July 25, 1863, it was merged into the Department of Tennessee. The Army of Kentucky, created in August 1862, was merged with the Army of Tennessee in November 1862. The department was disbanded by the War Department in October 1863 but reinstated in January 1864.

   Major General Edmund K. Smith, March 9, 1862–August 24, 1862.
   Major General John P. McCown, August 24, 1862–September 19, 1862.
   Major General Samuel Jones, September 19, 1862–October 20, 1862.
   Lieutenant General Edmund K. Smith, October 20, 1862–November 18, 1862.
   Brigadier General Henry Heth, November 18, 1862–December 23, 1862.
   Lieutenant General Edmund K. Smith, December 23, 1862–January 17, 1863.
   Major General Daniel S. Donelson, January 17, 1863–April 15, 1863.
   Major General Dabney H. Maury, April 15, 1863–May 12, 1863.
   Major General Simon B. Buckner, May 12, 1863–September 6, 1863.
   Lieutenant General James Longstreet, January 8, 1864–March 8, 1864.
   Major General Simon B. Buckner, March 8, 1864–March 18, 1864.
   Lieutenant General James Longstreet, March 18, 1864–April 12, 1864.
   Major General Simon B. Buckner, April 12, 1864–May 2, 1864.
   Brigadier General William "Grumble" Jones, May 2, 1864–May 31, 1864.

Department of Florida— Created August 21, 1861. On November 4, 1862, it was divided into District of East Florida and District of Middle Florida.

   Brigadier General John B. Grayson, August 21, 1861–October 21, 1861.
   Colonel William S. Dilworth, October 21, 1861–November 17, 1861.
   Brigadier General James H. Trapier, November 17, 1861–March 19, 1862.
   Colonel William S. Dilworth, March 19, 1862–April 18, 1862.
   Brigadier General Joseph Finnegan, April 18, 1862–November 4, 1862.

Department of Louisiana— Created February 22, 1861, from the various militia forces in and around New Orleans. On April 17, 1861, it was merged into the Military District of Louisiana.

   Major General Braxton Bragg, February 22, 1861–April 17, 1861.

Department of Mississippi and East Louisiana— Organized October 21, 1862, and divided into two districts. Was abolished September 2, 1863.

   1. First Military District

   Brigadier General Daniel Ruggles, October 21, 1862–September 2, 1863.

   2. Second Military District— Surrendered by Lt. Gen. Pemberton to Union officials on July 4, 1863, with the fall of Vicksburg.

   Brigadier General Martin L. Smith, October 21, 1862–December 30, 1862.
   Major General Carter L. Stevenson, December 30, 1862–May 4, 1863.
   Major General John H. Forney, May 4, 1863–July 4, 1863.

Department of Northern Virginia— Created October 22, 1861, and was composed of the Districts of Potomac, the Aquia District and the Army of the Shenandoah. On June 1, 1862, the Departments of Norfolk and the Peninsula were combined into this department. Upon the appointment of General Robert E. Lee, the Department of Northern Virginia was often referred to as the Army of Northern Virginia.

   Major General Joseph E. Johnston, October 22, 1861–May 31, 1862, upon the wounding of General Johnston.
   Major General G.W. Smith, May 31, 1862–June 1, 1862.
   Major General Robert E. Lee, June 1, 1862–April 9, 1865.

Department Number One— Formed May 27, 1861, to be composed of Louisiana and the southern parts of Alabama and Mississippi. Louisiana was added on October 14, 1861. On June 25, 1862, it was merged into Department Number Two.

Major General David E. Twiggs, May 31, 1861–October 7, 1861.

Major General Mansfield Lowell, October 18, 1861–June 25, 1862.

Department Number Two (Also known as the Western Department)— Came into existence on July 4, 1861, to encompass part of Alabama, Tennessee, Arkansas, and all military operations in Missouri. On July 25, 1863, it was renamed Department of Tennessee.

Major General Leonidas Polk, July 13, 1861–September 15, 1861.

General Albert S. Johnston, September 15, 1861–April 6, 1862.

General P.G.T. Beauregard, April 6, 1862–June 17, 1862.

General Braxton Bragg, June 17, 1862–October 24, 1862.

Lieutenant General Leonidas Polk, October 24, 1862–November 3, 1862.

General Braxton Bragg, November 3, 1862–July 25, 1863.

Department of South Carolina— Created August 21, 1861, and was formed from forces gathered in and near Charleston, South Carolina. On March 6, 1861, Brigadier General P.G.T. Beauregard had been ordered to set up an area to take in and receive incoming soldiers into the Confederate service. On November 5, 1861, the Department of South Carolina was merged into the Department of South Carolina, Georgia and Florida.

Brigadier General P.G.T. Beauregard, March 6, 1861–May 27, 1861.

Brigadier General R.H. Anderson, May 27, 1861–August 21, 1861.

Brigadier General R.S. Ripley, August 21, 1861–November 5, 1861.

Department of Tennessee and Georgia— Organized August 15, 1864. Was made up of the remnants of the Army of Tennessee and portions of Georgia.

Lieutenant General John B. Hood, August 15, 1864–January 23, 1865.

Lieutenant General Richard Taylor, January 23, 1865–February 25, 1865.

General Joseph E. Johnston, February 25, 1865–March 17, 1865.

Major General Howell Cobb, Sr., March 27, 1865–April 20, 1865.

Department of Texas— Created April 11, 1861, when Earl Van Dorn was given the assignment to organize troops in Texas. Various military districts were created within the state. On August 20, 1862, it was merged into the District of Texas.

Colonel Earl Van Dorn, April 21, 1861–September 4, 1861.

Colonel Henry E. McCulloch, September 4, 1861–September 18, 1861.

Brigadier General Paul O. Hebert, September 18, 1861–August 20, 1862.

District of East Tennessee— Created November 10, 1861, when the planned invasion of Southeastern Kentucky was in the works. Was renamed Department of East Tennessee on March 9, 1862.

Brigadier General Felix K. Zollicoffer, July 26, 1861–November 10, 1861.

Colonel Danville Leadbetter, November 10, 1861–March 9, 1862.

District of the Gulf— Created July 2, 1862, and was a subsection of Department Number Two. Was composed of areas east of the Pearl River to the Apalachicola River. Later the area ran to the Georgia state line. In May 1864, portions of the Florida coast were incorporated into the District of the Gulf.

Brigadier General John H. Forney, July 2, 1862–December 14, 1862.

Brigadier General William W. Mackall, December 14, 1862–December 23, 1862.

Major General Simon B. Buckner, December 23, 1862–April 27, 1863.

Major General Dabney H. Maury, May 21, 1863–August 23, 1864.

Major General Franklin Gardner, August 23, 1864–September 12, 1864.
Major General Dabney H. Maury, September 12, 1864–November 28, 1864.
Major General Martin L. Smith, November 28, 1864–December 12, 1864.
Major General Dabney H. Maury, December 12, 1864–May 4, 1865.

District of Mississippi—Was a subsection of Department Number Two. Created July 2, 1862, and was later merged into the Department of Mississippi and East Louisiana on October 1, 1862.
Major General Earl Van Dorn, July 2, 1862–September 5, 1862.
Brigadier General Daniel Ruggles, September 5, 1862–October 1, 1862.

District of Tennessee—Originally a subsection of Department Number Two. Organized June 21, 1862, and merged into the Department of Mississippi and East Louisiana on October 1, 1862.
Major General Sterling Price, July 21, 1862–October 1, 1862.

District of Texas—Created August 20, 1862, from troops in Texas and the Territory of Arizona. In November, was renamed District of Texas, New Mexico and Arizona.
Brigadier General Paul O. Hebert, August 20, 1862–November 27, 1862.
Brigadier General Hamilton P. Bee, November 27–29, 1862.

District of the Trans-Mississippi—Created January 10, 1862, and was to consist of that part of Louisiana north of the Red River, the Indian Territory west of Arkansas and the states of Arkansas and Missouri. Merged into the Trans-Mississippi Department (Army of Trans-Mississippi) on May 26, 1862.
Major General Earl Van Dorn, January 29, 1862–May 26, 1862.

District of Upper Arkansas—Created July 22, 1861, to be composed of that part of Arkansas lying west of the White and Black rivers and north of the Arkansas River to the Missouri line. Merged into the Trans-Mississippi District on January 10, 1862.
Brigadier General William J. Hardee, July 22, 1861–October 1861.
Colonel Solon Borland, November 5, 1861–January 10, 1862.

Arizona Territory—Created August 1, 1861, with the passage of the Arizona Secession Ordinance. Merged into the Department of Trans-Mississippi on August 20, 1862.
Lt. Colonel John R. Baylor, August 1, 1861–December 14, 1861.
Brigadier General Henry H. Sibley, December 14, 1861–May 4, 1862.

There were many other districts, subsections, subdivisions and departments of those listed above. Some were in existence for a few days to a few months before they became part of another organization.

Appendix III. The Ships

United States of America Naval Ships

USS *Abeona* A stern-wheel steamer converted to a tinclad gunboat. She was 157 feet long with a beam of 31 feet and a draft of 4 feet. Commanded by Samuel Hall.

USS *Abraham* Formerly known as the CSS *Victoria*. Captured by Union forces as the ship was moored in the harbor at Memphis, Tennessee. After the war, the ship was sold and renamed the *Lexington*. She caught fire on February 3, 1869, at Algiers, Louisiana. (See also CSS *Victoria*.)

USS *Adolph Hugel* A mortar schooner, 114-feet long with a beam of 29 feet and a draft of 9 feet. Part of the mortar flotilla on the Gulf Coast. In 1864, she was transferred to the Atlantic, where she became part of the defenses of Washington.

USS *Agamenticus* A 3,295-ton, twin-turret monitor. After the war it was renamed the USS *Terror*.

USS *Agawam* A side-wheel with a wooden hull, she carried a crew of 200 men and officers and had 10 guns.

USS *Albatross* A commercial steamship converted into wooden gunboat. After the war, she reverted to a commercial sailing ship.

USS *Alexandria* A captured ship formerly known as the CSS *St. Mary*. She was approximately 90 feet in length with a beam of 15 feet and a draft of four feet. (See also CSS *St. Mary*.)

USS *Alligator* The Union's only true submarine, 45 feet long and 66 inches deep. Unable to purify the air while submerged. Sank in a gale in 1863.

USS *Argosy* A 219-ton tinclad gunboat.

USS *Atlanta* Formerly the CSS *Atlanta*. Sank off the coast of Cape Hatteras in December 1869. (See also CSS *Atlanta*.)

USS *Baron DeKalb see* USS *St. Louis*)

USS *Bazeley* A 50-ton tugboat serving the North Carolina sounds. On December 9, 1864, while operating at Rainbow Bluff, North Carolina, on the Roanoke River, she struck a mine and sank.

USS *Belle* A steam tugboat used as a dispatch ship. She was equipped with a spar-torpedo apparatus.

USS *Benton* An ironclad gunboat with 16 guns and a crew of 176. She was 202 feet long and her sides were protected by iron armor 3.5 inches thick. After the war, she was stripped of her plating and sold for scrap.

USS *Black Hawk* Converted steamer known as the *New Uncle Sam*. She was 260 feet long with a 45-foot beam and carried eight guns. Served as flagship for Admiral David D. Porter. On April 22, 1865, the ship caught fire and sank near Cairo, Illinois. (Porter kept his horses aboard the ship and rode them down the gangplank when he went ashore.)

USS *Brooklyn* A wooden sloop of war 233 feet long with a beam of 43 feet and a draft of 16.3 feet. Her crew numbered 335 officers and men.

USS *Cairo* A "Pook Turtle" ironclad. Blown up and sank on December 12, 1862, when she struck a mine planted by the Confederates in the Yazoo River.

USS *Camanche* An ironclad. She was 200 feet long and 46 feet wide and, displacing 1,875 tons, destined to serve and protect California. Her revolving gun turret held two 15-inch guns and was steam powered. Not designed to operate on the open seas, she sank on November 16, 1863, while being towed to California in sections aboard the *Aquila*. Never saw combat.

USS *Canonicus* A 2,100-ton monitor.

USS *Carondelet* "Pook Turtle" ironclad. Armed with 13 guns, she was 175 feet long and weighed 512 tons. Her draft of six inches allowed her to maneuver in shallow waters. Saw more action than any of the Pook Turtles.

USS *Casco* A 1,175-ton torpedo monitor. When built in 1864, she did not have an armored gun turret. She was part of the Potomac Flotilla fleet serving in the defense of Washington in 1865. After the war, she was renamed *Hero* and scrapped for parts in 1875.

USS *Catawaba* A monitor which was never commissioned and when delivered, was placed in a reserve status.

USS *Catskill* A monitor severely damaged by Confederate gunfire in the attack on Fort Sumter on April 7, 1863. Repaired, she was again damaged later that summer in Charleston Harbor. Saw action as part of the coastal defense during the Spanish American War.

USS *Cayuga* A steam gunboat.

USS *Ceres* A side-wheel steamer converted into a gunboat in 1861. In April and May 1864, she was involved in several incidents with the Confederate ram *Albemarle*.

USS *Champion* A 115-ton side-wheel tinclad gunboat.

USS *Chattanooga* A "home-made" steamboat whose purpose in 1863 was to carry supplies to the Union troops starving in Chattanooga, Tennessee.

USS *Chickasaw* An ironclad river monitor that participated in the Battle of Mobile Bay. After the war, she was converted into a railroad ferry, named The *Gouldsboro* and served on the Mississippi River near New Orleans until she was destroyed in 1944.

USS *Chillicothe* An ironclad gunboat, 165 feet long with a beam of 50 feet and a draft of 4 feet.

USS *Chimo* A 1,175-ton light draft monitor converted to a spar torpedo ship. After the war, she was sold and renamed *Orion* and later *Piscataqua*.

USS *Choctaw* An side-wheel ironclad ram 260 feet long that was part of the Mississippi fleet river gunboat.

USS *Cincinnati* An ironclad that was 175 feet long, with a beam of 51 feet and weighing 512 tons. She carried 14 guns and 251 men, and had a draft of six feet. The ship was powered by a single paddle wheel located amidship.

USS *Commodore Barney* A side-wheel ferry known as the *Ethan Allen*. She was 143 feet long with a beam of 33 feet and a draft of 9 feet.

USS *Commodore Hull* A 376-ton gunboat.

USS *Commodore Jones* An armed side-wheel ferry that operated on the James River. She was destroyed by a torpedo on May 6, 1864.

USS *Commodore Morris* A gunboat.

USS *Commodore Perry* A ferryboat converted into an armed side-wheel ferry.

USS *Conestoga* A side-wheel steamer converted into a timberclad gunboat. She sank on March 8, 1864, after a collision with the USS *General Price.*

USS *Congress* A frigate.

USS *Connecticut* Originally known as the *Mississippi,* she was a steamship that was converted into a warship and named the USS *Connecticut.* She was decommissioned in August 1865 and renamed the *South America.*

USS *Constellation* A frigate 186 feet long with a beam of 41 feet, she carried a crew of 285 men and officers.

USS *Covington* A 224-ton side-wheel steamer converted into a tinclad river gunboat. On May 5, 1864, she was attacked by Confederate gunfire on the Red River. To prevent her capture, her crew set fire to her.

USS *Cricket* An 178-ton ironclad.

USS *Dahlia* Originally known as the *Firefly,* this 54-ton tug, built by the Army in 1861, was transferred to the Navy in 1862, where she saw service as a tug under the name of USS *Dahlia.*

USS *Daisy* Originally known as the *Mulford,* she was a tug doing service along the Mississippi. After the war, she was sold and renamed *Little Queen.*

USS *Dictator* A 4,338-ton monitor with a single turret commissioned in November 1864 and decommissioned in September 1865.

USS *Dunderberg* An oceangoing ironclad, she was the longest wooden ship ever built, having a ram in excess of fifty feet. When she was delivered to the Navy, the war was over and she was returned to the builder.

USS *Eastport* An ironclad river gunboat that struck a mine at Grand Ecore, Louisiana. She was blown up on April 26, 1864, to prevent her capture.

USS *Elk* An 162-ton side-wheel tinclad.

USS *Essex* Originally a ferryboat known as the *New Era.* She was converted into a gunboat.

USS *Fairplay* A side-wheel tinclad ferry used by the Confederates as a transport; it was captured on August 18, 1862, at Milliken's Bend. Converted into a gunboat, she served the Union army until the end of the war.

Fanny A steam transport.

USS *Fawn* A tinclad formerly known as the *Fanny Barker.*

USS *Fern* A tugboat.

USS *Forest Rose* A 260-ton tinclad river gunboat.

USS *Fort Henry* A side-wheel steamer, known as the *Aleck Scott.* She was renamed as the *Fort Henry* when she was used by the Army for a quartermaster ship. When she was transferred to the Navy, she was converted into an ironclad and renamed USS *Lafayette.* (See also USS *Lafayette.*)

USS *Fort Hindman* A 286-ton side-wheel tinclad river gunboat.

USS *Galena* An ironclad sloop with three-inch iron plating. After the Battle of Drewry Bluffs, she was stripped of her heavy iron and outfitted as a gunboat.

USS *General Bragg* Was originally a side-wheel steamer known as the CSS *General Bragg.* She was captured on June 6, 1862, by Union forces at Memphis. Her named was changed to USS *General Bragg.* (See also CSS *General Bragg.*)

USS *General Lyon* A Confederate 390-ton side-wheel river gunboat known as the *De Soto.* She was captured on April 7, 1862, and renamed the USS *General Lyon.* After the war, she was sold and renamed *Alabama.* (See also CSS *De Soto.*)

USS *General Price* A side-wheel river steamer converted into a ram by the Confederate Navy. She was sunk during the Battle of Memphis on June 6, 1862. Raised and refitted, she became the USS *General Price.* On March 8, 1864, she accidentally rammed and sank the USS *Conestoga.*

USS *General Sherman* A 187-ton tinclad river gunboat.

USS *Genesee* A 1,120-ton double-ender side-wheel steam gunboat.

USS *Glide* A 232-ton stern-wheel tinclad river gunboat. After the war, she was sold. She was destroyed in a boiler explosion in January 1869.

USS *Grand Gulf* Originally known as the *Onward*, she was a wooden steamship converted into a gunboat and named the USS *Grand Gulf*. At the end of the war, she was sold and served as the *General Grant* until she caught fire in New Orleans on April 19, 1869.

USS *Great Western* A tinclad.

USS *Hartford* A wooden frigate rigged with sails and a steam engine that powered the screw propeller. She was 225 feet long with a 44 foot beam and she displaced 2,900-tons. Armed with 24 guns, she served as the flagship for Captain David G. Farragut. It was while aboard the USS *Hartford* that Farragut uttered his famous saying, "Damn the torpedoes! Full speed ahead!" during the Battle of Mobile Bay on August 5, 1864.

USS *Harvest Moon* A steamer which served as the flagship for Admiral John A. Dahlgren. She sank after striking a Confederate torpedo/mine on March 1, 1865, off the coast of Winyah Bay, South Carolina.

USS *Hatteras* A side-wheel steamer known as *Saint Marys*, she was converted into a gunboat. On January 11, 1863, as she was on patrol near Galveston, she came across the CSS *Alabama* masquerading as a British warship. After a brief fight, the *Hatteras* was sunk.

USS *Hornet* A side-wheel gunboat that was formerly known as the Confederate *Lady Sterling*.

USS *Housatonic* A sloop-of-war, she was the first ship to be sunk by a submarine when she met the CSS *Hunley* while anchored off Charleston on February 17, 1864.

USS *Hunchback* A side-wheel ferryboat, approximately 180 feet long, with a draft of 9 feet. She was converted into a gunboat.

USS *Indianola* An ironclad river gunboat 174 feet long with a 50 foot beam and three inch iron plating on her sides. Mounted forward were two 11-inch Dahlgren guns. The USS *Indianola* was captured on February 26, 1863, by Confederate forces who blew up the ship.

USS *Itasca* A schooner, known as a "90-day gunboat," was 158 feet long with a beam of 28 feet and a draft of 9 feet. Though she did not function well under sail, she did have what was termed "good steaming performance."

J. R. Williams A steamboat.

USS *Kansas* A gunboat.

USS *Kearsarge* A steam sloop-of-war, she was 200 feet long and had 3 masts in addition to a steam-powered screw propeller. She carried a crew of 163 men and officers and possessed eight guns and two 11-inch Dahlgren pivot guns mounted amidships. She spent most of her time at sea chasing the CSS *Alabama*, a Confederate ship. Upon learning that the *Alabama* was in Cherbourg, France, for repairs, Captain Winslow of the *Kearsarge* waited offshore for her. On June 19, 1864, the two ships engaged in combat on the open seas and after an hour's combat, the *Alabama* went down. The *Kearsarge*'s only action during the war was her fight with the CSS *Alabama*. Later that year, the *Kearsarge* was sold and went to the bottom of the sea in 1894 when she sank off the coast of Central America. (See also CSS *Alabama*.)

USS *Keokuk* Originally named the *Moodna*. A 677-ton twin-turret monitor that participated in the attack on Fort Sumter on April 7, 1863. Struck numerous times by Confederate fire, the *Keokuk* sank the following morning.

USS *Key West* A steamer converted into a river gunboat. Near Johnsonville, Tennessee, she was destroyed to prevent her capture on November 4, 1864.

USS *Kickapoo* A 1,300-ton double turret ironclad river monitor.

USS *Lafayette* Formerly an army quartermaster ship known as the *Fort Henry*. She was converted into an ironclad river gunboat that operated mostly on the lower Mississippi. (See also USS *Fort Henry*.)

Lancaster A side-wheel towboat converted into a ram.

USS *Lehigh* A 1,335-ton monitor. After the war, she served as a training ship for the U.S. Naval Academy.

USS *Lexington* A side-wheel passenger steamer converted into a timberclad steamer with 5-inch oak plating. She was 177 feet long with a seven-foot draft.

USS *Leyden* A steam tugboat that also saw action off Cuba during the Spanish-American War.

Linda A transport.

USS *Linden* A 177-ton tinclad river gunboat. Sank while assisting a transport steamer on February 22, 1864.

Lioness A 198-ton stern-wheel steamer converted into a ram.

USS *Louisville* A 512-ton ironclad gunboat.

USS *Mahopac* A 2,100-ton monitor.

USS *Malvern* A steamship 240 feet in length with an 8-foot draft, seized by the governor of Louisiana for use as a blockade runner. Captured by Union ships in 1864 off the North Carolina coast when she ran against the USS *Niphon,* she was converted to a Union ship. During the attacks of Fort Fisher, she served as the flagship for Admiral Porter.

USS *Manayunk* A 2,100-ton monitor delivered to the Navy at the end of the war. She did not see service during the Civil War, but as the USS *Ajax,* she saw service during the Spanish-American War.

USS *Manhattan* A 2,100-ton monitor.

USS *Maria Denning* An 870-ton side-wheel river steamer that was transferred to the Army in December 1862 for use as an Army transport.

USS *Marmora* A 207-ton stern-wheel tinclad river gunboat.

USS *Mattabesett* A 974-ton *Sassacus* class "double-ender" side-wheel steam gunboat.

USS *Mendota* A side-wheel gunboat.

USS *Merrimack* (USS *Merrimac*) A frigate that had 40 guns. While at the Gosport Naval Yard, she was burned by the Union officials in 1861 to prevent her from being taken and used by the Confederates. Raised and repaired by the Confederates, she served the Confederacy as the CSS *Virginia.* (See also CSS *Virginia.*)

USS *Miami* A side-wheel gunboat involved in a fight with the CSS *Albemarle* on April 19, 1864.

USS *Michigan* An ironclad side-wheel steamer which was the Navy's first iron-hulled warship. She had a length of 163 feet and a beam of 27 feet with a draft of 9 feet. In 1905, her name was changed to the USS *Wolverine* so a new and more modern ship could be named the *Michigan.* In 1949, the *Wolverine* was cut up and sold for scrap.

USS *Milwaukee* A river monitor that was 209 feet long with a 56 beam and a six-foot draft. In April 1865 while patrolling the Blakely River, the USS *Milwaukee* struck a torpedo and sank. It was reported that Confederate soldiers manning Spanish Fort fired shots in celebration as she went down.

Mingo A stern-wheel steamer converted into a ram. She sank accidentally in November 1862 while at Cape Girardeau, Missouri.

USS *Minnesota* One of the few warships in the Navy at the time of the war, she carried 47 guns on two decks and had a crew of 646 sailors and officers. She was the flagship of the North Atlantic Blockading Squadron. During the Battle of Hampton Roads, the *Minnesota* ran aground on March 9, 1862, and while aground, fired over fifty shells at the Confederate monitor, the CSS *Virginia.* The CSS *Virginia* returned fire, causing an explosion on board the USS *Minnesota.* She was saved from further damage with the arrival of the USS *Monitor,* which then engaged the CSS *Virginia* in the famous sea battle between the *Monitor* and the *Merrimack.*

USS *Mississippi* A frigate.

USS *Monadnock* A 3,295-ton twin-turret monitor.

Monarch A 406-ton side-wheel towboat converted into a ram.

USS *Monitor* The small warship was 172 feet long and 41.5 feet wide and carried only two guns. She had a 10.5-foot draft that allowed her to operate in rivers and streams. She gave the appearance of a large raft with a tin can in the middle. She sat about 18 inches above the water and was covered with two layers of half-inch iron plates. The tinclad actually had a 9-foot high revolving turret, 20 feet in diameter. After her famous battle with the CSS *Virginia* in March 1862, the USS *Monitor* sank while being towed to Cape Hatteras on December 30, 1862.

USS *Monongahela* A 2,078-ton steam screw sloop. After the war, she served as a training ship for the U.S. Naval Academy from 1894 to 1899, when she was assigned as a store ship at Guantanamo Bay, Cuba. She caught fire and was destroyed on March 17, 1908.

USS *Montauk* On this ship in April 1865, the body of John Wilkes Booth was brought aboard to be examined by physicians. The ship also served as a prison for some of the Lincoln conspirators.

USS *Monticello* A steam ship built in 1859, which was converted into a gunboat.

USS *Morning Light* An 8-gun ship captured by the Confederates at Sabine Pass, Texas, on January 21, 1863.

USS *Mound City* An ironclad river gunboat.

USS *Nahant* A monitor that assisted in the capture of the CSS *Atlanta* on June 17, 1863.

USS *Naiad* A tinclad river gunboat.

USS *Nantucket* A 1,335-ton monitor that took part in the firing on Fort Sumter in April 1863 and assisted in the attack on Battery Wagner in September 1863. As a monitor, she saw action during the Spanish-American War when she took part in the defense of Port Royal, South Carolina.

USS *Neosho* A 523-ton single-turret ironclad river monitor.

USS *New Hampshire* A store ship.

USS *New Ironsides* An ironclad frigate 230 feet in length, with only 170 feet covered in 4.5-inches of plating over her wooden hull. She carried 18 guns, including two 200-pounders. She became the flagship for Admiral Samuel F. DuPont on January 17, 1863. She was decommissioned after the war and was destroyed when she caught fire on December 1, 1866.

USS *Niagara* A steam frigate.

USS *Nymph* A steamer known as *Cricket Number 3*, converted into a stern-wheel tinclad river gunboat.

USS *Onondaga* A twin-turret monitor 226 feet in length; one of the first double turreted monitors in the Navy. She carried two fifteen-inch Dahlgren guns in addition to two 150-pound Parrott guns.

USS *Osage* An ironclad monitor that had a rear turret that revolved on iron ball bearings which were protected by gun port shutters that closed automatically after the guns had fired. She struck a torpedo on the Blakely River during the Battle for Mobile Bay in March 1865 and sank.

USS *Ossipee* A steam screw sloop.

USS *Otsego* A 974-ton double-ender side-wheel gunboat. She sank after striking a Confederate mine near Rainbow Bluff on the Roanoke River on December 9, 1864.

USS *Ouachita* A tinclad.

USS *Ozark* An ironclad river monitor.

USS *Passaic* A 1,335-ton ironclad monitor. Saw duty in the Florida waters during the Spanish-American War.

USS *Pensacola* A steam frigate.

USS *Peosta* A tinclad.

USS *Pittsburgh* An ironclad.

USS *Planter* A side-wheel steamship.

USS *Powhatan* A steam frigate.

USS *Prairie Bird* A tinclad.

USS *Preble* A sloop of war.

USS *Princeton* A screw steamer.

USS *Queen City* A tinclad.

USS *Queen of the West* *see* CSS *Queen of the West*

USS *Rattler* A tinclad.

USS *Red Rover* A side-wheel steamer.

USS *Richmond* A steam frigate.

USS *Roanoke* An ironclad steam frigate.

USS *Rodolph* A tinclad.

USS *Sabine* School ship.

USS *Sacramento* A steam screw sloop.

USS *St. Clair* A tinclad.

USS *St. Louis* A gunboat 175 feet long with a 51.2 inch beam. She carried a crew of 251 men and had 13 heavy guns. It was while she was shelling Fort Donelson that she was hit by a Confederate shell, which took out the wheel and caused the ship to drift downstream. In September 1862, she was rebuilt and renamed *Baron DeKalb*. On July 13, 1863, the ship was sunk after she was hit by two torpedoes while on duty on the Yazoo River.

Samson A stern-wheel steamer.

USS *San Jacinto* A wooden sloop-of-war that carried 12 guns. She was one of the ships that stopped and detained James M. Mason and John Slidell as they were about to leave Cuba for England in December 1860 aboard a British ship. The men were taken prisoner and transported on the San Jacinto to the United States, creating an international incident which came close to war with Great Britain. At the same time, the United States was also facing the secession crisis. On January 1, 1865, the ship struck a reef in the Bahama Islands and sank.

USS *Sangamon* A monitor.

USS *Sassacus* A double-ender side-wheel steam gunboat, which suffered severe damage after ramming the CSS *Albemarle*. She remained on duty until September 14, 1864, when she was refitted.

USS *Saugus* An ironclad monitor 235 feet long and 44 feet wide. She had a draft of 13.6 feet and carried a crew of 86. She had 11 inches of iron plating on her turret and 5 inches of iron plating on her sides. In her turret were two 15-inch guns. She was later fitted with a torpedo rake designed to trap and detonate mines before they could damage the ship. During the January 1865 attack on Fort Fisher, her guns exploded, putting the ship out of commission. Repaired, she became a transport ship, transporting and housing a few of Lincoln's conspirators: Michael O'Laughlin, Lewis Payne, Samuel Arnold, and George Atzerodt.

USS *Shamrock* A side-wheel gunboat.

USS *Shawnee* A monitor.

USS *Signal* A tinclad.

USS *Silver Cloud* A tinclad.

USS *Silver Lake* A gunboat.

USS *Southfield* A double ended side-wheel gunboat. On April 19, 1864, while lashed to the USS *Miami*, she was attacked by the CSS *Albemarle*. Cutting the ropes that bound her to the USS *Miami*, the *Southfield* sank, allowing the *Miami* to make a run for safety.

USS *Spuytin Duyvil* A torpedo boat.

USS *Sultana* A steamship used as a transport vehicle after the war. It was on this ship that over

2,000 Union prisoners of war who had recently been released from Andersonville Prison were going home. The ship's boilers exploded during the morning hours of April 27, 1865, killing 1,547 soldiers and civilians.

Switzerland A side-wheel towboat converted into a ram.

USS *Tacony* A side-wheel gunboat.

USS *Tecumseh* A single turret monitor with armor of ten inches covering the turret and five inches covering the sides. She also was equipped with an iron guard 15 inches high and 5 inches thick running around the base of her revolving turret. She was 223 feet long and weighed 1,034 tons. She carried two 15-inch Dahlgren guns in her turret. As she led the way into Mobile Bay on August 5, 1864, she ran into an underwater mine and sank within 30 seconds, losing 93 of her 114-man crew.

USS *Tennessee* A 52 foot long, 13 foot wide horse ferry that was converted into a warship. She was mounted with a 10-pound Parrott gun as she set off for Chattanooga on June 7, 1862. Unable to pass over the rapids, she was stripped of her gun and returned to duty as a horse ferry. Her only combat was firing on some Confederate soldiers on the river bank who had shot at her.

USS *Ticonderoga* A screw sloop.

USS *Tuscumbia* An ironclad river gunboat.

USS *Tyler* A 575-ton timberclad gunboat that carried a 32-pound cannon in addition to other guns. She had 5-inch-thick oak planks on her decks.

USS *Unadilla* A gunboat.

USS *Underwriter* A side-wheel steamer converted into a gunboat. On February 2, 1864, Confederate forces commanded by John Taylor Wood, the grandson of President Zachary Taylor, led a group of Confederate raiders aboard the ship while it was moored at New Bern, North Carolina. Nine of the crew were killed, including her captain. After capturing the Union crew, the Confederates set the ship on fire.

USS *United States* A frigate captured by the Confederates and renamed the CSS *United States*. (See also CSS *United States*.)

USS *Vermont* A store ship.

USS *Vincennes* A sloop-of-war.

USS *Vindicator* A side-wheel ram.

USS *Volunteer* A side-wheel steamer.

USS *W. H. Brown* A side-wheel steamer.

USS *Wabash* A steam screw frigate.

USS *Wachusett* A screw sloop-of-war. In October 1864, her commander, Napoleon Collins, took her to Brazil, where he and his crew captured the Confederate ship CSS *Florida*. (See also CSS *Florida*.)

USS *Washington Irving* A transport ship.

USS *Wassuc* A monitor.

USS *Water Witch* An 150-foot-long side-wheel sloop with a bow of 23 and a draft of 9 feet. On June 3, 1864, she was captured by Confederate forces as she was moored in Ossabaw Sound. On December 19, 1864, the Confederates set her on fire to prevent her from being re-captured by Union forces.

USS *Weehawken* A monitor which sank in December 1863 as she took on water in a storm off the coast of Morris Island.

USS *Westfield* A gunboat 215 feet long with a beam of 35 feet. She carried two Dahlgren guns (a 19-inch and a 48-inch) in addition to a 100-pound Parrott rifle. On January 1, 1863, the Confederates made a surprise attack in an attempt to recapture Galveston. The *Westfield*, serving as the flagship for William B. Renshaw, ran aground near Pelican Spit. Upon finding that the ship could not be dislodged, the crew blew it up. Renshaw and a few of his crew were killed in the explosion. It is believed the men were killed as they returned to the ship believing the bombs had failed to detonate.

USS *Whitehead* A gunboat.

USS *William H. Brown* A stern-wheel steamer.

USS *Winnebago* An ironclad river monitor.

USS *Wyalusing* A side-wheel steam gunboat.

USS *Wyandotte* A monitor.

Confederate States of America Naval Ships

CSS *Admiral* A side-wheel steamer.

CSS *Alabama* A Confederate raider built in Liverpool, England. She was 220 feet long with a beam of 32 feet and capable of making 13 knots on water. Captained by Raphael Semmes, she carried a crew of 144 men and officers. The *Alabama* attacked Union ships on the open waters. She sailed into Cherbourg, France, on June 11, 1864, for needed repairs. As she left the harbor and sailed into open waters, she was met by the USS *Kearsarge.* After a two hour battle, on June 19, 1864, the CSS *Alabama* went to the bottom. (This ship, a Confederate raider, never entered any Confederate port during her 22-month service, in which she captured 66 Union merchant ships.) (See also USS *Kearsarge.*)

CSS *Albemarle* An ironclad ram, 152 feet long, equipped with a solid oak prow sheathed with two inches of iron whose sole purpose was to ram into the sides of wooden Union ships. On May 5, 1864, she rammed the USS *Sassacus*, causing severe damage to both ships. A planned Union raid led by Lt. William B. Cushing on October 27, 1864, found the *Albemarle* in Plymouth Harbor and the ship was destroyed.

CSS *Alert* A schooner.

Alexandra A screw steamer that never served. Built in Liverpool, England, she was launched in March 1863, but was seized the following month by the British government. Released the following year, her name was changed to the CSS *Mary.* She was again detained as she sailed into the Bahamas in December 1864, where she was held until the end of the war.

CSS *Arkansas* An ironclad ram 165 feet long with a beam of 35 feet and a draft of 12 feet. She was armed with various guns and had three 32-pounders on each side with two on her rear. She carried a crew of 200 officers and men. In an attempt to recapture the city of Baton Rouge, the CSS *Arkansas* moved to within four miles of the city before her engines stopped, causing her to run aground. Repaired, she once again moved toward the city only to run aground again. Knowing that they had been spotted by Union forces, her crew raced to set her on fire to prevent her capture.

CSS *Atlanta* A converted merchant ship known as the *Fingal,* she was 204 feet long with a beam of 41 feet. As a merchant ship, she had successfully run the Union blockade at Savannah, Georgia. When she was unable to leave the harbor, she was purchased by the Confederate Navy. Converted into an ironclad with an iron ram and a spar torpedo, she was renamed the CSS *Atlanta* in November 1862. As an ironclad, she attempted to break out of the harbor and, on her second attempt, she ran into two Union warships: USS *Nahant* and the USS *Weehawken.* She ran aground and was captured. As a captured ship, the *Atlanta* was renamed the USS *Atlanta* and finished out her military career on the James River as an Union warship. (See also USS *Atlanta.*)

CSS *Baltic* Originally a wooden river towboat, she was converted into an ironclad ram. She was 185 feet long with a beam of 38 feet and a draft of 6 feet, 6 inches. By early 1863, she was in such poor condition that her armor was removed and the ship abandoned. Captured by Union forces, she was sold for scrap in December 1865.

CSS *Beauregard* A side-wheel steamer used by the Confederacy as a transport. In December 1864, Union forces captured her near Savannah, Georgia.

CSS *Bermuda* A blockade runner that brought supplies in from England and returned to England with cotton. She was captured in Bermuda by a Union gunboat as she was transferring supplies to another ship. She was renamed the USS *General Meade.*

CSS *Bombshell* Originally an army transport ship that was sunk by Confederate forces near Albemarle Sound, North Carolina, on April 18, 1864. Raised by the Confederates, she was renamed the CSS *Bombshell.* As she was accompanying the CSS *Albemarle* on May 5, 1864, she was captured by the Union gunboats USS *Sassacus* and USS *Mattabesett.* (See also USS *Sassacus.*)

CSS *Capitol* A 499-ton side-wheel steamer destroyed by fire on June 28, 1862, while moored at Liverpool, Mississippi. To impede Union shipping, her hull was sunk in the Yazoo River.

CSS *Chattahoochee* A gunboat.

CSS *Chickamauga* Originally a blockade-runner known as the *Edith,* she was 175 feet long with a beam of 25 feet and a draft of 15 feet. In September 1864, she was purchased by the Confederate Navy and converted into a commerce raider, commanded by Lt. John Wilkinson. During the Battle for Fort Fisher in January 1865, the *Chickamauga,* located at Cape Fear, sent her shells into the Union ships as they moved against the fort. After the fort was captured and Wilmington fell, Union guns turned on the ship, sinking her.

CSS *Chicora* An ironclad measuring 150 feet long, which carried a multitude of various guns. She was assigned to protect Charleston Harbor. With the imminent arrival of General Sherman in January 1865, she was blown up to prevent her capture.

CSS *City of Vicksburg* Originally intended as a civilian steamer, she was used by the Confederacy as a transport ship. Damaged when rammed by the USS *Queen of the West,* she became a wharf boat at Vicksburg until March 29, 1863, when she went adrift and was later destroyed.

CSS *Colonel Love* A side-wheel steamer originally named *Hercules.* She was converted into a cottonclad ram.

CSS *Columbia* An ironclad 218 foot long covered with six-inch iron plating.

CSS *David* Designed as a torpedo boat, she was 50 feet long and 7 feet high. Her mission was to attach a torpedo or a bomb to the end of a 14-foot spar at the front of the boat and then ram the side of Union ships, detonating the torpedo or bomb. Then she would return to port to secure another torpedo. She was very successful in approaching Union ships. She could fill her ballast tanks with water to lower the ship until only her deck and smokestack remained afloat.

CSS *De Soto* A side-wheel river steamer captured by Union forces on April 7, 1862, then renamed the USS *General Lyon.* She served as a transport ship.

Denbigh A blockade runner which carried British registry.

CSS *Earl Van Dorn* A steamer that was burned on the Yazoo River.

Emily St. Pierre A blockade runner.

CSS *Firefly* A side-wheel steamer that was burned by her crew on December 21, 1864, to prevent her capture.

CSS *Flamingo* A blockade runner.

CSS *Florida* Secretly built in Liverpool, England, as a merchant ship, she was originally named the *Oreto.* She was 191 feet long and had a draft of 14 feet. It was against British neutrality laws to provide arms to the Confederacy and, as such, any ship built in her ports had to be a merchant ship and could not be fitted with guns. The *Oreto* left England in the summer of 1862 and headed to Mobile, Alabama, where she was fitted with guns and renamed the CSS *Florida.* For the next 18 months, she terrorized Union shipping. In October 1864, she was captured by Union forces as she cruised near Brazil in South America and was sunk later that year.

CSS *Fredericksburg* An ironclad ram with a draft of 11 feet. She was destroyed on April 4, 1865, by the Confederates when it looked as if Richmond was about to fall to Union troops.

CSS *Gaines* An ironclad steamer with a draft of 6 feet. She was sunk during the Battle of Mobile Bay on August 5, 1864.

CSS *General Beauregard* A side-wheel steamer known as *Ocean* which was converted into a cottonclad ram. She was sunk during the Battle of Memphis on June 6, 1862.

CSS *General Bragg* A side-wheel steamer used as a ram. On June 6, 1862, she was captured by Union forces in Memphis and renamed the USS *General Bragg*.

CSS *General Earl Van Dorn* A side-wheel steamer burned by the Confederates on the Yazoo River to prevent her capture.

General Lee A side-wheel steamer used as a transport.

CSS *General M. Jeff Thompson* A side-wheel steamer that was sunk in Memphis, Tennessee, on June 6, 1862.

CSS *General Polk* A side-wheel steamer sloop. Destroyed by the Confederates on June 26, 1862, on the Yazoo River to prevent her capture.

CSS *General Sumter* A cottonclad ram captured on June 6, 1862, at Memphis, Tennessee.

CSS *Georgia* Originally known as the *Japan*, she was purchased by the Confederate government in April 1863. Outfitted in France as an ironclad, she was commissioned the CSS *Georgia*, to be captained by Lt. William Lewis Maury. She captured and destroyed the USS *Dictator*. In October 1863, it was discovered that her hull was "fouled by marine growth" and she was decommissioned. Plans were made to remove her guns and place them aboard the CSS *Rappahannock*. The plan fell through and the ship was sailed to Liverpool and sold. Her guns were removed and she once again resumed her career as a steamer, but her reputation had preceded her. While sailing under her new owner's flag, she was captured by the USS *Niagara* in August 1864 and taken as a prize of war.

CSS *Governor Moore* A cottonclad side-wheel steamer.

CSS *Grampus* A 252-ton stern wheel steamer that served as a transport and gunboat on the Mississippi River. She was destroyed upon the fall of Island No. 10 on April 7, 1862. Believed raised by Union forces, she was once more destroyed on January 11, 1863.

H. L. Hunley The first submarine. She was 30 feet long, 5 feet high and 4 feet wide and was powered by an 8-man crew who turned cranks along the dive shift. She was capable of completely submerging when her ballast tanks were filled with water. She cruised under the surface of the water, staying submerged for up to two hours. She would tow a percussion-fused bomb at the end of a rope, and passing under a ship, the bomb would make contact with the ship above. When the bomb struck the ship, it would explode. General Beauregard gave the order that *Hunley* was to remain afloat, for she had sunk several times, losing some of her crew members. After the general's order, she was fitted with a 20-foot spar which enable her to deliver the bomb or torpedo by ramming Union ships. On February 17, 1864, the *Hunley* sank the blockade-runner USS *Housatonic*. The *Hunley* went down with the *Housatonic*. Two theories exist as to why the *Hunley* was lost: (1) the spar did not disengage, holding the *Hunley* to the sinking ship or (2) the *Hunley* was damaged by the explosion of the *Housatonic* and sank.

CSS *Huntsville* An ironclad that served as a floating battery. She sank twelve miles above Mobile in the Spanish River on April 12, 1864.

CSS *Ida* A side-wheel steamer that was captured and burned by Union troops on December 10, 1864.

Ivanhoe An iron-hulled paddleboat used as a blockade-runner. When she attempted to run the blockade at Mobile Bay, Alabama, on June 30, 1864, she was fired upon by the USS *Glasgow*. The *Ivanhoe* went aground. Within a few days, a Union raiding party slipped aboard the ship and set it on fire.

CSS *Jackson* Also known as the CSS *Muscogee*. She was an ironclad ram that was burned by Union forces in April 1865 while on the Chattahoochee River.

CSS *Jamestown* Originally a passenger side-wheel steamer seized by the Confederate government in 1861 and renamed the CSS *Thomas Jefferson*. She was sunk by the Confederates at Drewry Bluffs on May 13, 1862, in an attempt to obstruct the James River. Though known as the *Thomas Jefferson*, she was and still is referred to as the *Jamestown*.

Jefferson Davis Before the war, she was known by several names, the *Putnam* and as the *Echo*, a slave transport which had been captured in August 1858 by the USS *Dolphin*. Auctioned off, she reverted to her original name, the *Putnam*. When the war broke out, she became a privateer known as the *Jeff Davis*.

CSS *John Simonds* A side-wheel steamer.

CSS *Kanawha Valley* A side-wheel steamer.

CSS *Little Rebel* A screw steamer that served as a ram. She was captured by Union forces on June 6, 1862, at Memphis, Tennessee.

CSS *Livingston* Ferryboat.

CSS *Louisiana* An ironclad. She was destroyed by her crew after the fall of New Orleans on April 28, 1862, to prevent her from falling into the hands of the Union Army.

CSS *McRae* Formerly known as the *Marquis de la Habana*, she was a converted wood steamer rigged out as a sloop-of-war. She sank on the Mississippi River on April 28, 1862.

CSS *Manassas* An armored ram whose hull projected two and a half feet above the water line. She was 143 feet long and had a beam of 33 feet. She ran aground and was burned during the Union assault on New Orleans.

CSS *Mars* A side-wheel steamer.

CSS *Mississippi* An ironclad.

CSS *Morgan* A side-wheel steamer.

CSS *Nansemond* A gunboat.

CSS *Nashville* A side-wheel steamer converted into a warship. It was discovered that her decks were too weak to hold the large guns. She was sold and became a privateer known as the *Thomas L. Wragg*. The *Wragg* was sold in November 1862 and became a blockade runner under the name of the *Rattlesnake*. Ineffective as a blockade runner, she was sold once more to the Confederate Navy. At that time, she was again called the CSS *Nashville*. She ran aground on February 27, 1863, near Fort McAllister, Georgia, and sank. Another ship, a converted side-wheel sloop 217 feet long, was christened the CSS *Nashville* in 1864, and outfitted with heavy guns. However, before she could see action, the war came to an end. This ship was renamed the USS *Nashville*.

CSS *Neuse* An ironclad ram.

CSS *North Carolina* Measuring 174.5 feet, she had a beam of 45 feet with 4 inches of iron plating. She carried a crew of 183 men and officers and was assigned to clear the Wilmington harbor of Union ships trying to enforce the blockade. She never fought a battle or fired a shot. She sank on September 27, 1864, when her decaying hull took on water.

CSS *Ohio Belle* A side-wheel steamer.

CSS *Patrick Henry* Formerly known as the *Yorktown*, the 250 foot side-wheel steamer was seized by the state of Virginia and given to the Confederate Navy. She was renamed the CSS *Patrick Henry*, outfitted with 12 guns, and iron-plated. Her captain was Captain John R. Tucker. On April 3, 1865, as Richmond fell to the Union, her crew sank her to block the river channel.

Planter A 300-ton side-wheel steamer used as a transport ship. On May 13, 1862, Robert Smalls, her pilot, turned the ship over to Union officials at Charleston Harbor. She was renamed the USS *Planter* and served as an army transport.

CSS *Prince* A side-wheel steamer.

CSS *Queen of the West* A steamer converted into a tinclad and armed with a prow. Her main purpose was to be a floating ram. She previously had been known as the USS *Queen of the West* until her capture on February 14, 1863. She was renamed the CSS *Queen of the West* an aided in the capture of the USS *Indianola* ten days later. On April 14, 1863, she was surrounded by Union gunboats and was destroyed.

CSS *Raleigh* An ironclad. On May 6, 1864, she chased the USS *Britannia* from the Cape Fear River into the open seas. The following morning, the Union ships returned and surrounded the *Raleigh*. After opening on the Union ships, she ran aground as she returned to the inlet, breaking up and eventually sinking in the river.

CSS *Rappahannock* Originally a British dispatch boat known as the *Victor*. Bought at auction in 1863, she was outfitted with eight guns and renamed the CSS *Rappahannock*. After encountering numerous mechanical problems, the ship was taken to France for repairs and when ready for the open sea, was denied permission to sail by the French government because it believed the Confederacy was on the verge of losing the war. The ship was turned over to the United States after war.

CSS *Red Rover* A side-wheel steamer.

CSS *Richmond* A 180 foot ironclad. She was destroyed on April 4, 1865, by the Confederates when the City of Richmond fell.

Robert E. Lee A blockade runner.

Ruby A blockade runner.

CSS *St. Mary* A small side-wheel steamer protected by bales of cotton on her decks. Captured by the Union in July 1863 and renamed the USS *Alexandria*. (See also USS *Alexandria*.)

St. Philip A hospital ship.

CSS *Savannah* An ironclad used for protection of the Savannah harbor. Upon the arrival of General W.T. Sherman in December 1864, she was set ablaze to prevent her capture.

CSS *Selma* An ironclad.

CSS *Shenandoah* Formerly a merchant ship known as the *Sea King,* she was converted to a commerce raider to prey on Union shipping. The ship, 220 feet long and 32.5 feet wide, was renamed the CSS *Shenandoah* and set sail on October 19, 1864, under the command of Captain James I. Waddell on a round-the-world hunting party. It would not be until August 2, 1865, before Captain Waddell discovered the war had been over for months. Afraid of being tried as a pirate, Waddell set sail for England, where he surrendered his crew and ship to the British government.

CSS *Spray* A steam powered gunboat.

CSS *Squib* A torpedo boat that attempted to destroy the USS *Minnesota* on April 9, 1864. She delivered a spar torpedo into the sides of the *Minnesota* but the Union ship remained afloat and was repaired.

CSS *Stirling Price* A side-wheel river steamer.

CSS *Stonewall* Built in France and designed as an ironclad ram, she was 171 feet long with a beam of 33 feet. Covered with 3.5 inches of iron, she had one 300-pound cannon on her bow and two 70-pound guns on her rear. Her iron prow extended twenty feet under the water line. With the war going badly for the Confederate government, France refused to let the ship to leave port and she was sold many times over the next few months. In 1864, she was purchased by Lucien Arman and renamed the *Olinde.* Arman resold the ship to the Confederate government and it was renamed the CSS *Stonewall*. Captain Thomas J. Paige assumed command of the ship, but by the time it arrived in Cuba, the war was over.

CSS *Stonewall Jackson* A cottonclad ram.

CSS *Sumter* Originally known as the *Habana,* she became a commerce raider, capturing several Union merchant ships as she cruised from the South Atlantic to South America. Sailing into Gibraltar in early 1862 for repairs, Raphael Semmes, her captain, discovered he would have to escape the harbor to avoid capture by the Union. The ship was then sold to a British merchant and renamed *Gibraltar.* This ship had a successful run as a blockade runner.

CSS *Tallahassee* A ship of many names. Originally, she was known as the *Atlanta,* a ferry that operated on the English Channel. In July1864, she was purchased by the Confederate Navy and renamed the CSS *Tallahassee* and served as a raider. After numerous cruises, she returned to Wilmington, North Carolina, where she was renamed the *Olustee.* Under that name, she cruised the New England coast, capturing Union merchant ships. She returned to Wilmington and again her name was changed to the *Chameleon.* She was then outfitted as a merchant ship. After running the Union blockade, she sailed for Bermuda to obtain supplies for the Confederacy. Unable to pass or re-enter Confederate ports, she sailed for England. There, she was seized by the British government. The United States filed suit for possession of her and she was transferred to the custody of the U.S. government on April 26, 1866. She was promptly auctioned off and purchased by Japanese merchants. She ended her career as the *Haya-Maru* on June 17, 1868, when she went down between the Kobe and Yokohama, Japan.

CSS *Tennessee* An ironclad ram.

CSS *Texas* An ironclad.

CSS *Thomas Jefferson see* CSS *Jamestown*).

CSS *Tuscaloosa* An ironclad floating battery.

CSS *United States* A wooden frigate that was at the Gosport Naval Yard in Norfolk when it was abandoned by Union forces in early 1861. She was renamed the CSS *United States,* but often called the CSS *Confederate States.* She was used as a receiving ship. (See also USS *United States.*)

CSS *Vicksburg see* CSS *City of Vicksburg*)

CSS *Victoria* A side-wheeled steamer converted into a troop transport by the Confederate government. During the Battle of Memphis, she was captured by Union forces while moored in the Memphis harbor and renamed the USS *Abraham.* (See also USS *Abraham.*)

CSS *Virginia* Formally the USS *Merrimack,* which was deliberately sunk by the Union Navy in 1861. The Confederates raised and refitted her as an ironclad ram and covered her with two inches of iron plating. She was also outfitted with a four-foot cast-iron prow. She set sail on March 8, 1862, with Captain Franklin Buchanan at the helm. Sailing out of Hampton Roads, she took on the entire Union blockading squadron, ramming many and sinking the USS *Cumberland.* Union shells seemed to bounce off her armor. The following day, she engaged the USS *Monitor* to a draw in the waters off Newport News. On May 9, 1862, the *Virginia*'s crew sank her when Norfolk was captured by Union forces, for her draft was too great to maneuver into the nearby rivers.

CSS *William H. Webb* A 190-foot side-wheel steamer converted into a ram. She was one of the fastest steamships at the time. She was sunk on April 24, 1865, by her crew after they deliberately ran her aground to prevent her capture by the USS *Richmond.*

Appendix IV. The Commanders

Abercrombie, John Joseph. U.S.A.—Brigadier General. West Point Class of 1822. Born March 4, 1798, in Baltimore, Maryland. Main duties were confined to garrison and administrative duties because of his age. Died January 3, 1897, in Long Island, New York. Buried at Woodland Cemetery, Philadelphia, Pa.

Adams, John. C.S.A.—Brigadier General. West Point Class of 1846. Born July 1, 1825, in Nashville, Tennessee. Killed during the Battle of Franklin, November 30, 1864. Buried in Pulaski, Tennessee.

Alexander, Edward Porter. C.S.A.—Brigadier General. West Point Class of 1857. Born May 26, 1835, in Washington, Georgia. Artillery commander. Died April 28, 1910, in Savannah, Georgia. Buried in City Cemetery, Augusta, Georgia.

Anderson, Richard Heron. C.S.A.—Lieutenant General. West Point Class of 1842. Born October 7, 1821, in Sumter County, South Carolina. Assumed command of the Army of Northern Virginia's First Corps upon the wounding of General Longstreet in 1864. Died June 26, 1879, in Beaufort, South Carolina. Buried at Beaufort, South Carolina.

Anderson, Robert. U.S.A.—Major General. Born June 14, 1805, near Louisville, Kentucky. West Point Class of 1825. In command of Fort Sumter when fired upon by Confederate infantry. Died October 26, 1871, in Nice, France. Buried at West Point, New York.

Ashby, Turner. C.S.A.—Brigadier General. Born October 23, 1828, at Rose Bank in Fauquier County, Va. Cavalry commander. Died June 6, 1862, a few miles south of Harrisonburg. Buried: Stonewall Cemetery, Winchester, Va.

Augur, Christopher C. U.S.A.—Major General. West Point Class of 1843. Born July 10, 1821, in Kendall, New York. In command of the Union's XXII Corps from 1863 to the end of the war. Died January 16, 1898, in Georgetown, D.C. Buried in Arlington National Cemetery.

Averell, William W. U.S.A.—Major General. Born November 5, 1832, at Cameron, New York. West Point class of 1855. Cavalry commander. Died February 3, 1900, at Bath, New York. Buried in Bath, New York.

Baker, Edward D. U.S.A.—Colonel. Born February 24, 1811, in London, England. Member of the United States Senate when he was killed at Ball's Bluff on October 21, 1861. Buried in the San Francisco National Cemetery, San Francisco, California.

Banks, Nathaniel P. U.S.A.—Major General. Born January 30, 1816, at Waltham, Massachusetts. Commander of the Red River Campaign. Died September 1, 1894, in Waltham, Massachusetts. Buried in Grove Hill Cemetery.

Barksdale, William. C.S.A.—Brigadier General. Born August 12, 1821, in Smyrna, Tennessee. Infantry commander in General Pickett's Division. Killed during the Battle of Gettysburg, July 3, 1863. Buried in Greenwood Cemetery, Jackson, Mississippi.

Barlow, Francis C. U.S.A.—Major General. Born October 19, 1834, in Brooklyn New York. Infantry commander who entered politics after the war. Died January 11, 1896, in New York City. Buried in Brookline, Massachusetts.

Barton, Seth M. C.S.A.—Brigadier General. West Point Class of 1849. Born September 8, 1829, at Fredericksburg, Virginia. Was General Jackson's engineer officer when he operated in the Shenandoah Valley. Died in Washington, D.C., on April 11, 1900. Buried in Fredericksburg, Virginia.

Bate, William. C.S.A.—Major General. Born October 7, 1826, in what is now Castalian, Tennessee. Infantry commander. Died March 9, 1905, in Washington, D.C. Buried in Mount Olivet Cemetery, Nashville, Tennessee.

Bayard, George D. U.S.A.—Brigadier General. West Point Class of 1856. Born December 18, 1835, in Seneca Falls, New York. Cavalry commander of the Union's Third Corps. Killed during the Battle of Fredericksburg, December 13, 1862. Buried in Princeton, New Jersey.

Baylor, John R. C.S.A.—Colonel. Born July 27, 1822, in Paris, Bourbon County, Kentucky. Became the military governor of the Confederate Territory of Arizona. Died February 8, 1894, at Montell, Texas. Buried in Montell, Texas.

Beauregard, Pierre G.T. C.S.A.—Major General. Born May 28, 1818, in St. Bernard Parish, Louisiana. West Point Class of 1838. Infantry commander who ordered the first shot to be fired at Fort Sumter on April 12, 1861. Died February 20, 1893. Buried at Metairie Cemetery, New Orleans, Louisiana.

Bee, Barnard E. C.S.A.—Brigadier General. West Point Class of 1845. Born February 8, 1824, at Charleston, South Carolina. Wounded during the Battle of Bull Run on July 21, 1861, and died the next day. Buried in Pendleton, South Carolina.

Bee, Hamilton P. C.S.A.—Brigadier General. Born July 22, 1822, in Charleston, South Carolina. Younger brother of Barnard Bee, served as both an infantry and cavalry commander. Died October 3, 1897, in San Antonio, Texas. Buried in the Confederate Cemetery, San Antonio, Texas.

Benham, Henry W. U.S.A.—Brigadier General. West Point Class of 1837. Born April 17, 1813, in Connecticut. Commanded the engineer brigade of the Army of the Potomac from 1863 to the end of the war. Died June 1, 1884, in New York, New York. Buried in the Congressional Cemetery, Washington, D.C.

Bidwell, Daniel D. U.S.A.—Brigadier General. Born August 12, 1819, in Buffalo, New York. During the war was assigned to the Union's VI Corps. Died at Cedar Creek, Virginia, October 19, 1864. Buried in Forest Lawn Cemetery, Buffalo, New York.

Birney, David B. U.S.A.—Major General. Born May 29, 1825, in Huntsville, Alabama. Assumed command of the Union's III Corps at Gettysburg and was selected to command the X Corps prior to his death. Died October 18, 1864, of malaria in Philadelphia. Buried in Woodlands Cemetery, Philadelphia, Pa.

Blair, Francis P., Jr. U.S.A.—Brigadier General. Born February 19, 1821, in Lexington, Kentucky. Infantry commander who led both the Union's XV Corps and the XVII Corps. Died July 8, 1875, in St. Louis. Buried in Bellefontaine Cemetery in St. Louis.

Blunt, James G. U.S.A.—Major General. Born July 21, 1826, in Trenton, Maine. A doctor who became an infantry commander assigned to the western frontier. Died July 27, 1881, in Washington, D.C. Buried in Leavenworth, Kansas.

Bohlen, Henry. U.S.A.— Brigadier General. Born October 22, 1810, in Bremen, Germany. Infantry commander. Killed during the action at Freeman's Ford on August 22, 1862. Buried in Laurel Hill Cemetery, Philadelphia, Pennsylvania.

Bowen, John S. C.S.A.— Major General. Born October 30, 1830, in Savannah, Georgia. Infantry commander. Died July 13, 1863, in Raymond, Mississippi. Buried in the Confederate Cemetery, Vicksburg, Mississippi.

Bragg, Braxton. C.S.A.— Major General. West Point Class of 1837. Born March 22, 1817, in Warrington, North Carolina. Commander of the Army of Tennessee. Died September 27, 1876, in Galveston, Texas. Buried in Mobile, Alabama.

Branch, Lawrence O. C.S.A.— Brigadier General. Born November 28, 1820, in Enfield, North Carolina. Infantry commander who was killed during the Battle of Antietam (Sharpsburg) on September 17, 1862. Buried in Raleigh, North Carolina.

Breckinridge, John C. C.S.A.— Major General. Born January 15, 1821, in Lexington, Kentucky. Infantry commander appointed secretary of war under President Jefferson Davis in February 1865. Died May 17, 1875, in Lexington. Buried in Lexington.

Brown, Egbert B. U.S.A.— Brigadier General. Born October 4, 1816, in Brownsville, New York. Commanded the District of Central Missouri in 1864. Died February 11, 1902, in West Plains, Missouri. Buried in Cuba, Missouri.

Buckner, Simon B. C.S.A.— Lieutenant General. West Point Class of 1844. Born April 1, 1823, in Hart County, Kentucky. Infantry commander who in 1864 became chief of staff to General Kirby Smith. Died January 8, 1914, near Munfordville, Kentucky. Buried in the State Cemetery at Frankford, Kentucky.

Buell, Don Carlos. U.S.A.— Major General. West Point Class of 1841. Born March 23, 1818, in Lowell, Ohio. Infantry commander in Tennessee and Kentucky until relieved of his command in 1862. Died November 19, 1898, in Paradise, Kentucky. Buried in Bellefontaine Cemetery, St. Louis, Missouri.

Burbridge, Stephen G. U.S.A.— Brigadier General. Born August 19, 1831, in Scott County, Kentucky. Infantry commander. Died on December 2, 1894, in Brooklyn, New York. Buried in Arlington National Cemetery.

Burnside, Ambrose. U.S.A.— Major General. West Point Class of 1847. Born May 23, 1824, at Liberty, Indiana. Commander of the Army of the Potomac from November 1862 until January 1863. Died September 13, 1881, at Bristol, Rhode Island. Buried at Swan Point Cemetery in Providence, Rhode Island.

Butler, Benjamin. U.S.A.— Major General. Born November 5, 1818, in Deerfield, New Hampshire. Commander of the Army of the Gulf in 1862 and appointed military governor of New Orleans. Died January 11, 1893, in Washington, D.C. Buried in family cemetery in Lowell, Massachusetts.

Butterfield, Daniel. U.S.A.— Brigadier General. Born October 31, 1831, in Utica, New York. Infantry commander who for a time was General Joseph Hooker's chief of staff. Died July 17, 1901, in Cold Spring, New York. Buried at West Point.

Cabell, William L. C.S.A.— Brigadier General. West Point Class of 1850. Born January 1, 1827, in Danville, Virginia. Cavalry commander under General Sterling Price. Died February 22, 1911, in Dallas, Texas. Buried in Greenwood Cemetery, Dallas, Texas.

Caldwell, John C. U.S.A.— Brigadier General. Born April 17, 1833, in Lowell, Vermont. Infantry commander who served as one of the honor guards accompanying the body of President Lincoln from Washington to Springfield, Illinois. Died August 31, 1912, in Calais, Maine. Buried in East Machias, Maine.

Canby, Edward R.S. U.S.A.— Major General. West Point Class of 1839. Born November 9, 1817, at Piatt's Landing, Kentucky. In command of the Department of New Mexico until ordered east, where he served as commander of the Military District of West Mississippi. Died April

11, 1873, while fighting Indians in Siskiyou County, California. Buried in Crown Hill Cemetery, Indianapolis, Indiana.

Carter, John C. C.S.A.— Brigadier General. Born December 19, 1837, in Waynesboro, Georgia. Infantry commander who was mortally wounded during the Battle of Franklin on November 30, 1864, dying December 10. Buried in Rose Hill Cemetery in Columbia, Tennessee.

Carter, Samuel P. U.S.A.— Brigadier General. Naval Academy Class of 1846. Born August 6, 1819, in Elizabethton, East Tennessee. At the start of the war was a lieutenant in the U.S. Navy until he detailed from the navy to the War Department and was assigned to the infantry. Died May 26, 1891, in Washington, D.C. Buried in Oak Hill Cemetery, Georgetown, Washington, D.C.

Chalmers, James R. C.S.A.— Brigadier General. Born January 11, 1831, in Halifax County, Virginia. Infantry commander. Died April 9, 1898, in Memphis, Tennessee. Buried in Memphis, Tennessee.

Chambliss, John R. C.S.A.— Brigadier General. West Point Class of 1853. Born January 23, 1833, in Greensville County, Virginia. Cavalry commander who was killed during the Battle of Deep Bottom (Fussell's Mill) on August 16, 1864. Buried in Emporia, Virginia.

Churchill, Thomas J. C.S.A.— Major General. Born March 10, 1824, in Jefferson County, Kentucky. Infantry commander. Died May 14, 1905, in Little Rock, Arkansas. Buried in Mount Holly Cemetery, Little Rock, Arkansas.

Clark, John B. C.S.A.— Brigadier General. Born January 14, 1831, in Fayette, Missouri. Infantry commander. Died September 7, 1903, in Washington, D.C. Buried in Rock Creek Cemetery, Washington, D.C.

Clayton, Powell. U.S.A.— Brigadier General. Born August 7, 1833, in Delaware County, Pennsylvania. Infantry commander who served mainly in Missouri and Arkansas. Died August 25, 1914, in Washington, D.C. Buried in Arlington National Cemetery.

Cleburne, Patrick R. C.S.A.— Major General. Born March 17, 1828, near Cork, Ireland. Infantry commander who was killed during the Battle of Franklin on November 30, 1864. Buried in Helena, Arkansas.

Cobb, Thomas Reade R. C.S.A.— Brigadier General. Born April 10, 1823, in Jefferson County, Georgia. Infantry commander. Killed during the Battle of Fredericksburg, December 13, 1862. Buried in Oconee Hill Cemetery, Athens, Georgia.

Cooke, Philip St. George. U.S.A.— Major General. Born June 13, 1809, in Leesburg, Virginia. Commanded a brigade of cavalry until assigned to court-martial duty. Died March 20, 1985, in Detroit, Michigan. Buried in Elmwood Cemetery.

Cooper, Douglas H. C.S.A.— Brigadier General. Born November 1, 1815, in Mississippi. Infantry commander. Died April 29, 1879, at Old Fort Washita in the Chickasaw Nation (now Bryan, Oklahoma). Buried in the fort's cemetery in an unmarked grave.

Corse, John M. U.S.A.— Brigadier General. Born April 27, 1835, in Pittsburg, Pennsylvania. Served as General Sherman's Inspector-General during the Atlanta Campaign. Died April 27, 1893, in Winchester, Massachusetts. Buried in Aspen Grove Cemetery, Burlington, Massachusetts.

Couch, Darius N. U.S.A.— Major General. West Point Class of 1846. Born July 23, 1822, in Putnam County, New York. Infantry commander. Died February 12, 1897, in Norwalk, Connecticut. Buried in Taunton, Connecticut.

Crawford, Samuel. U.S.A.— Major General. Born November 8, 1829, in Franklin County, Pennsylvania. Before the war was an assistant surgeon but served as an infantry commander during the war. Died November 3, 1892, in Philadelphia, Pennsylvania. Buried in Laurel Hill Cemetery, Philadelphia, Pennsylvania.

Crittenden, Thomas L. U.S.A.— Major General. Born May 15, 1819, in Russellville, Kentucky.

Infantry commander. Died October 23, 1893, at Annandale, Staten Island, New York. Buried in Frankfort, Kentucky.

Crook, George. U.S.A.—Major General. West Point Class of 1852. Born September 8, 1828, in Dayton, Ohio. Cavalry commander in the Army of the Cumberland under General George Thomas. Died March 21, 1890, in Chicago, Illinois. Buried in Arlington National Cemetery.

Curtis, Samuel R. U.S.A.—Brigadier General. West Point Class of 1831. Born February 3, 1805, in Clinton County, New York. Commander of the Department of the Mississippi and later the Department of Kansas. Died December 26, 1866, in Council Bluffs, Iowa. Buried in Oakland Cemetery, Keokuk, Iowa.

Custer, George A. U.S.A.—Major General. West Point Class of 1861. Born December 5, 1839, in New Rumley, Ohio. Cavalry commander. Killed during the Battle of Little Big Horn on June 25, 1876. Remains believed to be Custer were reburied at West Point.

Dahlgren, John A. U.S.A.—Admiral. Born November 14, 1809, in Philadelphia, Pennsylvania. Naval commander. Died July 12, 1870, in Washington, D.C. Buried in Laurel Hill Cemetery, Philadelphia, Pennsylvania.

Dana, Napoleon J.T. U.S.A.—Major General. West Point Class of 1842. Born April 15, 1822, in Eastport, Maine. Infantry commander. Died July 15, 1905, in Portsmouth, New Hampshire. Buried in Portsmouth, New Hampshire.

Davidson, John W. U.S.A.—Major General. West Point Class of 1845. Born August 18, 1824, in Fairfax, Virginia. He served most of his military career in the west. In 1863, he was named commander of the Army of Southwest Missouri and later the Army of Arkansas. Died June 26, 1881, in St. Paul, Minnesota. Buried in Arlington National Cemetery.

Dent, Frederick T. U.S.A.—Major General. West Point Class of 1843. Born December 17, 1820, near St. Louis, Missouri. Infantry commander. His sister was the wife of Ulysses S. Grant. Died December 23, 1892, in Denver, Colorado. Buried in Arlington National Cemetery, Washington, D.C.

Doles, George P. C.S.A.—Brigadier General. Born May 14, 1830, in Milledgeville, Georgia. Served with the infantry and was killed when shot by a sniper near the Bethesda Church during the Battle of Cold Harbor on June 2, 1864. Buried in Milledgeville, Georgia.

Doubleday, Abner. U.S.A.—Major General. West Point Class of 1842. Born June 26, 1819, in Ballston Spa, New York. Before the war was assigned to the artillery but when the war broke out, switched to the infantry. Died January 26, 1893, in Mendham, New Jersey. Buried in Arlington National Cemetery.

Dumont, Ebenezer. U.S.A.—Brigadier General. Born November 23, 1814, in Switzerland County, Indiana. Resigned from the U.S. Army on February 28, 1863, to become a U.S. Congressman. Died April 16, 1872, in Indianapolis, Indiana. Buried in Crown Cemetery in Indianapolis, Indiana.

Duncan, Johnson K. C.S.A.—Brigadier General. West Point Class of 1847. Born March 19, 1827, in York, Pennsylvania. Artillery commander until he died of fever on December 18, 1862, in Knoxville, Tennessee. Buried in McGavock Cemetery, Franklin, Tennessee.

DuPont, Henry. U.S.A.—Lieutenant Colonel. West Point Class of 1861. Born July 30, 1838. Artillery commander. Died December 31, 1926, in Delaware. Buried in DuPont Cemetery, New Castle, Delaware.

DuPont, Samuel. U.S.A.—Rear Admiral. Born 1803 in Bergen Point, New Jersey. Naval commander. Died June 23, 1865, in Philadelphia, Pennsylvania.

Early, Jubal A. C.S.A.—Lieutenant General. West Point Class of 1837. Born November 3, 1816, in Franklin County, Virginia. Infantry commander given command of Ewell's Second Corps. Died March 2, 1894, and was buried in Lynchburg, Virginia.

Echols, John. C.S.A.—Brigadier General. Born March 20, 1823, in Lynchburg, Virginia. Infantry commander. Died May 24, 1896, in Staunton, Virginia. Buried in Thornrose Cemetery, Staunton, Virginia.

Ellet, Alfred W. U.S.A.— Brigadier General. Born October 11, 1820, in Penn's Manor, Pennsylvania. With his brother, Charles, was ordered by the War Department to purchase ships for conversion into rams. Served with both the army and naval forces, especially near Vicksburg. Died January 9, 1895, in El Dorado, Kansas. Buried in El Dorado, Kansas.

Elliott, Jr., Stephen. C.S.A.— Brigadier General. Born October 26, 1830, in Beaufort, South Carolina. Artillery commander whose entire service was in South Carolina, his home state. Died February 21, 1866, in Aiken, South Carolina. Buried in the Episcopal Churchyard, Beaufort, South Carolina.

Ellsworth, Elmer Ephriam. U.S.A.— Colonial New York Fire Zouaves. Born April 11, 1837, in Malta near Saratoga Springs, New York. Died when shot on May 24, 1861, as he was taking down a Confederate flag hanging from the Marshall House Inn, Alexandria, Virginia. Buried in Mechanicville, NY.

Emory, William H. U.S.A.— Major General. West Point Class of 1831. Born September 7, 1811, in Queen Annes County, Maryland. Infantry commander. Died December 1, 1887, in Washington, D.C. Buried in the Congressional Cemetery, Washington, D.C.

Evans, Clement A. C.S.A.— Brigadier General. Born February 25, 1833, in Stewart County, Georgia. Infantry commander. Died July 2, 1911, in Atlanta, Georgia. Buried in Oakland Cemetery, Georgia.

Evans, Nathan G. "Shanks." C.S.A.— Brigadier General. West Point Class of 1848. Born February 3, 1824, in Marion, South Carolina. Infantry commander. Died November 23, 1868, in Midway, Alabama. Buried in Cokesbury, South Carolina.

Ewell, Richard Stoddert. C.S.A.— Lieutenant General. West Point Class of 1840. Born February 8, 1817, in Georgetown, Washington, D.C. Infantry commander of the Army of Northern Virginia's Second Corps. Died January 25, 1872, in Spring Hill, Tennessee. Buried in Old City Cemetery, Nashville, Tennessee.

Fagen, James F. C.S.A.— Major General. Born March 1, 1828, in Clark County, Kentucky. Infantry commander. Died September 1, 1893, in Little Rock, Arkansas. Buried in Mount Holly Cemetery, Little Rock, Arkansas.

Farragut, David. U.S.A.— Rear Admiral. Born July 5, 1801, near Campbell's Station, Tennessee. Died August 14, 1870, in Portsmouth, New Hampshire. Buried in Westchester County, New York.

Field, Charles W. C.S.A.— Major General. West Point Class of 1849. Born April 6, 1828, in Woodford County, Kentucky. Was a cavalry commander at the start of the war, but was transferred to the infantry in 1862. Died April 9, 1892, in Washington, D.C. Buried in Loudon Park Cemetery in Baltimore, Maryland.

Finegan, Joseph. C.S.A.— Brigadier General. Born November 17, 1814, in Clones, Ireland. Commander of the District of Middle and East Florida until the Battle of Olustee in February 1864. Died October 29, 1885, in Rutledge, Florida. Buried in Old City Cemetery, Jacksonville, Florida.

Floyd, John B. C.S.A.— Major General. Born June 1, 1806, in Montgomery County, Virginia. Was President James Buchanan's secretary of war. Resigned his position to become a Confederate infantry commander. Died August 26, 1863, in Abingdon, Virginia. Buried in Abingdon, Virginia.

Forrest, Nathan Bedford. C.S.A.— Lieutenant General. Born July 13, 1821, in Bedford County, Tennessee. Cavalry commander. Died October 29, 1877, in Memphis, Tennessee. Buried in Forrest Park Cemetery, Memphis, Tennessee.

Foster, John G. U.S.A.— Major General. West Point Class of 1846. Born May 27, 1823, in Whitefield, New Hampshire. Engineer before the war, became an infantry commander. Died September 2, 1874, in Nashua, New York. Buried in Nashua Cemetery, New York.

Franklin, William B. U.S.A.—Brigadier General. West Point Class 1843. Born February 27, 1823, in York, Pennsylvania. Infantry commander. Died March 8, 1903, in Hartford, Connecticut. Buried in York, Pennsylvania.

Fremont, John Charles. U.S.A.—Major General. Born January 21, 1813, in Savannah, Georgia. Assigned by Lincoln as commander of the Department of the West. Died July 13, 1890, in New York City. Buried in Rockland Cemetery, Piermont-on-the-Hudson, New York.

French, Samuel G. C.S.A.—Major General. West Point Class of 1843. Born November 22, 1818, in Gloucester, New Jersey. Artillery and infantry commander. Died April 20, 1910, in Florala, Florida. Buried in St. John's Cemetery, Pensacola, Florida.

French, William H. U.S.A.—Major General. West Point Class of 1837. Born January 13, 1815, in Baltimore, Maryland. Briefly commanded the Union's III Corps after General Sickles was wounded at Gettysburg. Died May 20, 1881, in Washington, D.C. Buried in Rock Creek Cemetery, Washington, D.C.

Gano, Richard M. C.S.A.—Brigadier General. Born June 17, 1830, in Bourbon County, Kentucky. Cavalry and artillery commander. Died March 27, 1913, in Dallas, Texas. Buried in Dallas, Texas.

Gardner, Franklin. C.S.A.—Major General. West Point Class of 1843. Born January 29, 1823, in New York, New York. Commanded the District of Middle Florida until 1864. Died April 29, 1873, near Lafayette, Louisiana. Buried in St. John's Episcopal Church Cemetery, Lafayette, Louisiana.

Garfield, James A. U.S.A.—Major General. Born November 19, 1831, in Cuyahoga County, Ohio. Infantry commander. Garfield, elected president of the United States in 1881, was shot by Charles J. Guiteau in Washington, D.C., on July 2, 1881. Died September 19, 1881, in Elberon, New Jersey, of the assassin's bullet.

Garland, Samuel. C.S.A.—Brigadier General. Virginia Military Institute Class of 1849. Born December 16, 1830, in Lynchburg, Virginia. Infantry commander who was killed during the Battle of South Mountain on September 14, 1862. Buried in Lynchburg, Virginia.

Garnett, Richard Brooke. C.S.A.—Brigadier General. West Point Class of 1841. Born November 21, 1817, in Essex County, Virginia. Infantry commander. Killed during the Battle of Gettysburg on July 3, 1863 (body not recovered). Has a memorial in Hollywood Cemetery for Gettysburg unknown dead, Richmond, Virginia.

Garnett, Robert Selden. C.S.A.—Brigadier General. West Point Class of 1841. Born December 16, 1819, in Essex County, Virginia. Infantry commander. Died July 13, 1861. Buried in Green Wood Cemetery in Brooklyn, New York.

Geary, John. U.S.A.—Major General. Born December 30, 1819, at Mount Pleasant, Pennsylvania. Infantry commander. Died February 8, 1873, in Harrisburg, Pennsylvania. Buried in Mount Kalma Cemetery in Harrisburg, Pennsylvania.

Gibbon, John. U.S.A.—Major General. West Point Class of 1847. Born April 20, 1827, in Philadelphia, Pennsylvania. Commander of the Union's II Corps after the wounding of General Hancock and named commander of the Union's XXIV Corps, Army of the James in 1865. Died February 6, 1896, in Baltimore, Maryland. Buried in Arlington National Cemetery, Washington, D.C.

Gillem, Alvan C. U.S.A.—Brigadier General. West Point Class of 1851. Born July 29, 1830, in Gainesboro, Tennessee. Named as adjutant governor of Tennessee in June 1863. Died December 2, 1875, near Nashville, Tennessee. Buried in Mount Olivet Cemetery, Nashville, Tennessee.

Gillmore, Quincy A. U.S.A.—Major General. West Point Class of 1849. Born February 28, 1825, in Lorain, Ohio. Was an engineer instructor at West Point prior to the war and during the war served as commander of the Union's X Corps. Died April 7, 1888, in Brooklyn, New York. Buried at West Point.

Gist, States Right. C.S.A.— Brigadier General. Born September 3, 1831, in Union District, South Carolina. Infantry commander killed in the Battle of Franklin, November 30, 1864. Buried in Trinity Episcopal Churchyard, Columbia, South Carolina.

Gordon, John Brown. C.S.A.— Major General. Born February 6, 1832, in Upson County, Georgia. Infantry commander. Died January 9, 1904, in Miami, Florida. Buried in Oakland Cemetery, Atlanta, Georgia.

Granbury, Hirem. C.S.A.— Brigadier General. Born March 1, 1831, in Copiah County, Mississippi. Infantry commander. Killed during the Battle of Franklin on November 30, 1864. Buried in Granbury, Texas.

Granger, Gordon. U.S.A.— Major General. West Point Class of 1845. Born November 6, 1822, in Joy, New York. Originally with the cavalry, he became commander of the Union's IV Corps during the Battle of Chattanooga. Died January 10, 1876, in Lexington, Kentucky. Buried in Lexington, Kentucky.

Granger, Robert S. U.S.A.— Major General. West Point Class of 1838. Born May 24, 1816, in Zanesville, Ohio. Assigned to garrison duty in Kentucky, Tennessee and North Alabama. Died April 25, 1894, in Washington, D.C. Buried in Zanesville, Ohio.

Grant, Ulysses Simpson (Real name Hiram Ulysses Grant). U.S.A.— Lieutenant General. West Point Class of 1843. Born April 27, 1822, in Point Pleasant, Ohio. Named commander of the Union Army in March 1864. Served two terms as president of the United States. Died July 23, 1885, in Mount McGregor, New York. Buried in a mausoleum on Riverside Drive (Grant's Tomb), New York City, New York.

Green, Martin E. C.S.A.— Brigadier General. Born June 3, 1815, in Fauquier County, Virginia. Infantry commander. Died June 27, 1863, after being shot in the head during the Siege of Vicksburg. According to reports he was buried in a private lot in Vicksburg's city cemetery, but the exact location of his remains are unknown now.

Green, Thomas. C.S.A.— Brigadier General. Born January 8, 1814, in Amelia County, Virginia. Cavalry commander. Killed April 12, 1864, during the battle of Blair's Landing, Louisiana. Buried in Oakwood Cemetery, Austin, Texas.

Gregg, David M. U.S.A.— Brigadier General. West Point Class of 1855. Born April 10, 1833, in Huntingdon, Pennsylvania. Cavalry commander. Died August 7, 1916, in Reading, Pennsylvania. Buried in the Charles Evans Cemetery, Reading, Pennsylvania.

Gregg, John. C.S.A.— Brigadier General. Born September 28, 1828, in Lawrence County, Alabama. Infantry commander. Killed during the skirmish known as Derbytown Road (Johnson Farm), Virginia on October 7, 1864. Buried in Aberdeen, Mississippi.

Gregg, Maxcy. C.S.A.— Brigadier General. Born August 1, 1814, in Columbia, South Carolina. Infantry commander. Killed during the Battle of Fredericksburg, December 13, 1862. Buried in Columbia, South Carolina.

Grover, Cuvier. U.S.A.— Brigadier General. West Point Class of 1850. Born July 29, 1828, in Bethel, Maine. Infantry commander. Died June 6, 1885, in Atlanta, Georgia. Buried at West Point.

Hagood, Johnson. C.S.A.— Brigadier General. South Carolina Military Academy Class of 1847. Born February 21, 1829, at Barnwell, South Carolina. Infantry commander. Died January 4, 1898, in Columbia, South Carolina. Buried in Episcopal Churchyard, Barnwell, South Carolina.

Halleck, Henry W. U.S.A.— Major General (General-in-Chief, Chief of Staff). West Point Class of 1839. Born January 16, 1815, in Westernville, New York. Died January 9, 1872, in Louisville, Kentucky. Buried in Green Wood Cemetery, Brooklyn, New York.

Hampton, Wade. C.S.A.— Lieutenant General. Born March 28, 1818, in Charleston, South Carolina. Originally assigned to the infantry, became a cavalry commander in 1862. Died April 11, 1902, in Columbia, South Carolina. Buried in Columbia, South Carolina.

Hancock, Winfield Scott. U.S.A.—Major General. West Point Class of 1844. Born February 14, 1824, in Montgomery Square, Pennsylvania. Infantry commander of Union's Second Corps during the Battle of Gettysburg. Died February 9, 1886, at Governors Island. Buried in Montgomery Cemetery, Norristown, Pennsylvania.

Hardee, William J. C.S.A.—Lieutenant General. West Point Class of 1838. Born October 12, 1815, in Camden County, Georgia. Infantry commander. Died November 6, 1873, at Wytheville, Virginia. Buried in Selma, Alabama.

Harding, Abner C. U.S.A.—Brigadier General. Born February 10, 1807, in East Hampton, Connecticut. Infantry commander. Died July 19, 1874, Monmouth, Illinois. Buried in Monmouth, Illinois.

Hatch, Edward. U.S.A.—Major General. Born December 22, 1832, in Bangor, Maine. Cavalry commander. Died April 11, 1889, in Fort Robinson, Nebraska. Buried in National Cemetery, Fort Leavenworth, Kansas.

Hazen, William B. U.S.A.—Major General. West Point Class of 1855. Born September 27, 1830, in West Hartford, Vermont. Infantry commander. Died January 16, 1887, in Washington, D.C. Buried in Arlington National Cemetery.

Hebert, Louis. C.S.A.—Brigadier General. Born March 13, 1820, in Iberville Parish, Louisiana. Infantry commander and commander of the Department of Texas. Died January 7, 1901, in Iberville Parish, Louisiana. Buried in Breaux Bridge, Louisiana.

Heintzelman, Samuel P. U.S.A.—Major General. West Point Class of 1826. Born September 30, 1805, in Manheim, Pennsylvania. Infantry commander. Died May 1, 1880, in Washington, D.C. Buried in Forest Lawn Cemetery, Buffalo, New York.

Herron, Francis J. U.S.A.—Major General. Born February 17, 1837, in Pittsburgh, Pennsylvania. Infantry commander who assumed command of the Union's XIII Corps. Died January 8, 1902, New York, New York. Buried in Calvary Cemetery, Long Island, New York.

Heth, Henry. C.S.A.—Major General. West Point Class of 1847. Born December 16, 1825, in Chesterfield County, Virginia. Infantry commander. Died September 27, 1899, in Washington, D.C. Buried in Hollywood Cemetery, Richmond, Virginia.

Hill, Ambrose Powell. C.S.A.—Lieutenant General. West Point Class of 1847. Born November 9, 1825, in Culpeper, Virginia. Infantry commander, in command of the Army of Northern Virginia's Third Corps. Killed during the Petersburg Siege on April 2, 1865. Buried under a monument to him at the intersection of Laburum and Hermitage Road in Richmond, Virginia.

Hill, Daniel Harvey. C.S.A.—Lieutenant General. West Point Class of 1842. Born July 12, 1821. Infantry commander. Died September 24, 1889. Buried at Davidson College, Davidson, North Carolina.

Hindman, Thomas C. C.S.A.—Brigadier General. Born January 28, 1828, in Knoxville, Tennessee. Infantry commander. Died September 28, 1868, by an assassin's bullet in Helena, Arkansas. Buried in Maple Hill Cemetery, Helena, Arkansas.

Hobson, Edward H. U.S.A.—Brigadier General. Born July 11, 1825, in Greensburg, Kentucky. Infantry commander. Died September 14, 1901, in Cleveland, Ohio. Buried in family cemetery in Greensburg, Kentucky.

Hodge, George B. C.S.A.—Brigadier General. Born April 8, 1828, in Fleming County, Kentucky. Commanded a cavalry brigade under Joseph Wheeler. Died August 1, 1892, in Longwood, Orange County, Florida. Buried in Newport, Kentucky.

Hoke, Robert F. C.S.A.—Major General. Born May 27, 1837, in Lincolnton, North Carolina. Infantry commander. Died July 3, 1912, in Raleigh, North Carolina. Buried in Raleigh.

Holmes, Theophilus H. C.S.A.—Lieutenant General. West Point Class of 1829. Born November 13, 1804, in Sampson County, North Carolina. Infantry commander. Died June 21, 1880, near Fayetteville, North Carolina. Buried in Fayetteville, North Carolina.

Hood, John Bell. C.S.A.—Lieutenant General. West Point Class of 1853. Born June 1, 1831, in Owingsville, Kentucky. Was an infantry commander and served as a corps commander under General Joseph Johnston. Died August 30, 1879, in New Orleans, Louisiana. Buried in Metairie Cemetery in New Orleans.

Hooker, Joseph. U.S.A.—Major General. West Point Class of 1837. Born November 13, 1814, in Hadley, Massachusetts. Named commander of the Army of the Potomac in January 1863 and relieved of his command after the Battle of Chancellorsville. Died October 31, 1879, in Garden City, New York. Buried in Cincinnati, Ohio.

Howard, Otis O. U.S.A.—Major General. West Point Class of 1854. Born November 8, 1830, in Leeds, Maine. Assumed command of the Union's XI Corps. Died October 26, 1909, in Burlington, Vermont. Buried in Lake View Cemetery, Burlington, Vermont.

Huger, Benjamin. C.S.A.—Brigadier General. West Point Class of 1825. Born November 22, 1805, in Charleston, South Carolina. Artillery and chief ordnance officer with the Trans-Mississippi Department. Died December 7, 1877, in Charleston, South Carolina. Buried in Green Mount Cemetery, Baltimore, Maryland.

Humphries, Andrew W. U.S.A.—Major General. West Point Class of 1831. Born November 2, 1810, in Philadelphia, Pennsylvania. Served as chief of staff for General George G. Meade. Died December 27, 1883, in Washington, D.C. Buried in the Congressional Cemetery, Washington, D.C.

Hunt, Henry J. U.S.A.—Major General. West Point Class of 1839. Born September 14, 1819, in Detroit, Michigan. Artillery commander for the Army of the Potomac. Died February 11, 1889, in Washington, D.C. Buried in the Soldier's Home Cemetery, Washington, D.C.

Hunter, David. U.S.A.—Major General. West Point Class of 1822. Born July 21, 1802, in Washington, D.C. Infantry commander. Died February 2, 1886, in Washington, D.C. Buried in Princeton, New Jersey.

Imboden, John D. C.S.A.—Brigadier General. Born January 16, 1823, near Staunton, Virginia. Entered the war as an artillery officer. Died August 15, 1895, in Damascus, Virginia. Buried in Hollywood Cemetery, Richmond, Virginia.

Jackson, Alfred E. C.S.A.—Brigadier General. Born January 11, 1807, in Davidson County, Tennessee. Infantry commander. Died October 30, 1889, in Jonesborough, Tennessee. Buried in Jonesborough, Tennessee.

Jackson, Claiborne. C.S.A.—Governor of Missouri. Born April 4, 1806, in Kentucky. Died December 6, 1862, of stomach cancer in Little Rock, Arkansas.

Jackson, Conrad J. U.S.A.—Brigadier General. Born September 11, 1813, in Berks County, Pennsylvania. Infantry commander who was killed during the Battle of Fredericksburg, on December 13, 1862. Buried in Allegheny Cemetery, Pittsburgh, Pennsylvania.

Jackson, Henry R. C.S.A.—Major General. Born June 24, 1820. Infantry commander. Died May 23, 1898, in Savannah, Georgia. Buried in Bonaventure Cemetery, Savannah, Georgia.

Jackson, Thomas "Stonewall." C.S.A.—Lieutenant General. West Point Class of 1846. Born January 21, 1824, in what is now Clarksburg, West Virginia. Commander of General Lee's Second Corps until his death. Died after the Battle of Chancellorsville on May 10, 1863. Buried in Jackson Cemetery at Lexington, Va.

Jackson, William H. C.S.A.—Major General. Born October 1, 1835, in Paris, Tennessee. Cavalry commander. Died March 30, 1903, at "Belle Meade," Nashville, Tennessee. Buried in Mount Olivet Cemetery, Nashville, Tennessee.

Jenkins, Albert G. C.S.A.—Brigadier General. Born November 10, 1830, in what is now Cabell County, West Virginia. Cavalry commander. Died May 21, 1864, from wounds received on May 9, 1864, during the skirmish at Cloyd's Mountain. Buried in Spring Hill Cemetery, Huntington, West Virginia.

Johnson, Bradley. C.S.A.—Brigadier General. Born September 29, 1928, in Frederick, Maryland. Infantry commander instrumental in the burning of Chambersburg, Pennsylvania, in 1864. Died October 5, 1903, in Amelia, Virginia. Buried in Loudon Park Cemetery, Baltimore, Maryland.

Johnson, Bushrod R. C.S.A.— Major General. West Point Class of 1840. Born October 7, 1817, in Belmont County, Ohio. An engineer who became an infantry commander. Died September 12, 1880, near Brighton, Illinois. Buried in City Cemetery, Nashville, Tennessee.

Johnson, Edward. C.S.A.— Major General. West Point Class of 1838. Born April 16, 1816, in Salisbury, Chesterfield County, Virginia. Infantry commander. Died March 2, 1873, in Richmond. Buried in Hollywood Cemetery, Richmond, Virginia.

Johnston, Albert S. C.S.A.— Full General. West Point Class of 1826. Born February 2, 1803, in Washington, Kentucky. In command of the troops west of the Alleghenies. He was mortally wounded during the Battle of Shiloh on April 6, 1862. Buried in the State Cemetery, Austin, Texas.

Johnston, Joseph Eggleston. C.S.A.— Lieutenant General. West Point Class of 1825. Born February 3, 1807, in Farmville, Va. Commander of the Army of Tennessee. Died March 21, 1891. Buried at Green Mount Cemetery, Baltimore, Maryland.

Jones, William E. "Grumble." C.S.A.— Brigadier General. West Point Class of 1848. Born May 9, 1824, in Washington County, Virginia. Cavalry commander. Killed during the Battle of Staunton (Piedmont) on June 5, 1864. Buried in Old Glade Spring Presbyterian Church Cemetery, Glade Springs, Virginia.

Kautz, August V. U.S.A.— Major General. West Point Class of 1852. Born January 5, 1828, near Baden, Germany. Cavalry commander. Died September 4, 1895, in Seattle, Washington. Buried in Arlington National Cemetery.

Kearny, Philip. U.S.A.— Major General. Born June 2, 1815, in New York, New York. Infantry commander. Killed during the Battle of Chantilly on July 4, 1862. Buried in Arlington National Cemetery.

Kelly, Benjamin F. U.S.A.— Major General. Born April 10, 1807, in New Hampton, New Hampshire. Infantry commander. Died July 16, 1891, in Oakland, Maryland. Buried in Arlington National Cemetery.

Kershaw, Joseph B. C.S.A.— Major General. Born January 5, 1822, in Camden, South Carolina. Infantry commander. Died April 13, 1894, in Camden, South Carolina. Buried in the Quaker Cemetery, Camden, South Carolina.

Keyes, Eramus D. U.S.A.— Major General. West Point Class of 1832. Born May 29, 1810, Brimfield, Massachusetts. Infantry commander. Died October 14, 1895, in Nice, France. Buried at West Point.

Kilpatrick, Hugh Judson. U.S.A.— Major General. West Point Class of May 1861. Born January 14, 1836, near Deckertown, New Jersey. Cavalry commander. Died December 4, 1881, in Santiago, Chili. Buried at West Point.

Kimball, Nathan. U.S.A.— Major General. Born November 22, 1822, in Fredericksburg, Indiana. Infantry commander. Died January 21, 1898, in Ogden, Utah. Buried in Weber, Iowa.

Lander, Frederick W. U.S.A.— Brigadier General. Born December 17, 1821, in Salem, Massachusetts. Infantry commander who died March 2, 1862, of illness while at Camp Chase, Virginia. Buried in Broad Street Burial Ground, Salem, Massachusetts.

Lee, Fitzhugh. C.S.A.— Major General. West Point Class of 1856. Born November 19, 1835, in Fairfax County, Virginia. Cavalry commander. Died April 28, 1905, in Washington, D.C. Buried in Hollywood Cemetery, Richmond, Virginia.

Lee, Robert Edward. C.S.A.— General. West Point Class of 1825. Born January 19, 1807, at Stratford, Va. Commander of the Army of Northern Virginia and named commander of the Army in 1865. Died October 12, 1870, in Lexington, Virginia. Buried at Lee Chapel at Washington and Lee University, Lexington, Va.

Lee, Stephen Dill. C.S.A.—Lieutenant General. West Point Class of 1854. Born September 22, 1833, in Charleston, South Carolina. Artillery commander. Died May 28, 1908, in Vicksburg, Mississippi. Buried in Columbus, Mississippi.

Lee, William H. "Rooney." C.S.A.—Major General. Born May 31, 1837, in the Custis Home in Arlington, Virginia. Cavalry commander. Died October 15, 1891, in Alexandria, Virginia. Buried in the Lee Chapel, Washington and Lee University, Lexington, Virginia.

Logan, John A. U.S.A.—Major General. Born February 9, 1826, in Jackson County, Illinois. Infantry commander. Died December 26, 1886, in Washington, D.C. Buried in Soldier's Home National Cemetery, Washington, D.C.

Longstreet, James. C.S.A.—Lieutenant General. West Point Class of 1842. Born January 21, 1821, in the Edgefield District, South Carolina. Commander of Lee's First Corps. Died January 2, 1904, in Gainesville, Georgia. Buried in Alta Vista Cemetery, Gainesville, Georgia.

Loring, William W. C.S.A.—Major General. Born December 4, 1818, in Wilmington, North Carolina. Infantry commander. Died December 30, 1886, in New York, New York. Buried in St. Augustine, Florida.

Lynde, Isaac. U.S.A.—Major. Born July 27, 1804, in Williamstown, Vermont. Commander of the Mounted Infantry. Died April 10, 1886, in Picolata, Florida.

Lyon, Hylan Benton. C.S.A.—Brigadier General. West Point Class of 1856. Born February 22, 1836, in Caldwell, Kentucky. Cavalry commander. Died April 25, 1907. Buried in Eddyville, Kentucky.

Lyon, Nathaniel. U.S.A.—Brigadier General. West Point Class of 1841. Born July 14, 1818, Ashford, Connecticut. Infantry commander who was killed during the Battle of Wilson Creek, Missouri, on August 10, 1861. Buried in a cemetery in Eastford, Connecticut.

McCausland, John. C.S.A.—Brigadier General. Virginia Military Institute Class of 1857. Born September 13, 1836, in St. Louis, Missouri. Infantry commander who operated in the Shenandoah Valley. Died January 27, 1927, in Mason County, West Virginia. Buried in Henderson, West Virginia.

McClellan, George B. U.S.A.—Major General. West Point Class of 1846. Born December 3, 1826, in Philadelphia, Pennsylvania. Placed in command of the Army of the Potomac until relieved on November 7, 1862. Died October 29, 1885, in Orange, New Jersey. Buried Riverview Cemetery, Trenton, New Jersey.

McClernand, John A. U.S.A.—Major General. Born May 30, 1812, in Hardinsburg, Kentucky. Commanded the Union's XIII Corps during the Vicksburg Campaign. Died September 20, 1890, in Springfield, Illinois. Buried in Springfield, Illinois.

McCook, Alexander M. U.S.A.—Major General. West Point Class of 1852. Born April 22, 1831, in Columbiana County, Ohio. Infantry commander. Died June 12, 1903, in Dayton, Ohio. Buried in Cincinnati, Ohio.

McCook, Edward M. U.S.A.—Brigadier General. Born June 15, 1833, in Steubenville, Ohio. Infantry commander. Died September 9, 1909, in Chicago, Illinois. Buried in Union Cemetery, Steubenville, Ohio.

McCulloch, Henry E. C.S.A.—Brigadier General. Born December 6, 1816, in Rutherford County, Tennessee. Brother of Ben McCulloch. Served mostly in Texas as part of the Texas Mounted Riflemen. Died March 12, 1895, in Rockport, Texas. Buried in Seguin, Texas.

McCullock, Ben. C.S.A.—Brigadier General. Born November 11, 1811, in Rutherford County, Tennessee. Infantry commander. Killed during the Battle of Pea Ridge (Elkhorn Tavern) on March 7, 1862. Buried in the State Cemetery, Austin, Texas.

McDowell, Irvin. U.S.A.—Major General. West Point Class of 1838. Born October 15, 1818, in Columbus, Ohio. Corps commander under General John Pope. Died May 4, 1885, in San Francisco, California. Buried at the Presidio, California.

McIntosh, James M. C.S.A.—Brigadier General. West Point Class of 1849. Born in 1828 in Fort

Brooke, Florida, the older brother of John McIntosh. Cavalry commander. Killed during the Battle of Pea Ridge (Elkhorn Tavern) on March 7, 1862. Buried in the State Cemetery, Austin, Texas.

McIntosh, John B. U.S.A.— Major General. Born June 6, 1829, at Fort Brooke, Florida, the younger brother of James McIntosh. Cavalry commander. Died June 29, 1888, in New Brunswick, New Jersey. Buried in Elmwood Cemetery, New Brunswick, New Jersey.

McLaws, Lafayette. C.S.A.— Major General. West Point Class of 1842. Born January 15, 1821, in Augusta, Georgia. Infantry commander. Died July 24, 1897, in Savannah, Georgia. Buried in Savannah, Georgia.

McNeil, John. U.S.A.— Brigadier General. Born February 14, 1813, in Halifax, Nova Scotia. Infantry commander. Died June 8, 1891, in St. Louis, Missouri. Buried in Bellefontaine Cemetery, St. Louis, Missouri.

McPherson, James Birdseye. U.S.A.— Major General. West Point Class of 1853. Born November 14, 1828, near Clyde, Ohio. Commander of the Union's XVII Corps, was killed July 22, 1864, during the Battle of Snake Creek Gap, during the Battle for Atlanta, Georgia. Buried in a family orchard near Clyde, Ohio.

Mackall, William W. C.S.A.— Brigadier General. West Point Class of 1837. Born January 18, 1817. Named as chief of staff to General Joseph Johnston. Died August 12, 1891, Fairfax, Virginia. Buried on private land near McLean, Virginia.

Magruder, John Bankhead. C.S.A.— Brigadier General. West Point Class of 1830. Born May 1, 1807, in Port Royal, Virginia. Known as "Prince John." Infantry commander. Died February 18, 1871. Buried in Galveston, Texas.

Mahone, William. C.S.A.— Major General. Virginia Military Institute Class of 1847. Born December 1, 1826, in Southampton County, Virginia. Infantry commander. Died October 8, 1895, in Washington, D.C. Buried in Blandford Cemetery, Petersburg, Virginia.

Major, James P. C.S.A.— Brigadier General. West Point Class of 1856. Born May 14, 1836. Cavalry commander. Died May 7, 1877, in Austin, Texas. Buried in Donaldson, Louisiana.

Marmaduke, John Sappington. C.S.A.— Major General. West Point Class of 1857. Born March 14, 1833, in Arrow Rock, Missouri. Cavalry commander. Died December 28, 1887. Buried at Jefferson City, Missouri.

Marshall, Humphrey. C.S.A.— Brigadier General. Born January 13, 1812, in Frankfort, Kentucky. Infantry commander. Died March 28, 1872, in Louisville, Kentucky. Buried in the State Cemetery, Frankfort, Kentucky.

Martin, William T. C.S.A.— Major General. Born March 25, 1823, in Glasgow, Kentucky. Infantry commander. Died March 10, 1910, near Natchez, Mississippi. Buried in the City Cemetery, Natchez, Mississippi.

Maxey, Samuel B. C.S.A.— Major General. West Point Class of 1846. Born March 30, 1825, in Tompkinsville, Kentucky. Infantry commander. Died August 16, 1895, in Eureka Springs, Arkansas. Buried in Paris, Texas.

Meade, George G. U.S.A.— Major General. West Point Class of 1835. Born December 31, 1815, in Cadiz, Spain. Placed in command of the Army of the Potomac in June 1863 and served in that position until the end of the war. Died November 6, 1872, in Philadelphia. Buried in Laurel Hill Cemetery, Philadelphia, Pennsylvania.

Meagher, Thomas F. U.S.A.— Brigadier General. Born August 3, 1823, in Waterford, Ireland. Infantry commander. Died July 1, 1867, as he fell overboard from the deck of a steamboat in Benton, Montana. His body was never recovered.

Merritt, Wesley. U.S.A.— Major General. West Point Class of 1860. Born June 16, 1834, in New York, New York. Cavalry commander. Died December 3, 1910, at Natural Bridge, Virginia. Buried at West Point.

Miles, Nelson A. U.S.A.— Brigadier General. Born August 8, 1839, at Westminster, Massachusetts. Infantry commander. Died May 15, 1925, in Washington, D.C. Buried in Arlington National Cemetery.

Milroy, Robert H. U.S.A.— Brigadier General. Born June 11, 1816, in Salem, Indiana. Infantry commander. Died March 29, 1890, in Olympia, Washington. Buried in the Masonic Cemetery, Olympia, Washington.

Morgan, John Hunt. C.S.A.— Brigadier General. Born June 1, 1825, in Huntsville, Alabama. Cavalry commander. Killed in Greensville, Tennessee, on September 3, 1864, as he tried to elude Union forces. Buried in Lexington, Kentucky.

Moulton, Alfred (Jean Jacques Alfred). C.S.A.— Brigadier General. West Point Class of 1850. Born February 18, 1829, in Opelousas, Louisiana. Infantry commander who was killed during the Battle of Sabine Crossroads (Mansfield) on April 8, 1864. Buried in Lafayette, Louisiana.

Mower, Joseph A. U.S.A.— Brigadier General. Born August 22, 1827, in Woodstock, Vermont. Corps commander. Died January 6, 1870, in New Orleans, Louisiana. Buried in Arlington National Cemetery.

Nelson, William. U.S.A.— Major General. Born September 27, 1824, in Maysville, Kentucky. Infantry commander who was killed in a duel on September 29, 1862, when shot by Union General Jefferson C. Davis. Buried in Maysville, Kentucky.

Newton, John. U.S.A.— Major General. West Point Class of 1842. Born August 25, 1822, in Norfolk, Virginia. Infantry commander. Died May 1, 1895, in New York, New York. Buried at West Point.

Ord, Edward O.C. U.S.A.— Major General. West Point Class of 1839. Born October 18, 1818, in Cumberland, Maryland. Corps commander. Died July 22, 1883, in Havana, Cuba. Buried in Arlington National Cemetery.

Palmer, Innis N. U.S.A.— Brigadier General. West Point Class of 1846. Born March 30, 1824, in Buffalo, New York. Served both as a cavalry commander and an infantry commander. Died September 9, 1900, in Chevy Chase, Maryland. Buried at Arlington National Cemetery.

Parke, John G. U.S.A.— Major General. West Point Class of 1849. Born September 22, 1827, in Coatesville, Pennsylvania. An engineer assigned to the Corps of Topographical Engineers. Died December 16, 1900, in Washington, D.C. Buried in the churchyard of St. James the Less, Philadelphia, Pennsylvania.

Patterson, Robert. U.S.A.— Major General. Born January 12, 1792, in Cappagh County, Ireland. Oldest soldier in the Union army, mustered out on July 27, 1861. Died August 7, 1881, in Philadelphia, Pennsylvania.

Peck, John J. U.S.A.— Major General. West Point Class of 1843. Born January 4, 1821, in Manlius, New York. Infantry commander. Died April 21, 1878, Syracuse, New York. Buried in Oakwood Cemetery, Syracuse, New York.

Pegram, John. C.S.A.— Brigadier General. West Point Class of 1854. Born January 24, 1832, in Petersburg, Va. Assigned to the infantry, he served as chief-of-staff for General Kirby Smith. Also served as a cavalry commander under General Forrest and later as infantry commander in the Army of Northern Virginia. Died February 6, 1865, when struck with a Minie ball near Hatcher's Run. Buried in Hollywood Cemetery, Richmond, Va.

Pelham, John. C.S.A.— Colonel. Resigned from West Point in 1861. Born September 7, 1838, near Alexandria, Alabama. Artillery commander who was killed during the Battle of Kelly's Ford on March 17, 1863. Buried in Calhoun County, Alabama.

Pemberton, John C. C.S.A.— Lieutenant General. West Point Class of 1837. Born August 10, 1814, in Philadelphia, Pennsylvania. Commander of the Department of Mississippi and Eastern Louisiana. Died July 13, 1881, in Penllyn, Pennsylvania. Buried in Philadelphia, Pennsylvania.

Pendleton, William N. C.S.A.—Brigadier General. West Point Class of 1830. Born December 26, 1809, in Richmond, Virginia. The Army of Northern Virginia's artillery chief. Died January 15, 1883, in Lexington, Virginia. Buried in Jackson Cemetery, Lexington, Virginia.

Perrin, Abner. C.S.A.—Brigadier General. Born February 2, 1827, in Edgefield District, South Carolina. Infantry commander. Killed during the Battle of Spotsylvania on May 12, 1864. Buried in City Cemetery in Fredericksburg, Virginia.

Pickett, George E. C.S.A.—Major General. West Point Class of 1846. Born January 28, 1825, in Richmond, Virginia. Infantry commander. Died July 30, 1875, in Norfolk. Buried in Hollywood Cemetery, Richmond, Virginia.

Pillow, Gideon Johnson. C.S.A.—Major General. Born June 8, 1806, in Williamson County, Tennessee. Infantry commander. Died October 8, 1878, near Helena, Arkansas. Buried in Memphis, Tennessee.

Pleasonton, Alfred. U.S.A.—Major General. West Point Class of 1840. Born July 7, 1824, in Washington, D.C. Cavalry commander. Died February 17, 1897, in Washington, D.C. Buried in the Congressional Cemetery, Washington, D.C.

Polk, Leonidas. C.S.A.—Lieutenant General. West Point Class of 1827. Born April 10, 1806, in Raleigh, North Carolina. Infantry commander. He was killed after being hit by a Union artillery shell while watching the Union artillery from a position atop Pine Mountain, near Marietta, Georgia, on June 14, 1864. Buried in Christ Church Cathedral in New Orleans, Louisiana.

Pope, John. U.S.A.—Major General. West Point Class of 1842. Born March 16, 1822, in Louisville, Kentucky. Union corps commander. Died September 23, 1892, in Sandusky, Ohio. Buried in Bellefontaine Cemetery, St. Louis, Missouri.

Porter, David D. U.S.A.—Full Admiral, U.S. Navy. Born June 8, 1813, in Chester, Pennsylvania. Naval commander. Died February 13, 1891, in Washington, D.C. Buried in Arlington National Cemetery.

Porter, Fitz John. U.S.A.—Major General. West Point Class of 1845. Born August 31, 1822, in Portsmouth, New Hampshire. Infantry commander. Died May 21, 1901, in Morristown, New Jersey. Buried in Green Wood Cemetery, Brooklyn, New York.

Prentiss, Benjamin M. U.S.A.—Brigadier General. Born November 23, 1819, in Belleville, Virginia (now West Virginia). Infantry commander. Died February 8, 1901, in Bethany, Missouri. Buried in Miriam Cemetery, Bethany, Missouri.

Price, Sterling. C.S.A.—Major General. Born September 20, 1809, in Prince Edward County, Virginia. Infantry commander who led raids through Missouri. Died September 29, 1867, in St. Louis, Missouri. Buried in Bellefontaine Cemetery, St. Louis, Missouri.

Quantrill, William C. C.S.A.—Guerrilla. Born in 1837 in Canal Dover, Ohio. Shot by Union troops while he was making a raid in Taylorsville, Kentucky, on May 10, 1865. Died as a result of those wounds on June 6, 1865.

Rains, James Edward. C.S.A.—Brigadier General. Born April 10, 1833, in Nashville, Tennessee. Infantry commander. Killed on December 31, 1862, during the Battle of Stone River (3rd Battle of Murfreesboro). Buried in Mt. Olivet Cemetery, Nashville, Tennessee.

Ramseur, Stephen D. C.S.A.—Major General. West Point Class of 1860. Born May 31, 1837, in Lincolnton, North Carolina. Infantry commander who was shot during the Battle of Cedar Creek on October 19, 1864. He died in Union hands, surrounded by his former West Point classmates. Buried in Lincolnton, North Carolina.

Randolph, George Wythe. C.S.A.—Brigadier General. Born March 10, 1818, at Monticello, Charlottesville, Virginia, the grandson of Thomas Jefferson. Artillery commander. Died April 3, 1867, at Edgehill. Buried at Monticello in Charlottesville, Virginia.

Ransom, Robert. C.S.A.—Major General. West Point Class of 1850. Born February 12, 1828, in Warren County, North Carolina. Infantry commander who served as a cavalry commander under General Early in 1864. Died January 14, 1892, in New Bern, North Carolina. Buried in New Bern, North Carolina.

Ransom, Thomas E. U.S.A.— Brigadier General. Born November 29, 1834, in Norwich, Vermont. Infantry commander. Died October 29, 1864, near Rome, Georgia, of illness and infection from a wound received during the Battle of Sabine Cross Roads during the Red River Campaign. Buried in Rosehill Cemetery, Chicago, Illinois.

Reilly, James W. U.S.A.— Brigadier General. Born May 20, 1828, in Akron, Ohio. Infantry commander. Died November 6, 1905, in Wellsville, Ohio. Buried in St. Elizabeth's Cemetery, Wellsville, Ohio.

Reno, Jesse. U.S.A.— Major General. West Point Class of 1846. Born June 20, 1823, in Wheeling, West Virginia. Infantry commander who was mortally wounded on September 14, 1862, near South Mountain. Buried in Oak Hill Cemetery, Georgetown, D.C.

Reynolds, John F. U.S.A.— Major General. West Point Class of 1841. Born September 20, 1820, in Lancaster, Pennsylvania. Union corps commander who was killed on July 1, 1863, during the opening shots of the Battle of Gettysburg. Buried in Lancaster, Pennsylvania.

Richardson, Israel B. U.S.A.— Major General. West Point Class of 1841. Born December 26, 1815, in Fairfax, Vermont. Infantry commander. Wounded by an artillery shell during the Battle of Antietam on September 17, 1862, and died on November 3. Buried in Pontiac, Michigan.

Ripley, Roswell Sabine. C.S.A.— Brigadier General. West Point Class of 1843. Born March 14, 1823, in Franklin County, Ohio. Infantry commander. Died March 29, 1887, in New York, New York. Buried in Charleston, South Carolina.

Robertson, Beverly H. C.S.A.— Brigadier General. West Point Class of 1849. Born June 5, 1827, in Amelia County, Virginia. Cavalry commander. Died November 12, 1910, in Washington, D.C. Buried in Amelia County, Virginia.

Rodes, Robert E. C.S.A.— Major General. Virginia Military Class of 1848. Born March 29, 1829, in Lynchburg, Virginia. Infantry commander. Mortally wounded during the Battle of Winchester September 19, 1864. Buried in Lynchburg, Virginia.

Rosecrans, William S. U.S.A.— Major General. West Point Class of 1842. Born September 6, 1819, in Delaware County, Ohio. Commander of the Army of the Cumberland. Died May 17, 1902, near present day Redondo Beach, California. Buried in Arlington National Cemetery.

Ross, Lawrence S. C.S.A.— Brigadier General. Born September 27, 1838, in Bentonsport, Iowa. Cavalry commander. Died January 3, 1898, in College Station, Texas. Buried in Waco, Texas.

Ross, Leonard F. U.S.A.— Brigadier General. Born July 18, 1823, near Lewistown, Illinois. Infantry commander. Died January 17, 1901, in Lewistown, Illinois. Buried in Oakhill Cemetery, Lewistown.

Rosser, Thomas. C.S.A.— Brigadier General. Resigned from West Point in 1861. Born October 15, 1836, in Campbell County, Virginia. Artillery commander who became a cavalry commander at the insistence of General J.E.B. Stuart. Died March 29, 1910, in Charlottesville, Virginia. Buried in Riverview Cemetery, Charlottesville, Virginia.

Rousseau, Lovell H. U.S.A.— Major General. Born August 4, 1818, near Stanford, Kentucky. Infantry commander. Died January 7, 1869, in New Orleans, Louisiana. Buried in Arlington National Cemetery.

Rust, Albert. C.S.A.— Brigadier General. Born in 1818 in Fauquier County, Virginia. Infantry commander. Died April 4, 1870, in Little Rock, Arkansas. Buried in Mount Holly Cemetery, Little Rock, Arkansas.

Schenck, Robert C. U.S.A.— Major General. Born October 4, 1809, in Franklin, Ohio. Infantry commander. Died March 23, 1890, in Washington, D.C. Buried in Woodland Cemetery, Dayton, Ohio.

Schofield, John M. U.S.A.— Major General. West Point Class of 1853. Born September 29, 1831, in Gerry, New York. Commander of the Army of the Ohio. Died March 4, 1906, in St. Augustine, Florida. Buried in Arlington National Cemetery.

Schurz, Carl. U.S.A.—Major General. Born March 2, 1829, near Cologne, Prussia. Infantry commander. Died May 14, 1906, in New York, New York. Buried in Sleepy Hollow Cemetery, Tarrytown, New York.

Scurry, William R. C.S.A.—Brigadier General. Born February 10, 1821, in Galletin, Tennessee. Cavalry commander who died April 30, 1864, when mortally wounded during the Battle of Jenkins Ferry. Buried in Texas State Cemetery, Austin, Texas.

Sedgwick, John. U.S.A.—Major General. West Point Class of 1837. Born September 13, 1813, in Cornwall Hollow, Connecticut. Infantry commander who was killed during the Battle of Spotsylvania on May 9, 1864. Buried in Cornwall Hollow, Connecticut.

Semmes, Paul J. C.S.A.—Brigadier General. Born June 4, 1815, at Munford's Plantation, Wilkes County, Georgia. Brother of Rear Admiral Raphael Semmes. Infantry commander. Mortally wounded during the Battle of Gettysburg, Pennsylvania, on July 2, 1863. Died on July 10, 1863, at Martinsburg, West Virginia. Buried in Linnwood Cemetery, Columbus, Georgia.

Semmes, Raphael. C.S.A.—Rear Admiral, CSA Navy. Born September 27, 1809, in Charles County, Maryland. Naval commander. Died August 30, 1877, in Point Clear, Alabama.

Seymore, Truman. U.S.A.—Major General. West Point Class of 1846. Born September 24, 1824, in Burlington, Vermont. Infantry commander. Died October 30, 1891, in Florence, Italy. Buried at Cimitero degli Allori, Florence, Italy.

Shackelford, James M. U.S.A.—Brigadier General. Born July 7, 1827, in Lincoln County, Kentucky. Cavalry commander. Died September 7, 1909, in Port Huron, Michigan. Buried in Cave Hill Cemetery, Louisville, Kentucky.

Shaw, Robert G. U.S.A.—Colonel. Born October 10, 1837, in Boston, Massachusetts. Infantry commander who was killed during the Battle of Fort Wagner, July 18, 1863. Buried at Fort Wagner, South Carolina.

Shelby, Joseph. C.S.A.—Brigadier General. Born December 12, 1830, in Lexington, Kentucky. Cavalry commander. Died February 13, 1897, in Adrian, Missouri. Buried in Forest Hill Cemetery, Kansas City, Missouri.

Sheridan, Philip. U.S.A.—Major General. West Point Class of 1853. Born March 6, 1831, in Albany, New York. Cavalry commander. Died August 5, 1888, at Nonquitt, Massachusetts. Buried in Arlington National Cemetery.

Sherman, Thomas W. U.S.A.—Brigadier General. West Point Class of 1836. Born March 26, 1813, in Newport, Rhode Island. Infantry commander. Died March 16, 1879, in Newport, Rhode Island. Buried in Island Cemetery, Newport, Rhode Island.

Sherman, William T. U.S.A.—Major General. West Point Class of 1840. Born February 8, 1820, in Lancaster, Ohio. Commander of all Union troops in the western theater in 1864–65. Died February 14, 1891, in New York, New York. Buried in Calvary Cemetery, St. Louis, Missouri.

Shields, James. U.S.A.—Brigadier General. Born May 10, 1810, in County Tyrone, Ireland. Infantry commander. Died June 1, 1879, in Ottumwa, Iowa. Buried in St. Mary's Cemetery, Carrollton, Missouri.

Sibley, Henry Hastings. U.S.A.—Brigadier General. Born February 29, 1811, in Detroit, Michigan. Cousin of Henry Hopkins Sibley. Union commander who fought Indians rather than Confederates. Died February 18, 1891, in St. Paul, Minnesota. Buried in Oakland Cemetery, St. Paul, Minnesota.

Sibley, Henry Hopkins. C.S.A.—Brigadier General. West Point Class of 1838. Born May 25, 1816, in Natchitoches, La. Cousin of Henry Hastings Sibley. In command of the expedition into New Mexico. Died August 23, 1886. Buried in Fredericksburg, Va.

Sickles, Daniel E. U.S.A.—Major General. Born October 20, 1819, in New York, New York.

Commander of the Army of the Potomac's Third Corps. Died May 3, 1914, in New York, New York. Buried in Arlington National Cemetery.

Sigel, Franz. U.S.A.—Major General. Born November 18, 1824, in Baden, Germany. Union commander in charge of the Department of West Virginia. Died August 21, 1902, in New York, New York. Buried in Woodlawn Cemetery, New York, New York.

Sill, Joshua. U.S.A.—Brigadier General. West Point Class of 1853. Born December 6, 1831, in Fort Sill, Oklahoma. Infantry commander. Killed on December 31, 1862, during the Battle of Stone River (3rd Battle of Murfreesboro). Buried in Grand View Cemetery near Chillicothe, Ohio.

Slemmer, Adam J. U.S.A.—Brigadier General. West Point Class of 1850. Born January 24, 1829, in Montgomery County, Pennsylvania. Infantry commander. Died October 7, 1868, at Fort Laramie, Wyoming. Buried in Montgomery Cemetery, Norristown, Pennsylvania.

Slocum, Henry W. U.S.A.—Major General. West Point Class of 1852. Born September 24, 1827, in Delphi, New York. Union corps commander. Died April 14, 1894, in Brooklyn, New York. Buried in Green Wood Cemetery, Brooklyn, New York.

Smith, Andrew J. U.S.A.—Major General. West Point Class of 1838. Born April 28, 1815, in Bucks County, Pennsylvania. Infantry commander. Died January 30, 1897, in St. Louis, Missouri. Buried in Bellefontaine Cemetery, St. Louis, Missouri.

Smith, Charles F. U.S.A.—Major General. West Point Class of 1825. Born April 24, 1807, in Philadelphia, Pennsylvania. Infantry commander. Died April 25, 1862, of an infection in Savannah, Tennessee. Buried Laurel Hill Cemetery, Philadelphia, Pennsylvania.

Smith, Edmund K. C.S.A.—Lieutenant General. West Point Class of 1845. Born May 16, 1824, in St. Augustine, Florida. Commander of the Trans-Mississippi Department. Died March 28, 1893, in Sewanee, Tennessee. Buried in Sewanee, Tennessee.

Smith, Gustavus W. C.S.A.—Major General. West Point Class of 1842. Born December 1, 1821, in Georgetown, Kentucky. Infantry commander. Died June 24, 1896, in New York, New York. Buried in New London, Connecticut.

Smith, Martin L. C.S.A.—Brigadier General. West Point Class of 1842. Born September 9, 1819, in Danby, New York. An engineer. Died July 29, 1866, in Savannah, Georgia. Buried in Athens, Georgia.

Smith, Thomas K. U.S.A.—Brigadier General. Born September 23, 1820, in Dorchester, Massachusetts. Infantry commander. Died December 14, 1887, in New York, New York. Buried in Torresdale, Pennsylvania.

Steele, Frederick. U.S.A.—Major General. West Point Class of 1843. Born January 14, 1819, in Delhi, New York. Infantry commander. Died January 12, 1868, in San Mateo, California, when he fell out of a buggy. Buried in Woodlawn Memorial Park, Colma, California.

Stevens, Isaac I. U.S.A.—Brigadier General. West Point Class of 1939. Born March 25, 1818, in Andover, Massachusetts. Infantry commander who was killed during the Battle of Chantilly on September 1, 1862. Buried in Island Cemetery, Newport, Rhode Island.

Stewart, Alexander P. C.S.A.—Lieutenant General. West Point Class of 1842. Born October 2, 1821, in Rogersville, Tennessee. Was in the artillery until promoted to Lieutenant General and given command of a corps under General Polk. Died August 30, 1908, in Biloxi, Mississippi. Buried in St. Louis, Missouri.

Stone, Charles P. U.S.A.—Brigadier General. West Point Class of 1845. Born September 30, 1824, in Greenfield, Massachusetts. Infantry commander. Died January 24, 1887, in New York, New York. Buried at West Point.

Stoneman, George. U.S.A.—Major General. West Point Class of 1846. Born August 22, 1822, in Bustion, New York. Cavalry commander. Died September 5, 1894, in Buffalo, New York. Buried in Lakewood, New York.

Strahal, Otho. C.S.A.—Brigadier General. Born June 3, 1831, in McConnelsville, Ohio. Infantry commander who was killed during the Battle of Franklin on November 30, 1864. Buried in Dyersburg, Tennessee.

Strong, George. U.S.A.— Brigadier General. West Point Class of 1857. Born October 16, 1832, in Stockbridge, Vermont. Infantry commander. Wounded during the Battle of Fort Wagner on July 18, 1863, coming down with lockjaw, dying July 30, 1863, in New York, New York. Buried in Greenwood Cemetery, Brooklyn, New York.

Stuart, James Ewell Brown. C.S.A.— Lieutenant General. West Point Class of 1854. Born February 6, 1833, in Patrick County, Virginia. Cavalry commander who was killed on May 11, 1864, during the Battle of Yellow Tavern. Buried in Hollywood Cemetery, Richmond, Virginia.

Sturgis, Samuel D. U.S.A.— Brigadier General. West Point Class of 1846. Born June 11, 1822, in Shippensburg, Pennsylvania. Cavalry commander. Died September 28, 1889, in St. Paul, Minnesota. Buried in Arlington National Cemetery.

Sullivan, Jeremiah C. U.S.A.— Brigadier General. Born October 1, 1830, in Madison, Indiana. Infantry commander. Died October 21, 1890, in Oakland, California. Buried in Mountain View Cemetery, Oakland, California.

Sully, Alfred. U.S.A.— Major General. West Point Class of 1841. Born May 22, 1820, in Philadelphia, Pennsylvania. Infantry commander. Died April 27, 1879, in Fort Vancouver, Washington. Buried in Laurel Hill Cemetery, Philadelphia, Pennsylvania.

Sumner, Edwin V. U.S.A.— Major General. Born January 30, 1797, in Boston, Massachusetts. Infantry commander. Died March 21, 1863, in Syracuse, New York. Buried in Oakwood Cemetery, Syracuse, New York.

Sykes, George. U.S.A.— Major General. West Point Class of 1842. Born October 9, 1822, in Dover, Delaware. Corps commander. Died February 8, 1880, in Brownsville, Texas. Buried at West Point.

Taliaferro, William B. C.S.A.— Brigadier General. Born December 28, 1822, in Gloucester County, Virginia. Infantry commander. Died February 27, 1898, in Gloucester County, Virginia. Buried in Ware Church Cemetery, Gloucester County, Virginia.

Taylor, George W. U.S.A.— Brigadier General. Born November 22, 1808, in Hunterdon County, New Jersey. Infantry commander. Mortally wounded during the Battle of Manassas Junction on August 27, 1862, dying September 1 in Alexandria. Buried in Rock Church Cemetery, Hunterdon, New Jersey.

Taylor, Richard. C.S.A.— Lieutenant General. Born January 27, 1826, the son of President Zachary Taylor. Infantry commander. Died April 12, 1879, in New York, New York. Buried in Metairie Cemetery, New Orleans, Louisiana.

Terrill, James B. C.S.A.— Confirmed Brigadier General a day after his death. Virginia Military Institute, 1857. Born February 20, 1838, in Bath, Virginia. Was the younger brother of William Terrill, a Union officer. Infantry commander who was killed during the Battle of Cold Harbor (Bethesda Church) on May 30, 1864.

Terrill, William R. U.S.A.— Brigadier General. West Point Class of 1853. Born April 21, 1834, in Covington, Virginia. Older brother of James B. Terrill, a Confederate brigadier general. Artillery commander. Killed during the battle of Perryville on October 8, 1862. Buried at West Point.

Terry, Alfred H. U.S.A.— Brigadier General. Born November 10, 1827, in Hartford, Connecticut. Infantry commander. Died December 16, 1890, in New Haven, Connecticut. Buried in Grove Street Cemetery, New Haven, Connecticut.

Terry, William. C.S.A.— Brigadier General. Born August 14, 1824, in Amherst County, Virginia. Infantry commander. Drowned as he attempted to cross Reed Creek near Wytheville, Virginia, on September 5, 1888. Buried in Wytheville, Virginia.

Terry, William R. C.S.A.— Brigadier General. Virginia Military Academy Class of 1850. Born

March 12, 1827, in Liberty, Virginia. Infantry commander. Died March 28, 1897, near Chesterfield Court House, Virginia. Buried in Hollywood Cemetery, Richmond, Virginia.

Thomas, George H. U.S.A.— Major General. West Point Class of 1840. Born July 31, 1816, in Southampton, Virginia. Infantry commander. Died March 28, 1870, in San Francisco, California. Buried in Oakwood Cemetery, Troy, New York.

Tilghman, Lloyd. C.S.A.— Brigadier General. West Point Class of 1836. Born January 18, 1816, near Claiborne, Maryland. Infantry commander. Died when struck by a shell fragment during the Battle of Champion's Hill (Baker's Creek) on May 16, 1863. Buried in Woodlawn Cemetery, New York, New York.

Torbert, Alfred. U.S.A.— Major General. West Point Class of 1855. Born July 1, 1833, in Georgetown, Delaware. Infantry commander. Died August 29, 1880, in a shipwreck off the coast of Cape Canaveral, Florida. Body was recovered and is buried in Methodist Episcopal Cemetery in Milford, Delaware.

Trimble, Isaac R. C.S.A.— Major General. West Point Class of 1822. Born May 15, 1802, in Culpeper County, Virginia. Infantry commander. Died January 2, 1888, in Baltimore, Maryland. Buried in Green Mount Cemetery, Baltimore, Maryland.

Turchin, John B. U.S.A.— Brigadier General. Imperial Military School at St. Petersburg (Leningrad) Class of 1841. Born January 30, 1822, in the Province of Don, Russia. Infantry commander. Died June 19, 1901, in Anna, Illinois. Buried in the National Cemetery at Mound City, Illinois.

Twiggs, David D. C.S.A.— Major General. Born 1790 in Richmond County, Georgia. Infantry commander. Died July 15, 1862. Buried in Richmond County, Georgia.

Tyler, Daniel. U.S.A.— West Point Class of 1819. Born January 7, 1799. Infantry commander. Died November 30, 1882. Buried in Hillside Cemetery, Anniston, Alabama.

Tyler, Erastus. U.S.A.— Brigadier General. Born April 24, 1822, in West Bloomfield, New York. Infantry commander. Died January 9, 1891, in Calverton, Maryland. Buried in Greenmount Cemetery, Baltimore, Maryland.

Tyler, Richard O. U.S.A.— Major General. West Point Class of 1853. Born December 22, 1831, in Hunter, New York. Infantry commander. Died December 1, 1874, in Boston, Massachusetts. Buried in Cedar Hill Cemetery, Hartford, Connecticut.

Van Dorn, Earl. C.S.A.— Major General. West Point Class of 1842. Born September 17, 1820, in Port Gibson, Mississippi. Cavalry commander who died when shot by a jealous husband on May 7, 1863, in Spring Hill, Tennessee. Buried in Port Gibson, Mississippi.

Vandever, William. U.S.A.— Brigadier General. Born March 31, 1817, in Baltimore, Maryland. Infantry commander. Died July 23, 1893, in Ventura, California. Buried in Ventura Cemetery, Ventura, California.

Walcutt, Charles C. U.S.A.— Brigadier General. Kentucky Military Academy Class of 1858. Born February 12, 1838, in Columbus, Ohio. Infantry commander. Died May 2, 1898, in Omaha, Nebraska. Buried in Greenlawn Cemetery in Columbus, Ohio.

Wallace, William Harvey L. U.S.A.— Brigadier General. Born July 8, 1821, in Urbana, Ohio. Infantry commander. Mortally wounded during the Battle of Shiloh, he died April 10, 1862, at Savannah, Tennessee. Buried in a private cemetery near Ottawa, Illinois.

Wallace, William Henry. C.S.A.— Brigadier General. Born March 24, 1827, in Laurens District, South Carolina. Infantry commander. Died March 21, 1901, in Union, South Carolina. Buried in Union, South Carolina.

Warren, Gouverneur K. U.S.A.— Major General. West Point Class of 1850. Born January 8, 1830, in Cold Spring, New York. Chief engineer for the Army of the Potomac. Died August 8, 1882, in Newport, Rhode Island. Buried in Island Cemetery, Newport, Rhode Island.

Watie, Stand. C.S.A.— Brigadier General. Born December 12, 1806, near Rome, Georgia. Member of the Cherokee Indian Tribe. Commander of the Cherokee Mounted Rifles. Died

September 9, 1871, in Delaware County, Oklahoma. Buried in Old Ridge Cemetery, Delaware County, Oklahoma.

Wheeler, Joseph. C.S.A.—Major General. West Point Class of 1859. Born September 10, 1836, in Augusta, Georgia. Cavalry commander in the Army of Tennessee. Died January 25, 1906, in Brooklyn, New York. Buried in Arlington National Cemetery.

Whiting, William H.C. C.S.A.—Major General. West Point Class of 1824. Born March 22, 1824, in Biloxi, Mississippi. Engineer who became an infantry commander. Wounded during the Battle of Fort Fisher on January 15, 1865, dying of those wounds on March 10, 1865. Buried in Oakdale Cemetery, Wilmington, North Carolina.

Wietzel, Godfrey. U.S.A.—Major General. West Point Class of 1855. Born November 1, 1835, in Cincinnati, Ohio. Infantry commander. Died March 19, 1884, in Philadelphia, Pennsylvania. Buried in Spring Grove Cemetery, Cincinnati, Ohio.

Wild, Edward. U.S.A.—Brigadier General. Born November 25, 1825, in Brookline, Massachusetts. Infantry commander. Died August 28, 1891, in Medellin, Colombia. Buried in Cementerio de San Pedro, Medellin, Colombia.

Williams, John S. C.S.A.—Brigadier General. Born July 10, 1818, in Mount Sterling, Kentucky. Infantry commander. Died July 17, 1898, at Mount Sterling, Kentucky. Buried in Winchester, Virginia.

Williams, Thomas. U.S.A.—Brigadier General. West Point Class of 1837. Born January 10, 1815, in Albany, New York. At the start of the war was an artillery commander but later led an infantry brigade. Killed on August 5, 1862, during the Battle for Baton Rouge. Buried in Elmwood Cemetery, Detroit, Michigan.

Williamson, John S. U.S.A.—Brigadier General. Born February 8, 1829, in Adair County, Kentucky. Infantry commander. Died September 7, 1902, in Jamestown, Rhode Island. Buried in Rock Cemetery, Georgetown, D.C.

Wilson, James H. U.S.A.—Major General. West Point Class of 1855. Born September 2, 1837, near Shawneetown, Illinois. Cavalry commander. Died February 23, 1925, in Wilmington, Illinois. Buried in Olds Swede Churchyard, Wilmington, Illinois.

Winder, Charles S. C.S.A.—West Point Class of 1850. Brigadier General. Born October 18, 1829, in Talbot County, Maryland. Infantry commander. Killed on August 9, 1862, during the Battle of Cedar Mountain. Buried at Wye House, Easton, Maryland.

Winthrop, Theodore. U.S.A.—Major. Born September 22, 1828, in New Haven, Connecticut. Assigned to the infantry when he was killed during the Battle of Big Bethel on June 10, 1861.

Wise, Henry A. C.S.A.—General. Born December 3, 1806, in Drummondtown, Virginia. Infantry commander. Died September 124, 1876, in Richmond, Virginia. Buried in Hollywood Cemetery, Richmond, Virginia.

Wood, Thomas J. U.S.A.—Brigadier General. West Point Class of 1845. Born September 25, 1823, in Munfordville, Kentucky. Cavalry commander. Died February 25, 1906, in Dayton, Ohio. Buried at West Point.

Wright, Ambrose R. C.S.A.—Major General. Born April 26, 1826, in Louisville, Georgia. Infantry commander. Died December 21, 1872, in Augusta, Georgia. Buried in City Cemetery, Augusta, Georgia.

Wright, Horatio G. U.S.A.—Major General. West Point Class of 1841. Born March 6, 1820, in Clinton, Connecticut. Corps commander. Died July 2, 1899, in Washington. Buried in Arlington National Cemetery.

Zollicoffer, Felix K. C.S.A.—Brigadier General. Born May 19, 1812, in Maury County, Tennessee. Infantry commander. Killed during the Battle of Mill Springs on January 19, 1862. Buried in City Cemetery, Nashville, Tennessee.

Chapter Notes

CHAPTER 4. THE OFFICERS

1. Moxley Sorrell, *Recollections of a Confederate Staff Officer* (New York: Konecky and Konecky, 1994), 129.

CHAPTER 6. THE WAR

1. Slave States: Alabama, Arkansas, Delaware, Florida, Missouri, North Carolina, South Carolina, Tennessee, Texas, Virginia. Free States: California, Connecticut, Illinois, Indiana, Iowa, Maine, Massachusetts, Michigan, Minnesota, New Hampshire, New Jersey, New York, Ohio, Oregon, Pennsylvania, Rhode Island, Vermont, Wisconsin.
2. *James Madison's Writings*, edited by Jack Rakove (New York: Library of America, 1999), 806.
3. President Abraham Lincoln's First Inaugural Speech delivered on March 4, 1861.
4. U.S. Constitution, art. IV, sec. 3 par. 1.

CHAPTER 8. 1862

1. United States War Department. *The War of the Rebellion: A Compilation of the Official Records of the Union and Confederate Armies*, 128 volumes (Washington, D.C.: Government Printing Office. 1880–1901) (referred to hereafter as OR), Series I, Vol. VII (S7), 863. Letter to J.P. Benjamin, Secretary of War, by A.S. Johnston, dated February 8, 1862.
2. U.S. Constitution, art. I, sec. 8, par. 5.
3. OR, Series I, Vol. XV (S#21), 466.
4. *Ibid.*, Vol. XVI/I (S#22), 770.
5. Stephen T. Foster, *Atlas Edition of Civil War Cards: Battles, Leaders, Armies, Medical and Uniform* (Later identified as *Atlas Cards*), (Durham, Conn.: 1994–5) Card #D3 602 99–04.

CHAPTER 9. 1863

1. Longstreet, James, "Manassas to Appomattox," 1896, Dallas Publishing, Pg. 386–7.
2. OR, Series I, Vol. XXII/I (S#32), 355.

CHAPTER 10. 1864

1. OR, Series I, Vol. XXXII/3 (S#59), 246, Letter to Maj. Gen. W.T. Sherman from U.S. Grant, dated April 4, 1864.
2. David D. Porter, "Torpedo Warfare," *North Americana Review* (University of Northern Iowa, Cedar Falls: September–October 1878), and Web page: http://cdl.library.cornell.edu/cgi-bin/moa/moa-cgi?notisid= ABQ75780 127&byte=99127352), accessed September 9, 2004.
3. Edward A. Miller, Jr., "David Hunter: The General Who Burned VMI," VMI *Alumni Review*, Vol. 73. No. 4 (Spring 1997), 6.
4. Jubal A. Early, *Autobiographical Sketch and Narrative of the War Between the States.* (Philadelphia: J.B. Lippincott, 1912), 392.
5. Web pages: http://www.absoluteastronomy. com/encyclopedia-/O/Ol/Oliver_Wendell_Holmes, _Jr.htm and http://www.us-civilwar.com/stevens. htm, accessed October 15, 2004.
6. Bruce Catton, *The American Heritage: New History of the Civil War*, edited by James M. McPherson (New York: Viking Press, 1988), 493.
7. OR, Series I, Vol. XXXVIII/5 (S#76), 777. Letter to General H. Halleck from General Sherman dated September 3, 1864.
8. *Ibid.*, 795. Letter to General H. Halleck from General Sherman dated September 4, 1864.
9. *Ibid.*, Vol. XLI/3 (S#85), 488. Letter to General Rosecrans from General Clinton B. Fisk dated September 29, 1864.

10. *Ibid.*, Series IV, Vol. III (S#129), 491.

11. *Ibid.*, Series I, Vol. VLI/1 (S#83), 640.

12. *Ibid.*, Vol. XXXIX/2, (S#79) 162.

13. Southern Historical Papers, Vol. XXVI, 1898, p. 81: *Atlas Cards*, Card #D3–602–106–08.

14. OR, Series I, Vol. XLV/2 (S#94), 70. Letter to General Thomas from General Grant dated December 6, 1864.

15. *Ibid.*, 114. Letter to General Halleck from General Thomas dated December 9, 1864.

16. *Ibid.*, 143. Letters between General Grant and General Thomas dated December 11, 1864.

17. *Ibid.*, Vol. XLIV/2 (S#92), 783. Letter to President Lincoln from W.T. Sherman, dated December 22, 1864.

CHAPTER 11. 1865

1. OR, Series I, Vol. XLIV/2 (S#92), 799.

2. Erza J. Warner, *Generals in Blue: Lives of the Union Commanders* (Baton Rouge: Louisiana State University Press, 1992), 439 and *Atlas Cards*, Card #D3–602–13–11.

3. OR, Series I, Vol. XLVI/2 (S#96), 824. Letter to General Grant from Robert E. Lee dated March 2, 1865.

4. *Ibid.*, 802. Letter to General Grant from Edwin Stanton dated March 3, 1965.

5. President Abraham Lincoln's Second Inaugural Address delivered Saturday, March 4, 1865.

6. OR, Series I, Vol. XLVII/1 (S#98), 1055. Letter to General Lee from General Johnston.

7. *Atlas Cards*, Card #D3–602–75–10.

8. OR, Series I, Vol. XLIX/I (S#103), 616. Letter to Major General George H. Thomas from General U. S. Grant.

9. *Atlas Cards*, Card #D3–602087–08.

10. OR, Series I, Vol. XXXIV/1 (S#61), 54. Letter to General Lee from General Grant dated April 7, 1865.

11. *Ibid.*, 55, Letter to General Grant from General Lee dated April 7, 1865.

12. *Ibid.*

13. Walter Taylor, *General Lee: His Campaigns in Virginia, 1861–1865* (Lincoln: University of Nebraska Press, 1906, reprinted by Bison Book Press 1994), 288.

14. OR, Series 1, Vol. XLVI/3 (S#97), 664. Letter to General Grant from General Lee dated April 9, 1865.

15. *Ibid.*, 663. Letter to Edwin Stanton from General Grant dated April 9, 1865.

16. Joshua Lawrence Chamberlain, *The Passing of the Armies: The Last Campaign of the Armies* (New York: 1915 Reprinted by Stan Clark Military Books, Gettysburg 1994), 260.

17. *Atlas Cards*, Card #D–602–19–10.

18. OR, Series III, Vol. V (S#126), 18.

19. Sherman, William T. *Memoirs of General W.T. Sherman*, 2 Volumes (New York: D. Appleton, 1889), Vol. II 389.

20. *Ibid.*, Series II, Vol. VIII (S#121), 579–580.

21. *Ibid.*, 700.

CHAPTER 12. CASUALTIES

1. William F. Fox, *Regimental Losses in the American Civil War: 1861–1865* (Albany: Albany Publishing, 1889), 1.

2. *Ibid.*, 225.

3. *Ibid.*, 2.

4. OR, Series 1, Vol. XIX/2 (S#28) Pg. 718–19.

Bibliography

Published Materials

Axelrod, Alan. *The Complete Idiot's Guide to the American History, Second Edition.* Indianapolis: Alpha Books, division of Macmillan, 2000.

_____. *The Complete Idiot's Guide to the Civil War.* New York: Alpha Books, Division of Macmillan Reference, 1998.

Beller, Susan Provost. *Medical Practices in the Civil War.* Charlotte, Vermont: Susan Provost Beller, 1992.

Blair, Jayne E. *Tragedy at Montpelier: Untold Story of Ten Confederate Deserters from North Carolina.* Bowie, Maryland: Heritage Books, 2003.

Catton, Bruce. *American Heritage: New History of the Civil War.* Edited and with an introduction by James M. McPherson. New York: Viking, 1988.

_____. *Mr. Lincoln's Army.* Garden City, New York: Doubleday, 1951.

Chamberlain, Joshua Lawrence. *The Passing of the Armies: The Last Campaign of the Armies.* New York, 1915. Reprint, Gettysburg: Stan Clark Military Books, 1994.

Crute Jr., Joseph H. *Units of the Confederate States Army.* Gaithersburg, Maryland: Olde Soldier Books, 1987.

Davis, Burke. *The Civil War: Strange and Interesting Facts.* New York: Wings Books, distributed by Random House, 1960.

Davis, Kenneth C. *Don't Know Much About the Civil War.* New York: Avon Books, 1996.

Davis, William C. *The Campaign to Appomattox: Civil War Times Special Edition.* Eastern Acorn Press, nd.

_____. *The Commanders of the Civil War.* New York: Gallery Books, 1990.

_____. *Confederate General,* 6 volumes. National Historical Society, 1991.

_____, ed. *Touched by Fire: A National Historical Society Photographic Portrait of the Civil War.* New York: Black Dog and Leventhal, 1997.

Davis, William C. Foreword, *Civil War Wall Chart.* Lincolnwood, Illinois. Publications International, 1990.

Dyer, Frederick H. *A Compendium of the War of the Rebellion.* Des Moines: Dyer, 1908.

Early, Jubal A. *Autobiographical Sketch and Narrative of the War Between the States.* Philadelphia: J.B. Lippincott, 1912.

Ethier, Eric. "Who Was the Common Soldier of the Civil War." *Civil War Times Illustrated.* Volume XLII, Number 5 (December 2003).

Evans, E. Chris. "I Almost Tremble at Her Fate." *Civil War Times Illustrated.* Volume XXXVII, Number 5 (October 1998).

Faust, Patricia L., ed. *Historical Times Illustrated: Encyclopedia of the Civil War.* New York: Harper Perennial, 1986.

Fowler, Robert H. "The Assassination of Abraham Lincoln." *Civil War Times, Special Edition.* Harrisonburg, Pennsylvania: Eastern Acorn Press, original publisher, Historical Times, 1965.

Fox, William F. *Regimental Losses in the American Civil War 1861–1865.* Albany: Albany Publishing, 1889.

Freeman, Douglas. *Lee's Dispatches: Unpublished Letters of General Robert E. Lee to Jefferson Davis and the War Department of the Confederate States of America 1862–1865.* Baton Rouge: Louisiana State University Press, 1957.

Gallagher, Gary, ed. *Lee the Soldier*. Lincoln: University of Nebraska Press, 1996.

Garrison, Webb. *Civil War Trivia and Fact Book*. Nashville, Tennessee: Rutledge Hill Press, 1992.

_____. *Encyclopedia of Civil War Usage*. Nashville: Cumberland House, 2001.

_____. *2,000 Questions and Answers About the Civil War: Unusual and Unique Facts About the War Between the States*. New York: Gramercy Books, 1992.

Goff, Alan D. "Two Died at Sumter." *Civil War Times Illustrated*. Volume XL, Number 1 (March 2001).

Griess, Thomas E., ed. *West Point Atlas for the American Civil War*. Wayne, New Jersey: Avery, 1986.

Houch, Peter W., ed. *Confederate Surgeon: Personal Recollections of E.A. Craighill*. Lynchburg, Virginia: W.E. Howard, 1989.

Howard, McHenry. *Recollections of a Maryland Confederate Soldier and Staff Officer Under Johnston, Jackson and Lee*. Dayton: Morningside Press, 1975.

Huebner, Michael. "The Regulars." *Civil War Times Illustrated*. Volume XXXIX, Number 3 (June 2000).

Johnson, Robert Underwood, and Clarence Clough Buel, eds. *Battles and Leaders of the Civil War*, 4 volumes, reprint edition. Secaucus, New Jersey: Castle, nd.

Joiner, Gary D. *Up the Red River and Down to Defeat*. America's Civil War. Volume 17, Number 1 (March 2004).

Lanier, Robert S., ed. *The Photographic History of the Civil War*. 10 volumes. Secaucus, New Jersey: Blue and Gray Press, 1987.

Long, E.B. and Barbara Long. *The Civil War Day by Day: An Almanac 1861–1865*. New York: DaCapo Press, 1971.

Longacre, Edward G. *The Cavalry at Gettysburg: A Tactical Study of Mounted Operations during the Civil War's Pivotal Campaign 9 June–14 July 1863*. Lincoln and London: University of Nebraska Press, 1986.

_____. "John Hunt Morgan's Ohio Raid." *Civil War Times Illustrated*. Volume XLII, Number 3 (August 2003).

Lutz, Stuart. "Terror in St. Albans." *Civil War Times Illustrated*. Volume XL, Number 3 (June 2001).

McAfee, Michael. "Uncommon Soldier." *Civil War Times Illustrated*. Volume XLII, Number 5 (December 2003).

McPherson, James M. "What Caused the Civil War." *North and South*. Volume 4, Number 1 (November 2000).

Mathless, Paul, ed. *Voices of the Civil War: Vicksburg*. Alexandria, Virginia: Time-Life Books, 1997.

Meade, George G. *The Life and Letters of George G. Meade*. New York: Scribner's, 1913.

Miller, Edward A., Jr. "David Hunter: The General Who Burned VMI." *VMI Alumni Review*, Vol. 73. No. 4 (Spring 1997).

Miller, William. *In Camp and Battle with the Washington Artillery of New Orleans*. New Orleans: Louisiana State University Press, New Orleans, 1885, New material introduced by Nathaniel Cheairs Hughes, Jr., 1999.

Mitchell, Reid. "The Infantryman in Combat." *North and South*. Volume 4, Number 6 (August 2001).

Naisawald, L. Van Loan. *Grape and Canister: The Story of the Field Artillery of the Army of the Potomac*. Washington, D.C.: Zenger, 1983.

Nevins, Allan. *Ordeal of the Union* (4 Volumes). New York: Scribner's, 1947.

_____. *The War For the Union* (4 volumes). New York: Scribner's, 1971.

Nofi, Albert A. *A Civil War Journal: A Fascinating Collection of Facts, Episodes and Anecdotes*. New York: Galahad Books, 1993.

Owens, Richard H. "Battle of Pea Ridge." *America's Civil War*. Volume 12, Number 6 (January 2000).

Page, Dave. "A Fight For Missouri." *Civil War Times Illustrated*. Volume XXXIV, Number 3 (July–August 1995).

Rakove, Jack, ed. *James Madison's Writings*. New York: Library of America, 1999.

Robertson Jr., James I. and the editors of Time-Life Books, eds. *The Civil War: Tenting Tonight The Soldier's Life*. Alexandria, Virginia: Time-Life Books, 1984.

Salecker, Gene Eric. "The Tragic Sinking of Sultana." *America's Civil War*, Volume 15, Number 2 (May 2002).

Sherman, William T. *Memoirs of General W.T. Sherman* (2 Volumes). New York: D. Appleton, 1889.

Simmons, Henry E., ed. *A Concise Encyclopedia of the Civil War*. New York: Bonanza Books, 1965.

Sorrell, Moxley. *Recollections of a Confederate Staff Officer*. New York: Konecky and Konecky, 1994.

Suderow, Bryce A. "War Along the James." *North and South*, Volume 6, Number 3 (April 2003).

Swanberg, W.A. *Sickles the Incredible*. Gettysburg, Pennsylvania: Stan Clark Military Books, 1956.

Taylor, Walter H. *General Lee: His Campaigns in Virginia, 1861–1865*. Lincoln: University of Nebraska Press, 1994.

Thomas, Emory M. *Bold Dragoon: The Life of J.E.B. Stuart*. Norman: University of Oklahoma Press, 1986.

United States War Department. *The War of the Rebellion: A Compilation of the Official Records of the Union and Confederate Armies*, 128 volumes. Washington, D.C.: Government Printing Office, 1880–1901.

Virginia Regimental History Series, Lynchburg, Virginia: H.G. Howard, 1987.

Walker Jr., Frank S. *Remembering: A History of*

Orange County, Virginia. Orange, Virginia: Orange County Historical Society, 2004.

Warner, Erza J. *Generals in Blue: Lives of the Union Commanders.* Baton Rouge: Louisiana State University Press, 1994.

_____. *Generals in Gray: Lives of the Confederate Commanders.* Baton Rouge: Louisiana State University Press, 1987.

Watts, J. Carter. "Confederate General's Dawn Duel." *America's Civil War*, Volume 12, Number 5 (November 1999).

Welsh, Jack D. *Medical Histories of Confederate Generals.* Kent, Ohio: Kent State University Press, 1995.

_____. *Medical Histories of Union Generals.* Kent, Ohio: Kent State University Press, 1996.

Woodhead, Henry, ed. *Voices of the Civil War: Atlanta.* Alexandria, Virginia: Time-Life Books, 1996.

_____. *Voices of the Civil War: Charleston.* Alexandria, Virginia: Time-Life Books, 1997.

_____. *Voices of the Civil War: Soldier Life.* Alexandria, Virginia. Time-Life Books, 1996.

Young III, Alfred C. "Numbers and Losses in the Army of Northern Virginia." *North and South.* Volume 3, Number 3 (March 2000).

Internet Sites

The American Civil War: http://www.vectorsite.net/twcw.html

America's Civil War: http://home.ptd.net/~nikki/civilwar.htm

Army of Tennessee: http://encyclopedia.thefreedictionary.com/Army%20of%20the%20Tennessee

Civil War Archive, Regimental Index: http://www.civilwararchive.com/regim.htm

Civil War Armies: http://www.civilwarhome.com/civilwararmies.htm

Civil War Battles Page: http://www.fortunecity.com/victorian/pottery/1080/index.htm

Civil War Generals Burial Places: http://www.cwc.lsu.edu/cwc/projects/dbases/generals.htm

Civil War Medical Links: http://home.nc.rr.com/fieldhospcsa/Links.html

Civil War National Parks: http://www.nps.gov

Civil War Naval Forces Index: http://www.tarleton.edu/~kjones/CSNavy.html

http://www.tarleton.edu/~kjones/USNavy.html

Civil War Terminology: http://civilwarmini.com/terms.htm#top

Confederate Navy: http://www.csnavy.org/alpha,ships.htm

Confederate Regimental History Links: http://www.tarleton.edu/~kjones/confeds.html

Confederate States of America: http://www.civil-warhome.com/csa.htm

David D. Porter: http://cdl.library.cornell.edu/cgi-bin/moa/moa-cgi?notisid=ABQ7578-0127&byte=99127352

Fort Stevens: http://www.us-civilwar.com/stevens.htm

http://www.nps.gov/rocr/ftcircle/stevens.htm

Genealogy Site: http://www.Ancestry.com

Heritage Preservation: http://www2.cr.nps.gov/abpp/battles

Museum of the Confederacy: http://www.moc.org

Oliver Wendell Holmes: http://www.absolute astronomy.com/encyclopedia/O/Ol/Oliver_Wendell_Holmes,_Jr.htm

Teach PD Law's Civil War: http://members.aol.com/teachpdlaw/civilwar.htm

United States Civil War: http://www.us-civilwar.com

United States Civil War Center: http://home.nc.rr.com/fieldhospcsa/Links.html

Virginia Military Institute Archives: http://www.vmi.edu/archives/cwsource.html

West Point Military Academy: http://american history.si.edu/westpoint

http://www.west-point.org/family/bicent/history.html

CD-ROM

Confederate Military History (CD-ROM). Carmel, Indiana: Guild Press of Indiana.

Southern Historical Papers (52 volumes). (CD-ROM). Carmel, Indiana: Guild Press of Indiana.

Other References

Brown, Joseph E. "Message of His Excellency Joseph E. Brown, to the Extra Session of the Legislature, Convened March 10th, 1864, Upon the Currency Act; Secret Sessions of Congress; The Late Conscription Act; The Unconstitutionality of the Act Suspending the Privilege of the Writ of Habeas Corpus, in Cases of Illegal Arrests Made by the President; The Causes of the War and Manner of Conducting It; And the Terms Upon Which Peace Should be Sought," 48 p. Milledgeville, Ga.: Boughton, Nisbet, Barnes and Moore, State Printer 1864. Call number 1569 Conf., Rare Book Collection, University of North Carolina at Chapel Hill.

Foster, Stephen T., *Civil War Cards.* The People, the Places, the Politics, the Action. Atlas Editions, Durham, Conn.: 1995.

Index